RHYTHMS IN POLITICS AND ECONOMICS

INTERNATIONAL STUDIES ASSOCIATION

New Dimensions in International Studies
Published in Cooperation with
the International Studies Association

Rhythms in Politics and Economics

Edited by
Paul M. Johnson and
William R. Thompson

PRAEGER

PRAEGER SPECIAL STUDIES • PRAEGER SCIENTIFIC

New York • Philadelphia • Eastbourne, UK
Toronto • Hong Kong • Tokyo • Sydney

LIBRARY OF CONGRESS CATALOGING IN PUBLICATION DATA
Main entry under title:

Rhythms in politics and economics.

(New dimensions in international studies)
"Published in cooperation with the International
Studies Association."
   Includes index.
   1. Political stability--Economic aspects—Addresses,
essays, lectures. Business cycles--Political aspects--
Addresses, essays, lectures. I. Johnson, Paul M.
II. Thompson, William R. III. International Studies
Association. IV. Series.
JC330.2.R49 1985   306'.2   84-18130
ISBN 0-03-002032-8 (alk. paper)

Published in 1985 by Praeger Publishers
CBS Educational and Professional Publishing
A Division of CBS Inc.
521 Fifth Avenue, New York, NY 10175 USA

56789 052 987654321

Printed in the United States of America
on acid-free paper

Foreword

Economic fluctuations affect political conditions, including the prospects for political stability and peace. We sense that, and can point to many instances where we think it has happened. But systematic theorizing and empirical evidence on these effects have not been extensive. Furthermore, interest in them has itself fluctuated— possibly cyclically, in response to changes in the international system itself, perhaps erratically.

In any case, the level of interest is now relatively high, and it should be. The global economy recently sustained its most severe economic setback since the 1930s. The political effects have to this point probably been felt most accurately in the less developed countries, as authoritarian regimes have been discredited and more democratic ones have struggled against adverse conditions only very partially of their own making. The industrialized countries so far have coped rather better—due in some degree to their ability to export many of the economic difficulties to others in the form of higher debt payments and lower commodity prices.

Two questions stand out regarding the industrialized countries: First, why have we not seen more political and social unrest as a consequence of the recent economic adversity? Many theories of political instability would have us expect much protest and insurgency to have resulted from such a difficult period of economic stagnation and decline. Why has this not occurred, and can we expect continued relative political quiescence in the face of continued or renewed economic adversity? Second, can the industrialized states continue to succeed in exporting such a large share of the economic difficulties, and, if not, will the result be the kind of political instability they have so far been able to avoid?

These and related questions are addressed by this volume. The chapters are concerned both with the domestic or intranational

v

effects of economic change, and with the effects of such change on the international system. They are written from a variety of disciplinary perspectives, representing, among other things, a determination of the program chairs to bring substantial representation from sociology and economics, as well as political science, into deliberations at the International Studies Association. They show an impressive range of methodological, theoretical, and ideological perspectives. The explicit concern of much of the volume with the security consequences, for producing or avoiding large-scale political violence, is notable, and linkage between the hitherto all-too-separate fields of international political economy and international security has been, in my opinion, delayed far too long. The chapters also show some representation of non-U.S. perspectives, though not, I am sure, as much as the editors would prefer. In short, the characteristics of the chapters and contributors to this volume reflect rather well the characteristics of the International Studies Association itself, in some combination of achievement and aspiration. It is a pleasure to introduce this volume to readers.

Bruce Russett

Preface

We are pleased to present this, the second annual volume in the Praeger series "New Dimensions in International Studies," which is published by special arrangement with the International Studies Association. Our last mission as 1984 ISA program chairs was to select about a dozen papers from the approximately 200 panels at Atlanta, develop a rationale for presenting them as a reasonably representative, coherent, and interesting collection, and then to bully the authors into revising their conference presentations within an extremely brief period of time. The contributions to this volume, accordingly, represent versions of papers originally presented in Atlanta at the ISA's Twenty-Fifty Annual Meeting, March 27 to 31, 1984.

The unifying theme of this volume is a common interest of all the contributors in investigating one or another example of a particular kind of phenomenon: the interaction between recurrent economic and political cycles or fluctuations, either at the international level or within nation-states. As editors, we have made a conscious effort to cast our nets widely so as to include a diversity of disciplinary backgrounds, methodological approaches, and ideological commitments. That being the case, we should note for the record that the ideas and conclusions expressed herein are those of the individual authors and do not necessarily reflect the views of the editors or of the ISA.

We would like to take this opportunity to express our thanks to our contributors for their stoic acceptance of our heavy-handed demands to abridge their intellectual handiwork and for their mostly exemplary cooperation in meeting what we freely concede was an unconscionably demanding schedule. We are indebted as well to Marjorie Smith, who typed much of the manuscript.

Contents

Introduction

Paul M. Johnson
William R. Thompson

In more prosperous years, there is a tendency to think in terms of straight lines. Political and economic processes are viewed as trending upward, downward, or else remaining relatively stationary. In less prosperous years, interest in cyclical or recurring fluctuations seems to revive. Whether this latter tendency can be related to the greater clarity of peaks and valleys when viewed from the vantage point of a trough or simply wishful thinking (some troughs are easier to accept if one can look forward to another peak) remains an open question. Still another tendency with a perhaps somewhat similar periodicity is the fluctuating interest in the interaction of political and economic processes of social scientists. In this case, however, there is less room for the wishful-thinking explanation. The interdependence of politics and economics is far more evident when economic problems seem more acute. Evident or not, though, we really do not have anything resembling a confident grasp on precisely how economic and political processes interact. Is it possible that there is a connection between this less-than-firm grasp on political-economic interdependencies and our reluctance to think nonlinearly?

This volume cannot hope to even begin to resolve the numerous controversies surrounding the study of political economy. Indeed, its contents may only add a bit more fuel to the flames of disagreement. However, the purpose of this collection is to focus more attention on the possible existence of several types of cyclical interactions between politics and economics at various levels of analysis. In arranging the 13 chapters, we have fallen back on an old-fashioned and convenient fiction: separating analyses that focus primarily on "internal/domestic/within-nation" behavior and policy from those that concentrate on "external/foreign/between-nation" behavior and policy. Clearly, this is an artificial distinction and one that the very nature of the chapters should help to expose as an only sometimes useful myth. Our sole defense is editorial license.

Domestic Policy and Behavior

The first chapter, by Desmond King and Ted Gurr, focuses on the political interaction between local and national states within the context of economic change. The degree of local political autonomy tends to be cyclical. Historically, for example, European towns were initially surbordinated to feudal lords, then they enjoyed variable periods of relative autonomy, only to be resubordinated by national states—but not without continuing resistance from the cities. In the post-World War II era, King and Gurr argue that local state autonomy in advanced capitalist states is a twin function of its relationships with local groups—the primary source of revenue and political support—and the national state. The fundamental dynamic of local autonomy fluctuations is keyed to local economic decline and/or the expansion of the scope of local state activities. Either or both phenomena can lead to the problem of insufficient funds, which require local states to seek financial assistance from the national state. The accompanying loss of local autonomy may be either temporary or long-lived depending upon the nature of national assistance and how successfully it is applied in developing new sources of local revenues. Replacing traditional manufacturing activities with lighter industry or service enterprises can serve as one example of a successful response to local decline. Even so, the problems of local versus national control are complicated further by the economic dislocation consequences of the ongoing internationalization of industrial economies in addition to intermittent business cycles.

Chapters 2 and 3 shift the cyclical focus to Eastern Europe and the persistence of economic fluctuations in centrally planned economies designed in part to eliminate business cycles and their political-economic consequences. Antoni Moskwa and Timothy Kearney point out some similarities between capitalist and socialist cycles, but they feel that the two remain fundamentally different and therefore require different explanations. Concentrating on Poland in the post-war period, Moskwa and Kearney examine a number of economic series and conclude that the Polish economy has experienced four seven-to-eleven-year cycles since 1949. Their explanation centers on the role of capital investment decisions in the Polish economy. Planners rely on capital investment to increase future output and tend to expand investment through a process of bureaucratic bargaining in more prosperous years (as indicated by rising per capita income and good harvests). However, increased investment comes at the expense of the production of consumption goods, which leads to shortages and political unrest. In the absence of corrective processes within the economic system, Moskwa and Kearney argue ironically that it is only political unrest that functions as a form of economic stabilizer—in the sense that it sometimes leads to changes in priorities and leadership.

While Zbigniew Fallenbuchl's analysis is broader in geographical scope, his conclusions complement those of Moskwa and Kearney. Reviewing the economic experiences of six East European states, Fallenbuchl also finds four "socialist business cycles" in the postwar era. The six economic systems are not exactly identical in terms of structure or in their cyclical records, but their actual functioning is sufficiently similar to permit generalizations. The basic problem is traced to an interaction between the natures of the economic systems, the development strategies employed, and the errors in planning decisions. Beginning in the late 1940s and early 1950s, high priority was given to the development of heavy industry in all six states. Other economic sectors such as agriculture and consumption goods were given relatively little attention. The results were shortages, declining productivity and work incentives, and social tension. Decision-makers would eventually respond to these probelms by reducing their emphases on savings and investment. But the responsiveness has usually been quite short-lived and followed by a renewed push for rapid development and a repetition of the dysfunctional consequences. Moreover, this cyclical syndrome is aggravated by the structural inefficiencies inherent to these particular economic systems and by the associated barriers to expanding foreign trade. Both of these factors serve as additional brakes on the course and length of economic upswings. The end results are far less development than planned and variable amounts of political instability (depending on the country).

A number of analysts do not feel the centrally planned economies and their five-year plans possess a monopoly on non-Keynesean, cyclical attempts by government to stimulate economic growth. Mitchell Kellman and Oded Izraeli's chapter returns the focus to political-economic practices in Western industrialized states and what they refer to as the "PBC" (political business cycle). Kellman and Izraeli choose to examine the relationships among wages, inflation, unemployment, and election years in 15 countries. For the most part, their initial results are statistically insignificant but the authors are unsure whether this reflects an absence of evidence for political business cycles or aggregation bias. Accordingly, they proceed to explore the relationships between a set of economic variables and PBC "intensity" and find that greater intensity is positively associated with inflation and unemployment levels. These findings suggest that governmental efforts to resort to "macroeconomic bribery" for reelection purposes are facilitated by high rates of inflation and unemployment, which afford governments greater degrees of opportunity to influence the economy. Kellman and Izraeli conclude with a brief comparison of Western European states and the United States and find little evidence that the hypothesized U.S. political business cycle differs fundamentally from European behavior.

The last two chapters in the first half of this volume concentrate on political responses to specific economic shocks: the world depression of the 1930s and the oil price increases in the 1970s. Ekkart Zimmermann provides a preliminary report on his project investigating how half a dozen European states' political systems reacted to economic crisis in the decade prior to World War II. After carefully describing and contrasting the specific ways in which the depression affected the various economic systems, Zimmermann aggregates the multiple indicators in order to create a rough scale of the impact of economic crisis. Germany appears to have suffered the greatest decline in economic performance and Great Britain the least. Zimmermann then discusses a relatively complex causal model of the political impact of economic crisis that revolves around the interplay among swings in the electorate, governmental stability, and economic and political measures taken by governments in response to mounting economic problems. As the author suggests, a great deal more work is needed to determine why some political systems were radically changed while others managed to survive with little overt change.

Barry Hughes feels that the oil shocks of the 1970s provide another excellent opportunity (in addition to the 1930s) to explore the relationships between economic crisis and political conflict. A series of hypotheses are first generated linking the 1973-74 oil shock to postshock increases in domestic as well as international conflict. Although the findings are complicated by an intervening economic development variable, they tend to provide at best only partial support for increased conflict expectations. Domestic conflict, for instance, tends to increase in industrialized states while it decreases in poorer states. On the other hand, postshock international conflict decreased in general, as did international cooperation. These unexpected findings underscore how little we know about how economic downturns are translated into politics. While data availability problems have restricted Hughes's analysis to the first oil shock, it will be interesting to see whether the uncovered economic downturn–political conflict relationships remain the same after the second oil shock of the 1970s is investigated.

Foreign Policy and Behavior

In addition to an emphasis on the domestic level of analysis (with some exceptions), much of the attention in the first six chapters is concentrated on relatively short-term cyclical behavior such as a seven-to-eleven year "socialist business cycle," a four-year "political business cycle" (at least in states with a fixed four-year electoral cycle), or occasional oil shocks. In the next seven chapters, the level of analysis shifts predominately to external policy and behavior and the dynamics of the world system. Frequently, the cyclical behavior that is highlighted will be relatively long term in nature—as exemplified by interests in cycles of capability concentration, the rise and decline of system leaders, or the Kondratieff long wave. These shifts in cyclical time need not follow axiomatically the shifts in level of analysis. Short-run cyclical behavior influences "external" behavior just as long-run cycles affect "internal" behavior. For example, the Zimmermann and Hughes chapters could conceivably have been analyzed from a systemic point of view and, as we will see, some of the authors in the second section of this volume pursue interests in short- and long-run cycles. Nor are their analytical interests necessarily confined to a single level of analysis.

Mark Rupert and David Rapkin are interested in the rise and fall of hegemonic leadership. Several analysts have argued that behavior in periods characterized by the concentration of important capabilities in one preponderant state tends to be different from that displayed in periods characterized by diffused capabilities. But as Rupert and Rapkin suggest, we do not have much precise information on various facets of this phenomenon. They choose to focus on the decline of economic leadership as manifested, presumably, in the ongoing case of the United States. Conceptualizing the problem as a joint "scissoring" process of the loss of leadership in capability shares and the leader's increasing interdependence with the economic system that it has shaped, the authors review a large number of pertinent indicators. The share indicators exhibit steady decay patterns while the interdependence indicators display abrupt increases in the 1970s. The implications of this uneven closing of the scissors' blades (which departs from conventional images of hegemonic decline) remains an intriguing question for further research.

Mark Amen pursues a much different approach to the consequences of changes in power concentration in the international system. Amen is interested in explaining the causes of foreign and domestic economic policies and their interrelationships. Within this context, the international distribution of power is but one of six factors (in addition to external and internal market conditions, domestic politics, decision-making, and policy beliefs) that might possess some explanatory value. All six approaches are applied to the evolution of balance of payments and fiscal policies in the Kennedy and Reagan administrations. This comparative case study generates a number of observations about the relative potency of the explanatory factors. One is particularly interesting for the theme of this volume. Amen argues that while change in the international distribution of economic power was of some significance, market conditions were relatively unimportant other than as sources of problems requiring some type of policy change. Bureaucratic, cognitive, and organizational forces functioned as important filters to eliminate or distort policies designed, or that might have been designed, to accommodate changing economic circumstances.

In contrast to Amen's emphasis on forces affecting the development of policies, Robert Kudrle's chapter compares and contrasts three perspectives that have been utilized to account for the historical evolution of U.S. tariff and protectionist policies. These policies have been of particular interest to students of cyclical economic influences on politics. For example, does a position of economic hegemony dictate a free-trade stance? If so, what happens as the hegemonic position erodes? Alternatively, do protectionist impulses oscillate in unison with recession and recovery? Kudrle touches upon these questions and a number of others in his critique of the realist, "conventional political science," and public choice literatures on tariffs. In brief, he concludes that the public choice "bottoms-up" stress on perceptions and definitions of group interest is essential to interpreting the development of trade policy in the United States. Ideological learning, major economic shocks, and the conjunction of systemic structure also have explanatory roles to play. But it is an appreciation for a combination of powerful economic interests in place and a generation or more of socialization in the legitimacy of free trade that lead Kudrle to predict continued U.S. adherence to a free-trade position—despite the decline of its predominance in the world economy and barring another economic catastrophe on the scale of the early 1930s.

Robert Elder and Jack Holmes explore a completely different perspective from the preceding chapter in explaining U.S. policies or orientations. Rather than pursuing Kudrle's "bottoms-up" strategy, Elder and Holmes attempt to match the periodicities of the Kondratieff long wave to fluctuations in the intensity of U.S. interest in foreign policy questions. After examining data on foreign policy moods, presidential psychological attributes, war, and economic fluctuations, the authors conclude that there is an impressive degree of fit between domestic and international cycles. They generalize these findings by arguing that phases of expansionist foreign policies and war tend to overlap with relatively prosperous economic conditions that facilitate higher defense expenditures. Conversely, periods of less foreign involvement cooccur with periods characterized by postwar economic deterioration and declining governmental revenues. Elder and Holmes do not develop the causal interconnections between these overlapping periodicities, but they do feel they have established that U.S. political and economic cycles operate in a mutually supportive manner. Further analysis will be required to assess the range of implications of this close political-economic interdependence.

While the Elder-Holmes chapter essentially does not attempt to go beyond establishing correlation patterns, Pat McGowan's chapter is explicitly concerned with developing causal connections between capital accumulation, imperialism, and international conflict. Restricting his model-building efforts to the important case of Great Britain between 1870 and 1914, McGowan begins with the assumptions of a laissez-faire regime, an approximately nine-year business cycle, and a class of people seeking profitable investments. In periods of domestic decline, foreign investment provides an attractive alternative to domestic investment. But economic outreach tended to lead to territorial imperialism, military expansion, and interstate conflict/violence. These ideas, of course, are hardly novel. What is novel (that is, unless one views lateral-pressure theory as an attempt to generalize Marxist-Leninist et al. theories of imperialism) is the attempt to utilize them in the construction of a testable, complex, simultaneous equations model. In this fashion, it may prove possible to probe empirically some of the international consequences of the nineteenth-century's lead economy's business cycles as well as the interactions between short-term economic fluctuations and the longer-term decline of Great Britain's economic leadership.

In earlier analyses, Charles Doran has developed a power cycle theory that contends that the national capability of states follows a cyclical pattern of rise and decline vis-à-vis one another. As states pass through critical turning points on their relative power curve, expectations and assumptions developed earlier in the cycle are no longer applicable. As a consequence, the destabilizing implications of these critical points bring about an increased probability of major war involvement. In this chapter, Doran translates these national cyclical movements to the systemic level of analysis by demonstrating that the periods prior to World War I and II were characterized by an unusually large number of major power critical points. This finding leads Doran to conclude that both world wars resulted from systems transformation or the collective "inability of governments to adapt to rapid and unexpected changes in role and position on their respective power cycles."

Albert Bergesen's chapter pursues further this idea that wars are a consequence of systemic crisis—albeit from a perspective more closely linked to McGowan's than to Doran's. For Bergesen, war is rooted in the reproductive dynamics of the world system's political economy. These reproductive dynamics, in turn, are associated with a number of causally interconnected cyclical processes. Bergesen names six: war/peace, economic expansion/contraction, mercantilism/free trade, colonization/decolonization, hegemony/multicentrism, and firm expansion/mergers. Of the six, economic expansion/contraction appears to be the most central: economic downturn is said to be associated with mercantilism, colonization, multicentrism, firm mergers, and war. But war also helps bring about systemic reorganization, peace, hegemony, economic expansion, and so forth. From this perspective, then, war is not a consequence of systems transformation but rather a component in the continuity of the system's recurring or cyclical dynamic of reproduction.

Thus, in the aggregate, the authors brought together within these covers suggest that there are a large number of cyclical phenomena—ranging from city-state relations through several kinds of business cycles to the longer-term structural changes—that have considerable significance for our attempts to understand how economics and politics intertwine. Many of us may think it is too soon to say that for every thing there is a season. But the 13 chapters of this volume do help to illustrate the need to at least explore further the possibility of significant economic and political periodicities and the ways in which they may be interdependent. That there are indeed economic and political cycles and they do make some difference is beyond question. What remains questionable is which, and to what extent and consequence, political and economic processes are cyclical. Arguments and data have been advanced here and elsewhere both for and against the existence of various types of cycles as well as on the variable impact of economic cycles on political decisions and vice versa. But as the authors assembled here indicate, we have a considerable way to go in sorting out which processes are related and why.

RHYTHMS IN POLITICS AND ECONOMICS

I. Domestic Policy and Behavior

1

The State and the City: Economic Transformation and the Autonomy of the Local State in Advanced Industrial Societies

DESMOND S. KING AND TED ROBERT GURR

The extent to which the state—both national and local—is constrained by economic processes has gained prominence as a central issue in social science recently. This mirrors both a renewed interest in the state as an object of analysis (Skocpol 1982) and the emergence of political economy as a framework for studying political phenomena. In urban studies, political economy approaches have developed a strong challenge to traditional urban studies by emphasizing the extent to which cities and patterns of urbanization are derivative of underlying economic processes (Castells 1977; Procter 1982). In a series of papers, we have constructed a state-centered theory of state-city relations in advanced industrial societies with specific reference to the political economy of urban growth and decline (Gurr and King 1984, 1985). This work is derived from a general theory of the contemporary state and aims to delineate its neglected role as an autonomous agent of urban change—neglected, that is, by much of the extant literature on urban political economy.

In this chapter we are concerned with the changing character and capacities of the local state in advanced industrial societies. The concept of the "local state" is itself problematic. From a traditional perspective it can be argued that municipal governments are so sharply circumscribed by national governments that they are little more than agencies of the national state. Cockburn, whose 1977 study of the Lambeth Borough Council (London) introduced the concept of the "local state" into recent social science discourse, writes from a neo-Marxist perspective according to which both the national and local state act mainly to facilitate capital accumulation. In her conceptualization, what is distinctive about the local state is its detailed management of families and local organizations, not its interests—which are, derivatively, those of the capitalist class. We disagree with both the traditional and neo-Marxist perspectives. The local states of Western cities have significant (though variable) autonomy from both the national state and private economic forces, and are capable of using that autonomy in the pursuit of their own distinctive interests.

The State and the City: Key Theoretical Assumptions

This is a very cursory summary of our key theoretical arguments. We argue that the rulers and officials of the contemporary state pursue their own interests in the aggrandizement of power and resources. They also have what we call *programmatic commitments* to social and political objectives that may have ideological or historical origins outside the state, but are shaped and given institutional momentum by the state's own legal and normative order. Thus ruler and officials can be said to have interests distinct from other societal groups (see Nordlinger 1981). The national state is conceptualized, both contemporaneously and historically, as a bureaucratically institutionalized pattern of authority whose rulers claim to exercise ultimate control over the inhabitants of a territory, and who demonstrate an enduring capacity to enforce that claim. A definition of the local state is offered below. State positions are filled by elective and appointive officials: in modern states they are legislators, chief executives, and higher-ranked bureaucrats of national, regional, and local governments. Two types of interests—short run and long run—can be ascribed to officials: the former concern mainly the maximization of incumbency (for elected officials) and of agency resources (for bureaucrats); the latter concern the perpetuation of the state and of the institutions of authority, legitimacy, and finance necessary for realization of those objectives. We do not assume a monolithic state; there is recurrent conflict of interests between elected and bureaucratic officials and between national and local authorities. The latter conflict informs our concern with the nature and scope of local autonomy discussed below.

The principal constraint on the national state's pursuit of its own interests in industrial societies has been the countervailing interests of dominant economic actors. The state *can* be subordinated to a dominant economic class, as it came to be during the middle stages of European capitalism, but there are strong tendencies for the autonomous interests of state power to be reasserted by officials pursuing their own interests. Of course the state's political interests are not and can never be regarded as wholly independent of the base of production, and especially not in advanced industrial societies. As Block observes in a neo-Marxist analysis of the capitalist state, "those who manage the state apparatus—regardless of their own political ideology—are dependent on the maintenance of some reasonable level of economic activity" (1977, p. 15). But whether the requisite economic activity is carried out independently by entrepreneurs, or by state managers, or in partnership between them is in principal and in historical fact an open question. It is in the self-interest of officials to subordinate economic activity to state authority, directly or indirectly, both to minimize constraints on state power and to ensure an ample and reliable flow of revenue, just as it is in the narrow self-interest of entrepreneurs to maximize profits and minimize state intervention in economic activity. Although our state-centered analysis is non-Marxist, it converges with one line of development in neo-Marxist analysis of states, represented in Block's work, summarized above (see also Miliband 1983).

We argue that the state-centered theoretical perspective implies two sorts of state interest in cities (see Gurr and King 1985). In relation to municipalities, this perspective assumes that officials generally pursue their own interests in the protection and expansion of state power and resources, and specifically have interests in the viability of cities that do not simply reflect the interests of private capital or any other societal groups. Their general interests derive from the concrete interests of officials, elective and appointive, in maintaining the political institutions and relationships that underpin their power, status, and privilege. A broad, twofold distinction is made between those state functions necessary for the perpetuation of the state (maintenance of public order, legitimacy, durable political institutions, and revenue base) and those necessary for the perpetuation of cities (general and special collective goods, developmental policies, and provision of social services).

As already noted, in this paradigm the state is not a monolithic entity: there is conflict between different agencies each pursuing its particular interests, and there is likely to be conflict between officials of the national and various local states. These latter clearly share the national officials' intrinsic interests in the maintenance of local authority, but from a different position within the state structure. Each set of local officials has an overriding interest in the perpetuation and economic health of their municipality; national officials' interests in city viability, however, is likely to be unevenly distributed across municipalities.

The Local State in Advanced Industrial Societies

Analysis of the national state's interests in urban processes and in municipalities has been stimulated by the neglect of this central issue in the new urban political economy of the 1970s (Zukin 1980). Since much of this latter literature uses a neo-Marxist framework and is particularly influenced by Castells' (1977) application of Althusserian Marxist structuralism to processes of urbanization, its primary emphasis has been on documenting the impact of economic dynamics on those processes. Urban political economy has been criticized for neglecting the national state (see Harloe 1981; Elliott and McCrone 1982) and also for emphasizing economic to the neglect of political factors as determinants of urban forms and forces.

Within the same urban political economy literature, however, some attention has been paid to the development of a theory of the local state (Broadbent 1977; Cockburn 1977; Dear and Clark 1978; and Saunders 1979). It is not entirely unjust to suggest that, aside from these works, the new urban political economy does little more than ascribe some specific functions to local state managers deriving from their linkage with the national state. Here we explicate the concept of local autonomy and identify the kinds of constraint within which officials of the local state operate while seeking to maintain their own cities' economic vitality and relative political autonomy.

Defining the Local State

Various arguments underscore the significance of the local state of analyses of urban political economy. If the state is important at all, then the local state has intrinsic importance because it is a key point of contact for most citizens with the apparatus of the national state structure. Second, the local state is the point at which most public/

private controversies and interactions become manifest to citizens and officials. The local state is typically responsible for the implementation of many centrally formulated programs, and hence frequently for arbitration between public and private interests. Private interests resistant to public interventions thus are likely to focus on the local state, which then must attempt to mediate disagreements. The fact that it sometimes suits the national state to delegate such interventions to the local state is an additional problematic (Friedland et al. 1977; Dear 1981). Such arguments have led Cawson (1982) to conclude that a corporatist analysis offers the most adequate theoretical framework for understanding the local state's status within the national state structure. Cawson criticizes scholars for having failed to give sufficient attention to the local state as a semiautonomous component of the whole state structure. Most studies assume

> that the state can be explained as a whole, and that its operation at the local level can be shown through the identification of local government as the local arm of the central state. But this conception implies a very simplistic notion of central-local relationships which fails to capture the evident complexity of the real world. (Cawson 1982: p. 29)

Cawson goes on to argue that the national and local states are differentially accessible to penetration by competitive and corporate interest groups. Dearlove (1979) and Webman (1982) provide evidence of this complexity: the latter study, for example, details the considerable independence enjoyed by the local state in Birmingham (Britain) from the national government in its execution of urban renewal policy from the 1930s to the 1970s.

At a metatheoretical level, it is necessary to pose more fundamental questions about the local state: In what sense is it a state? Can it be demonstrated that local states have some autonomy? What are the nature and sources of this autonomy? Contemporary municipalities are evidently not states if these are defined by reference to the notion of sovereignty: local states have clear constitutional, statutory, and legal limitations on the extent of their independent activities. However, by the same token, local states are semiautonomous concentrations of authority that can be used in the pursuit of a variety of interests. They have (variable) powers of revenue raising; they have specific functions, whether nationally or locally formulated, whose performance affects their political environment; they have (variable) discretion on how they carry these functions out; they are headed by elected officials and thus somewhat accountable to local electoral forces and to voters' interests.

The historical way in which municipalities have evolved is relevant here. In significant parts of Continental Europe, including northern Italy, the Lowlands, parts of Germany, and the Hanseatic League, cities were precursors of nation-states. Only after a period of semisovereignty, beginning as early as the twelfth century and lasting as late as the nineteenth century, were they effectively subordinated to the authority of the rulers of emerging national states. This means that historically, and in some regions of Europe, it makes sense to speak about politically autonomous city-states, some of whose features and aspirations continue to characterize the contemporary local state. Elsewhere, especially in France and Britain, state-formation and the growth of cities occurred more or less simultaneously, but was accompanied by the development of strong sentiments of localism, centered on regional cities and often at odds with the nationalizing political forces emanating from Paris and London.

In the United States the historical heritage is different again. With some Eastern seaboard exceptions, cities were founded and grew within the established authority of state and federal governments. But in the U.S. tradition of decentralized governments, municipal authorities also were legally accorded significant degrees of self-rule by state governments. As cities grew in relative size and economic importance, they used their political influence in state legislatures to defend and extend the scope of legal authority. Inasmuch as the contemporary local state in the United States has some discretion over how it allocates federal and state funds, implements federal policy, and chooses which services to provide and how, then it continues to exercise some autonomy.

Accordingly, for both historical and contemporary reasons, we concur with Duncan and Goodwin's (1982, p. 77) judgment that

> despite the semantic confusion of the term [local state] . . . the term does seem to refer to an important dimension of social relations in the advanced capitalist societies. It does appear that social and political consciousness is focused around local issues

and experiences just as much as—if not more than—national issues. Indeed, for most of the time national issues can only be directly experienced in a local context.

This is our definition of the local state. In contrast to fairly general conceptions such as Johnston's (1982, p. 187)—"the term local state applies to any non-sovereign body concerned with the government of a constituent area of a sovereign state"—we propose a definition specific to municipalities. There are four key elements in our conception of the local state (see also Dear 1981). First, it has the primary, formally constituted authority for the governance of city population. In practice, responsibility for various public services is often divided among levels of government and among functionally specialized authorities: the "local state" is the *primary* governing and coordinating entity at the level of the city. Second, it exercises jurisdiction over all people and activities within a geographically bounded space— which may include only central cities, as in the United States, or larger metropolitan regions. Third, the local state's structure consists of both bureaucratic (career and appointive) and governmental (elective) offices, with the former substantially responsible to the latter. Fourth, the local state has the legal authority (whether conferred from within or without) to collect some revenues from citizens within its jurisdiction and to make allocative decisions about the use of these and other resources. The fact that these powers are always constrained does not call into question the existence of the local state; the degree to which they are constrained is one dimension of local state autonomy (see below).

Dimensions of the Local State's Authority

Analysis of the local state in advanced industrial societies suggests that its autonomy derives from a flux of relevant factors: its constitutional status, historical formation, revenue base, power relations between national and local elites, incorporation of social groups, and so forth. Fundamentally, however, these factors can be parsimoniously organized into two groups. Accordingly, we argue that the autonomy of the local state in advanced capitalist societies at any given historical juncture is a function first of its relationship with local economic and social groups, and second of its relationship with the national state. The former have historically constituted the indispensable sources of revenue and political support upon which the autonomous power of the local state is based. The national state in all Western societies now has extensive legal powers over the local state, the cumulative result of the growth of the nation-state and the centrally guided expansion of the public sector (see Gurr and King 1985). The extant literature disagrees about the relative importance of each of these two sets of constraints on the local state, and there is a general propensity to focus on only one to the neglect of the other. Wolman (1982), for instance, compares local autonomy in Britain and the United States only with respect to the local state's relationship with the national state (for other emphases see, for example, Broadbent 1977; Cockburn 1977; and Dear 1981). The two sets of relationships provide us with a basis for specifying two crucial dimensions of local state autonomy, which we designate as Type I and Type II.

Local State Autonomy Type I

Type I concerns the local state's autonomy from local economic and social forces. The local state is autonomous to the extent that it can pursue its interests without being substantially constrained by local economic and social conditions. More concretely, the conditions most likely to constrain local state autonomy are of three kinds: limits on the revenues that can be extracted from the local economy; resistance of dominant local interests to the policies of the local state; and the activities of locally based (or focused) political organizations and social movements that aim at reshaping the content of local public policy or at thwarting its implementation.

Whether the local state is part of a federal or unitary political system, it needs revenues from the local economy to ensure its perpetuation. The local state's revenue-raising capacities are a function of the carrying capacity of its local economy and of the statutory stipulations (whether national or regional) as to what within its jurisdiction is taxable and how much it can be taxed (for the United States, see Bingham et al. 1978). At a formal level, the relationship between the local state and its local economy has traditionally been relatively uncomplicated: the local economy has historically been the principal revenue base for the local state, thereby providing the latter with a certain (financial, not necessarily political) autonomy. This formalistic relationship has been considerably reshaped, however, by the increasing amount of local state revenues supplied by the national state. Broadbent (1977, p. 128) contends that unlike the national economy

> it is immediately clear that the local economy is a much more *open* system than the national economy, and by the same token . . . the link between the local state and the local urban economy is much less direct than that between the national state and the national economy.

This implies that there are sharp limitations on what the local state can do to maintain a locally healthy economy. Nonetheless, there are significant policy tools available to local states to initiate public-private partnerships, create enterprise zones, make rate or tax changes, offer tax incentives to new industry, and so forth.

Shortfalls in local revenues may be the result of relative expansion of the public sector, that is, a consequence of the state's past pursuit of its interests in programmatic expansion. Or shortfalls may be the result of local or regional economic decline. In either case, when insufficient funds are generated locally, the local state is likely to seek additional revenues from external sources, from either the national state or, in federal systems, the state or province of which it is part. The fiscal constraints on Type I local autonomy thus can be overcome, but at the cost of increased fiscal reliance on the national state. If increased national control of local policy follows from increased fiscal responsibility, as it usually does, the effect is a decrease in Type II autonomy (see below). Thus there are likely tradeoffs between Type I and Type II autonomy.

The other two processes relevant to Type I local state autonomy are powerful economic interests and social movements or political organizations concerned with influencing the content and execution of the local state's policies. The former included corporations, banks, developers, and labor unions, either locally based or agents of national or—in the case of corporations—transnational organizations. Friedland (1976, 1980, 1983) has argued from empirical analysis that War on Poverty and urban renewal funds in the United States were distributed in disproportionate ratio to cities in which corporate and union headquarters were located. In the case of Britain, Kirk contends that the local state's autonomy with respect to decisions to grant or deny planning permissions is considerably chastened by powerful economic interests, whether locally based or organized through the national state:

> compared with capital or national governments, a local authority has only limited powers. In land-use planning matters this is exemplified by the limited control local councils have over the commercial development process and the location of firms. (Kirk 1980, p. 182).

Molotch's (1976) conception of the city as a "growth machine" is somewhat analogous to this: the goal of growth acts as a unifying force for the local political elite and investors. Since the key growth-and-wealth-generating commodity at the local level is land, over whose use the local state has some control, it becomes the focus of growth-related political activity.

Local State Autonomy Type II

Type II concerns the local state's autonomy from the national state. The local state is autonomous to the extent it can pursue its interests without substantial interference by the national state. Clearly there are always some national constraints on local policy, encroaching even on functional areas in which the local state has exclusive responsibility. These range from constitutionally specified limitations to more recondite guidelines accompanying grants, to national political pressures aimed at specific policies of particular municipal administrations. At issue generally is how much decisional latitude the local state has, legally and in practice, within each functional area of activity. Like Type I autonomy, Type II autonomy is a composite of opportunities for and constraints on local policy options across the entire range of governmental activity.

Just as officials of the local state have recurrently sought to enhance their relative economic autonomy, they have sought autonomy in their relations with the national state. Thus Elliott and McCrone (1982, pp. 46-48) contend that despite nation-specific differences, one common characteristic of the development of national-municipal relations in Europe was the quest for political autonomy by the local state. However, municipalities were forced by the dynamics of state centralization and industrialization to become jurisdictional subunits of the national state:

> by the sixteenth century, the independent city had everywhere lost ground to more powerful monarchs and princelings and the new authority of the state. Thus, Weber describes a cyclical process for the city: from subordination to feudal or territorial lords, a brief though important autonomy, the decay of that freedom and then the subordination of the city to the patrimonial state. Cities become rich sources of tax revenue for the ambitious monarchs and their courtiers and the control and manipulation of the cities and their corporations was a matter of statecraft. (Elliott and McCrone 1982, p. 48)

With some national variations, the growth of the nation-state and the diffusion of capitalism combined with a new bourgeoisie to subordinate the city to the jurisdiction of expanding national authority.

National state constraints have traditionally taken two main forms. First are constitutional and legal constraints, which are formally stated and embodied in explicit institutional arrangements (for example, in Britain the stipulation that local governments must maintain a balanced budget). This constraint varies across federal and unitary systems, reflecting country-specific factors. Wolman (1982, p. 172) provides the following instance:

> the primary formal difference with respect to government's effect on local autonomy is that in the United Kingdom local government may undertake no activity not explicitly authorised by the central governments (the doctrine of ultra vires), whereas in the United States local government is not prevented by the federal government from undertaking any activity not contrary to the United States constitutional or federal legislation.

This formal constitutional difference is, of course, much modified by administrative and political practice. The range of activities the local state can assume in the United States is not quite as wide as this formal distinction would imply, nor is it as narrow in the Unted Kingdom.

Second are administrative constraints that emerge from the intrinsically political nature of the national-local state relationship, as Webman's (1982) comparative study of urban renewal programs in Lyons and Birmingham reveals. He concludes that the extent of central intervention or control is markedly greater in Britain than in France:

> the British pattern of local-national relations consistently stressed rule-making in London and rule-application by local authorities. . . . In contrast, the French pattern stressed overlapping, shared, or contested control over individual projects among a mix of central and local agencies all enjoying legal, financial and technical grounds for insisting upon details of design and implementation. (1981, p. 144)

Thus municipal autonomy in Britain may be notably less than suggested by formal administrative arrangements (though see Broaden 1970).

The Role of the Local State in the Transformation of Western Cities

The "crisis" of cities in advanced industrial societies expressed in the loss of industrial jobs and population, and often associated with urban decay and social malaise, is mainly the result of an economic transition that has arisen, most fundamentally, from the internationalization of industrial economies in the postwar period. Here we explore, in a preliminary way, some implications of these changes for the local states in Britain and the United States that have sought either to manage or to ride the tide of change.

The internationalization of industrial economies in the postwar period is reflected in the shift in manufacturing production away from developed countries and within the United States away from the industrial Northeast and Midwest. This has resulted in an interregional shift in manufacturing employment opportunities. The composition of international trade has changed too, with a smaller proportion of industrial goods and an increase in agricultural commodities. Translated into U.S. urban and regional terms, Glickman (1981a, p. 8) observes:

the decline of sales of heavy manufacturing (in particular, transportation equipment, nonelectrical and electrical machinery and chemicals) abroad has had deleterious effects on the old Industrial Heartland of the Northeast and Midwest. A production hierarchy has evolved world wide and within the United States in which high-technology industry and services are concentrated in the larger cities of the United States and other industrialized nations, while production processes have dispersed throughout the rest of the country and to the Third World.

The picture for capital mobility is similar: there are large outflows of capital from the United States and increasing investment by multinational corporations in the United States. These latter have played a significant role, Glickman contends, in the development of the Sunbelt region. At national, regional, and urban levels, the increasing mobility of capital and investment makes the formulation of effective public policy more complex and difficult. Investment tends to be uneven in spatial distribution and devastating in impact when disinvestment occurs:

> the problem relates to the relative speed of movements of capital relative to labor—workers cannot move as fast as capital and often are reluctant to relocate from areas where they have deep family and other ties. The affected communities cannot often find replacement industries. (Glickman 1981a, p. 12)

Also working on urban areas are the effects of business cycles and long-term economic growth.

The principal urban consequence of these trends has been a general decline (indexed by population loss, declining productivity, and increased incidence of hardship and social stress) in many once-prosperous industrial cities. Approximately half the larger cities of Europe and the United States were losing population during the 1970s. Of 150 functional urban regions (cities and their peripheries) examined in the Urban Europe project (Van den Berg et al. 1982, Ch. 7), 19 percent experienced population loss in 1970-75, while these plus another 29 percent lost population in their core cities. Three-quarters or more of the urban regions in Britain, the Netherlands, and Belgium were in these two groupings. Other concentrations of declining old industrial cities are to be found in northern France and

the German Ruhr. In the United States the incidence of urban decline
in 1970-75 was quite similar. Of 121 Standard Metropolitan Statistical Areas (SMSAs), 26 (21 percent) lost population during these five
years and 51 (42 percent) of them had core cities with shrinking
populations. As in Europe, declining U.S. urban regions are concentrated in old industrial regions. In the Northeastern United States, 23
of 24 metropolitan areas had absolute or core-city decline, and in the
North Central region 29 of 33 (Bradbury, Downs, and Small 1982,
Ch. 3). Shifts in economic patterns are not the only factor to
population decline in these regions and cities; social preferences for
exurban living and governmental policies of decentralization (as in
Britain and the Netherlands) also are at issue. But the economic
dynamic is evidently the most important.

In terms of our analysis, these economic changes constitute a
decline in Type I autonomy for the local state in two respects. Most
obviously, the more seriously affected municipalities are no longer
able to generate sufficient revenues from declining local economies to
meet rising social costs. More fundamentally, the internationalization
of production means that the controlling nodes of urban economic
change are increasingly distant from the local economy, and thus are
less subject to manipulation or control by the local state.

One major implication for the local state that follows from these
economic shifts is that it is pushed into greater reliance on the
national state for funds. The growing fiscal reliance of local governments on the national state is well-documented. In six countries we
have examined for the 1970s, national and regional contributions to
local government expenditures consistently increased. In the United
Kingdom, for example, grants increased from 39.3 percent of local
budgets to 44.6 percent in 1980. In the United States the percentage
increased from 38.6 percent in 1972 to 48.6 percent in 1979 (King and
Gurr 1983, table 3). The increased flow of national funds to the local
state has been interpreted as leading to a diminution of the latter's
autonomy. Newton (1980, p. 11), for example, concludes from a six-
country study of local finance in Europe that "since local authorities
are less and less able to rely upon their own resources, they are also
less and less able to determine how much money they will raise and
how it will be raised." Harold Wolman (1982, p. 178) places a more
general interpretation on this trend: "central-local relations in mod-

ern states to a large extent occur in the context of the *system* of intergovernmental assistance."

Two different questions need to be asked about the connection between increased national contributions to municipal budgets and the autonomy of the local state. One is the extent to which the uses of those funds are mandated by central authorities or are the subject of local discretion: unrestricted revenue-sharing and block grants imply greater Type II autonomy. The second concerns the economic dynamics of growing national-to-local transfers of funds. If the result of shrinking local revenues, then a real decrease in Type I autonomy has occurred. If the result of the general expansion of local state services and activities, the net result may well be an increase in Type I autonomy. The expanding local state financing its expansion by drawing upon extralocal sources of revenue may be able to substantially increase its relative autonomy over local economic and social interests. The hypothetical relations among fiscal dependence, national restrictions on local use of funds, and our two types of autonomy are shown in Table 1.1

This line of analysis has implications for the local state's capacity for formulating public policies capable of controlling or ameliorating economic decline and its social stresses. The local state is often trapped between the extralocal source of many of its economic difficulties and the differential, potentially conflicting interests of the national state upon which it is fiscally dependent. Thus local attempts to control and respond to changing conditions often bring it into

Table 1.1 Implications of Growing Fiscal Dependence on the Autonomy of the Local State

Cause of Increased Fiscal Dependence	*Restrictions Imposed by the National/Regional State on Increased Grants to Localities*	
	Low	High
Expanding scope of local state activities	Type I autonomy + Type II autonomy 0	Type I autonomy + Type II autonomy -
Contraction of local economy	Type I autonomy - Type II autonomy 0	Type I autonomy - Type II autonomy -

conflict with central state objectives. This point is well made by Young and Mills (1982) in their study of the conditions of declining municipal economies in Britain. They contend that a fundamental conflict between the objectives of central and local states has emerged:

> different agencies and levels of government pursue different and often contradictory purposes. City governments must deploy policies against the tide, if only in the hope of reducing its rate of flow, so buying further time for adaptation. National governments, for their part, follow the tide because ultimately they will go where the market advantage leads. Conflict avoidance dictates that this diversity of purpose is not made over-explicit, and for this reason national and local responses to fiscal stress in cities are likely to remain contradictory and confusing. (Young and Mills 1982, p. 99)

Referring to Table 1.1, the most benign situation, from the point of view of local officials concerned to maintain local autonomy, is that in which the expanding scope of local state activity leads (say, by statutory requirements) to an increased flow of funds from higher levels of government that carry a minimum of new restrictions. The Houstons and San Joses of the U.S. Sunbelt may be in this enviable position. The worst situation is faced by officials attempting to maintain existing activities in declining cities who find that the price of increased aid is increased dictation of policy. This was the price paid by New York City officials for a federal and state bailout in 1975: they were forced to retrench municipal services and employment across the board (Tabb 1982). Under fiscally conservative governments in both the United States and Britain, retrenchment is the price exacted by the national and regional state for continued aid to local states in fiscal crisis. It has recently been the source of a sharp confrontation between the Labour-controlled municipal government of Liverpool, which seeks to maintain social services even if this means an unbalanced budget, and the Conservative government's determination to force a reduction in local public expenditure.[1] In our terms, the local state in Liverpool has too little autonomy to deal effectively with the crisis: Type I autonomy is restricted by both the shrinking revenue-generating capacity of the local economy and Labour's political commitment to a constituency that resists cuts;

Type II autonomy is restricted by the national government's fiscal policies.

We conclude by noting that some cities have fared better in dealing with the crises of shifting economic patterns and urban decline of the post-1960 period. It is useful to distinguish among three types of postindustrial cities: those that were once industrially prosperous but are now in absolute decline, typified by Newark and St. Louis in the United States and Newcastle and Glasgow in Britain; those that are no longer industrially prosperous but are stabilizing decline by shifting to a mix of old industrial and new service enterprises, for example Baltimore and Oakland (U.S.) and Bristol (U.K.); and those whose economic viability now rests firmly on a mix of financial, administrative, and service activities, such as Boston and Edinburgh. All of these cities have lost population and industrial jobs; those in the latter two categories are much better places in which to live and work.

The conventional explanations for these differential responses to urban adversity emphasize economic factors: locational advantages and investment decisions in an internationalized economy (conditions determined outside the city); or, if one accepts Jane Jacobs's (1984) new urban economics, creative import-substitution (a condition generated within the city). From a state-centered perspective, the policies of the national and local state do not only shape these economic conditions, but also redistribute public-sector investment, jobs, and grants across the social landscape in ways that differentially benefit some cities (see Gurr and King 1984). Boston's revival, for example, is due to both the substantial development of light industry and public-sector expansion funded by national and state governments.

The local state plays a crucial part in such development. Some have been consistently more effective than others in attracting both public and private funds. In effect, these are exercises of local autonomy: autonomy in shaping the local social and economic environment to provide a climate that stimulates local technological innovation and attracts investment, and political autonomy—or clout—in inducing higher levels of government to channel greater shares of public resources to the city. In this conception, the local state in declining cities is a political entrepreneur. We need more research as to why some are more effective in this role than others.

Such research needs to relate local state behavior to the two distinct dimensions of its autonomy formulated in this chapter, as a means of advancing our general understanding of the local state's part in cities' changing economic and political circumstances.

Note

1. As reported in the British press and journals. See, for example, "Liverpool Docked," *New Statesman*, 3 February 1984, pp. 8-10.

Bibliography

Bingham, Richard D., Brett Hawkins, and F. Ted Herbert. 1978. *The Politics of Raising State and Local Revenue*. New York: Praeger.

Block, Fred. 1977. "The Ruling Class Does Not Rule: Notes on the Marxist Theory of the State." *Socialist Revolution* 33 (May-June), pp. 6-28.

Bradbury, Katherine L., Anthony Downs, and Kenneth A. Small. 1982. *Urban Decline and the Future of American Cities*. Washington, D.C.: Brookings Institution

Broadbent, Andrew. 1977. *Planning and Profit in the Urban Economy*. London: Methuen.

Broaden, Noel. 1970. "Central Departments and Local Authorities: The Relationship Examined." *Political Studies* 18, pp. 175-86.

Castells, Manuel. 1977. *The Urban Question*. Cambridge, MA: MIT Press.

Cawson, Alan. 1982. "Corporatism and State Theory in the Analysis of Urban Policy." In *Applied Urban Research, Vol. 1*, ed. Gerd-Michael Hellstem, Frithjof Spreer, and Hellmutt Wollmann, pp. 291-300. Bonn: Federal Research Institute for Regional Geography and Regional Planning.

Cockburn, Cynthia. 1977. *The Local State: Management of Cities and People*. London: Pluto Press.

Dear, Michael. 1981. "A Theory of the Local State." In *Political Studies from Spatial Perspectives*, ed. Alan D. Burnett and Peter J. Taylor, pp. 183-200. New York: Wiley.

——————————— and Gordon Clark. 1978. "The State and Geographical Process: A Critical Review." *Environment and Planning* 10, pp. 173-83.

Dearlove, John. 1979. *The Reorganization of British Local Government*. Cambridge: Cambridge University Press.

Duncan, S.S. and M. Goodwin. 1982. "The Local State: Functionalism, Autonomy and Class Relations in Cockburn and Saunders." *Political Geography Quarterly* 1, pp. 77-96.

Elliott, Brian and David McCrone. 1982. *The City: Patterns of Domination and Conflict*. New York: St. Martin's Press.

Friedland, Roger. 1983. *Power and Crisis in the City: Corporations, Unions and Urban Policy*. New York: Schocken.

——————————. 1980. "Corporate Power and Urban Growth: The Case of Urban Renewal." *Politics and Society* 10, pp. 203-24.

——————————. 1976. "Class Power and Social Control: The War on Poverty." *Politics and Society* 6, pp. 459-89.

——————————————, Francis Fox Piven, and Roger Alford. 1977. "Political Conflict, Urban Structure and the Fiscal Crisis." In *Comparing Public Policies,* ed. Douglas Ashford, pp. 197-225. Beverly Hills: Sage.

Glickman, Norman J. 1981a. "National Urban Policy in an Age of Economic Austerity." Report to the President's Commission for a National Agenda for the Eighties. University of Pennsylvania, Department of Regional Science, Working Paper 33.

——————————————. 1981b. "Emerging Urban Policies in a Slow-Growth Economy." *International Journal of Urban and Regional Research* 5, pp. 492-527.

Gurr, Ted Robert and Desmond S. King. 1985. "The State and the City: A Theory of State-City Relations in Western Societies." *Comparative Politics,* forthcoming.

——————————————. 1984. "The Postindustrial City in Transition from Private to Public." In *The Politics of the Public and the Private,* ed. Jan-Erik Lane. London: Sage.

Harloe, Michael, ed. 1981. *New Perspectives in Urban Change and Conflict.* London: Heinemann Educational Books.

Hill, Richard C. 1977. "State Capitalism and the Urban Fiscal Crisis in the United States." *International Journal of Urban and Regional Research* 1, pp. 76-100.

Jacobs, Jane. 1984. *Cities and the Wealth of Nations: Principles of Economic Life.* New York: Random House.

Johnston, R.J. 1982. *Geography and the State.* London: Macmillan.

King, Desmond S. and Ted Robert Gurr. 1983. "State Fiscal Crisis and Urban Decline in Western Societies." Paper read to the American Political Science Annual Meetings, Chicago.

Kirk, Gwyneth. 1980. *Urban Planning in a Capitalist Society.* London: Croom Helm.

Miliband, Ralph. 1983. "State Power and Class Interests." *New Left Review* 138, pp. 57-68.

Molotch, Harvey. 1976. "The City as a Growth Machine; Toward a Political Economy of Place." *American Journal of Sociology* 82, pp. 309-32.

Newton, Kenneth. 1980. *Balancing the Books: Financial Problems of Local Government in Western Europe.* London and Beverly Hills: Sage.

Nordlinger, Eric. 1981. *On the Autonomy of the Democratic State.* Cambridge, MA: Harvard University Press.

Procter, Ian. 1982. "Some Political Economies of Urbanization and Suggestions for a Research Framework." *International Journal of Urban and Regional Research* 6, pp. 83-97.

Saunders, Peter. 1981. *Social Theory and the Urban Question.* London: Hutchinson.

——————————————. 1979. *Urban Politics: A Sociological Approach.* London: Hutchinson.

Skocpol, Theda. 1982. "Bringing the State Back In: A Report on Current Comparative Research on the Relationship between States and Social Structures." *SSRC Items* 36 (June), pp. 1-8.

Tabb, William K. 1982. *The Long Default.* New York: Monthly Review Press.

Van den Berg, L., R. Drewett, L.H. Klaasen, A. Rossi, and C. H. T. Vijverberg. 1982. *Urban Europe Vol. 1: A Study of Growth and Decline.* Oxford: Pergamon.

Webman, Jerry A. 1982. *Reviving the Industrial City: The Politics of Urban Renewal in Lyons and Birmingham.* New Brunswick: Rutgers University Press.

—————————————. 1981. "Centralization and Implementation: Urban Renewal in Great Britain and France." *Comparative Politics* 13, pp. 127-48.

Wolman, Harold. 1982. "Local Autonomy and Intergovernmental Finances in Britain and the United States." In *Fiscal Stress in Cities,* ed. Richard Rose and Edward Page, pp. 168-97. Cambridge: Cambridge University Press.

Young, Ken and Liz Mills. 1982. "The Decline of Urban Economies." In *Fiscal Stress in Cities,* ed. Richard Rose and Edward Page, pp. 77-106. Cambridge: Cambridge University Press.

Zukin, Sharon. 1980. "A Decade of the New Urban Sociology." *Theory and Society* 9, pp. 575-601.

2

The Crises of Development
Or the Development of Crises

ANTONI MOSKWA AND TIMOTHY KEARNEY

Introduction

Since the founding of the USSR as the first so-called scientific
socialist state in 1917, its leaders have professed to be applying
Marxist insights to construct a politicoeconomic and social system
markedly superior to that of the capitalist world. Their system,
which has been diffused to other subsequently established "Socialist
Republics" and "People's Democracies" around the world, is
broadly based on the public ownership of the means of production
and the centralized planning of virtually all economic activity, with
the Communist Party preeminent in the leadership positions of all
strategic economic institutions, buttressed by their parallel domination of state, political, social, and cultural organizations. The wasteful "anarchy of production" characteristic of capitalism, which led
inexorably to the "regular and periodic recurrence" of industrial
cycles punctuated by periodic "overproduction, crisis, and stagnation," is said to have been decisively overcome. Social ownership and
scientific planning would "open a new era in history of utilizing the
principles of a rational economy." Socialist institutions would ensure
"a high rate of steady growth, free from fluctuations, inflation, and
crisis."

The view that economic production cycles are a phenomenon
peculiar to the capitalist mode of production and hence not a suitable
subject for research in the elaboration of the political economy of
socialism quickly solidified into unquestioned dogma among economists in the Soviet sphere of influence. (Interestingly, Western economists studying the Soviet-style economy tended also to leave this

assumption unquestioned, perhaps because their tendency to focus upon institutional analysis rather than dynamic processes obscured the problem.) Nevertheless, the death of Stalin in 1953 led to circumstances in which Soviet bloc economists could once again begin to research and publish on topics that had hitherto been taboo without the need to worry about the more extreme consequences suffered by such predecessors as Bukharin, Kondratieff, or Voznesensky. Established theory (or at least selected portions of it) could now be confronted with the facts of socialist economic life by the new breed of more empirically oriented analysts. By the mid-1950s, the institutional foundations of socialism had been more or less completely in place in the Soviet Union for two decades, and consequently there were nearly two decades of empirical evidence to consider. The central concern with the triumphs and failures of Soviet methods of rapid industrialization quite naturally directed the attention of economists to the closer analysis and more elaborate specification of formal models of the dynamics of socialist industrialization, drawing attention to variations over time in the development tempo of various crucial macroeconomic variables.

A survey of the Polish economic literature uncovers some discussion on this topic, such as Sulnicki's *Economic Structure* (1962) or Minc's *The Political Economy of Socialism* (1963). It was hypothesized that this industrialization, funded in the main by forced savings, had raised the production possibility curve. Following this period of industrialization, production would be switched to consumer goods from investment goods, and society would enjoy a higher level of consumption and welfare. According to the literature, this was a costly but fruitful way to industrialize. We must emphasize, however, that it was believed that the economy would undergo this one fluctuation, and thereafter reap the benefits of smooth, continued growth. Similar conclusions were drawn by Chelinski (1964) and Beksiak (1965). An empirical study of the "investment cycle" of the 1950s was also done by Kliszko (1967), who recognized and predicted additional cycles, which she called the "investment echo." The conclusions drawn, in general, were that the investment cycle was the result of technical factors, due to the size and scale of the initial investment drive undertaken during the transition to socialism. As such, this cycle was not regarded as the product of the political and economic system.

The first Marxist economist who proposed that the socialist countries could be susceptible to permanent economic fluctuation was the Czech Goldman. He raised this proposition in his famous work "Fluctuations and Trends in the Rate of Economic Growth in Some Socialist Countries" (1966). By the beginning of the 1970s, additional empirical studies supported the idea of regular fluctuation of the socialist economies. Research done by Sudra (1972) and Zebrok (1974) now concentrated not on establishing the possibility of fluctuation in socialism, but rather on why the socialist economies fluctuate.

We propose to continue this line of research on the nature of the socialist economy as practiced in East Europe in general, but in Poland specifically. While "court economists" inside Poland continue to proclaim to the public that there are no business cycles in a socialist planned economy, the facts are clearly otherwise. Inside the country, there are serious shortages of goods, rising prices, long lines, and labor unrest. Poland cannot meet its external obligations. Thirty-plus years of socialism have left the media mute, and there is no vocabulary to describe negative economic results.[1] Strikes in August 1980 were described as "work breaks" *(przerwy w pracy)*. There is no concept of depression, recession, or structural imbalance; inflation, unemployment, the underutilization of capacity, even exchange rates have all been stripped of meaning, remaining as vessels of anticapitalist rhetoric.

In the face of such facts, we must define what we mean by a crisis or business cycle in a capitalist economy. Only armed with such knowledge can we begin to investigate the nature of the situation in Poland.

Business Cycles

The study of business cycles is not new in economics, though Keynes revolutionized this field. During the postwar era in the West, "the effort to explain business cycles had been directed at identifying institutional sources of instability, with the hope that . . . their sources could be removed or their influence mitigated by appropriate institutional changes" (Lucas 1981, p. 216). This work has been directed at capitalist economies, even by economists working in socialist countries.

Lucas poses the essential question that must be answered in order to obtain a theory of trade cycles: "Why is it that . . . aggregate variables undergo repeated fluctuations about trends all of essentially the same character?" (p. 215). To answer this question for the Polish case, we must first understand the cycle in a Western sense. As the economy undergoes a cyclical upswing, aggregate demand increases. Inventories rise, adding to that demand. Unemployment falls as additional workers are added, but wages also increase, lowering labor productivity. Increasing labor costs and the greater demand combine to push up prices. Firms, besides increasing stocks, invest more to meet the increased demand. However, as prices increase and consumers, firms, and the government push for capital, interest rates climb. Rising prices and higher interest rates act to slow demand, and once the desired stock/sales ratio is reached, inventory stocking too is cut back, further reducing demand. With demand falling, workers are laid off, which also acts to reduce demand, and investment is cut back, reducing aggregate demand even more. Wages and prices, though rigid, do experience a slowing of their respective rates of increase during this cyclical downturn. The reduction in consumer and firm demand for funds, combined with lowered inflation rates, acts to lower interest rates. Generally, the government steps in to increase aggregate demand through the use of fiscal and monetary instruments (though the effectiveness of such intervention is far from clear). The effect of government policy is to spur demand (short term at least) and falling interest rates prod interest-rate-sensitive consumer spending, as well as business investment, all which combine to increase demand, and the process is started again.

The ability to characterize a Western business cycle in a few sentences is the result of the accumulation of knowledge of a few generations of economists. The Polish crisis is quite similar in its effects to the Great Depression of the 1930s, but no one seems to know why this crash happened and how long it is likely to last. What we will attempt to show is a crisis in a capitalist economy and compare it with a crisis in a socialist economy, namely, Poland.

A recession in a capitalist economy can usually be described by the following:

- Diminishing aggregate demand, which is a cause of diminishing aggregate supply.

- Decreasing income levels.
- Decreasing price levels.
- Decreasing interest rates.
- Falling capacity utilization.
- Reduced investment.
- Increasing unemployment.
- Overall decreased economic activity, measured by falling GNP.

Currently, Poland is in the midst of the deepest crisis any socialist country has yet to face. What are the symptoms, then, of the Polish crisis? A first glance at the Polish situation gives rise to the following picture:

- Aggregate demand exceeds aggregate supply.
- Increasing prices.
- No unemployment (but widespread underemployment).
- Falling investment.
- Increasing nominal wages, but decreasing real wages.
- Overall decreasing national income.
- Falling labor and capital productivity.

Comparing the socialist and capitalist crises, we see that while there are some similarities, for the most part they are different. Therefore, theory developed to account for a capitalist crisis cannot simply be adapted to elucidate the nature and mechanism of this phenomenon in a socialist state. We must turn to the available empirical evidence, and start at the beginning.

Empirical Evidence

In order to demonstrate fully the fluctuating nature of the Polish economy, we will develop further the work done by Moskwa et al. (1981). While the original research investigated the 1948-78 time period, we will extend the analysis through 1982, the most recent year for which data are available.[2] The existing literature on the socialist trade cycle clearly points to the key role of fluctuations in investment spending in the generation of cyclical phenomena. Investment is a crucial determinant of the future growth trend. Investment is also an important decision-making variable in Poland, since the system rewards managers who make investments, be it by ministries, enterprises, or plants. We hypothesize that the propensity to make capital investments is the key variable in the study of Polish business cycles.

In order to decide if the Polish economy exhibits cyclical behavior, we analyzed the following time series, covering the years 1949-82:

- Exports in billions of devisa zloty in constant 1971 prices (EX).
- Imports in billions of devisa zloty in constant 1971 prices (IM).
- Produced national income in billions of 1971 zloty (PNI).
- Distributed national income in billions of 1971 zloty (DNI).
- Employment (excluding services) in millions (L).
- Productive capital stock in billions of 1971 zloty (KS).
- Consumption as a percentage of distributed national income (PC).
- Consumption in billions of 1971 zloty (CON).
- Harvests of four main grains (rye, oats, wheat, and barley) in quintiles per hectare.
- Capital investment outlays in billions of 1971 zloty (I).
- Capital investment as a percentage of distributed national income (PKI).
- Population, in millions (POP).

Using these data as a base, we formulated the following variables:

- The trade balance in billions of 1971 devisa zloty.
- The growth rate of real exports (X).
- The growth rate of real imports (M).
- The lagged growth rate of M.
- The growth rate of PNI.
- The growth rate of DNI.
- The growth rate of KS.
- Harvests lagged one year (HARLAG).
- The growth rate of DNI per capita (CAPNI).
- Consumption growth rates (both CON and PC).
- Investment growth rates (both PKS and I).
- The growth rate of KS.
- Labor productivity (LP).
- Capital productivity (CP).
- The growth rate of LP and CP.
- The growth rate of harvests.

Taking capital investment as the dependent variable, we are able to eliminate consumption from consideration, as consumption plus accumulation equals DNI, and capital investment makes up 75-80 percent of accumulation. Therefore, changes in CON are directly reflected by changes in capital investment, and vice versa. We further rejected I as the dependent variable, since it is the capital investment proportion of DNI that we are calling the "propensity to invest," and it is this variable, and not the stock of capital investment in a given year, that matters.

Further, the growth of capital stock was rejected as it is in reality a function of investment, and as such is the other side of the coin under investigation. Since global export and import figures were given in devisa zloty, the growth rates of X and M were considered. Inasmuch as Poland is a capital good importer, and exports represent the effects of investment, only the growth rate of imports (M) was utilized. Previous research indicated strong correlations among the following variables in the postulated general functional form:

$$
\begin{aligned}
PKI &= f(IM, CP, LP, GNI, H); \text{ where} \\
M &= \text{imports} \\
KP &= \text{capital productivity} \\
LP &= \text{labor productivity} \\
GNI &= \text{growth rate of NI} \\
H &= \text{harvests}
\end{aligned}
$$

Theory can accommodate all the variables except those pertaining to the harvests of the four main grains. The following analysis, however, shows that this agricultural factor plays an important role in the decision-making process. This point can be expanded below. Regression analysis on the data led to the following equation, with the standard errors in parentheses under the coefficients:

$$PKI = 7.4 + .38 \text{ Harlag} - 1.2 \text{ CP} + 1.33 \text{ CAPNI} - .07 \text{ M}$$
$$\quad\; (1.58) \quad (.11) \qquad (.22) \qquad (.18) \qquad\qquad (.04)$$

$$\bar{R}^2 = .938 \qquad F = 126.3 \qquad \text{Durbin-Watson} = 1.883$$

We see from the Durbin-Watson statistic that despite an extremely high adjusted R square, we need not reject the hypothesis of zero autocorrelation. All variables are significant at the 95 percent confidence level, and three (HLAG, CP, and CAPNI) are significant at the 99 percent level. The model, however, showed strong multicollinearity.

Labor productivity was found to be not significant when entered into this equation, though the data show that both capital and labor productivity fluctuate in the same direction (though not in the same degree).

Import growth, however, remains a problematic variable to enter into the equation. First of all, imports as expressed in devisa zloty are not necessarily a good measure of actual imports, as this is merely an accounting convention. In any case, it is the growth of capital goods imports/DNI that would give a true measure of the impact of imports on PKI, rather than, say, the import of consumer items. Recognizing these shortcomings, the regression was run again, without the inclusion of import growth, and the following equation was specified:

$$PKI = 7.44 + .37\ HARLAG - 1.24\ KP + 1.27\ CAPNI$$
$$(1.64)\ (.12)\qquad\qquad (.22)\qquad (.18)$$

with the D-W statistic of 1.61, in the indeterminate range. The F-statistic increased to 156 in this model, and all t-statistics as well as the F-statistic are at the 99 percent confidence level.

The model still continued to exhibit a high degree of multicollinearity. As a result of this strong correleation among the independent variables, it was decided to track the behavior of PKI, CP, HARLAG, and CAPNI over the 1949-82 period. While multicollinearity does serve to reduce our confidence in the value of the independent regressors, our analysis suggests that the model is correctly specified and that indeed the independent variables are statistically significant. It was decided to add the growth of labor productivity (LP) to the historical analysis, since it does exhibit cyclical behavior quite similar to that of the growth of capital productivity.

Some tentative conclusions can be drawn from the regression analysis. Most important, the propensity to make capital investments in Poland has been strongly correlated with the growth of distributed national income per capita and the harvest levels of the preceding year. This suggests that investment tended to be higher when income was growing and food more plentiful and vice versa. Economic theory does not fully explain the significance of these two variables. We hypothesize that investment decisions are primarily of a political nature. For example, the bad harvest of 1975 was nevertheless the second-best harvest during the postwar period. It seems highly unlikely that the central plan was balanced only on the lack of continued record harvests. Thus the change in the development strategy was covered by the fig leaf of an act of God in the form of a bad harvest. Furthermore, our regression analysis showed investment to be a negative function of the growth of capital productivity, pointing up the inefficient use of capital under Poland's socialist system. In the Polish system of national accounts, outlays on unfinished projects are included in the capital stock. Measuring the capital productivity as KS/DNI, we see KS increasing faster than DNI as investment increases during the cyclical upswing. Capital productivity falls as the system continues to add to the stock of unproductive capital.

Our study revealed a number of changes in the data over the time period studied (see Figure 2.1), and we have attempted to analyze these changes over time.

The Propensity to Invest (PKI)

During the 1949-82 period, four local peaks or turning points in investment's share of national income were observed: 1953, 1962, 1969, and 1974. From 1949 to 1953, PKI increased by 10 percent per annum, reaching 16.2 percent in 1953. From 1954-57, PKI fell by 13 percent to 14.1 percent in 1957. The following year represented the starting point for the second fluctuation. During the 1958-62 period, PKI grew by over one-third and equalled 19.1 percent in 1962. There were small decreases in 1963-64 (2.6 percent per year), and 1965-69 registered annual increases. By 1969, gross capital formation had reached 22.3 percent of DNI, at that time the highest level yet recorded. Again, the downturn was short (two years) and small (2.6 percent), to 21.8 percent.

The early 1970s (1972-74) were characterized by the largest

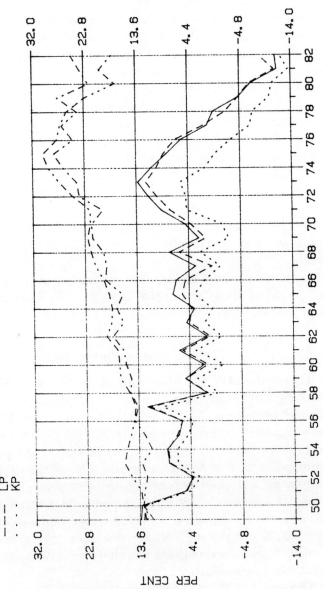

Figure 2.1 Polish Macroeconomic Variables, 1949-82

----- HARLAG
---- PKI
····· CAPNI
-- LP
·· KP

QUINTILES/HA

PER CENT

32

increases in PKI in Polish history, fully 39 percent from a relatively high starting point, and in 1975 reached 30.2 percent. PKI began its long slide in 1976, and fell to 17.3 percent in 1980. Since then, the Polish authorities have slightly modified their definition of PKI. Data are entered in the statistical yearbook per the previous definition to 1980, and per the new definition from 1980 onwards. Thus, while the new definition increases PKI to 22.7 percent in 1980 from 17.3, it also records a fall by 17.9 percent in 1982.

In sum, we see four cycles in postwar Poland:

- 1949-57, with a peak in 1953.
- 1958-64, with a peak in 1962.
- 1965-71, with a peak in 1969.
- 1972-82, with a peak in 1975.

We are not able to say with certainty if in fact the fourth cycle is over, but we will return to this point. The first cycle lasted nine years, the second and third seven, while the fourth has gone on for at least 11 years. During the first cycle, investment increased for five years and decreased for four years. During the second and third cycles, the increase was again over five years, but the decrease was a relatively short two years and the decrease was rather small. The fourth cycle started with a strong increase over four years, but the decrease has lasted for at least seven years.

Growth in Distributed National Income Per Capita (CAPNI)

The first phase shows growth in national income per capita falling during 1949-53 from 13.5 percent to 8.3 percent as PKI increased. During the second phase (1954-57), CAPNI increased to 12 percent as PKI fell. The second cycle (1958-64) saw no simple monotonic increase or decrease, but in 1962, when PKI reached a peak, PACNI had fallen to 1.3 percent, and growth picked up to 4.9 percent in 1963 and 3.5 percent in 1964 as PKI fell. For the third cycle (1965-71) there is again no smooth pattern but rather sharp fluctuation. Nevertheless, in 1969, when PKI reached a local peak of 21.6 percent, CAPNI had fallen to 2.6 percent; while PKI fell during both 1970 and 1971, CAPNI increased to 5 percent (1971) and 9.2 percent (1972). CAPNI continued to rise until 1973 when it reached 13.3 percent, as the Gierek regime followed its policy of "consumption as the engine of growth." But as PKI continued to rise, CAPNI began a fall in its growth rate, which turned negative in 1978 and reached −11.5 percent in 1981 and −11.2 percent in 1982. The Polish economy virtually collapsed.

Labor (LP) and Capital (CP) Productivity Growth

Labor and capital productivity growth follow nearly identical growth patterns during the 1949-82 period and as such will be treated together. Figure 2.1 shows that labor productivity growth generally has been stronger in Poland.

During the first cycle, LP and CP both fall from over 12 percent in 1949 to 4 percent (LP) and 2.74 percent (CP) in 1952, the year before the peak of 1953. Growth jumps in 1953 for LP to 8.1 percent and CP to 6.7 percent, but falls annually until 1956, the year before the trough. In 1957, LP (11.5 percent) and KP (9.3 percent) show strong growth, which is again not sustained. During the second cycle, as for CAPNI, LP and CP fluctuate without a definite pattern, but both fall off sharply in 1962 (CP = −1.3 percent, LP = 0.7 percent), as PKI reaches a local peak. This pattern is repeated in 1969, when LP falls to 1.4 percent from 6.1 percent in 1968, and CP falls to −2.7 percent from 2.4 percent. As the 1972-82 cycle begins, LP reaches a maximum growth rate of 11 percent in 1972, with KP peaking at 5.8 percent in 1973. Growth again falls thereafter for both ratios, with growth of KP turning negative in 1975, and LP in 1977. Neither had turned positive by 1982.

Near or at the local peaks in national income growth, we see the smallest increases of LP. The situation is even more pronounced for capital productivity growth, since at the local peaks of 1962, 1969, and 1975 capital productivity growth was actually negative. A drastic fall in capital productivity is a leading indicator of impending crisis. The increasingly inefficient use of resources becomes more pronounced before each swing. Despite large-scale importation of technology from the West in the 1970s, the efficiency of both labor and capital is lower than it was in the early 1970s.

Harvests Lagged One Year (HARLAG)

In the first years of the downturn (1954, 1963, 1970, and 1976), HARLAG shows either a reduction or little growth. In other words, during the peak year harvests fall significantly, forcing planners to switch resources to consumption from capital formation. Likewise, in the first year of increase in 1958 and 1972, the lagged harvests show strong increases. That is to say, the harvest in the fall of the last year of the downturn is such that the authorities feel they can again begin to redirect resources to the investment sector. The availability and price of food has played an important role in Poland since World War II. The disturbances of 1956, 1970-71, and 1980, which began to protest food increases, eventually led to the changing of the first secretary of the Communist Party. By examining the difference between growth rates of food prices on state and free markets, we can see if there was excess demand pressure. A value below zero indicates higher free market price growth and vice versa. We see market equilibrium obtained (among other times) in 1963 and 1970 (right after achieving the local peak in PKI), in 1953 and 1975 (during the local peak), and in 1956 and 1968 (years right before reaching a local peak) (see Figure 2.2).

Political Conflict

It is impossible to understand the cyclical behavior of the Polish economy since 1949 without an investigation of political changes during that period. Since Poles lack the ability to voice political concerns peacefully—the result of the lack of free elections with competitive candidates or parties—it is difficult to introduce an explicit "political" variable to our analysis. We can nonetheless note that the accumulation of popular dissatisfaction crystalized in the form of protests in 1956, 1968, 1970, 1976, and 1980. The protests of 1956, 1970, and 1980 were strong enough to force changes in the leadership of the Communist Party. With the exception of the unrest in 1968, we can see that the peaks of overt political conflict occur in the periods just following the peaks of PKI. According to Taylor and Jodice's (1983) World Handbook of Political and Social Indicators (which contains data for the 1948-77 period), Poland experienced political strikes in the following pattern:

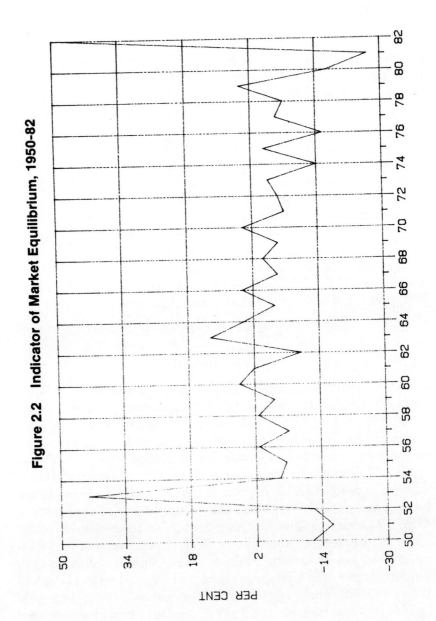

Figure 2.2 Indicator of Market Equilibrium, 1950-82

Period	Strikes
1948-52	0
1953-57	4
1958-62	0
1963-67	0
1968	6
1969	0
1970-71	8
1972-75	0
1976	1
1977	0

Of course Poland had undergone a number of political strikes since then, and the number has been especially high since 1980. We see that, with the exception of 1968, all political strikes occurred during the downside of the cycle, somewhat lagging the peak year (especially in 1970-71 and 1976). We hypothesize a direct connection between the two phenomena. Increasing PKI automatically lowers consumption and the shortages of goods become more pronounced. Unrest increases and creates an explosion, which in 1956, 1970, 1976, and 1980 was triggered by food price increases. In short, we feel that this political behavior is a slow reflex reaction to the economic changes. Political change has been generally the result of mass demonstrations during which hundreds are injured or killed.

Although each cycle is of a somewhat different time frame and exhibits somewhat different behavior, we will try to present a "typical cycle."

The Cycle

A typical cycle begins from relative market equilibrium, as measured above. Investment begins to take an increasing portion of DNI. The total value of uncompleted investment achieves a peak usually one year before the local peaking of PKI. Simultaneously, CAPNI begins to decrease. Almost automatically, the decrease in the efficiency of capital is larger than that of labor. Two years before the turning point, the gestation period of investment drastically increases. The authorities then switch a large share of the available construction workers and materials from projects in housing, schools, hospitals, and so forth to industrial capital construction. Market disequilibrium becomes more visible as inflationary pressures intensify. These problems are compounded by real or statistically created bad harvests. After the turning point, national income decelerates and the authorities are faced with reducing PKI. New investments are curtailed until unfinished projects are completed. Industrial capacity increases as projects come on stream, and both labor and capital productivity begin to improve, but with a longer and longer lag in each cycle.

Immediately after the turning point, change in the investment policy does not lead to a spectacular improvement in the economy's performance. Bad harvest and shifting of resources from service-oriented construction projects to industrial projects to break bottlenecks have an almost immediate impact on living standards. The public begins to realize the depth of the economic problems. The longer the lines, the less the patience, which serves to increase political tensions among the masses. In Poland, this heightening of tensions generally has found its outlet in protests, mass demonstrations, and strikes, which three times have been strong enough to change the leadership of the Communist Party. The new leadership normally has shifted resources quickly from investment to consumption as a political stopgap (sometimes assisted by foreign emergency aid) and then later generally has benefitted from the delayed coming-on-stream of capital projects begun much earlier. The economy gradually approaches equilibrium, planners recover their self-confidence, and the process begins again.

In both the socialist and capitalist cases, we see that investment plays a key role in economic fluctuation. Thus, understanding the fluctuation of investment is the key to understanding the economic changes an economy undergoes over time. It is not our intention to discuss comprehensively the investment mechanism in a socialist country in this chapter, as it is a separate topic in its own right. We will, therefore, limit our discussion to a few major points.

The political-economic authorities in a socialist country treat investment as the main factor in economic growth. They believe that a high level of current investment will increase the welfare of the public in the future. With some qualifications, this is theoretically true. The highest sustainable level of investment should be allocated efficiently to the various sectors of the economy. The model being used during the planning process, however, does not lead to this goal. In our view, the market is the one tool for the efficient allocation of investment, but it is not generally used in socialist states. The market mechanism has been replaced by a specific type of bureaucratic bargaining. The planned allocation of investment is the result of the bargaining position and strategies of enterprises, of private friendships, and of access to semiclassified documents. The incentive system is not profit-oriented, and therefore the marginal efficiency of investment is scarcely taken into account by decision-makers. Additionally, the planners can manipulate prices to support their decisions: that is, having decided to make certain investments, the parameters can than be changed to give the appearance of "optimality" to the plan. Stankiewicz (1980-81) and Staniszkis (1980), among others, have shown that the propensity for managers, the regional nomenklatura, enterprises, and ministries to seek new investment is very high. Without an interest rate that plays an economically significant role, investment is free to the direct beneficiaries and therefore demand is not satiable. There is no organized opposition to increased investment within the planning process, and bargaining is chiefly concerned with the distribution of the expanding investment pie. The only effective brakes on investment are the periodic crises.

Conclusions

As we can see, the Polish economy does exhibit cyclical behavior. The current, deep depression in Poland is not the result of the mistakes made by particular politicians, nor aggravated by the banned trade union Solidarity or private farmers (kulaks). Rather, the crisis is a consequence of the system operating in Poland for nearly 40 years. Rational scientific central planning is a myth. Was the current recession planned? Certainly not. One must then conclude that the plan does not direct, and in fact is quite separate from reality. Other mechanisms, as we mention above, run the economy.

Armed with this knowledge of the three previous crises, what can we expect from the current situation? As the investments of the recent past come on line, especially in the areas of raw materials and semimanufactured goods, production should again begin to increase as bottlenecks are eased. The level of investment will increase, partly as the result of Soviet direct investment, exemplified by the recent signing of an agreement to run 150 large plants in Poland. This will produce a short-term increase in national income growth. However, the recent reforms have not altered greatly the Polish planning and managerial system. (This point is even made in Polish publications, that behind proud pronouncements stand empty words!) Producers are still to be evaluated on their success in fulfilling physical output targets, rather than on profitability. Therefore, their interest is to continue to increase output (in certain numerical quantities rather than by product mix or quality). The surest way to increase output, and thereby pad one's position, remains the securing of additional "free" capital and labor resources. There is no room to maneuver on the part of the plant managers in any meaningful way. The political authorities and planners remain unwilling to share power with any other group that might oppose overambitious development plans at the expense of short-term living standards. Thus, there is no mechanism to check the growth of investment before reaching the next turning point. This threshold is probably much lower now than the 30 percent registered in the 1970s, or even lower than the 20 percent in the 1950s. Due to the fact that Polish society is poorer and probably will not accept many more restrictions on consumption, we see no way to increase the marginal propensity to save of a people who spend 40 percent of their disposable income on food, and one-third of whom live below the government's definition of the poverty line. Further, Poland can no longer import capital from the West on the scale of the 1970s as the result of its debt problems; it must even orient production to exports to repay its debts. Thus, the recovery in Poland will probably be very weak and the next turning point will be very low.

We see nothing in place to forestall the next crisis. Economic changes alone, no matter how deep, cannot create the apparatus to produce solid growth. As we have pointed out briefly, this problem is one of a political nature that actively fights reform. There are many automatic stabilizers in a capitalist economy. They turn back the economy from recession to recovery. In other words, the economy moves along in a rough balance generally, groping for equilibrium. The Polish economy does not seem to have any endogenous economic stabilizers. The planners conduct the economy along the twisting road of development by periodically "dropping the hammer" of investment, with no braking mechanism but the brick wall of political unrest.

As we understand this problem, any effective reform must first be political. The means of production must be returned to the owners—the public—who then will have control of the economic decision-making process.

The necessity for reform in the Eastern bloc is self-evident. Such reform would be useful for both the bloc and the West. This remains a deep, political-economic question, too large to even initiate here. Understanding the nature and origin of the crisis should help in addressing this question in the future.

Notes

1. Nove (1978) gives an example of this phenomenon in the Soviet Union: "Even the word 'statistics' was replaced by 'accounting', because 'statistics' suggested random and uncontrollable results."

2. All statistical data are taken from *Rocznik Statystyczny* (statistical yearbook) published in Poland.

Bibliography

Baka, W. 1978. *Planowanie Gospodarki Narodowej*. Warszawa: PWE.

Bartnicki, Z. 1983. "Kryzys Gospdarczy w PRL." *Kultura* 11, Paris.

Beksiak, Janusz. 1965. *Wzrost Gospodarczy i Niepodzielnosc Inwestycji*. Warszawa: PWN.

Campbell, Robert. 1974. *The Soviet-type Economies*. Boston: Houghton Mifflin.

Chelinski, R. 1964. "Ftapowy Charakter Rozwoju Gospodarczego w Polsce Ludowej." *Economista* 5, Warszawa.

Erdos, P. 1971. *Contribution to the Theory of Capitalist Money, Business Fluctuation and Crises*. Budapest: Akademiaikiado.

Goldman, Josef. 1964. "Fluctuation and Trend in the Rate of Economic Growth in Some Socialist Countries." *Economics of Planning* 4, pp.13-19.

Kalecki, Michael. 1969. *Theory of Economic Dynamics*. New York: Kelley.

Keynes, John. 1964. *The General Theory of Employment, Interest and Money*. New York: Harcourt Brace Jovanovich.

Kliszko, A. 1967. "Proba Weryfikacji Hipotezy Wystepowania Ogolnego Cyklu Inwestycyjnego w Polsce Ludowej." *Gospodarka Planowa* 7-8, Warszawa.

Kolodko, G. 1979. "Fazy Wzrostu Gospodarczego w Polsce." *Gospodarka Planowa* 3, Warszawa.

Kuczynski, W. 1981. *Po Wielkim Skoku*. Warszawa: PWE.

Lange, Oskar. 1978. *Ekonomika Polityczna*. Warszawa: PWE.

Lenin, Vladimir I. 1971. *Selected Works*. New York: International.

Lucas, R. 1981. *Studies in Business-Cycle Theory*. Cambridge: MIT Press.

Minc, Bronislaw. 1963. *Ekonomia Polityczna Socjalizmu*. Warszawa: KIW.

Mitchell, Wesley C. 1975. *Business Cycles: The Problem and Its Setting.* New York: Arno.

Moskwa, Antoni. 1981. "Udane Proby Nieudanych Reform." *Wektory,* Warszawa.

—————————————, M. Socha, and J. Wilkin. 1981. "Kierunki Zmian Politycznogospodarczych w Polsce." In *Reforma Gospodarcza.* Warszawa: PWE.

Neuberger, Egon and R. Petty. 1976. *Comparative Economic Systems.* Boston: Allyn & Bacon.

Nove, Alec. 1978. *The Soviet Economic System.* London: Allen & Unwin.

Pajestka, Josef. 1981. *Polski Kryzys Lat 1980-81.* Warszawa: KIW.

—————————————. 1965. "Analiza Niektorych Aspektow Polityki Rozwoju Gospodarczego Polski." *Ekonomista* 2, Warszawa.

Rocznik Statystyczny. Various years, Gus Warszawa.

Staniszkis, Jadwiga. 1980. "Systemowe Uwarunkowania Funkczonowania Przedsiebiorstwa Przemyslowego w Polsce." *Przeglad Socjologiczny* 32, Warszawa.

Stankiewicz, T. 1980-81. Seminar at Warsaw University, Department of Economics.

Sudra, T. 1972. "Pryczyny Etapowosci Wzrostu Gospodarczego w Socjalizmie." *Ekonomista* 2, Warszawa.

Sulnicki, P. 1962. *Struktura Ekonomiczna.* Warszawa: PWN.

Taylor, Charles and David Jodice. 1983. *World Handbook of Political and Social Indicators.* 3d edition, Volume 2. New Haven: Yale University Press.

Taylor, Charles and Michael Hudson. 1972. *World Handbook of Political and Social Indicators,* 2d edition. New Haven: Yale University Press.

Tucker, Robert, ed. 1978. *The Marx-Engels Reader.* New York: Norton.

Zebrok, J. 1974. "Proba Periodyzacji Rozwoju Przemyslu w Polsce Ludowej." *Gospodarka Planowa.* Warszawa.

3

Sources of Periodic Economic Crises Under the Centrally Planned Socialist System

ZBIGNIEW M. FALLENBUCHL

By the late 1940s, Communist governments had become firmly established in all East European countries. A highly centralized Soviet-type economic system and a development strategy modelled closely on the Soviet policy of forced-pace industrialization and agricultural collectivization were adopted in every country, irrespective of size, level of development, factor endowment, or specific national features or traditions. A drastic redirection of foreign trade away from market economies to the USSR and other Communist countries was accomplished with extreme rapidity and institutionalized by the creation in 1949 of the Council for Mutual Economic Assistance (CMEA). The span of over 30 years beginning with the first five-year plans in 1951 represents a period of development in Eastern Europe guided with remarkable consistency by the institutions and distinctive policy priorities of the centrally planned socialist system.

Contrary to the official claims that socialist central planning would virtually eliminate wasteful economic fluctuations along with the "anarchy of the marketplace," the actual record of developments in Eastern Europe during the period 1951-82 indicates that the main macroeconomic variables have continued to display quite substantial fluctuations in every country (although some countries have experi-

The author wishes to thank Professor Paul M. Johnson of Florida State University for his many valuable editorial suggestions.

enced considerably more instability than others). This is true even when we confine our analysis to the official statistics, with all of their well-known weaknesses.

The present chapter examines this phenomenon of fluctuating rates of economic growth in Eastern Europe, with an eye to untangling and elucidating factors that combine to produce the distinctive boom-and-bust pattern of the "socialist business cycle."

Growth Role Volatility

The volatility of growth rates of Domestic Net Material Product (DNMP) can be gauged in several ways. Table 3.1 displays summary statistics for the period 1951-82 for the volatility of DNMP and several other key macroeconomic indicators. Space precludes extended analysis here, but the following relatively elementary descriptive generalizations may be a useful background for the more detailed treatment of the period below.

Regardless of the particular measure taken, the GDR, Czechoslovakia (CSSR), and the USSR show greater stability in their DNMP growth rates than the other four countries. The difference between the two groups of countries corresponds closely to their relative degrees of industrialization at the beginning of the period as measured by the share of industrial employment in total employment. The greatest absolute fluctuations are observed in Bulgaria and Romania, the two least industrialized countries, but since they also maintained the highest average rates of growth by a considerable margin, they show up as somewhat more stable than Hungary and Poland by the coefficient of variation criterion.

The close correspondence between level of industrialization and volatility in the growth rate suggests immediately the thought that the differences between the more and less industrialized countries' stability might be largely accounted for by the differing relative importance of agriculture in total output, since the vagaries of the weather tend everywhere to make agriculture one of the more volatile elements of the national economy. Table 3.1 indeed shows the index of gross agricultural production to be particularly unstable compared to the other components of the national income. However, multiple correlation analysis produces somewhat surprising results. Accepting the rates of growth of DNMP as the dependent variable and taking the rates of growth of gross agricultural production and gross indus-

Table 3.1 Measures of Volatility in Economic Growth Rates, 1951-82

	Bulgaria	Romania	Hungary	Poland	GDR	CSSR	USSR
DNMP							
Max-Min	42	38	34	23	20	13	11
Variance	55.3	42.4	33.0	29.1	14.0	9.1	8.7
Coefficient of Variation	0.87	0.71	1.07	1.00	0.61	0.33	0.40
Gross Agricultural Production							
Max-Min	56	44	45	21	30	18	23
Variance	105.5	103.3	68.8	23.3	35.4	18.1	34.7
Coefficient of Variation	2.38	2.11	2.89	2.62	2.24	2.13	1.81
Gross Industrial Production							
Max-Min	16	23	32	29	20	19	13
Variance	15.5	18.0	34.3	28.7	14.4	14.1	9.2
Coefficient of Variation	0.37	0.35	0.80	0.64	0.50	0.53	0.36
Investment Outlays							
Max-Min	74	47	77	48	31	32	19
Variance	157.9	99.9	188.4	104.2	64.2	46.9	18.7
Coefficient of Variation	1.17	0.86	2.01	1.54	0.91	1.05	0.55

45

trial production as independent variables, we can derive the partial correlation coefficients shown in Table 3.2. Only in Bulgaria was agriculture relatively more important than the industrial sector in influencing the DNMP rates of growth, although dependence upon agriculture was also fairly strong in Romania and Hungary as well. For highly industrialized Czechoslovakia, GDR, and the USSR, as might be expected, the role of agricultural fluctuations in overall DNMP fluctuations was so minor as to fall short of conventional thresholds of statistical significance. Except in the least developed country, the principal sources of instability are to be found in the modern sector rather than in agriculture.

Fluctuations in investment policy seem to have represented a particularly important source of instability during the period 1951-82. Investment outlays fluctuated more widely than the DNMP in every country (see Table 3.1), and the fluctuations of the two variables were very highly correlated (Pearson's r of .844 for the USSR, .576 for Romania, .554 for Czechoslovakia, .553 for Poland, .509 for GDR, .492 for Bulgaria, and .266 for Hungary—all but the last significant at the .05 level). The major role of investment as a source of instability is of particular interest, since close control of investment policy by the planners and their political bosses has been a principal feature of the system of planning and management.

The degree of dependence upon imports to sustain growth might

Table 3.2 Relative Contribution of Gross Agricultural Production and Gross Industrial Production to Accounting for Fluctuations in Growth Rates of Domestic Net Material Product in Seven East European Countries, 1951-82

| | Partial correlation coefficients for | | | | | | |
	Bulgaria	CSSR	GDR	Hungary	Poland	Romania	USSR
Growth rate of agricultural production	.579*	.231	.060	.409*	.360*	.417*	.218
Growth rate of industrial production	.546*	.664*	.804*	.572*	.636*	.607*	.778*

*Significant at .05 level

be expected to influence the stability of growth rates, since external market conditions are largely beyond the control of the planners. East European trade data are scarce and subject to more than the usual number of reservations, but data on the volume of total imports are available for all seven countries for the years 1959-82. Correlation coefficients between growth of imports and growth of DNMP were as follows: Poland, .420; Bulgaria, .412; Czechoslovakia, .375; Romania, .364; GDR, .334; USSR, .313; and Hungary, .301 (only the figures for Poland and Bulgaria are significant at the .05 level). The figures for the period as a whole reflect the relatively autarkic development policies pursued and suggest that fluctuations in imports could have played an important role in generating instability only in Poland and Bulgaria. However, because of the changing approaches to international trade in the 1970s, this is a particularly complicated question and requires a separate and more detailed study before drawing such conclusions.

Large-scale political disturbances might be expected to have an impact on the stability of economic growth rates. However, because of the relative success of the Communist regimes in maintaining public order over the years, such factors played an important role in only a few subperiods for only a few of the countries. During the first half of the 1950s, riots in Berlin and the large outflow of population to the West clearly increased the GDR's economic instability. The mass uprising of 1956 clearly had a very strong impact on Hungary's economic performance during the second half of the 1950s. In Poland, riots in Poznan and the turmoil accompanying Gomulka's return to power in 1956 seem to have had a small but appreciable impact on the stability of economic growth. In Czechoslovakia, the stagnation in the rates of growth of the early and mid-1960s was a major factor in bringing about the political ferment of 1968 and thus in precipitating the Soviet invasion of that summer, which in turn disrupted production for some time thereafter. Similarly, in Poland, economic difficulties helped precipitate riots and a massive turnover in economic and political leadership in 1970-71, more riots and strikes in 1976, and the massive wave of strikes in 1980 that brought about a third enforced change of leadership. While quantitative proof is difficult, it would seem that only in Poland was political turmoil a major determinant of economic instability over the period as a whole, and even there the direction of causation remains highly uncertain.

Cyclical Patterns in Growth Rates

We concentrated above on analyzing instability for the entire 1951-82 period. Instability does not, however, constitute an unambiguous indication of the existence of periodical or semiperiodical fluctuations, and when it is measured for such a long period it may even conceal many instructive developments that tend to cancel each other out. We will now focus more closely on particular sequences in particular subperiods. As is usual in cyclical analysis, the division of the period into cycles is inescapably somewhat arbitrary. Their length depends on how they are measured. Moreover, not all minor turning points should be taken into consideration.

Figure 3.1 suggests three comments: except in a few special cases the fluctuations in the DNMP rates of growth were above their zero values—that is, there were only rarely instances of absolute decline, at least until the difficulties of the late 1970s and early 1980s; upswings and downswings tended to be very short; and fluctuations were more pronounced during the early years than during the middle period, but they seem to have increased again in some countries during more recent years.

The First Cycle: 1951-56

The pattern of fluctuations during the first few years of the 1951-82 period seems to be very similar across countries. Very ambitious five-year plans were introduced in 1951 in all countries of Eastern Europe (except Poland, where the six-year-plan started in 1950). The years 1951-56 may be accepted as the first cycle. The share of accumulation (forced saving) in the national net material product (NNMP, or the "allocated national income" according to Marxist terminology, which differs from DNMP by deducting the value of export and adding the value of import) was extremely high in Romania, Bulgaria, Hungary, and Poland. It was more moderate in Czechoslovakia and, especially, in the GDR. Everywhere the rates of growth of investment were very high in 1951-52 and in Romania, GDR, and Poland also in 1953. In all countries the DNMP rates of growth were unsustainably high and the savings and investment effort too extreme. They created distortions and maladjustments throughout the economy and destabilized it. In 1952 the DNMP rate of growth declined to −2 percent in Hungary, −1 percent in

Figure 3.1   Domestic Net Material Product and Investment

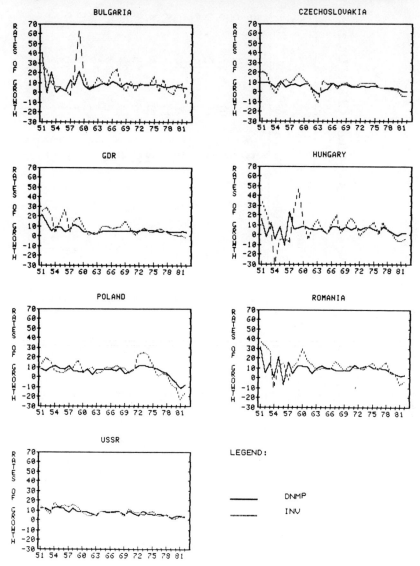

LEGEND:

—————— DNMP

············· INV

49

Table 3.3   Gross Investment Outlays and Domestic Net Material Product (Official Data, Annual Rates of Growth, Constant Prices)

Year	Bulgaria		Czechoslovakia		GDR		Hungary		Poland		Romania		USSR	
	Inv.	DNMP	Inv.	DNMP	Inv.	DNMP	Inv.	DNMP	Inv.	DNMP	Inv.	DNMP	Inv.	DNMP
1951	27	41	21	10	25*	22	35	16	12	8	37	31	14	12
1952	22	-1	18	10	29*	14	22	-2	19	6	32	5	11	12
1953	9	21	4	7	21*	5	5	12	15	10	27	15	5	9
1954	6	0	-2	4	3	9	-30	-5	6	11	-10	0	18	13
1955	5	5	8	11	15	9	-5	8	4	8	12	22	13	12
1956	2	1	13	5	27	4	-4	-11	5	7	15	-7	15	11
1957	-3	13	9	7	4	7	-8	23	8	11	-2	16	13	7
1958	22	7	13	8	15	11	23	6	10	6	11	4	16	12
1959	63	22	19	6	19	9	47	7	17	5	16	12	13	8
1960	18	7	12	8	10	4	13	9	6	4	30	11	7	8
1961	4	3	8	7	1	4	-5	6	7	8	18	11	4	7
1962	7	6	-3	1	3	2	9	5	10	2	13	4	5	6
1963	15	7	-11	-2	2	3	15	6	3	7	8	10	5	4
1964	10	10	11	1	10	5	4	5	5	7	10	12	9	9
1965	8	7	7	3	10	5	1	1	10	7	9	10	8	7

Year													
1966	20	11	10	9	7	5	11	8	8	7	9	10	7	8
1967	24	9	3	6	9	5	20	8	11	6	17	7	8	9
1968	9	6	8	7	10	5	2	5	9	9	12	7	8	8
1969	1	10	10	7	15	5	8	8	8	3	7	7	3	5
1970	11	7	6	5	7	6	17	5	4	5	12	7	11	9
1971	2	7	5	5	1	4	11	7	7	8	10	13	7	6
1972	10	8	9	6	5	6	-1	5	23	11	10	10	7	4
1973	7	8	9	5	8	6	4	7	25	11	8	11	5	9
1974	8	8	9	6	4	6	9	7	22	10	13	13	7	6
1975	17	9	8	6	5	5	13	5	11	9	15	10	9	5
1976	1	7	4	4	7	4	0	3	1	7	8	10	4	6
1977	14	6	3	4	6	5	13	8	3	5	12	9	4	5
1978	1	6	4	4	3	4	4	5	2	3	16	8	6	5
1979	-2	7	2	3	1	4	1	2	-8	-2	4	6	1	2
1980	8	6	1	3	0	4	-6	-1	-12	-6	3	3	2	4
1981	10	5	-5	0	1	5	-6	2	-23	-12	-7	2	4	3
1982	-11	4	-4	0	-2	3	-3	2	-16	-8	-3	3	2	3

* Current prices.

Sources: G.U.S., *Rozwoj gospodarczy krajow RWPG, 1950-1968* (The Economic Development of the CMEA Countries, 1950-1968), Warsaw 1969; G.U.S., *Kraje RWPG* (The CMEA Countries), Warsaw 1972; G.U.S., *Kraje RWPG, 1960-1975* (The CMEA Countries, 1960-1975), Warsaw 1976; statistical yearbooks of the above countries.

Bulgaria, 5 percent in Romania, 6 percent in Poland, and 14 percent in GDR. Only in Czechoslovakia, where the rate of growth in 1951 was relatively moderate, was it maintained unchanged in 1952. In 1953 the rate of growth increased in Bulgaria (to 21 percent), Romania (to 15 percent), Hungary (to 12 percent), and Poland (to 10 percent), but declined in Czechoslovakia (to 7 percent) and the GDR (to 5 percent). The decline continued in 1954. In Romania and in Bulgaria there was zero growth and in Hungary an absolute decline (−5 percent). In Czechoslovakia the rate of growth declined to 4 percent. Only in GDR and in Poland did the rates of growth increase (to 9 percent and 11 percent respectively). There was some revival of the rates of growth in 1955 in Bulgaria (5 percent), Hungary (8 percent), and Czechoslovakia (11 percent) and a big increase in Romania (22 percent). In the GDR the same rate of growth was maintained as in 1954 (9 percent), but in Poland there was a decline (to 7 percent). Everywhere the rates of growth declined in 1956. They were: −11 percent in Hungary, where an uprising took place, −7 percent in Romania, 1 percent in Bulgaria, 4 percent in GDR, 5 percent in Czechoslovakia, and 7 percent in Poland despite riots and a change in leadership.

The pattern during the first cycle can be explained by the interaction of the strategy of development and the economic system (Fallenbuchl 1964), together with mistakes in planning that the system made possible. The strategy required the highest possible rates of forced saving and investment. Top priority was given to highly capital-, material-, and energy-intensive heavy industry in order to produce the largest possible range of producers' goods for the continuation of the domestic investment program (Fallenbuchl 1965). The gestation period of investment (the period of time between the initial investment outlays and the beginnings of actual utilization in production of the new capital assets) was inescapably rather long in the priority sector. Moreover, an excessively wide investment front resulted in dissipating scarce resources over a large number of unfinished projects and consequent waste. Industries producing consumption goods, agriculture, and infrastructure were largely neglected. Moreover, the harsh political struggle for rural collectivization, which at that time was regarded as a necessary condition for a successful "socialist industrialization," created additional instability in the agricultural sector (Fallenbuchl 1967).

This was basically an inward looking strategy based on import substitution (Fallenbuchl 1966). Developments in other countries were not taken into consideration, except for current Soviet import requirements, which mandated still further expansion of heavy industry. As the result of almost identical priorities, "parallel industrial structures" were created in all East European countries, making it difficult to expand trade among them, since they were offering each other almost the same goods and had the same requirements for raw materials and machines (Nagy 1957, p. 189). Despite strong autarkic tendencies, the import of raw materials, fuels, and machines increased while no viable export sector was created and some prewar markets in the West were lost (Fallenbuchl 1968).

Standards of living declined, shortages of consumption goods appeared, housing deteriorated, and incentives to work were correspondingly reduced. A politically explosive situation appeared, first in the GDR and Czechoslovakia, then subsequently in Hungary and Poland and, to a considerably more controllable extent, elsewhere.

The system of the command economy made all these excesses possible. In the absence of the rate of interest and with prices and wages controlled, with foreign trade a state monopoly, and a high degree of insulation of the economy thus assured, the planners had no automatic warnings that they were exceeding the optimum rate of saving and investment. Instead of increasing the rate of growth of social product, in their zeal they caused its collapse (Fallenbuchl 1963).

Without market signals they created industrial structures that were not only inefficient and heavily capital-, material- and energy-intensive, but also to a considerable extent technologically obsolete, unable to produce competitive exports. In effect, a built-in balance-of-payments deficit and inflationary pressures were created at that time that have had serious consequences for the whole postwar period (Fallenbuchl 1981a).

When the economies became excessively destabilized, numerous serious bottlenecks slowed down development, especially in the areas of construction, raw materials, and energy supply. Balance-of-payments difficulties created the so-called foreign trade barrier, limiting the planners' ability to overcome bottlenecks through increased imports. Productivity declined and social tensions were exacerbated. The planners were forced to reduce the planned rates of saving and investment. But no sooner had they begun to achieve stabilization than, under the pressure of the expansive nature of the system and in accordance with the accepted strategy of development, the planners again decided to introduce still another "big push" during 1957-58 (Beksiak 1972, p. 113; Karpinski 1958, pp. 138-41).

The Second Cycle: 1957-1961/3

There was an increase in the share of forced saving (accumulation) in DNMP and in the rates of growth of investment at the end of the 1950s and the beginning of the 1960s in all countries, although not exactly at the same time (see Figure 3.1). In Bulgaria the DNMP rates of growth were increasing from 1956 to 1959 (from 1 percent to 22 percent) with considerable fluctuations and collapsed in 1960 and 1961 when the rate was only 3 percent. In Czechoslovakia the rates fluctuated slightly, increasing from 5 percent in 1956 to 8 percent in 1960, and then declined, reaching 1 percent in 1962 and −2 percent in 1963. In GDR they increased from 4 percent in 1956 to 11 percent in 1958 and then declined until they reached 2 percent in 1962. In Hungary there was a sudden big increase from −11 percent in 1956 to 23 percent in 1957, which was followed by a decline to 5 percent in 1958. The highest rate in this cycle was reached in 1960 (9 percent) and it was followed by a downswing that lasted until 1965 when the rate was only 1 percent. In Poland the rates increased from 7 percent in 1956 to 11 percent in 1957. This increase was followed by a downswing in the three subsequent years (6 percent, 5 percent, 4 percent), another increase in 1961 (8 percent), and decline to 2 percent in 1962. In Romania the rates increased from −7 percent in 1956 to 16 percent in 1957, declined to 4 percent in 1958, increased to 12 percent in 1959, and a downswing followed until 1962 when the rate was 4 percent.

The pattern of the second cycle can again be explained by the three elements of the mechanism that tend to create periodic economic fluctuations in the centrally planned economies: the system, the development strategy, and mistakes in planning that each were to commit because the system removed various barriers and warning signals that the market would usually provide. It is precisely because the system makes it possible to ignore market forces that it permits the creation of new enterprises and industries in accordance with the planners' preferences, regardless of the short-run, or even the long-run profitability of these investment projects. However, it is also because of the lack of market signals that the planners have no guidance as to the industrial structure they should attempt to create and the order in which various industries, or stages of production, should be developed. This is particularly true when the economy is insulated from the impact of foreign competition and has no links with the leading world producers through direct investment, industrial cooperation, or other arrangements for technology transfer (Fallenbuchl 1971).

One of the consequences of the investment drive that took place at the beginning of the first cycle was the overexpansion of manufacturing industry, especially heavy industry, in relation to other sectors of the economy. Further development was impeded by shortages of raw materials, difficulties in financing the necessary imports, and the lagging of agriculture, which under the combined impact of collectivization and principled underinvestment was unable to supply adequate quantities of food and other products for the domestic market and for export (Iskra 1967, pp. 85-86). For this reason a new investment drive was started at the end of the 1950s or the beginning of the 1960s in all East European countries. The stated objective was reduction or even elimination of structural disproportions regarded as the main sources of domestic and external disequilibria as well as the effective barrier to further growth. Partly as the result of the pressure of the CMEA, a large part of investment outlays was allocated for the expansion of the "domestic raw material base," often of very poor quality (Fallenbuchl 1974, p. 91). These projects had a high degree of capital intensity, long gestation periods, and low efficiency. This investment policy directly contributed to the lowering of the rates of growth of industrial production and national income that appeared in the first half of the 1960s (Karpinski 1969, pp. 28-29, 389-92).

At the same time there was a further rapid development of the engineering industry. Despite the efforts of the CMEA bodies, very little specialization and cooperation among the member countries took place and strong autarkic tendencies continued to exist in planning practice (Knyziak 1970, p. 1; Bognar 1969, pp. 29-30). In all countries a very wide range of products was produced and only small shares of output were exported. In Czechoslovakia this policy led to the establishment of about 80 percent of all possible branches of the machine-building industry, and the price list of the heavy machinery industry alone included about 250,000 items (Toman et al. 1968). It was difficult to export the products of industries that were enjoying priority in order to pay for the import of necessary raw materials. This was especially true in trade with the West, but it became increasingly difficult to export machines to other CMEA countries, since domestic production was expanding in the less developed socialist countries, crowding out imports. In addition, planners and production managers had a strong preference for obtaining technologically more advanced machines from the West (Polaczek 1968, pp. 19-20; Krolak 1970, p. 32), particularly since the use of relatively inefficient machines was increasingly cited as one of the factors behind the deceleration of growth throughout the region (Karpinski 1969, pp. 105, 400).

Because of the difficulties that were encountered in exporting manufactured goods to the West, to pay for imports it was necessary to revitalize the long neglected branches of light industry (burdened by an obsolete and rundown capital stock) and/or agriculture. Except in Bulgaria and Hungary, where greater stress was put on the modernization of agriculture and on the export of specialized food products, the rates of growth of export were low and uneven around the middle of the decade and serious balance-of-payments difficulties continued.

The often staggering inefficiency of showpiece industries that had been created at the cost of enormous sacrifices of consumption by the population, led to the rehabilitation of the principle of comparative advantage by Marxist economists. A more efficient international division of labor within the bloc was accepted as an important objective in the early 1960s. The formerly unquestioned concept of the "comprehensive development" of a very large number of industries and products, mainly for domestic needs, was replaced by the concept of "structural policy" (GDR, Czechoslovakia) or "selective development" (Poland) in the party programs of all East European countries during the second half of the 1960s (Köves 1978).

By the middle of the 1960s, it was also recognized in Eastern Europe that the "sources of extensive growth" would be exhausted in the near future. Faced with slowing increases in the labor force and unable to enlarge the share of accumulation beyond a certain point without reducing incentives to work or even endangering internal political stability, all East European economic experts recognized the need to switch from "extensive" to an "intensive" pattern of development during the late 1960s. That is, sustaining satisfactory rates of growth of DNMP and industrial production would depend mainly on increasing the productivity per unit of labor and capital rather than on further increases in the sheer quantities of these inputs (Fallenbuchl 1973d).

It was recognized that the necessary increases in productive efficiency would require three kinds of measures: institutional reforms in the systems of planning and management; the restructuring of the economy to give priority to sectors where comparative advantage was evident despite ideological preconceptions of the priority of heavy industry; and the acceleration of technological progress. The relative priority that a given country allocated to these three demands during the second half of the 1960s helps to explain the scope and the nature of reforms in different countries in Eastern Europe. Only in Czechoslovakia (temporarily, from 1965 to 1968) and in Hungary (from 1968) were institutional reforms attempted on a scale that could measurably reduce the built-in obstacles to an intensive pattern of development inherent in the old command system. Even in Hungary, however, the impact of reforms was limited by the inefficient industrial structure created in the 1950s and the early 1960s. In the GDR, Poland, Romania, and Bulgaria, priority was given to sectoral restructuring and technological modernization of the economy. This task implied yet another new investment drive (Fallenbuchl 1973b).

The Third Cycle: 1966-1970/2

The third cycle started around 1966. The rate of growth of forced saving (accumulation) accelerated in that year in Bulgaria, Czechoslovakia, and GDR. In Hungary a brief acceleration took place in 1967, but after the new economic mechanism was inaugurated at the beginning of 1968, accumulation actually declined in that year and, again, in 1969. In Poland the "selective growth strategy" introduced in 1968 involved a sudden big acceleration in the rate

Table 3.4 National Net Material Product Consumption and Accumulation (Official Data, Rates of Growth, Constant Prices)

	Bulgaria		Czechoslovakia		GDR		Hungary			Poland		
	NNMP Cons	Acc.	NNMP Cons	Acc.	NNMP Cons	Acc.	NNMP	Cons	Acc.	NNMP	Cons	Acc.
1951	–	–	3	–	–	–	17.0	5.0	71.0	7.5	8.0	5.4
1952	–	–	8	–	–	–	-0.9	6.7	-22.8	8.1	3.1	19.3
1953	–	2.3	1	29.2	–	–	10.3	6.3	28.0	10.3	3.1	35.6
1954	–	–	12	–	–	–	-3.1	5.0	-30.2	10.6	17.7	-8.4
1955	11	-29	4	-5	–	–	4.8	2.4	17.8	8.9	10.1	5.1
1956	5	58	6	28	–	–	-9.2	5.5	-1.4	7.8	10.4	-1.6
1957	10	5	7	36	–	16.5	32.2	7.4	52.6	13.6	11.2	23.8
1958	12	100	1	12	–	–	-4.5	3.5	-29.2	3.2	3.2	3.3
1959	7	-6	5	4	–	–	9.4	6.0	22.3	7.0	6.3	9.7
1960	8	-18	9	26	–	–	12.3	5.7	38.7	3.0	1.7	7.5
1961	5	24	4	-8	2	2.3	2.2	2.4	2.4	7.3	6.1	10.9
1962	6	32	3	-28	1	–	7.0	5.8	8.6	2.7	3.6	0.9
1963	7	18	2	-5	1	16	6.5	4.4	14.7	6.3	8.1	11.4
1964	7	-6	3	0	4	11	6.1	5.3	7.8	4.9	4.7	5.6
1965	–	–	5	–	4	–	-2.2	1.0	-12.5	8.3	6.2	14.4

Year															
1966	10.9	6.2	7.4	11.6	4.5	5.9	13	4		26	5		40	6	
1967	1.9	5.4	4.5	32.3	6.6	12.4	6	4		5	6		8	10	
1968	14.0	6.6	8.5	-1.8	5.3	3.4	-6	4		10	9		1	9	
1969	-0.8	5.1	3.5	-2.3	5.9	4.0	21	5		10	5		10	5	
1970	7.4	4.1	5.0	22.0	8.8	11.7	11	4		-1	6		-1	6	
1971	15.2	7.7	9.8	30.5	5.5	11.4	-2	4		-11	7		-11	7	
1972	20.9	9.1	12.5	-21.4	3.1	-3.7	2	7		21	6		21	6	
1973	27.8	8.1	14.3	-4.3	3.7	2.1	6	6		16	7		16	7	
1974	20.5	7.3	12.0	34.2	6.8	12.6	6	5	6.0	24	7	8.0	24	7	9.0
1975	7.0	11.1	9.5	11.4	4.6	5.8	0	4	2.7	19	7	4.5	19	7	11.0
1976	2.4	8.8	6.5	-1.4	2.3	1.2	8.8	4.8	5.7	-11.0	6.4	3.1	-11.0	6.4	0.7
1977	-6.5	6.8	2.2	10.9	4.6	6.2	5.0	4.7	4.8	-7.0	5.9	1.6	-7.0	5.9	2.2
1978	-2.0	1.7	0.5	23.9	4.6	10.0	-6.1	3.5	1.4	-7.9	5.1	2.7	-7.9	5.2	1.8
1979	-19.2	4.8	-3.7	-24.9	3.1	-5.5	-5.4	3.3	1.6	5.0	3.0	1.1	5.0	3.0	3.5
1980	-29.6	2.1	-6.0	-12.3	1.5	-1.9	12.5	3.0	4.9	9.5	3.6	2.7	9.5	3.6	5.1
1981	-60.4	0.0	-12.3	-8.1	2.4	0.1	-2.4	2.6	1.5	14.8	5.3	-4.5	14.8	5.3	7.7
1982			-8.0			-2.0			1.0			-2.0			-2.0

Sources: G.U.S., *Rozwoj gospodarczy krajow RWPG, 1950-1965* (Economic Development of the CMEA Countries, 1950-1965), Warsaw 1969; K.S.H., *Statisztikai evkonyv 1980* (Statistical Yearbook 1980), Budapest 1981; G.U.S., *Rocznik statystyczny 1980* (Statistical Yearbook 1980), Warsaw 1980; *1982*, Warsaw 1982; U.N. Economic Commission for Europe, *Economic Survey of Europe*, Geneva, 1974, 1975, 1977, 1979, 1982.

of growth of accumulation. Accumulation's share of NNMP like-wise increased in Bulgaria, Czechoslovakia, and the GDR (see Table 3.4).

There was an increase in the rates of growth of investment (see Table 3.3 and Figure 3.1). In Bulgaria the rate of growth of DNMP increased in 1966 but declined in 1967 and 1968, increased in 1969, and dropped in 1970. Almost the same pattern was repeated in Czechoslovakia and Hungary. In GDR the rate increased only slightly in 1969 and 1970. In Poland there was an increase in 1968 and a downswing in 1969 and 1970. In Romania there was an increase in 1966 that was followed by a considerable instability (see Table 3.3 and Figure 3.1).

The GDR's ambitious "structural policy" soon resulted in seri-ous disproportions and a downswing in 1971. The "selective growth strategy" in Poland, with its consequent program of austerity, was derailed by the workers' riots of December 1970 (Fallenbuchl 1973a). In Romania, where the policy of modernization and restructuring coincided with the expansion of economic relations with the West, foreign borrowing and technology transfer somewhat reduced the adverse effect of a new investment drive.

Neither the limited systemic reforms undertaken without a sufficiently far-reaching restructuring and modernization (as hap-pened in Hungary), nor attempts to restructure and to modernize the economy "from above" by arbitrary decisions of the central planners without the benefits of market signals or the adaptability of more decentralized decision-making (as was the case in GDR, Poland, and Romania) seemed to give satisfactory results. The annual planned rates of growth of DNMP were not achieved in 1968-70 in Bulgaria, GDR, and Romania. In Hungary the targets were not met for the two years for which data are available (1968 and 1970), in Poland in 1968-69, and in Czechoslovakia in 1969.

The investment drive at the beginning of the third cycle was smaller than the drives at the beginnings of the previous two cycles. The subsequent decline in the growth rates was also less pronounced. The cycle was much shorter. It is possible that the downswing was actually interrupted by the beginning of the fourth cycle, which started in the early 1970s as the joint result of the political caution induced by the Polish riots of December 1970 and of some new developments in the international field that seemed to present new opportunities.

The Fourth Cycle: 1970/3-1983

East European countries could now benefit from political de-tente, a slack world demand for investment goods, and the liquid position of Western bankers to pursue a more intensive pattern of development via large-scale imports of capital and technology from the West. Because such a course could be financed in large part on credit, both investment and consumption could be simultaneously expanded at a rapid rate. Increases in consumption were badly needed to provide incentives to work after the damage done to morale by prolonged periods of austerity while large-scale invest-ments (embodying an accelerated transfer of Western technology) were needed for correcting sectoral imbalances and modernization. The share of advanced capitalist countries in the total trade of East European countries, calculated at current prices, increased and defi-cits in visible trade with the advanced countries appeared for the first time or became much larger.[1]

The policy was based on an assumption that, with the help of Western exporters' credits and bankers' loans, a large inflow of machines and equipment of the latest vintage, licenses, and other forms of disembodied technology transfer would result in the expan-sion of the production of modern, and efficiently produced, high-quality manufactured goods. It was expected that it would not be difficult to export these goods in rapidly growing quantities to other CMEA countries, to the less developed countries, and even to the West. The scale of production would be large and a considerable proportion of the industrial capital stock would be composed of the most modern machines. Productivity would therefore be high, unit costs low, and the pattern of development would become more intensive, while the debts would be repaid by the export of the products made with the help of imported machines and equipment. In effect, at the beginning of the 1970s, the large-scale import of Western capital and technology was accepted as a substitute for further systemic reforms (Fallenbuchl 1978)

This policy was applied to a smaller or greater extent in all East European countries and in the Soviet Union. It was explicitly formu-lated as a "new development strategy" in Poland, where it was introduced later than in Romania, GDR, and Czechoslovakia, but was subsequently pushed further than in any other country of the region (Fallenbuchl 1977).

The fourth cycle started with a rapid acceleration in the rates of growth of accumulation: in 1971 in Hungary, in 1972 in Bulgaria, Czechoslovakia, and Poland, and in 1973 in the GDR (see Table 3.4). We do not have information for Romania, but the rate of growth of investment accelerated in that country in 1971 (see Table 3.3) This cycle was novel in that the availability of foreign credit neutralized what would normally have been the adverse impact on consumption of such an increased share for accumulation (NNMP exceeded DNMP by the excess of import over export). With the popular protest barrier thus temporarily removed, the share of accumulation soon exceeded the extremely high level of 30 percent. Of course the consequence was that deficits in trade with the advanced countries dramatically increased (see Table 3.5). Growth rates of investment increased in all countries at the beginning of the 1970s, but due to deteriorating efficiency in utilization, they failed to pull up the rates of growth of DNMP to any significant extent. The one exception was Poland. But even in that country the investment bulge greatly exceeded the DNMP bulge. The suddenly accelerated transfer of embodied and disembodied technology exceeded the country's capacity to absorb it (Fallenbuchl 1983a). The investment front became so wide that it became unmanageable. It was impossible to complete many projects. The gestation period of investment grew, waste became enormous, and the capital-output ratio increased.

East-West trade expanded very rapidly but in an asymmetrical way: imports to the CMEA countries greatly exceeded exports from those countries. The actual rates of growth of DNMP exceeded the planned rates in Poland, Czechoslovakia, and, in two years, in Hungary and GDR. The difference was, however, negative every year in Romania and Bulgaria, where the planners clearly overestimated the capacity of the economy to accelerate growth.

Unanticipated difficulties appeared in expanding exports to the advanced countries, and trade deficits persisted and grew. The world stagflation and the oil crisis undoubtedly had some impact, especially in Hungary (Fallenbuchl et al. 1977; Brown et al. 1978), although Poland, as a major exporter of coal, benefited greatly at first from more favorable terms of trade (Fallenbuchl 1980a). The main reason for these difficulties was the inability of the central planners to effect the required changes in the structure of production "from above" without the benefit of market signals. The investment policy of the

Table 3.5 Share of Accumulation in NNMP in Domestic Currencies and Prices-Percentages (A) Balance of Visible Trade With Advanced Countries in Million U.S. Dollars (B)

		1969	1970	1971	1972	1973	1974	1975	1976	1977	1978	1979	1980	1981
Bulgaria	A	31.4	29.2	23.5	26.7	34.1	35.4	32.8	29.0	26	24	23	22	27
	B	-31	-65	-56	-41	-74	-515	-838	-474	-361	-390	-22	-1	-665
Czechoslovakia	A	26.0	27.1	22.3	22.8	33.7	34.7	26.0	25.5	25	25	25	25	20
	B	-17	-130	-144	-118	-231	-381	-542	-746	-703	-759	-774	-450	-569
GDR	A	21.6	22.8	22.0	n.a.	29.2	28.6	22.3	22.9	23	22	20	23	22
	B	-46	-290	-303	-521	-837	-890	-1,012	-1,432	-1,304	-1,154	-1,997	-697	-1,045
Hungary	A	23.8	27.2	31.0	28.3	34.1	34.5	25.9	25.2	32	34	26	23	23
	B	-1	-54	-230	-66	-5	-524	-534	-686	-1,058	-1,838	-723	-697	-1,045
Poland	A	26.4	27.1	28.5	30.6	34.1	36.7	35.2	34.3	31.4	30.6	25.7	20.3	9.1
	B	-50	78	52	-319	-1,291	-2,307	-2,944	-3,258	-2,504	-2,099	-1,611	-834	-564
Romania	A	n.a.	29.5	n.a.	n.a.	36.2	36.5	39.7	n.a.	n.a.	n.a.	n.a.	n.a.	n.a.
	B	-265	-185	-115	-184	-120	-447	-314	-77	-444	-736	-373		

n.a.: not available.
Sources: G.U.S., *Rocznik handlu zagraniczncgo* (Statistical Yearbook of Foreign Trade), Warsaw, 1972, 1974, 1978, 1979, 1980; G.U.S., *Rocznik statystyczny* (Statistical Yearbook), Warsaw 1981, 1982, 1983.

early 1970s was supposed to restructure the economy so as to increase its efficiency, expand its ability to export to the West, and generally facilitate the switch to an intensive pattern of development. Instead, the planners' decisions created an industrial structure even more capital-, material-, and energy-intensive than the old one. Since even the most able and dedicated central planners could not decide what foreign importers would be ready to purchase, and since the unreformed system was still too inflexible for quick adjustments to changes in foreign demand, the investment policy was not, in effect, geared to the requirements of foreign trade (Fallenbuchl 1980b). It became clear that a large-scale import of capital and technology from the West could not serve as a substitute for economic reform. Systemic reforms were needed to ensure full absorption and diffusion of imported technology and to expand profitable exports to the world markets, without which it was difficult to repay the debts.

In other words, while the system made the credit-financed overexpansion of investment possible, it was also the system that made the repayment of the loans difficult. In Poland the lack of systemic modifications was particularly damaging because of the extremism with which the new strategy was applied in that country. But similar developments took place on a smaller scale in all other CMEA countries, except Hungary, where the new economic mechanism had been introduced in 1968 and structural changes were therefore somewhat rationalized by greater attention to cost factors in microeconomic decisions at the enterprise level. All other East European countries used import of capital and technology in the classic "extensive" style to maximize the rate of growth of output rather than to improve economic efficiency. As in the past, priority was given to the further strengthening of the engineering industry. Unfortunately, quality and other considerations made it very difficult for East European countries to expand the profitable export of machines and equipment to the advanced countries, even when the products were made on the basis of Western licenses (Fallenbuchl 1982). To expand this type of export to the less developed countries, it would have been necessary to grant much larger credits and to provide a more regular supply of parts and servicing in various regions of the world.

By the middle of the 1970s, frightening deficits had appeared in trade with the advanced countries (see Table 3.5). Unable to expand exports to the West at the requisite pace, East European countries were forced to cut imports. As the inflow of capital goods decreased and debt service absorbed ever higher proportions of available foreign exchange, a major deterioration in economic performance marked the second half of the decade. As might be expected, the situation became most acute in Poland, where the DNMP began declining absolutely in 1979, setting the stage for the wave of strikes in August-September 1980, the establishment of free labor and farmers unions, a third enforced change of political leadership, and, finally, the imposition of martial law (Fallenbuchl 1981b, 1982, 1983b, 1983c, 1983d). All other East European countries experienced serious downswings at the end of the 1970s and the beginning of the 1980s.

Implications

Over 20 years ago Julio H. G. Olivera (1960) suggested that, because the time preference of the planners under a centrally planned socialist system is necessarily lower than the ex-ante preference of the consumers, growth under that system must be subject to cyclical fluctuations.[2] In the middle of the 1960s, Czechoslovak economist Jozef Goldman (1964, 1965) discussed the existence of "quasi-cycles" in the centrally planned economies, explaining them by a tendency for the raw material base to lag behind the growth of manufacturing industries and "a certain voluntarism inherent in the traditional system of planning and management"—that is, attempts to enforce excessively high rates of growth that create disproportions and force the planners to reduce the pace of development in the subsequent years. Also in the middle of the 1960s, some Polish economists observed the existence of "stages" in the development of their country. They noted a tendency to concentrate excessively large volumes of investment in certain years, usually at the beginning of a five-year plan. Limitation of consumption creates pressures forcing a temporary deceleration of growth, to be again followed by yet another new concentration of investment (Chelinski 1964; Pajestka 1964). In Hungary, Janos Kornai (1972) demonstrated how attempts to enforce excessive rates of growth lead to a lowering of efficiency and structural maladjustments. He recommended a "harmonic growth" rather than "rush." Roughly at the same time, Janusz

Beksiak (1972) in Poland analyzed various aspects of the traditional system of planning and management of the socialist economy, pointing out that even when the planners formally balance the plan and attempt to avoid excessive rates of growth, the system forces all production enterprises to expand, to make excessive demands for the allocation of producers' goods, and to create excessive purchasing power in the hands of the employees at the time when there is a shortage of consumption goods created by the overexpansion of the production of producers' goods. When economic calculations ignore profit, prices are (at best) set on a cost-plus basis, incentives are offered for the overfulfillment of the plan targets, and production is directed by administrative commands, there will inevitably result excessive employment, excessive investments, high costs, and serious barriers to innovation. Barriers to growth appear and structural disproportions are created (Beksiak 1972). More recently there have appeared in Poland several additional studies that explain fluctuations in the growth rates of the CMEA countries by the politically established strategy of development based on the excessive expansion of investment (Wozniak 1981, 1983).

There seems to be, indeed, strong evidence that fluctuations are caused by the interaction of the system and the strategy of development. This interaction is not, however, limited to attempts to achieve excessively high rates of growth and to enforce, therefore, excessively high rates of accumulation (saving) that destroy incentives and create a politically explosive situation, and investment that leads to an excessively wide investment front, unfinished projects, and an increase in the capital-output ratio.

This interaction also adversely affects foreign economic relations. It makes the expansion of profitable export of manufactured goods difficult, and by limiting the availability of necessary import, reduces the rates of growth through the mechanism of the foreign trade supply multiplier (Holzman 1974). In the absence of expansion of imports, the upswing cannot be maintained. The foreign trade barrier has been encountered in every cycle but was particularly clearly seen during the 1970s, when the upswing was financed by the import of foreign capital on the premise that it would lead to an historically unprecedented expansion of export in very short order.

Finally, the interaction of the system and the development strategy leads to the creation of an inefficient industrial structure that makes a switch to a more intensive pattern of development impossible. It acts, therefore, as another barrier to the continuation of an upswing (Fallenbuchl 1973c).

It is important to realize that with a given system, only a certain range of development strategies is possible. On the other hand, the adoption of a particular strategy may necessitate the introduction of an economic system that would facilitate it. Some other systems could make the success of that strategy impossible. When an attempt is made to modify the system but there is no change in the development strategy, it may not be feasible to effect the necessary systemic modifications. When a new development strategy is adopted for which the system is not adjusted, the strategy may collapse. In other words, the economic system and the development strategy must be consistent with one another. This interrelation can be particularly clearly seen in Poland (Fallenbuchl forthcoming), but it has affected the pattern of growth of other East European countries as well.

Notes

1. It is, however, important to remember that until 1955 intra-CMEA trade was conducted at the world prices of certain base years, usually kept constant for a period of five years. Subsequently, intra-CMEA prices were based on the moving average of the world prices for the previous five years. During a period of rapid worldwide inflation, CMEA prices lagged and the share of intra-CMEA trade was understated. At the end of the decade, the reverse was true. Also, to some extent the negative balances in visible trade were offset by revenue from tourism (Bulgaria and Romania), shipping and transit (Poland), and by transfer payments from relatives abroad (important, for example, in GDR and in Poland).

2. For criticism of this analysis, see Nove (1960).

Bibliography

Beksiak, Janusz. 1972. *Spoleczenstwo Gospodarujace*. Warsaw.

Bognar, Jozsef. 1969. "A Contemporary Approach to East-West Economic Relations." *New Hungarian Quarterly* 34, pp. 29-30.

Brown, Alan A., Zbigniew M. Fallenbuchl, Joseph A. Licari, and Egon Neuberger. 1978. "The Impact of International Stagflation on Systemic Policy Changes in Eastern Europe." In *The Soviet Union and East Europe into the 80's*, ed. Simon McInnes, William McGrath, and Peter J. Potichnyj, pp. 309-23. Oakville, Canada: Mosaic Press.

Chelinski, R. 1964. "Etapowy Charakter Rozwoju Gospodarczego PRL." *Ekonomista* 5, pp. 1032-61.

Fallenbuchl, Zbigniew M. Forthcoming. "L'Interaction de la Strategie de Developpement et du Systeme Economique Source de Crises Socio-Economiques Periodiques en Pologne." *Revue d'Etudes Comparatives Est-Ouest*.

——————————. 1983a. *East-West Technology Transfer: Study of Poland, 1971-1980.* Paris: OECD.

——————————. 1983b. "Command Performance." *Wilson Quarterly 7,* pp. 69-76.

——————————. 1983c. "The Polish Economy Since August 1980." *Canadian Slavonic Papers* 25, pp. 361-79.

——————————. 1983d. "The Origins of the Present Economic Crisis in Poland and the Issue of Economic Reform." In *Solidarity,* ed. A. Jain, pp. 149-66. Baton Rouge: Oracle Press.

——————————. 1982. "East-West Economic Relations Since the Beginning of the 1970s." In *Soviet Foreign Policy and East-West Relations,* ed. Roger E. Kanet, pp. 77-93. New York: Pergamon.

——————————. 1981a. "Policy Alternatives in Polish Foreign Economic Relations." In *Background to Crisis: Policy and Politics in Gierek's Poland,* ed. Maurice D. Simon and Roger E. Kanet, pp. 329-69. Boulder, CO: Westview.

——————————. 1981b. "Poland: Command Planning in Crisis." *Challenge* 24, pp. 5-12.

——————————. 1980a. "The Impact of External Disturbances on Poland Since 1971." In *The Impact of Internal Economic Disturbances on the Soviet Union and Eastern Europe,* ed. Egon Neuberger and Laura D'Andrea Tyson, pp. 280-304. New York: Pergamon.

——————————. 1980b. "The Polish Economy at the Beginning of the 1980's." In *East European Economic Assessment,* ed. Joint Economic Committee, U.S. Congress, pp. 33-71. Washington, D.C.: U. S. Government Printing Office.

——————————. 1978. "Economic Developments." In *The Communist States in the Era of Détente,* ed. A. Bromke and D. Novak, pp. 315-54. Oakville, Ont.: Mosaic Press.

——————————. 1977. "The Polish Economy in the 1970's." In *East European Economies Post-Helsinki,* Joint Economic Committee, U.S. Congress, pp. 816-64. Washington, D.C.: U.S. Government Printing Office.

——————————. 1974. "East European Integration: Comecon." In *Reorientation and Commercial Relations of the Economies of Eastern Europe,* Joint Economic Committee, U.S. Congress, pp. 79-134. Washington, D.C.: U.S. Government Printing Office.

——————————. 1973a. "The Strategy of Development and Gierek's Economic Manoeuvre." *Canadian Slavonic Papers* 1-2, pp. 52-70.

——————————. 1973b. "Comecon Integration." *Problems of Communism* 22, pp. 25-39.

——————————. 1973c. "Industrial Structure and the Intensive Pattern of Development in Poland." *Jahrbuch der Wirtschaft Osteuropas* (Munich) 4, pp. 233-54.

——————————. 1973d. "Croissance Économique et Les Echange Exterieurs de l'Union Soviétique et de l'Europe de l'Est, 1971-75." *Revue de l'Est* 4, pp. 27-45.

——————————. 1971. "Growth Through Trade in the Socialist Economies." In *Current Problems of Socialist Economies,* ed. W.D.C. Hunter, pp. 97-131. Hamilton, Canada: McMaster University.

——————————. 1970. "The Communist Pattern of Industrialization." *Soviet Studies* 21, pp. 451-78.

—————————————. 1968. "The Role of International Trade in the Czechoslovakia Economy." *Canadian Slavonic Papers* 10, pp. 451-78.

—————————————. 1967. "Collectivization and Economic Development." *Canadian Journal of Economics and Political Science* 33, pp. 1-15.

—————————————. 1966. "International Economic Relations in the Communist Policy of Economic Development." In *East-West Trade,* ed. Philip E. Uren, pp. 67-86. Toronto: Canadian Institute of International Affairs.

—————————————. 1965. "Some Structural Aspects of the Soviet-Type Investment Policy." *Soviet Studies* 16, pp. 423-47.

—————————————. 1964. "How Does the Soviet Economy Function Without a Free Market?" *Queen's Quarterly* 70, pp. 559-75.

—————————————. 1963. "Investment Policy for Economic Development: Some Lessons of the Communist Experience." *Canadian Journal of Economics and Political Science* 29, pp. 26-39.

—————————————, Egon Neuberger, and Laura D'Andrea Tyson. 1977. "East European Relations to International Commodity Inflation." In *East European Economics Post-Helsinki,* Joint Economic Committee, U.S. Congress, pp. 816-64. Washington, D.C.: U.S. Government Printing Office.

Goldman, Jozef. 1965. "Short- and Long-Term Variations in the Growth Rate and the Model of Functioning of a Socialist Economy." *Czechoslovak Economic Papers,* 5, pp. 35-46.

—————————————. 1964. "Fluctuations and Trends in the Rate of Economic Growth in Some Socialist Countries." *Economics of Planning* 4, pp. 13-19.

Holzman, Franklyn D. 1974. *Foreign Trade Under Central Planning.* Cambridge, MA: Harvard University Press.

Iskra, W. 1967. *Rozwoj Przemyslowy Krajow RWPG.* Warsaw.

Karpinski, Andrzej. 1969. *Polityka Uprzemyslowienia Polski w Latach 1958-68.* Warsaw.

—————————————. 1958. *Zagadnienia Socjalistyczne Industrializacji Polski.* Warsaw.

Knyziak, Z. 1970. "Zasada Nakladow Komparatywnych w Rachunku Ekonomicznym Wspolpracy Gospodarczej Krajow Socjalistycznych." *Gospodarka Planowa* 2, pp. 1-4.

Kornai, Janos. 1972. *Rush Versus Harmonic Growth.* Amsterdam: North-Holland.

Koves, A. 1978. "Socialist Economy and the World Economy." *Acta Oeconomica* (Budapest) 21, pp. 299-311.

Krolak, Z. 1970. "Efektywnosc Pastepu Technicznego a Import Inwestycyjny." *Gospodarku Planowa* 7, pp. 31-33.

Nagy, Imre. 1957. *On Communism.* New York: Praeger.

Nove, Alec. 1960. "Some Observations on Professor Olivera's Article." *Kyklos* 17, pp. 256-60.

Olivera, Julio H.G. 1960. "Cyclical Economic Growth Under Collectivism." *Kyklos* 17, pp. 230-52.

Pajestka, Josef. 1964. "Analiza Niektorych Aspektow Polityki Rozwoju Ekonomicznego Polski." *Ekonomista* 2, pp. 229-44.

Polaczek, S. 1968. "Istotne Czynniki Integracji Krajow Socjalistycznych." *Gospodarka Planowa* 7, pp. 19-25.

Toman, Josef, Jozef Goldman, and Josef Flek. 1968. "Conjunctral Research in a Socialist Economy." *Czechoslovak Economic Papers* 10, pp. 29-46.

Wozniak, M.G. 1983. "Strategia Maksymalizacji Dynamiki Inwestycji a Wahania Tempa Wzrostv Gospodarczego Krajow RWPG." *Gospodarka Planowa* 4, pp. 155-62.

——————————————. 1981. "Okresowe Obnizanie Sie Tempa Wzrostu Gospodarczego w Krajach RWPG." *Gospodarka Planowa* 7, pp. 370-73.

4

The Political Business Cycle: An International Perspective

MITCHELL KELLMAN AND ODED IZRAELI

"The fact that economic conditions influence voters is a leading commonplace of conversation in election years. The question is: Is this fact in fact a fact?" (Stigler 1973, p. 163). Today, a full decade later, this question raised by George Stigler is still unresolved. Stigler argued that economic theory leads one to doubt the likelihood of the systematic existence of a political business cycle (PBC). "The main reason for this expectation is that a rational voter should not give much weight to short-run fluctuations in economic conditions" (Stigler 1973, p. 162). A rational economic agent would not react (or would resist) economic stimuli that were known to be temporary and reversible—a position consistent with the well-known "rational expectations" model of economic behavior. And yet, empirical studies of this issue continue to yield associational if not causal relationships that tend to cast doubt on the empirical validity of Stigler's intuitive rejection of the political business cycle (for example, see Fair 1978).

Combining a time series analysis of individual countries with a cross-country analysis, this study provides answers to the following questions:

Is the "practice" of artificial economic stimulation during election years by incumbent administrations generally and demonstrably prevalent in the Western European democracies?

The authors wish to gratefully acknowledge and thank the Schwager Fund for financial assistance for this project.

71

What economic and political characteristics may account for the inter-country differences in the resort to, or the successful implementation of, this form of macroeconomic bribery?

How does the phenomenon of PBC, as manifest in the United States, compare to that found in Western Europe?

Following the pioneering study by Nordhaus (1975), this study utilizes a standard macroeconomic Phillips curve framework in order to determine a reasonable trend value for nominal wage rate changes in each of the countries studied. Having specified and estimated this basic or underlying economic structural relationship, the degree to which nominal wages tended to systematically diverge from this trend, in each country, during years of nationwide parliamentary or presidential elections was examined utilizing an intercept dummy variable. In the process of answering the above three questions, this study provides an exploratory model that qualitatively defines the relevant parameters defining voter "rationality" in terms of shifting rates of social rate of time preference.

The Model

The methodology utilized here was pioneered by Nordhaus (1975), whose following statement comprises our working hypothesis:

> Under conditions where voting is an appropriate mechanism for social change, a democratic system will choose a policy on the Long Run (Phillips curve) trade-off that has lower unemployment and higher inflation than is optimal. . . . During an election period . . . U should . . . fall. (Nordhaus 1975, p. 178)

Following Nordhaus, we examine the phenomenon in the context of a Phillips curve. Our independent variable is the year-over-year rate of change of nominal wage earning, rather than Nordhaus's rate of employment. Our model utilizes one of the following alternative forms:

$$(1a) \quad WCH_{it} = f(PCH_{it}, UCH_{it}, T, EY_{it})$$

or

$$\text{(1b) } WCH_{it} = f(PCH_{it}, U_{it}, T, EY_{it})$$

where

> WCH is the rate of change in the average manufacturing wage
> earnings
> PCH is the rate of change in the Consumer Price Index
> UCH is the change in U, the rate of unemployment
> T is a time trend
> EY is an election year dummy variable, taking on a value of 1
> for each election year, and 0 for others.[1]

The finding consistent with Nordhaus's hypothesis and supportive of the empirically demonstrable existence of a political business cycle would be a finding of a statistically significant positive coefficient for the EY variable.

The Sample, Data, and Model Specification

The country sample utilized included all those Western democracies for which the necessary data were readily available. These were: Western Europe—Austria, Belgium, Denmark, Finland, France, West Germany, Ireland, Italy, Netherlands, Norway, Sweden, and the United Kingdom; and others—Canada, Japan, and the United States. For each of these countries, observations were obtained from 1964 to 1980 for wage, price, and unemployment series. These were primarily from either the International Financial Statistics of the International Monetary Fund, or from Data Resources Incorporated; in turn developed from national country sources.[2] The election years in each country were identified either in Mackie and Rose (1974) or through current newspaper files.

The two specifications were estimated using Ordinary Least Squares (utilizing the SPSS package). First specification (1a) was estimated for each country, from 1968 to 1979. In certain cases, negative values were found for the election year dummy variables (EY). In those cases, an alternative (1b) was estimated, which substituted the rate of unemployment for the change in this rate. In general, this did not affect the results. In two cases, Finland and Netherlands, it did yield positive coefficients for EY, which were utilized in the subsequent analysis.

The Results

Table 4.1 gives the estimated values for each country. The values for EY, in the first column, are the beta coefficients of the dummy variables. Since they are normalized by respective standard deviations, they are comparable across countries. The second column indicates the absolute values of the t statistics applicable to each respective EY coefficient. The third column is the coefficient of determination, adjusted for degrees of freedom, for the respective estimated equation.

An examination of the adjusted R squares in column 3 reveals that the overall "fit" of the Phillips curve model tended to be fairly good. That is, large portions of variations in wage changes over time tended to be explained in most of the countries sampled. The size of the R squares in this context has a sematic content in the context of our model, indicating one measure of the degree of certainty government authorities would tend to attach to the probability of success they could expect from any given infusion of election year "macroeconomic bribery." In this respect, the R squares would be an indication of the stability of the economic structure within which the government must operate in attempting to induce a PBC.

It is of some interest to note the degree to which our findings are consistent with those of the classic examination of such relationships internationally (Lucas 1973). In his equation 12, Lucas had estimated the effects on price inflation of real and of nominal output measures for 12 of our 15 countries (all except France, Finland, and Japan). The relevant R squares are summarized in his table 2 (Lucas 1973, p. 332).[3] A cursory examination suggests that the overall degree of explanation offered by the Phillips curve structures in the two studies is similar. The poor applicability of Lucas's model to the United Kingdom and Canada, R squares of interest since the two studies deal with different time periods (1953-67 and 1968-79), is particularly notable, and suggests a rather stable set of structural rankings over time in regard to the macroeconomic output-inflation tradeoff.

The second column of Table 4.1 gives the respective values of the t statistics applicable to each election year dummy variable. It is clear that, with few exceptions, they indicate a general absence of statistical significance. The straighforward inference of course is that the political business cycle is not systematically (or effectively) practiced by

Table 4.1   Election Year (EY) Dummy Variable Coefficients*

	EY	t	R^2
Western Europe			
Austria	.016	1.579	.898
Belgium	-.004	.213	.723
Denmark	.023	1.630	.683
Finland	.013	.625	.878
France	-.046	1.445	.883
W. Germany	-.009	.764	.745
Ireland	.030	1.471	.691
Italy	-.060	1.487	.429
Netherlands	.004	.268	.901
Norway	-.014	.293	-.189
Sweden	.012	.329	-.215
United Kingdom	.016	.585	.371
Others			
Canada	-.005	.190	.072
Japan	-.011	.849	.932
United States	.001	.158	.685

*Standardized beta coefficients.

incumbent regimes in today's modern Western European democracies. This would support Stigler's view that electorates (in this case in Western Europe) are indeed rational and cannot be "fooled." This interpretation, however, may be questioned since there are several reasons why this statistical interpretation should not be taken at face value. Phillips curves, estimated at aggregate national levels, have been suspected of overstated standard errors (and hence of understated significance levels) due to endemic aggregation bias (Lipsey 1960; Kaliski 1965; Hines 1969; Archibold 1978), a bias that has been empirically demonstrated to exist in the United States and Europe (see Kaun and Spiro 1970; Metcalf 1971; Mathur 1976; Izraeli and Kellman 1979). In addition, a recent empirical test for the presence of the PBC in the United States demonstrated that its estimated size and significance tends to be very sensitive to the exact specification chosen (Izraeli and Kellman 1982, p. 37).

Turning to the values of the actual beta coefficients of the election year dummies, we note a considerable spread between the

European countries, from a high of .03 for Ireland to negative values, especially in the bigger countries of France, West Germany, and Italy. In fact, the United Kingdom is alone of the European "big four" with a positive election year dummy.

How might we interpret the negatively signed coefficients? Per se, they indicate that for those countries, wages systematically tended to rise slower during election years than economic conditions warranted. Surely no sensible incumbent political party would engineer such a fiasco. Surely no rational expectations "overshooting" could sensibly explain such a finding. We are left with two possibilities: the negative coefficients indicate that in those particular countries the art of political macrobribery was not being practiced (successfully), or that the aggregation bias so seriously tended to overstate standard errors of estimate that what appear as negative coefficients may actually be positive.

The Economic Determinants of the Political Business Cycle

In this section we shall examine the relationships between a set of variables, primarily economic, and the degree of intensity with which the political business cycle was demonstrated to occur in each country from 1968 to 1979. The latter are the betas described above and listed in Table 4.1. The sample utilized here are all those European countries for which positive values were estimated for the election year betas. Table 4.2 describes the Pearson ("simple") correlation coefficients between the EY betas and a list of potentially interesting variables.

The results from Table 4.2 indicate that the successful utilization, or implementation, of a political business cycle in Western Europe was found to be (positively) associated with:

- A higher rate of overall price inflation.
- A higher rate of unemployment.
- A higher t statistic associated with the beta coefficient.

Though it is not the intention of this chapter to specify a fully articulated political-economic model of the PBC, we may attempt to interpret these findings. A weak working hypothesis that we require is that the basic idea quoted from Nordhaus above is understood and

Table 4.2   The Degree of Correlation Between Election Year "Bribery" and Various Factors

Variable	Correlation
TSTAT: the t statistic associated with the election year dummy variable estimated from equation (1a or 1b)	.78*
RSQ: the adjusted R^2 for the respective estimated equation	.03
EFREQ: the number of years (1965-80) in which elections were held	.34
G/GNP: the ratio of governmental expenditures for goods and services as a proportion of gross national product (IMF 1983)	-.08
GDP/P: the 1972 gross domestic product per capita, in current dollars (OECD 1980, p. 88)	-.42
CPICH: the average annual change in the Consumer Price Index from 1960 to 1980 (OECD 1981, Table 8.11)	.63*
GDPCH: the average annual change in real gross domestic product per employed person, 1960-80 (OECD 1981, Table 3.7)	.004
U: the mean rate of unemployment, 1968-79 (Data Resources, Inc.)	.82*
POP: 1972 population (IMF 1983)	-.17

*Indicates statistical significance at the 90 percent level.

accepted by all incumbent governments, who place a high priority on remaining in office. It follows that any lack of evidence of an operant PBC indicates not a lack of will, but rather an inability to overcome constraints external to the government decision-making process. Such constraints may reflect an unwillingness of a rational electorate to be "fooled" by a temporary (and reversible) government stimulatory policy (or a governmental perception that the public perceived the PBC in such terms).[4]

A greater tendency to apply PBC is seen to be associated with higher rates of inflation. Such a higher rate of inflation would also tend to be associated with a higher degree of price fluctuations, and would likely be accompanied by a relatively high degree of unexpected price changes. This would in turn tend to increase the degree of "money illusion" of the public, with consequent greater leeway available to government to effect short-run real resource shifts, resulting in a higher proportion of successful PBCs engineered by incumbent governments. Hence the positive correlation here is seen to reflect a greater degree of opportunity afforded governments to effect the PBC. This would tend to indicate that the rates of inflation prevalent in Western Europe during this period were beneath the threshold below which the public considers adjustments to perceived changes in the value of money as too costly.[5]

The positive correlation of the PBC variable with the average rate of unemployment may be interpreted in one of two ways. On the one hand, the greater degree of real slack would be a factor that would tend to enable a government to effect real resource shifts of the kind needed for a successful PBC policy. On the other hand, a public plagued by higher rates of unemployment may be more willing to be "fooled." That is, the social rate of time preference of the unemployed may be very high indeed, bringing about a willingness to grasp any short-run panacea, regardless of long-run implications.

Finally, the higher t values' positive association with the PBC is also readily explainable. The higher this value, the lower is the degree of variability of this variable, and the greater the degree of certainty the government may assign the probability of succeeding in effecting a successful PBC. Since any attempt of an administration to fine tune or manipulate the economy to favor its short-run political fortunes entails a gamble (which could backfire), the stability (degree of certainty of attaining success) of the PBCs generated may be an important factor in determining the extent to which this stratagem will be resorted to by incumbents.

A Multivariate Analysis

In order to have some idea of the explanatory power of a model that would include all three of these variables as determinants of the relative success in effecting PBCs in Western Europe, the election year variable (EY) was regressed on the rate of inflation (CPICH), the rate of unemployment (U), and the relative stability of the dependent variable (TSTAT). The results were:

(2) EY = $-.01 + .002$CPICH $+ .005$U $+ 009$TSTAT $\bar{R}^2 = .85$
          (2.05)   (.54)   (3.02)

where the figures in parentheses are t statistics.

The results indicate that both the average rate of inflation and the relative degree of reliability (or predictability) associated with the PBC mechanism explain close to 85 percent of the intercountry variability of the PBC variable. The rate of unemployment, on the other hand, exerted no independently significant effect. This is most likely explained by the relatively high (positive) degree of association between U and CPICH, as those European countries that suffered the greatest losses of real income from the oil shock recessions of the 1970s tended to also exhibit the highest rates of inflation (also associated with the same underlying supply-side shocks).

The United States in the European Perspective

How does the experience of the United States with regard to the PBC compare with that of Western Europe? To answer this we once more correlate the PBC variable with the same variables as before, with the United States added to the country sample. The results are in Table 4.3. Comparing the results here with those summarized in Table 4.2, it is apparent that the same set of correlates significant for Western Europe—inflation, unemployment, and the t statistic—remain significant explainers when the United States is added to the sample. While the statistical significance of both inflation and the t statistic became enhanced, that of the rate of unemployment dropped somewhat (from 99 percent to 91 percent level of significance).

However, three additional variables assume statistical significance in the new expanded country sample: the frequency of elections, per capita income (positive relationships), and the country (population) size (a negative relationship). That is, those countries with more frequently scheduled elections exhibit a greater success at "carrying off" PBCs in a systematic manner. This was also true the smaller and the poorer the country.

A careful examination of the data reveals that, while these two variables did not register a satisfactory level of statistical significance in the European sample, they may nevertheless be seen to be related to the PBC in Western Europe. In an enlarged sample that included

Table 4.3   The Degree of Correlation Between Election Year "Bribery" and Various Factors: Western Europe and the United States

Variable	Correlation	Variable	Correlation
TSTAT	.72**	GDP/P	-.62**
RSQ	-.02	CPICH	.71**
EFREQ	.47*	GDPCH	.36
G/GNP	-.28	U	.53**
		POP	-.59**

**Indicates statistical significance at the 85 percent level.
**Indicates statistical significance at the 90 percent level.
Note: Definitions of the variables may be found in Table 4.2.

all 12 European countries, the Spearman correlation coefficient between EY and population is $-.60$; and between EY and EFREQ (election frequency) is .50, both significant at the 95 percent level.

These three sets of correlation may be sensibly explained in the following terms. The larger a country, the less homogenous it tends to be. Provincial, regional, and local as well as other foci of power compete with and usurp from the central authority the administrative capability to flexibly and forcefully effect a PBC. As for the EFREQ variable, it may be posited that practice makes perfect; that is, the more often incumbents have an opportunity to observe the consequences of (experimental) attempts at PBC manipulation, the more likely they are to attempt it and to do it successfully. The more such successes or attempts are pushed back into the past, the less likely they are to serve as object lessons to incumbent politicians. Finally, the poorer the country the less resistance may be offered by even a rational electorate to (cynical) short-run political manipulation of the economy, since the social rate of time preference may be systematically (and negatively) associated with per capita income (the rich can afford to set aside for tomorrow). In general, it seems that the factors that tend to promote or hinder the successful implementation of PBCs in the United States are the same observed in Western Europe. The lower measured PBC indicator for the United States (.001 as against mean of .016 for the European sample) is largely explained by the larger size of the United States, the lower average rate of price inflation (5.3 percent versus 7.3 percent), and a lower frequency of elections.

Can one then say that the United States and Western Europe share a common experience with respect to the determinants of their respective political business cycles? This may be formally answered by regressing the PBC variable, EY, on those two variables that in equation (2) proved statistically significant, CPICH and TSTAT, first for the European sample, and then for the joint sample. A Chow test on the sums of squared residuals will then yield an answer.

The results for the European sample are:

$$(3a) \quad EY = -.01 + .0029CPICH + .099TSAT \quad \bar{R}^2 = .87$$
$$\qquad\qquad\qquad (3.76) \qquad\qquad (4.93)$$

with the United States:

$$(3b) \quad EY = -.02 + .0035CPICH + .0103STAT \quad \bar{R}^2 = .84$$
$$\qquad\qquad\qquad (3.92) \qquad\qquad (3.99)$$

The Chow test applied (Brown 1966, p.115) was the following:

$$F(p, n + m - 2p) = \frac{H - J - K}{J + K} \frac{(n + m - 2p)}{p}$$

where p is the number i of parameters
H is the SSR for the joint sample (inluding the United States)
J is the SSR for the initial sample (Europe only)
K is the SSR (or summed residual) for the United States

The results are:

$$F(3,2) = \frac{(.0000724 - .0000348 - .0000267) \times (2/3)}{.0000348 + .0000267} = 0.12$$

The United States is found not to be in a category of its own; it fits statistically with the European sample. An examination of the coefficient estimates in (3a) and (3b) suggests that to the extent that it does differ from Europe, it is primarily in that the efficacy of use of the PBC in the United States is more sensitive to the rate of price inflation. This may be associated with the more diffused perception of this variable in the United States (due to the size and decentralized nature of the U.S. policy). An alternative explanation may be that the

U.S. government was able, during this historic period, to take advantage of the public's "money illusion," since its public had less of an experience with price inflation, and hence was less likely to react to policies that were perceived to effect prices at a relative lower threshold level. Thus the very relative price stability enjoyed by the United States during that period rendered inflation a potent tool for incumbent administrations playing the PBC game.

Notes

1. We assume that even in countries characterized by volatile electorates and tenuous coalitions, the incumbent party typically has at least several months' notice of upcoming countrywide elections, and that one calendar year is sufficient time to engineer a PBC.

2. We wish to thank DRI's International Service for kindly providing us with the necessary data.

3. Since Lucas does not report R squares adjusted for degrees of freedom, the two sets of statistics are not exactly comparable. Removing from the sample the two cases with negative (adjusted) coefficients of determination, and one outlier (W. Germany), the Spearman correlation between the two sets of R squares is 0.517, significant at the 90 percent level.

4. See Stigler (1973) for a discussion of the perception by voters of government policies such as the PCB, and the resultant constraints placed on such policy.

5. See Izraeli and Kellman (1980) for a discussion and citation of the threshold effect.

Bibliography

Archibold, G. 1978. "The Structure of Excess Demand for Labor." In *Micro-Economic Foundations of Employment and Inflation Theory*, ed. E. Phelps. New York: Norton.

Brown, M. 1966. *On the Theory and Measurement of Technological Change*. London: Cambridge University Press.

Fair, R. 1978. "The Effect of Economic Events on Votes for President." *Review of Economics and Statistics* 60, pp. 158-73.

Hines, A. 1969. "Wage Inflation in the U.K.,1948-1962: A Disaggregated Study." *Economic Journal* 74, pp. 65-89.

IMF. 1983. *International Financial Statistics*. Washington, D.C.: International Monetary Fund.

Izraeli, O. and M. Kellman. 1979. "Changes in Money Wage Rates and Unemployment in Local Markets: The Latest Evidence." *Journal of Regional Science* 19, pp. 375-87.

—————. 1980. "The Rationality Hypothesis and the Spatially Disaggregated U.S. Labor Market." *Annals of Regional Science* (July), pp. 39-50.

—————. 1982. "Inflationary Expectations, Taxes and the Political Business Cycle: A Local Labor Market Perspective." *Urban Studies* 19, pp. 33-41.

Kaliski, S. 1965. "Unemployment and Money Wages." *International Economic Review* 6, pp. 1-33.

Kaun, D. and M. Spiro. 1970. "The Relationship Between Wages and Unemployment in U.S. Cities." *Manchester School of Economics and Social Studies* 38, pp. 1-14.

Lipsey, R. 1960. "The Relation Between Unemployment and the Rate of Change of Money Wage Rates in the U.K., 1862-1957." *Economica* 27, pp. 1-31.

Lucas, R. 1973. "Some International Evidence on Output-Inflation Tradeoffs." *American Economic Review* 63 (June), pp. 326-34.

Mackie, T. and R. Rose. *The International Almanac of Electoral History,* 2d ed. London: Macmillan.

Mathur, V. 1976. "The Relationship Between the Rate of Change of Money Wage Rates and Unemployment in Local Labor Markets: Some New Evidence." *Journal of Regional Science* 16, pp. 389-98.

Metcalf, D. 1971. "The Determinants of Earning Changes: A Regional Analysis for the U.K., 1960-1968." *International Economic Review* 12, pp. 243-83.

Nordhaus, W. 1975. "The Political Business Cycle." *Review of Economic Studies* 42, pp. 169-90.

OECD. 1980. *National Accounts: Main Aggregates, 1951-1980.* Paris: Organization for Economic Cooperation and Development.

——————. 1981. *Historical Statistics, 1960-1980.* Paris: Organization for Economic Cooperation and Development.

Stigler, G. 1973. "General Economic Conditions and National Elections." *American Economic Review, Papers and Proceedings* 63, pp. 160-67.

5

The 1930s World Economic Crisis In Six European Countries: A First Report on Causes of Political Instability and Reactions to Crisis

EKKART ZIMMERMANN

The worldwide economic and political turmoil that emerged from the crash of the New York stock exchange in October 1929 is one of the most challenging periods in the history of twentieth-century liberal democracies.[1] However, the lack of truly comparative studies of this period is puzzling. This study will not provide a complete remedy, even though I do hope to start from a more coherent cross-national design. There is no need here to discuss the theoretical literature on political (system) crises (see the reviews in Linz 1978; Zimmermann 1981, 1983, 1984). Rather, I shall concentrate on some of the preliminary findings of this study of the world economic crisis of the 1930s in six European countries. In doing so, the design of this study will gradually become apparent.

Sampling and Data Sources

Sample Selection

Since the focus is on Middle and Western European countries, the following six countries were selected for analysis: United King-

Collaborators, mostly on a part-time basis, in this research were and are Astrid Zitzelsberger-Eller, Ruth Seifert, Horst Länger, and Heinz Ulrich Brinkmann. At this early stage of our research project I am extremely grateful to them for their efforts at data collecting. For comments I am grateful to participants at the International Studies Association Meeting in Atlanta (March 1984) and at the European Consortium for Political Research Joint Sessions of Workshops in Salzburg (April 1984).

dom, France, Belgium, Netherlands, Austria, and Germany. The sample is not based on the idea of generalizing our findings as to how liberal democracies act under conditions of economic and political crises, but rather dictated by the criteria of "common" borders or "dense area sampling." Nevertheless, some interesting comparisons are suggested. The United Kingdom as a genuine democracy can be compared with France, a democracy oscillating between Caesarism and leftist mass participation. Developments in the Netherlands and Belgium can be compared with each other partly on the basis of the consociationalist model and—ex negativo—with those in Austria. Germany and Austria as "close cousins" are suited for comparison anyway.

Data Collection

The year 1927 is taken as a baseline. For some countries (such as Germany), in economic and political terms, this was a relatively calm or even successful year. Other countries, however, were shaken by considerable political turmoil. In Austria the burning of the Palace of Justice in Vienna took place on July 15; 89 people were killed in street fighting. France was suffering from an economic setback that partly was the price for Poincaré's policy for stabilizing the franc. Yet, in no instance do the economic indicators point to the slump that was soon to follow. A variety of macroeconomic indicators will be used, drawing on among other sources the newest and most complete cross-national data collection (Flora 1983/1984). I have also performed simple preliminary analyses drawing largely on the data collection of Mitchell (1981).

Indicators of Economic Crisis: Some Descriptive Findings

Unemployment

Among the three larger nations, Germany was affected most by the rise in unemployment (defined as percentage of appropriate work force).[2] From 1929 (9.3 percent)[3] till 1930 (15.3 percent), there was a factor increase of 1.6. In 1930 more than one of every seven Germans in the work force was out of work (not counting unregistered unemployment). In 1931 this figure climbed to almost one out of every four persons (23.3 percent) before reaching its all-time high of almost one out of three persons being without work in 1932 (30.1 percent).[4] It even took the Nazis, with their rigorously enforced public employment measures, more than three years before unemployment subsided below 10 percent (1936: 8.3 percent).

France was less severely hit by unemployment. Up till 1931, according to Mitchell's absolute figures, unemployment in France was below 70,000. It made the largest jump in 1932 when 301,000 were unemployed. This figure slowly and linearly rose till 1936 (470,000) and fluctuated around 400,000 until 1939. Apparently, only those people who received unemployment compensation were counted as unemployed. Kindleberger (1973, p. 160) notes that perhaps more than one million foreign workers of Polish, Italian, and Algerian origin left the country or had to leave it. Other workers went back from the cities to the countryside, where living conditions were less burdensome. These factors contribute to the relatively low rate of unemployment in France. Petzina (1977, pp. 16-17) lists percentage figures, but his numbers refer only to employed in the mining sector, the construction business, and industrial production. These figures and the percentages of the other five countries are presented in Table 5.1 and Figure 5.1.[5] Even though they are gross in definition, we use these figures here to facilitate at least some comparisons. According to Petzina, the rate of unemployment more than doubled from 1931 (6.5 percent) to 1934 (15.4 percent), stayed almost on this level till 1935 (14.5 percent), and then declined to 10.4 percent in 1936 and between 7 and 8 percent in 1937-38. Probably the real absolute figures lie considerably beyond those given by Mitchell.

Following Mitchell's figures, a country as small as Austria almost reached the French figure of unemployment in absolute numbers. From 1927 to 1929 the Austrian figure was fluctuating around 200,000 (about 9 percent, Botz 1982, p. 380) and then gradually climbed to a high of 406,000 in 1933 (20.3 percent), and then slowly declined again. Yet even in 1938 (245,000 or about 12.4 percent), the level of ten years earlier had not been reached again (estimation on the basis of figures given by Botz 1982, p. 380).

Britain more than doubled its rate of unemployment from 1927 (10.6 percent) till 1931 (21.5 percent), and then remained on that level until 1933. Only in 1936 was the rate of 1930 (14.6 percent) reached again. Compared to Germany, the peak and the fluctuations in unemployment were lower in Britain. Perhaps the greater "continu-

Table 5.1 Unemployment (percent)

Year	Germany	France	Austria	United Kingdom	Belgium	Netherlands
1927	8.8	11.0 (47)	9.2 (200)	10.6	2.5	7.5
1928	8.4	4.0 (16)	8.5 (182)	11.2	1.7	5.6
1929	9.3	1.0 (10)	8.9 (192)	11.0	1.9	5.9
1930	15.3	2.0 (13)	11.2 (243)	14.6	5.4	7.8
1931	23.3	6.5 (64)	14.2 (300)	21.5	14.5	14.8
1932	30.1	15.4 (301)	18.3 (378)	22.5	23.5	25.3
1933	26.3	14.1 (305)	20.3 (406)	21.3	20.4	26.9
1934	14.9	13.8 (368)	18.8 (370)	17.7	23.4	28.0
1935	11.6	14.5 (464)	17.7 (349)	16.4	22.9	31.7
1936	8.3	10.4 (470)	17.8 (350)	14.3	16.8	32.7
1937	4.6	7.4 (380)	16.3 (321)	11.3	13.8	26.9
1938	2.1	7.8 (402)	12.4 (245)	13.3	18.4	25.0

Sources: French percentage figures: Petzina 1977; Galenson and Zellner 1957. Austrian percentage figures for 1935-38 are estimated. All other data including the absolute figures (in parentheses and expressed in thousands) for France and Austria: Mitchell 1981.

ity" in crisis indicators had an effect—apart from numerous other factors—on the solutions to economic crisis to be pursued in Great Britain.

Belgium resembles Germany in that there is an enormous increase in the rate of unemployment: from less than 2 percent between 1928 and 1929 to 5.4 percent in 1930 and to a figure more than four times as high in 1932 (23.5 percent) lasting till 1935, after slight changes in 1933 and 1934, before going down to 13.8 percent in 1937 and rising again in 1938 to 18.4 percent. Prior to 1933 the Belgian pattern matches the German but on a lower level. After 1934, the rate of unemployment is higher in Belgium.

The pattern of the Netherlands shows some clear parallels to that of Belgium. However, in the Netherlands the highest value of all six countries was reached (32.7 percent in 1936) after a lag of four years with respect to Britain, Germany, and Belgium. Unemployment continuously rose from 7.8 percent in 1930 to 25.3 percent in 1932 and then for four more years gradually climbed beyond this figure, before going down to 25 percent in 1938. In terms of persistence, the

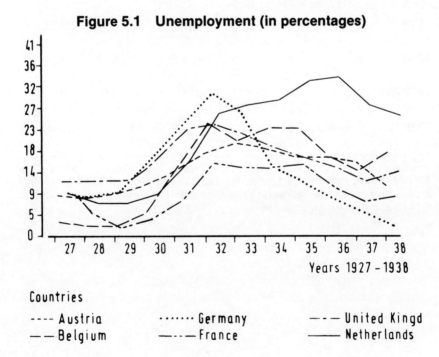

Figure 5.1 Unemployment (in percentages)

Years 1927 - 1938

Countries

---- Austria   ······ Germany   — - — United Kingd

— — Belgium   — - - — France   ——— Netherlands

Netherlands was even more strongly affected by unemployment than Germany (see also the comparisons in Galenson and Zellner 1957, pp. 458-59). It will be interesting to discover what political effects this economic distress had. The fact that the Netherlands was witnessing the developments in Germany and elsewhere in Europe may partly have influenced their reactions to internal political challenges. The figures of Galenson and Zellner (1957, p. 455) are identical for the Netherlands, slightly lower for Britain with the exception of 1930, and markedly higher for Germany from 1929 on, where Galenson and Zellner continue to rely on unemployment rates among members of reporting trade unions (till 1932; estimates afterwards). Their figures for 1930 to 1932 are 22.7, 34.3, and 43.8 percent respectively. Especially the last figure is often uncritically referred to in the literature. For Belgium, Mitchell reports generally higher figures than Galenson and Zellner.

Industrial Production

Taking 1937 as the base line, Germany in 1927 was more than one-fifth below this line, stagnated economically until 1929, before markedly declining in 1931 to almost one-half (56) of its 1937 industrial production. In 1932 the lowest value of 48 was reached. The drastic decline in industrial production becomes even more apparent in terms of relative changes: for three successive years from 1930 on, the rates of decline were 12.7, 18.8, and 14.3 percent. Moreover, this decline took place only after an explosive growth in industrial production of about 25 percent from 1926 to 1927, thereby reaching for the first time again the level of 1913 (Borchardt 1982, p. 194). These drastic economic changes have been described elsewhere in great statistical detail (Petzina 1977; Borchardt 1982; Conze and Raupach 1967); but even with the few figures used here, the economic collapse of Weimar Germany becomes apparent (see Figure 5.2). This pattern resembles that described in the famous J-curve hypothesis of rebellion by Davies (1962; for a critique see Zimmermann 1983, pp. 360-62).

The Austrian pattern of industrial production shows the closest parallel to developments in Germany (on whose economy Austria was partly dependent), the major differences being that Austria's lowest value (58 in 1932) was still higher than Germany's and

Austrian economic recovery lagged behind Germany's from 1935 onward. The two countries were the most affected by the decline of industrial production among our sample of six states.

Belgium's index of industrial production in 1927 (106), 1928, and 1929 (115 each) had already surpassed the value of 1937. Consequently, its economic decline from 1929 on was marked (lowest figure in 1932: 73), but by 1937 a fragile consolidation had been reached only to fall to 81 again in 1938.

France shows perhaps the closest parallel to the Belgian pattern, a rise from 1928 (111) to 1929 (123) and then a sharp decline to about 90. The major difference here is that in 1933 and 1936, industrial production rose by 8 and 7 points and from 1935 till 1937 by 12 points, but almost fell to the same degree in each subsequent year. The French pattern from 1933 on clearly indicates a stop-and-go path that one has come to associate with French political developments in the 1930s, with the fights between more conservative and leftist governments. This is also reflected in the economic and political

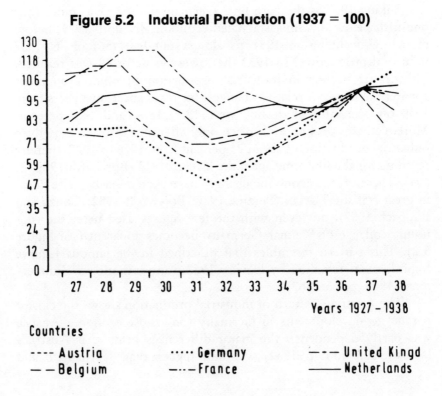

Figure 5.2   Industrial Production (1937 = 100)

Countries

---- Austria   ····· Germany   ——— United Kingd
——Belgium   —·—France   ———— Netherlands

measures taken by the respective governments. In terms of absolute differences between peaks and troughs France is, next to Belgium, most affected by the decline of industrial production. In relative terms, Germany and Belgium are more affected than France and Austria.

Great Britain (next to the Netherlands) is least affected in terms of industrial production. From 1929 till 1931 there was a decline from 76.9 to 68.9, to be followed by a steady recovery until 1937.

The Netherlands shows the lowest fluctuations of all six countries. There is a decline in industrial production from 99 to 82 within two years (1930 to 1932), to be followed by an economic recovery and an almost constant level of industrial production from 1933 to 1936. The steepest decline in industrial production is shown by Germany, Belgium, France, and Austria, whereas Germany exhibits the strongest rate of economic recovery, taking place under Nazi domination. There are, of course, many interdependencies between these national economies that cannot be dealt with at this stage.

A similar picture emerges if one compares the development of GNP in constant prices, or the net national product (NNP) for Germany, France, and the Netherlands. A fully adequate account would require the use of standardized measures of real purchase power, which are not available.

France, after a rise in NNP till 1929 and a subsequent decline till 1932, displays economic stagnation through the rest of the 1930s. Germany, in contrast, after a peak in 1928 experiences four years of marked decline, and from 1933 on the steepest rise of all the six countries. Britain goes through a much more modest decline after 1929 and from 1933 on experiences a considerably slower rate of growth than Germany. Belgium[6] in some respects seems to be a mixture of the German (strong rise in GNP from 1935 to 1936) and the British pattern (moderate decline from 1930 to 1934 and little change after 1936). The pattern of the Netherlands bears clear resemblance to the British, but has somewhat stronger oscillations. Finally, Austria is marked by the steepest decline and—next to France—the slowest recovery of all six countries.

Money Wages in Industry

The general rise in unemployment decreased the costs of labor. In Germany money wages in industry fell from 1929 in three successive years to about two-thirds of their level in 1929, before coming to a standstill in 1933 and gradually rising again afterwards so that after more than a decade (1938) the value of 1927 (85) was reached again. Since, however, the cost of living index also declined (see below), those who still had jobs in some instances were even better off in terms of purchasing power. Yet, for the vast majority, the personal economic situation seriously deteriorated.

With respect to the shape of the curve, Belgium comes closest to Germany, even though money wages as of 1929 went down one-fifth at the maximum. Note that in Belgium this trough occurred three years later (1935) than in Germany, as partly also holds for unemployment. After 1935 there was a steady increase in wages, which in 1938 (103) had passed the level of 1929.

Considering the fluctuations in industrial production and unemployment, Austria astonishingly shows little variation in money wages, as does Great Britain. The Netherlands, on the other hand, shows a slow but steady decline from 1931 to 1935 (15 percent altogether) and then stagnation for three consecutive years. Finally, France exhibits strong increases from 1927 (84) till 1930 (109), and then a minor decline until 1935. After 1935 steep rises occur until 1938 (values for Paris taken here; in the provinces there are, in general, first slightly higher, then lower figures). Thus, apart from Germany, Belgium, and perhaps the Netherlands, fluctuations in money wages have not been as strong as might have been expected on the basis of other economic indicators, such as unemployment or industrial production (see Figure 5.3).

Money Wages in Agriculture (1929 = 100)

For Germany the pattern of money wages is similar to that of industrial wages, except that agricultural wages were somewhat less affected from 1930 until 1932. There is a rise in both industrial wages up to 1929 and agricultural wages until 1930. Together with several other factors, this has led Borchardt (1982) to claim that the share of wages in the national product was too high in those years as well as throughout the entire Weimar Republic, leading to a "profit squeeze" and a lack of investment. According to Borchardt, this follows from long-time comparisons with developments in Imperial Germany (and the Federal Republic). GNP per capita in Weimar was below the rate

Figure 5.3   Money Wages in Industry (1929 = 100)

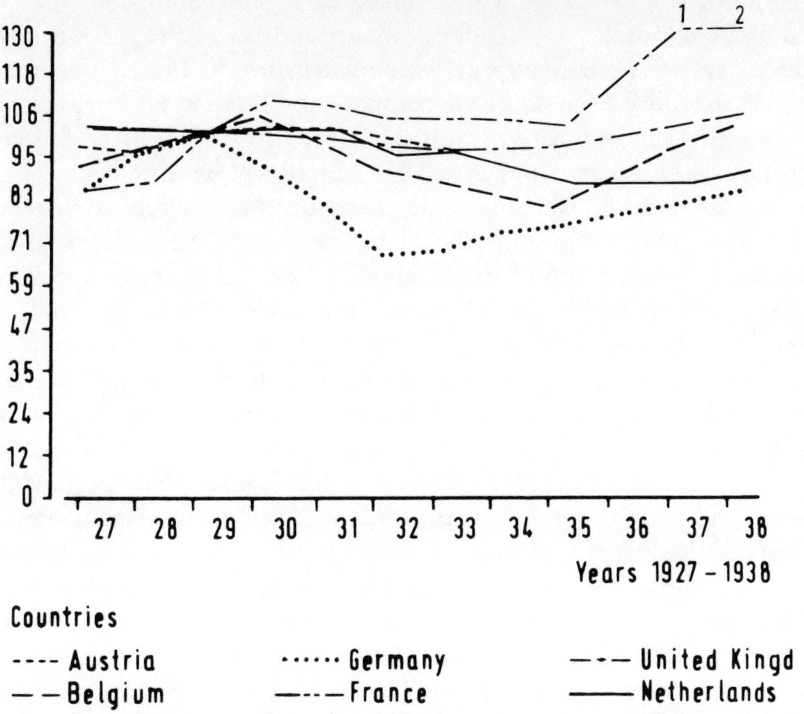

Outlying points 1 (1937 = 140) and 2 (1938 = 174) for France are estimates based on hourly wages in Paris. Austrian values for 1935-38 are missing.

Countries

---- Austria   ······ Germany   —·— United Kingd
— — Belgium   —·—France   ——— Netherlands

of growth to be expected when extrapolating data for 1850-1913 into the period of the Weimar Republic. Real investments in absolute figures were considerably below the values in Imperial Germany. Finally, unemployment in 1924-29 had already reached a relatively high level. All this made for a heavy structural burden for the Weimar economy.

Holtfrerich (1982, 1984; see also Krohn 1982), however, has called Borchardt's interpretation into question, pointing to important structural changes in the work force (a strong increase in the percentage of civil servants and clerks and slight decline in the relative number of workers) leading to more people being employed than before World War I—11 percent more in 1925. Geographical social mobility after the loss of former German territory in the Versailles

Treaty and the fact that former rentiers now had to participate in the work force also played a role in increasing the number of people employed. Borchardt also does not use indices of increases in productivity per hour of work, which according to Holtfrerich are a more appropriate measure of comparison. For 1925 he reports an increase of almost 6 percent over the figure of 1913 (Holtfrerich 1984, p. 127), whereas real wages had only increased by 3 percent. There were, however, considerable side-costs apart from wages to be paid.

This debate may put part of the blame for the collapse of the Weimar Republic and of its structurally "sick economy" (Borchardt 1982, p. 179) on the labor unions, the Social Democrats, and the state-guided forms of determining wage contracts. However, the figures given by Borchardt need further specification if such a claim is to be corroborated. Bourgeois cabinets were strongly involved in the years 1924 to 1928, when the wage explosion occurred (Krohn 1982, p. 417). Moreover, the governments of Weimar were plagued by many other economic problems, such as the external and internal costs of the lost war placing increased burdens on industry. Finally, and perhaps most convincingly in terms of statistical figures, Holtfrerich (1984) argues that the share of wages in the national product is generally higher in terms of economic crisis (he illustrates this with figures from Germany and the United States), with the share declining as the economy starts to boom again and profits increase. The high interest rates and international trade barriers also had an effect on the lack of investment so characteristic of the economy in Weimar. In sum, Holtfrerich maintains that the high share of wages is an indicator of the economic crisis, but that other factors were more relevant in bringing it about.

Actually, Borchardt's (1982, pp. 165-82) argument is much more complex (see also Borchardt's 1983 fierce reply to Krohn). He hardly could be accused of putting the blame on labor. Rather, he aims at demonstrating how the alternatives available to combat the economic crisis were successively diminished (here he reinterprets the role of Brüning). After the first success of the Nazis at the polls in 1930 and the July 1932 election that brought the Nazis an overwhelming triumph (see below), the economic crisis had broadened into a political crisis. The basic structural weakness of the economy (its lack of growth and investment leading to pessimism and, ultimately, withdrawal of support of the center coalitions of government by industrialists and other circles) now deprived it of an economically workable alternative.

Borchardt argues that Brüning could only have drawn on an alternative economic policy to his austerity measures after it was discovered that this economic crisis was different and more intense than preceding ones and therefore calling for different measures. According to Borchardt, this was not possible before summer 1931 when the international financial crisis set in. It would have been late in 1932 or in spring 1933 before any effect on such a new economic policy could have been realized. Moreover, Germany possessed little economic autonomy as far as manipulations of its currency or an inflationary policy to stimulate growth were concerned. Its export share in the international trade was also relatively high and such measures could have led to reprisals.

According to Mitchell, data on money wages in agriculture are available only for two other countries. The pattern resembles that of industrial wages in the respective countries. In Britain there is almost no change at all, with the exception of 1933 (minus 2 percent) and the increase by 5 percent from 1937 to 1938 (108). Agricultural workers in the Netherlands, on the other hand, were more seriously affected by the economic crisis. Their wages went down by almost a third within four years (from 1930 to 1934) and remained on that level until 1938. Workers in agriculture in the Netherlands were harder hit by the economic crisis than their colleagues in the industrial sector. The fascist movement of Anton Mussert drew its strongest support in the provincial election of April 1935 (Kwiet 1970, pp. 170-71) in some of the agrarian provinces suffering from the economic crisis.

Cost of Living (1929 = 100)

Within three years (1930-32) the cost of living index fell about one-fifth in Germany, before remaining almost constant for the next six years. In the Netherlands a similar pattern emerges, underlining the general trend of economic indicators during these years and the effects of deflationary economic decisions that at first were a dominant reaction to the economic crisis. Belgium also exhibits this pattern, but it is characterized by somewhat stronger fluctuations altogether. In Austria the cost of living went down by 5 percent from 1930 to 1931 and then remained on this level more or less for seven years. In Great Britain fluctuations were greater than in Austria but not as large as in Belgium and the Netherlands. Finally, France again exhibits a deviant pattern in that there is a rise of 25 percent from 1936 (80) to 1937 (101) and of another 14 percent in 1938 (115), whereas up to 1936 its pattern had resembled that of Britain.

Wholesale Price Indices

From the consumer's point of view, mostly similar effects are to be observed with respect to wholesale prices. In Germany there is a clear parallel to the cost of living index (r = .99). With the exception of Austria and Belgium, there are clear parallels in the curves of the wholesale price indices to about 1933. In Belgium the wholesale price index falls further in 1933 (59 in Belgium versus 68 in Germany), reaches its trough in 1934 (56), and starts to climb at a considerably faster rate than in Germany. In Belgium the value of 80 is reached in 1937, but then the index declines slightly again. In short, the Belgian fluctuations are greater than Germany's. In France the decline lasts until 1935 (56). Thereafter an even faster increase takes place, reaching a 1938 value of 103. This large increase from 1936 (65) to 1938 partly reflects the economic policies of the Popular Front Government. Overall, the pattern of the Netherlands bears a greater resemblance to the German pattern, although the trough of 61 is reached two years later (in 1935) as holds for other economic indicators, and the rise in wholesale prices is slightly less thereafter than in Germany. In Great Britain and Austria the decay in wholesale prices is considerably less. In Britain the lowest value is reached in 1932 (75). In 1937, however, a value of 96 is reached again, whereas in Austria wholesale prices, after declining to 84 in 1931, remain in the mideighties for the rest of the period. Note that in Great Britain, the Netherlands, and Belgium there is a slight reversal after 1937, which, for Britain and Belgium, can also be observed for unemployment and industrial production (see Figure 5.4).

Total Central Government Expenditure

The most dramatic change again occurred in Germany, where Brüning's austerity policy cut down total central government expenditure from 8.392 million marks in 1930 to 5.965 million in 1932, a decline of 28.9 percent. This pro-cyclical economic behavior of government can be observed in all six of the countries, most notably in Germany, Britain, and Austria (see Figure 5.5).

Keynes's *General Theory of Employment, Interest and Money* was published in 1936. In that year, four out of six countries (France, Germany, Belgium, and Great Britain) already followed some of the measures suggested. Military armament programs increasingly were being initiated as well. Other economic and political representatives had called already for state economic activities as a way of compensating for economic decline (with respect to Germany, see the references in Bombach et al. 1976).

In Great Britain, after a modest rise from 1928 on there is a decline of 7.6 percent in central government spending from 1932 to 1933, before a modest rise occurs from 1935 on (percentage increase in 1935: 5.6; in 1936: 7.2; in 1937: 2.2). In Belgium there is also first a rise from 1927 on and then an average decline in central government

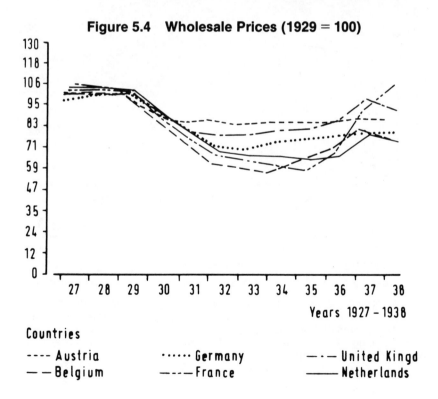

Figure 5.4 Wholesale Prices (1929 = 100)

Years 1927 - 1938

Countries

---- Austria ······ Germany —·— United Kingd
——Belgium ----France ——— Netherlands

spending of 4 percent for three successive years, 1931-33, before a rise takes place in 1935 that is especially remarkable (19.2 percent increase). (According to Flora's [1983, p. 361] data, this increase does not take place before 1936.)

The figures for Austria show an enormous drop in central government spending from 1931 to 1932 (17.5 percent decline). From 1933 until about 1937, the figure is more or less constant and on an average more than 20 percent below the figure for 1932. However, figures after 1932 (I still use the old figure for that year) do not include expenditure on tax collection and are thus not directly

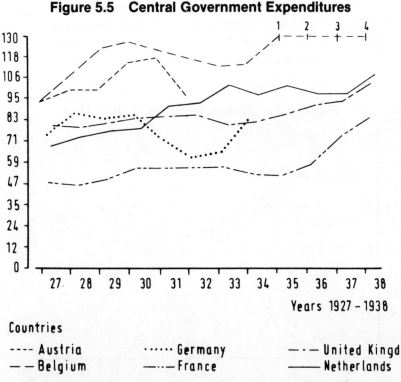

Figure 5.5   Central Government Expenditures

Years 1927 – 1938

Countries

---- Austria   ······ Germany   — · — United Kingd
— — Belgium   — ··· — France   ———— Netherlands

The outlying Belgian points are 1 (1935 = 136), 2 (1936 = 138), 3 (1937 = 142), and 4 (1938 = 145). Values for Austria (1933-1938) and Germany (1935-1938) are missing. Values are expressed in national currencies: Austria, twenty million shillings; Belgium, hundred million Belgian Francs; Germany, hundred million Marks; France, thousand million French Francs; United Kingdom, ten million Pounds; Netherlands, ten million Guilders.

comparable. If it were included, the percentage decline in central government spending should be lower than the 20 percent calculated here.

In the Netherlands, central government spending also shows some fluctuations. There is an increase up to 1933. In 1934 a percentage decline of 6.1 occurs before the level of 1933 is almost reached again, to be followed by a similar decrease. This pattern indicates that the economic crisis hit the Netherlands about two-and-a-half years later than most of the other five nations. In 1938, one year before World War II, however, central government spending was increased by 11.4 percent.

If one readjusts the figures for France given by Mitchell, total central government spending rises from 1928 to 1933 by 24.2 percent. Then a cut of 9.2 percent (1934) and no change for 1935 occurs. With the arrival of the Popular Front Government there are annual percentage increases of 11.9, 30.4, and 13.2 (which includes, of course, an inflationary push).

Although there are some increases in government spending after 1933, which need to be considered on a disaggregated base, in no instance could it be maintained that the new Keynesian economic theory calling for massively increased state activities and government spending had an immediate impact. (Nazi Germany is perhaps an exception to this.) Rather, government and the economy seem to have muddled through. The economy in most countries was still sagging. Germany with its strong rearmament program and the intimidation and reorganization of workers was the only country to experience an economic boom from 1936 on.

Industrial Disputes

In line with other cross-national analyses of strikes, there is a decline in strike behavior as the economic crisis widens. Some qualifications are, however, in order. In Germany the number of strikes declines from 1927 (844) to 1930 (353), and in the two final years of the Weimar Republic increases to 463 in 1931 and 648 in 1932. Yet the number of workers involved continually declines from 1928, where the peak is reached, until 1932. The most reliable figure in the present context is, however, the "product" of number of strikes and workers involved given as days lost. Here we note a rise by a factor of 3.3 from 1927, the year of economic boom, to 1928, and subsequent massive declines to about one-fifth of this level in 1930 and another decline of more than 70 percent until 1932. The number of days lost through strikes in 1932 amounts to only 5.6 percent of the figure in 1928. Clearly, the six million unemployed had a deterrent effect on individual willingness to engage in strikes.

In the United Kingdom all three figures (numbers of strikes, workers involved, and days lost) increase until 1929, where the highest number of days lost is reached (that amounts to about half of the German figure in 1928, taking the different population size into account). In 1930 the number of days lost declines by almost 50 percent, but rises again by 58.7 percent in 1931. The most massive decline in days lost occurs between 1932 and 1933 (83.5 percent), in the period when unemployment had reached its peak and the level of industrial production its trough. From 1935 to 1937 there again is an almost uniform slow rise in all three indicators, before another decline occurs in 1938.

France displays oscillations in the number of days lost from 1927 to 1935, with the highest figure reached in 1930. Most noteworthy in this period seems to be the rise in days lost by a factor of 6.1 from 1927 to 1928 and the strong decline by a factor of 7.6 from 1930 to 1931 as France was fully hit by the crisis in industrial production. The absolute peak in industrial disputes, however, was reached in 1936, followed by further massive strike waves in 1937. The political turmoil associated with the Government of the Popular Front also had a positive effect on the motivation of workers to go on strike, notwithstanding the relatively high rate of unemployment in those years. For 1936 till 1938, Mitchell does not give figures for the number of days lost (see Figure 5.6).

Belgium displays an erratic pattern of industrial disputes with rises and declines in workers involved almost alternating. Relative peaks in industrial disputes seem to have occurred in 1932 and 1935-37. Figures for days lost are not reported. However, this interpretation squares with developments in industrial production and unemployment in Belgium (see Figures 5.2 and 5.1).

The Netherlands experiences relatively higher levels of industrial disputes in 1929 and again in 1931 after a drop in 1930, as well as a peak in 1932 (altogether fewer workers than in Belgium were involved). Thereafter the level of industrial disputes almost continually declines, just as the economic crisis, in particular unemployment, starts to hit the Netherlands with full power after 1934 (see Figure 5.7).

In Austria, with some minor qualifications, industrial disputes from 1928 continually decline until 1933. In 1934 they level off totally, after the Dollfuss government had outlawed strikes on April 21, 1933.

Correlations between the three measures of industrial disputes in general are positive (see Table 5.2). On an average they are .66 (number of strikes and days lost; for Belgium the correlation cannot be calculated), .64 (number of strikes and workers involved; Britain is an exception here with a correlation of −.15, which seems to be

Figure 5.6   Industrial Disputes: Days Lost

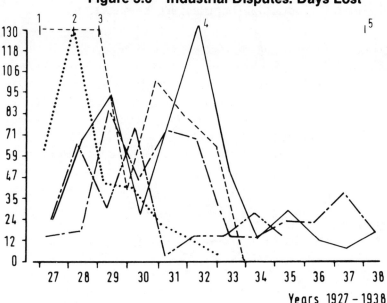

Years 1927 – 1938

Countries

		(hundred-		(hundred-
---- Austria (thous.)	····· Germany thous.)	---- United Kingd (thous.)

— — Belgium (thous.)   ——— France (hundred-   ——— Netherlands (ten-
                                            thous.)   thous.)

Values are missing from Belgium (1927-1937), Germany (1933-1938), France (1936-1938), and Austria (1938). Outlying points are 1 (Austria, 1927 = 477), 2 (Austria, 1928 = 563; Germany, 1928 = 203), 3 (Austria, 1929 = 287), 4 (Netherlands, 1932 = 164), and 5 (Belgium, 1938 = 241).

affected by the relatively low number of strikes and the high number of days lost between 1929 and 1932), and .88 (workers involved and days lost, which almost by definition is higher than the other two correlations; again no figure for Belgium). Correlations in some cases may be quite misleading considering our 12 points of observation at the maximum. The subsequent analysis should be read with this general warning in mind.

In 44 out of 68 cases (64.7 percent) the sign theoretically expected shows up, if indicators of economic success such as low unemployment, industrial production, wages in industry, and GNP are related to the three measures of industrial disputes (see Table 5.2). Also, eight correlations among the 24 "wrong" cases do not reach values beyond .15. In addition, the correlations that are in line with

Figure 5.7 Industrial Disputes: Workers Involved

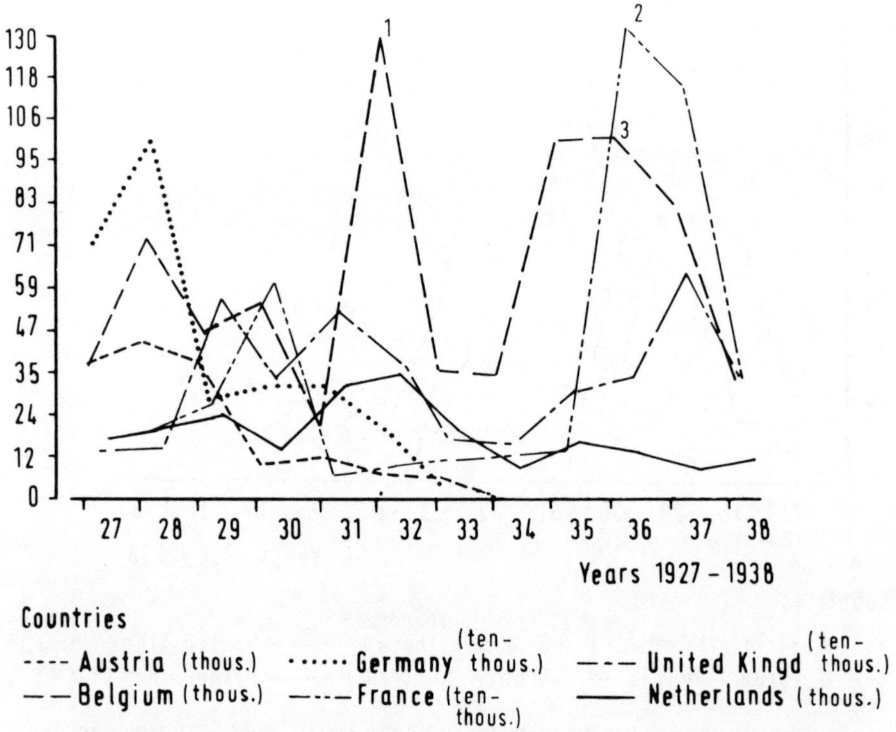

1
2
3
130
118
106
95
83
71
59
47
35
24
12
0
27 28 29 30 31 32 33 34 35 36 37 38
Years 1927 - 1938
Countries
---- Austria (thous.)
····· Germany (ten-thous.)
--- United Kingd (ten-thous.)
—— Belgium (thous.)
----France (ten-thous.)
—— Netherlands (thous.)

Values are missing from Austria (1938) and Germany (1933-1938). The outlying points are: 1 (Belgium, 1932 = 161); 2 (France, 1936 = 242). Point 3 (Belgium, 1936) has been estimated.

Table 5.2 Correlations Between Indicators of Economic Success and Three Measures of Industrial Disputes

	Expected Sign	Germany	France	UK	Austrtia	Netherlands	Belgium
Unemployment							
Numbers	-	-.21	.02	-.30	-.90	-.49	-.45
Workers involved	-	-.67	-.10	-.03	-.85	-.30	-.32
Days lost	-	-.61	-.66	-.20	-.73	-.23	n.a.
Industrial							
Numbers	+	.19	-.16	.93	.94	-.32	.66
Production							
Workers involved	+	.62	-.09	.25	.89	-.41	-.19
Days lost	+	.58	.61	-.37	.74	-.36	n.a.
Wages in industry							
Numbers	+	-.23	.15	.48	-.45	.67	-.001
Workers involved	+	.43	.27	.21	-.53	.52	-.32
Days lost	+	.54	-.08	-.06	-.67	.41	n.a.
GNP (NNP)							
Numbers	+	.31	-.35	.91	.82	-.02	-.26
Workers involved	+	.74	-.33	.24	.75	-.12	.43
Days lost	+	.68	.51	-.34	.58	-.10	n.a.

Underlined coefficients are commented on in the text.
n.a.: not available

103

conventional theoretical expectations in general are stronger than those disproving these expectations.

With respect to unemployment and industrial disputes, there are only two major deviations from the generally negative relationships. In the case of Belgium, data are incomplete and correlations are thus difficult to interpret. The correlation of .2 for Britain can be explained by the covariation of unemployment and days lost through strikes from the years 1930 to 1932.

The negative correlation of $-.16$ between industrial production and number of strikes in France is traceable to one extreme outlier: the year 1936. In Britain, 1929, 1931, and 1932 with their many days lost through striking affect the correlation of $-.37$, which otherwise would be considerably changed. Two of the three negative correlations for the Netherlands are not influenced by a particular outlier. In the case of industrial production and days lost through striking, 1932 with its massive striking in spite of low industrial production has such a strong effect that a negative sign emerges. The correlation of $-.19$ for Belgium is affected by values for 1932, when the number of strikers reached a maximum and industrial production fell to its lowest level.

The only deviation in the German case, the negative correlation between wages in industry and number of strikes ($-.23$), is based on six observations only (1927-32) and is strongly affected by 1927 and 1932. For Austria the correlation of $-.67$ between wages in industry and days lost through striking is greatly affected by 1928, when industrial disputes reached their highest value. At that time wages in industry were on a relatively low level. The same holds for 1927, but to a lesser degree. In a similar way the negative correlations between wages in industry and workers involved in strikes ($-.53$) as well as number of strikes ($-.45$) are affected. For Belgium, the correlation of $-.32$ between wages in industry and workers involved in strikes is strongly influenced by the values for 1932, when by far the maximum numbers of workers were involved in strikes, even though wages were on a relatively low level.

In France, 1936 with its extreme number of strikes and relatively low GNP again carries the burden for the negative correlation of $-.35$. The same holds true for the negative correlation in the case of workers involved ($-.33$). For Britain, the negative correlation with respect to days lost ($-.34$) again is caused by three years of turbulent striking: 1931, 1932, and above all 1929.

Germany and Austria altogether exhibit more consistent and theoretically expected relationships when relating the four simple measures of economic success to the three measures of industrial disputes. Observations are based, however, on only six (Germany) and seven (Austria) years. For France, Britain, and the Netherlands, the covariation between economic success or decline and industrial disputes is considerably weaker. What brought about these respective patterns of strike behavior needs to be discovered in further analyses.

Many other preliminary conclusions could be drawn from the correlation analyses performed thus far. A few summary evaluations will have to suffice here (see Table 5.3).

France is the only country that shows an extremely weak negative correlation ($-.08$) between unemployment and wages in industry, again having to do with the economic policies of the Popular Front Government from 1936 on. All countries show moderate (NL: $-.23$; UK: $-.45$) to strong (A: $-.70$; F: $-.83$; B and G: $-.94$) negative correlations between industrial production and unemployment (or vice versa for that matter). Again, mostly strong negative correlations show up across the board when relating the wholesale price index or living costs to unemployment as holds for GNP, with the exception of Belgium (.48). This positive correlation is partly created by the high GNP values that coincide with a sizable rate of unemployment during 1936-38. But this correlation is based on only seven values.

As should be expected, with the exception of France ($-.19$) there is a weak to moderate relationship between the wholesale price index and the number of strikes. (Austria with seven cases only and with a value of .96 is another "deviating" case here.) The negative coefficient for France is strongly influenced by the enormous number of strikes in 1936. France also shows the only noteworthy exception with respect to living costs and the number of strikes ($-.28$). Again, the "cause" is found in the year 1936. In Britain ($-.10$) there is no such single outlier.

With respect to workers involved in strikes and wholesale price index, France again displays a negative (but extremely weak: $-.08$) correlation, whereas in the case of Belgium ($-.26$) the year 1933 with the maximum number of workers involved has a strong effect in setting up this correlation. Concerning the number of workers involved in strikes and changes in living costs, Belgium ($-.35$: once more influenced by 1933) and France ($-.13$: 1936 as an extreme

Table 5.3 Correlations Between Various Economic (Crisis) Indicators

Indicators	Germany	Austria	France	Belgium	Netherlands	UK
Unemployment						
number of strikes	-.21	-.90	.02	-.45	-.49	-.30
workers involved	-.67	-.85	-.10	.32	-.30	-.03
days lost	-.61	-.73	-.66	n.a.	-.23	.20
wages in industry	-.58	-.22	-.08	-.62	-.93	-.74
industrial production	-.94	-.70	-.83	-.94	-.23	-.45
wholesale price index	-.42	-.84	-.74	-.98	-.94	-.91
living costs	-.31	-.44	-.66	-.86	-.98	-.82
GNP	-.82	-.97	-.71	.48	-.54	-.42
wages in agriculture	-.05	n.a.	n.a.	n.a.	-.97	-.45
Numbers of Strikes						
workers involved	.68	.99	.95	.12	.60	.49
days lost	.46	.92	.74	n.a.	.51	-.15
wages in industry	-.23	-.45	.15	-.001	.67	.48
industrial production	.19	.94	-.16	.66	-.32	.93
wholesale price index	.08	.96	-.19	.52	.29	.04
living costs	-.05	.25	-.28	.04	.49	-.10
GNP	.31	.82	-.35	.26	-.02	.91
wages in agriculture	-.80	n.a.	n.a.	n.a.	.57	.68
Workers Involved						
days lost	.92	.94	.84	n.a.	.93	.77
wages in industry	.43	-.53	.27	-.32	.52	.21
industrial production	.62	.89	-.09	-.19	-.41	.25

wholesale price index	.60	.94	-.08	-.26	.12	.02
living costs	.54	.15	-.13	-.35	.28	.04
GNP	.74	.75	-.33	.43	-.12	.24
wages in agriculture	-.12	n.a.	n.a.	n.a.	.45	.30

Days Lost

wages in industry	.54	-.67	-.08	n.a.	.41	-.06
industrial production	.58	.74	.61	n.a.	-.36	-.37
wholesale price index	.59	.86	.49	n.a.	.08	-.04
living costs	.54	-.10	.48	n.a.	.22	.11
GNP	.68	.58	.51	n.a.	-.10	-.34
wages in agriculture	.06	n.a.	n.a.	n.a.	.33	-.06

Wages in Industry

industrial production	.39	.00	-.35	.47	.03	.50
wholesale price index	.92	-.07	.18	.62	.78	.72
living costs	.91	.55	.58	.86	.90	.74
GNP	.14	.36	-.30	.21	.33	.53
wages in agriculture	.79	n.a.	n.a.	n.a.	.96	.88

Industrial Production

wholesale price index	.17	.48	.61	.95	.24	.13
living costs	.07	.10	.43	.72	.11	-.03
GNP	.96	.67	.85	-.32	.81	.98
wages in agriculture	-.09	n.a.	n.a.	n.a.	.07	.66

Wholesale Price Index

living costs	.99	.50	.82	.83	.95	.95

Table 5.3 Continued

Indicators	Germany	Austria	France	Belgium	Netherlands	UK
GNP	-.11	.84	.32	-.42	.56	.10
money wages in agriculture	.75	n.a.	n.a.	n.a.	.87	.34
Living Costs						
GNP	-.21	.68	.36	-.22	.40	-.03
money wages in agriculture	.82	n.a.	n.a.	n.a.	.94	.38
GNP Central Government Spending						
money wages in agriculture	-.29	n.a.	n.a.	n.a.	.42	.74
unemployment	-.82	.18	-.02	.37	.90	-.14
number of strikes	-.29	-.51	.10	.19	-.43	.84
workers involved	.45	-.57	.25	.22	-.27	.35
days lost	.59	-.64	-.24	n.a.	-.22	-.11
wages in industry	.78	.72	.98	.14	-.81	.58
industrial production	.80	-.25	-.36	-.22	.06	.79
wholesale price index	.66	-.63	.20	-.30	-.90	-.08
living costs	.67	.17	.58	-.21	-.91	-.08
GNP	.76	.07	-.35	.95	-.32	.85
money wages in agriculture	.56	n.a.	n.a.	n.a.	-.92	.88

Underlined coefficients are commented on in particular.
n.a.: not available

108

outlier in terms of industrial disputes) again are deviating from the general pattern.

More conclusive are the generally positive relationships between the wholesale price index and days lost through striking. Britain with a negative correlation of − .04 is an exception here, as is Germany with its − .10 with respect to the correlation between GNP and living costs. In half of the cases the relationship between industrial production and wages in industry is moderately positive. Surprising is the almost noncorrelation in the Netherlands (.03), which is partly affected by the limited variation in wages and the noncorrelation in Austria (eight cases only with a "random" pattern). Even more astonishing is the negative correlation of − .35 in France, which is caused by outlying values for 1938 when industrial production was relatively low but money wages in industry reached their maximum, and the preceding year when industrial production had increased somewhat but wages still remained on a relatively high level.

Relating wages in industry and the cost of living index leads to the most consistent and strongest positive correlations across the board and indicates perhaps how increasing costs of labor are converted into higher prices.

France once more is an exception, with its negative correlation of − .30 between GNP and wages in industry strongly influenced by income policies in 1936 and 1937. No surprise are the generally positive correlations between industrial production and the wholesale price index and living costs, with the minor exception of Britain in the latter instance. Also, there are strong positive correlations between industrial production and GNP, as should be expected. The negative correlation (− .32) in the case of Belgium is strongly affected by the relatively high level of industrial production paired with a low level of GNP in 1927 (also, only seven values are reported).

As to correlations with the index of wholesale prices in the lower half of Table 5.3, only the values for Belgium (− .42) and Germany (− .11), both with respect to GNP, deviate from the generally expected positive correlation. In the case of Belgium, only seven values are reported, whereas in Germany the years 1927-30 form a separate cluster. The three negative correlations between GNP and the cost of living are also surprising. In Germany (− .21) this is again influenced by the very same cluster of the years 1927-30. For Belgium (− .22), only seven values are reported, whereas in Britain the negative correlation (− .30) is almost negligible.

Less consistent are the correlations when relating central government spending to the other economic indicators as were the policies of many a government. Most noteworthy is the high negative correlation of − .82 between unemployment spending in the case of Germany, which, apart from Britain's less telling correlation of − .14 (and the − .02 of France), is unique in this row. It demonstrates how much Brüning with his extreme austerity policy deviates from policies pursued in the other five countries. Even if one grants that Germany was economically and politically in an extremely vulnerable position since it had lost the war and depended upon external credits, such an enormous difference between its economic policy and that of its neighbors is astonishing. It will need much further substantiation both in terms of statistical analysis and close description of economic and political measures and their impact. If one were to bet on a single figure in this correlation table as most revealing, it would be this figure. The very high positive correlation of .90 in the case of the Netherlands is strongly affected by two clusters of years: 1927 till 1930 and 1932 till 1938. Within these clusters there is no consistent increase of central government spending as unemployment increases. Between these clusters, however, the biggest relative increase in central government spending occurs, namely by 17.2 percent from 1930 to 1931, whereas unemployment increases by 7 percent. The other strong increase in central government spending occurs from 1932 to 1933 (by 12.5 percent). Unemployment, however, increases by only 1.6 percent. While impressive in its magnitude, a closer inspection of the correlation reveals there is no consistent increase of central government spending as unemployment increases, once the big jump in spending from 1930 to 1931 is taken into consideration, which occurred before the Netherlands was fully hit by the economic crisis.

There is no clear variation between central government spending and the three measures of industrial disputes and no compelling reason to expect it to occur. Welfare measures to buy off potential strike behavior were not yet a theme. Perhaps most noteworthy is the deviating positive correlation between central government spending and days of striking (.59) in Germany (the causes of which have been discussed just above), whereas all four other nations exhibit a negative relationship of a generally modest strength. The years of 1932 (lowest value) and of 1928 (highest value) strongly influence this correlation pattern restricted to only six cases.

The deviating high negative correlation of $-.81$ between central government spending and wages in industry in the Netherlands is strongly influenced by the limited variation in wages. Half of the values are 100. In the other cases positive correlations emerge as expected. What is surprising with respect to central government spending and industrial production is the high positive correlation of .79 for Britain. This partly has to do with increased central government spending in the military sector after 1936, which contributed to a rise in industrial production. Germany's .80 only shows the reverse of what has been noted a few lines above, but also the effects of its strong rearmament policies, whereas the three modest negative correlations for Austria, Belgium, and France demonstrate that there are at least some indications for increased government spending as the economic situation deteriorated. In Austria, however, this was the case only from 1929 to 1930 and—less so—to 1931. The trend was reversed in 1932. Values for the later years are based on a new index that could not be used for the present calculations. In Belgium increased central government spending does not start before 1934, and only occurs to a limited extent. The increase of 19.2 percent from 1934 to 1935 is the big exception. (Flora's [1983, p. 361] data also show a decline in spending for these two years.) If one traces the relationship between decline in industrial production and increased central government spending on a yearly basis, such a relation exists only for the years 1929 to 1930 and 1937 to 1938. Of course, various lag measures will also have to be used to discover in what ways, if at all, government tried to fight the economic crisis through increased spending. A similar graphical analysis for France reveals that only from 1937 to 1938 can such a tendency for increased spending be observed. The Government of the Popular Front may have been inclined for ideological reasons to increase government spending to combat the setback in industrial production. At the same time, however, it was besieged by other economic problems, as has become apparent even in the present simple correlation analysis.

Correlations between central government spending and the wholesale price index, the costs of living, and GNP, respectively, seem to be more strongly influenced by factors peculiar to each country. Also, the behavior of central government spending will probably show greater variations from country to country not merely in terms of how much is spent, but also under which circumstances (for example, composition and ideological orientation of government; relevancy of other economic indicators). In the case of central government spending, correlations are much more diverging, whereas in other instances patterns emerge that display a number of (almost) uniformities across the six countries. Perhaps this relative uniformity is one major finding in this still preliminary analysis.

The other major finding seems to be that some countries experienced greater shocks. Deviations from corresponding values in preceding years were considerably higher than holds for other countries. These patterns need further study through time series analysis and other techniques and corroboration both in statistical and substantive terms. A simple visual inspection (figures not reprinted here) of all economic indicators used thus far to characterize the six countries on their way into and out of their most serious economic crisis in this century reveals that the German, Austrian, Belgian, and French patterns show much stronger oscillations than the British and the Dutch (with the exception of unemployment). Will the political effects of and reactions to the economic (and perhaps political) crisis also show considerable variation in the six countries? Even if one were totally ingnorant of the history of the respective countries, one would assume that in Britain, the Netherlands, and in some respects perhaps Belgium,[7] the economic (and political) challenge came more smoothly than shockingly about and consequently left more chances for gradual adjustment than the abrupt, almost revolutionary pattern in other countries.

In Table 5.4 I have tried to rank the six countries on those six indicators that seem to be more unambiguously indicating situations of economic crisis in a polity. With respect to unemployment and industrial production, a rank order in terms of relative changes has also been established. All of these rank orders have been created simply on the basis of visual and tabular inspection. Rank correlation coefficients and more complex index measures will still have to be applied to more consolidated data. Furthermore, from year to year different rank orders emerge that have to be averaged in some way. Here I simply use peak and trough values in a very rough classification.

If for a start one simply adds the rank positions of each country, the country with the lowest sum should be the one most greatly afflicted in terms of these selected economic indicators. Such a procedure would assume that each indicator is equivalent with each

Table 5.4 A (Rough) Rank Order of Six European Countries According to Selected Indicators of Economic Crisis (1927-1938)

Declines in Industrial Production	Declines in Money Wages in Industry	Declines in Total Central Government Expenditure	Declines in GNP (NNP)	Declines in Industrial Production (rate of change)	Unemployment	Relative Increases in Unemployment	Wholesale Price Index (inverse order)
Germany	Germany	Germany	Germany	Germany	Netherlands	Belgium	Belgium
Austria	Belgium	Austria	Austria	Belgium	Germany	Netherlands	France
Belgium	Netherlands	Belgium	France	France	Belgium	Germany	Netherlands
United Kingdom	Austria	France	Netherlands	Austria	United Kingdom	United Kingdom	Germany
Netherlands	United Kingdom	United Kingdom	United Kingdom	Netherlands	Austria	Austria	United Kingdom
France	France	Netherlands	Belgium	United Kingdom	France	France	Austria

other and across all the six nations. Yet, some indicators, unemployment for example, may be much more important. They may cause considerable political trouble whereas the wholesale price index may be of minor relevance. Whether this is true and to what degree must be left to further analysis. Here it will suffice to present the summary ranking in terms of these selected economic crisis indicators:

1		Germany	14 points
2		Belgium	21 points
3 & 4	{	Austria	29 points
		Netherlands	29 points
5		France	36 points
6		United Kingdom	38 points

Although such an ordinal classification that does not take into account distances between ranking positions could indeed be corroborated through more substantial (and statistical) analysis, two things seem to be especially noteworthy. Germany is not only the most greatly afflicted country in terms of economic crisis; it also stands far apart from the two other large industrial states, France and the United Kingdom. The three smallest states more or less face similar economic challenges, which should make comparisons between them especially interesting. A more detailed inspection of Table 5.4 also reveals that depending on the economic indicator chosen, each of the six countries may be considered among the two most harshly affected with the exception of Britain, which never ranks first or second. This simple ranking and the less oscillatory pattern in the case of Britain— but also of the Netherlands, especially in comparison to the smaller countries—may point to much less dramatic political solutions finally reached to respond to the economic challenge.

Landes (1983, pp. 361-62), contrary to some other opinions in the literature (such as Aldcroft 1980, pp. 80-109), claims that France had to suffer most under the economic depression, but he does not list his indicators. The comparisons he presents, drawing on figures for industrial production, also disprove his contention. On the contrary, Germany is more afflicted than France and Britain (see also Kindleberger 1973, p. 293; Petzina 1977, pp. 17-18; Aldcroft 1980, pp. 80-96). For a full account, one obviously would also have to consider rates of recovery where Germany on many indicators is the leader, too, and France is massively lagging behind. In that respect, France perhaps suffered longer.

In terms of analysis, one point is basic here: all six countries were affected by the world economic crisis of the 1930s even though Germany experienced the worst impact. If, however, all were afflicted, there is no logical short-cut to treat the political radicalism occurring in Germany as a response to the widening economic crisis as "totally" explicable by such a precedent.[8] If a similar economic challenge was present in other countries, but other solutions were found, then in Germany additional factors besides economic ones must have played an important role in bringing about the collapse of the Weimar Republic. There is no lack of such factors, as the numerous "shopping lists" of alleged causal factors for the collapse of German democracy demonstrate:

- In the *long* run: The German tradition of the authoritarian state; the doctrine of Lutheranism preaching obedience to worldly authorities; the failure of the liberal bourgeoisie to constitute a strong and independent political force; anti-Western values in the political culture; and so forth.
- In the *middle* run: The lost war and the Treaty of Versailles, psychologically never accepted by a large majority; the inflation of 1923 with its dispossession of large segments of the middle strata; the strong reservations almost any social group had against the Republic of Weimar; the incompetence of party government; the remaining political isolation of Germany; and so forth.
- In the *short* run: The economic crisis from 1930 on with the ideological polarization of the electorate; the ill-conceived politics of financial austerity; the authoritarian form of government instituted through Brüning's and his successors' increased drawing on emergency measures according to §48 of the constitution (from Bracher's [1978] point of view, the beginning of the end of the Weimar Republic); the dual character of the constitution weakening the powers of the chancellor and thus encouraging parties to withdraw from responsible government and compromise finding; the role of the East German *Junker*; the *camarilla* around Hindenburg in finally aborting parliamentary government; and many others (for recent overviews see Broszat et al. 1983; Schulze 1982).

Consequently, the search for *differentia specifica* in each country must start from here. There are differences in terms of economic challenge, but more important differences will emerge as one turns to the political effects of those crisis indicators. In some instances these factors facilitated the mobilization of consensus to deal with the economic crisis. In other instances, notably Germany and Austria, but also France, political crisis factors emerge from this economic crisis or are reinforced by it and thus transform it into a general crisis of the political system. In later stages, some of these factors will be elaborated in a more qualitative way; others should be suited for quantitative analysis.

Political Effects

While the decline of economic performance can have a variety of political effects, we here are concerned only with three different categories of political effects: the impact of economic crisis on the electorate; the effects these two variables will have on government stability or durability; and the measures taken by government to react to economic downturn as well as political radicalization. Figure 5.8 illustrates the causal chains I want to analyze in quantitative terms in later stages of the project. At present, the causal model mainly serves a heuristic function. For adequate quantitative tests the model in the present form is, of course, underidentified.

Other political effects will have to be analyzed in qualitative terms. These more qualitative accounts will shed some light on the quantitative findings I hope to discover.

Swings in the Electorate

Is there a swing in the electorate, for example, to radical parties, as the economic situation deteriorates? In Table 5.5 the total net change (TNC) among voters during the elections between 1927 and 1938 (to 1932 for Germany and 1930 for Austria) has been listed drawing on the following formula (Pedersen 1983, p. 33):

$$V_t = \frac{1}{2} TNC_t$$

The data about seats won in parliament are taken from Mackie and Rose (1982). Unfortunately, there are computational errors in

Figure 5.8 A Raw Causal Model of Some Crisis Efforts

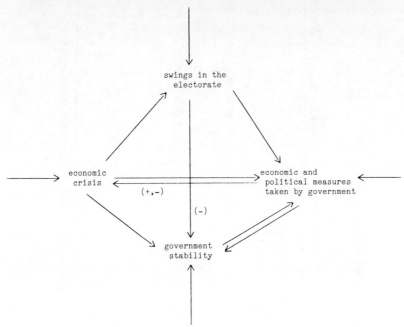

this data source (the French Radical-Socialist Party in 1928 won 120 seats, not 20; following Mackie and Rose the number of seats in the second German election of 1932 adds up to only 580 instead of the correct 584 given). Austria displays the lowest aggregate volatility, which has to do with the *Lagermentalität* so characteristic of the first Austrian Republic. The other two smaller countries also exhibit less volatility than the three larger nations. With the exception of Austria, maximum volatility is reached in the election closest to the trough of the economic crisis. For Belgium this was the case some time later than for the other four countries. The Netherlands reached its maximum economic decline even after Belgium; the maximum volatility of 14.9 in Belgium in 1936, and of 12 in Holland in 1937 thus comes as no surprise. The biggest surprise is, of course, the extreme figure of 44.3 volatility in the British election of October 1931, when Labour lost 241 seats (39.2 percent of all seats; unless otherwise indicated the number of all seats at each election is the base for all subsequent percentages) to the conservatives (214 seats gained or 34.8

Table 5.5 Aggregate Volatility in the Elections Between 1927 and 1938

Period	Germany	United Kingdom	France	Austria	Belgium	Netherlands
1927-28	compared to 1924 1928: 12.1		compared to 1924 1928: 10.8	compared to 1923 1927: <u>6.1</u>		
1929-30	1930: 18.8	compared to 1924 1929: 25.15		1930: 5.4	compared to 1925 1929: 6.95	compared to 1925 1929: 3
1931-32	July 32: <u>21.4</u> Nov. 32: 8.3	1931: <u>44.3</u>	1932: <u>19.1</u>		1932: 6.9	
1933-34						1933: 8
1935-36		1935: 17.9	1936: 14.2		1932: <u>14.9</u>	
1937-38						1937: <u>12</u>

Relative maximum values are underlined; for Austria (1927-33) and Germany (1927-32) a shorter period is utilized.

118

percent). The Liberal Party lost 27 seats or 4.4 percent. The majority system of voting has, of course, considerably contributed to this effect, since in terms of voters, Labour's defeat was not such a disaster (-7.8 percent). In that respect the Liberal Party was the big loser (-17.1 percent). In 1935 Labour took back 108 seats (17.6 percent) and thus partly recovered from the fatal blow in 1931, when MacDonald had headed the national government and the Labour Party had almost broken apart.

France reached the highest volatility in 1932 when the French economy was affected by the economic crisis. In 1932 the Radical-Socialist Party with 37 additional seats (6.1 percent of all seats) was the big winner, followed by the Socialist Party with 30 additional seats (5 percent), whereas the Republic Union experienced a dramatic loss of 106 seats (17.5 percent). In 1936 comparisons become more difficult since coalitions among the leftist parties and among the center parties were formed. The leftist block gained some 28 seats (4.6 percent), whereas the bourgeois block lost 37 seats (6.1 percent). The biggest loser, however, was the winner of 1932, the Radical-Socialist Party with 48 seats (7.9 percent). The biggest winner of the election in 1936 was the Communists, gaining 11.8 percent of all seats (60 seats, 9.8 percent more than in 1932), by far their best result in this period, which brought them into the government of the Popular Front (and at least temporarily made them less of an antisystem force).

Germany shows a dramatic increase in volatility from 1928 to the July election in 1932. Volatility almost doubles from 12.1 to 21.4 percent and is surpassed only by the British figures. Yet in the second election of 1932, the November election, volatility declines rapidly to 8 percent almost as if to document that voters at the polls had given up their efforts to change things by trying out different parties. In 1928 the Social Democratic Party was the big winner (4.5 percent, 22 additional seats), the Conservative Nationalist Party (DNVP) being the big loser (30 seats or 6.1 percent). All other parties were affected by only minor changes. In 1930 the first shock at the polls occurred when the Nazi Party drew 95 seats (16.5 percent) in addition and by itself made up for 44 percent of the entire volatility in that election. The Communist Party came in second with 23 additional seats (4 percent), while the DNVP again was the big loser (32 seats, -5.5 percent). The second blow to the democratic parties took place in

July 1932 when the Nazi Party won another 20.2 percent of the seats (123), accounted for almost half of the total volatility in that election, and for the first time became the largest party in parliament. The Communists again were the second winner (12 seats or 2 percent). The DNVP for the third time was a loser (− 4 seats or 0.7 percent), this time surpassed by the *Mittelstandspartei* (− 21 seats, 3.4 percent), the Peasants and Farmers Party (− 18 seats, 3 percent), the German Democratic Party (− 16 seats, 2.6 percent), the Social Democrats (− 10 seats, 1.6 percent), and losses of almost all other parties. The Nationalist-Conservative Party, however, recovered somewhat in the last free election of the Weimar Republic (2.6 percent or 15 additional seats). Again the Communists were the second winner (1.9 percent, 11 seats), being perceived by many bourgeois voters as more threatening than the Nazis. The Nazi Party this time was the big loser (− 6.5 percent, 38 seats, or 39 percent of the total volatility). The Nazis made up, however, for this painful loss in electoral prestige, which put a heavy burden on the morale of the party. In the *Landtagswahl* in January in Lippe they received 39.5 percent of the votes. On January 30, 1933, Hitler was made Chancellor by President Hindenburg. The Social Democrats also lost 2.1 percent or 12 seats in the November election of 1932. Since the July 1932 election the antisystem parties, the Nazis and the Communists, held the majority of seats in parliament. Bracher (1957, p. 645) has summarized these developments in Table 5.6.

While volatility in parliamentary seats in Britain was even higher than in Germany, it is remarkable that the British voters moved to the center to support the national government coalition (Conservatives, National Liberals, National Labour) in the election of October 1931 (522 seats or 84.9 percent). The antisystem radical parties achieved less than one percent of the vote and no seats in parliament. (In 1935 one communist deputy was elected.) The two elections of 1931 and 1935 brought overwhelming triumphs for the conservatives (77.1 percent and 63.1 percent of the seats, respectively).

Even in France electoral volatility did not further the consolidation of antisystem parties, with the exception of 1936 and it is at least debatable whether the communists were then any longer an antisystem party. Rather, the swing to the center taking place in the election of 1932 continued further to the left in the election of 1936. Also French rightist groups were not organized in the form of political

Table 5.6   Percentage of Parliamentary Seats by Type of Party

	Elections			
Parties	*May 1928*	*September 1930*	*July 1932*	*November 1932*
Democratic (SPD, Zentrum-BVP, Staats-partei- Wirt- schaftspartei)	56.7	47.3	38.8	36.6
Fascist (NSDAP)	2.5	18.5	37.8	33.6
Communist (KPD)	11.0	13.3	14.6	17.1
Conservative/ authoritarian/ monarchist (DNVP, DVP splinter)	29.4	20.8	8.5	12.7

Source: Bracher 1957: 645.

parties. While these groups were in command of sizable financial resources, their unwillingness to become political parties may have spared France some of the political trouble that was to occur in Germany, Austria, and Italy.

The volatility figures for Austria are not very revealing. The Christian Social Party lost seven seats (− 4.2 percent) in the election of 1930 as it did in 1927. The Heimwehr (eight seats or 4.8 percent) was the winner of the election, but also its main loser at the same time, since the massive financial backing (such as from Mussolini) did not lead to the electoral success expected. However, the door to government was opened to a party of the extreme right. The *Landtagswahlen* of April 24, 1932 brought the Nazi Party an electoral success and made it the third largest party.

For the three smaller countries, the Belgian figure of volatility is the highest, but a closer analysis reveals some stabilizing trends from election to election. In the election of 1932 the Catholic Party was the clear winner with an additional eight seats (4.3 percent). Altogether, however, volatility was limited as holds for 1929. Perhaps most noteworthy is the finding that every party that lost in 1929 won in 1932 and vice versa. The picture changes considerably in 1936 to look more stabilized again in 1939. The Catholic Party in 1936 was the big loser (minus 18 seats or 8.9 percent). The Flemish Nationalists won eight seats (4 percent). The real threat, however, came from the Fascist Rexists who claimed 21 seats (10.4 percent). Again with the exception of the Liberal Party (-1 seat, 0.5 percent), and the communists who won six seats (3 percent), every party winning in 1932 was losing in 1936 and vice versa. In 1939, however, the threat from the extreme right (Flemish Nationalists and above all Rexists) was fought off: the Catholic Party rose again (12 additional seats or 5.9 percent) followed by the Liberal Party (ten seats or 5 percent), while the Workers Party fell back to the second rank (minus six seats or 3 percent). The clear losers were the Rexists who had to give up 17 seats (-8.4 percent). For a moment the Belgian pattern of gradual electoral changes seemed to be challenged in the 1936 election, but the center parties were able to fight this threat off.

The Netherlands in electoral terms was least of all affected. If one did not know from economic indicators that there was a severe economic crisis, it could not be detected from the electoral statistics. Volatility does not go beyond 1 point per party in the election of 1929 and not beyond 2 points in 1933. Here the Anti-Revolutionary Party and the Communist Party each won two additional seats (in the Netherlands until 1956 the number of seats equals 100), whereas the Catholic Party and the Social Democratic Workers Party each lost two seats. In the election of 1933 the Catholic Party and the Social Democratic Workers Party each lost two seats. In the election of 1937 the Catholic Party made up for its losses and won three additional seats as did the Anti-Revolutionary Party. The Liberal States Party lost three seats. The biggest winner of 1937 was, however, the National Socialist Movement with four seats. Yet, altogether, this was an almost negligible threat to democratic order in the Netherlands. The enormous electoral stability is also demonstrated in the ruling coalition of the Catholic Party, the Anti-Revolutionary Party, and the Christian Historical Union under Prime Minister Colijn (Anti-Revolutionary Party), which only in 1933 and 1935 is enlarged by the Liberal States Party and the Radicals beyond the minimal winning status so as to broaden the legislative consensus (65 seats) for fighting the economic crisis that affected the Netherlands later than the other countries.

Duverger attributes remarkable stability to the political order of the Netherlands, Belgium, and also France during our period of observation. In his view the system of proportional representation as in the Netherlands and Belgium,

> when applied to countries that are naturally [?] stable . . . has the effect of petrifying representation. . . . National temperament also plays an important part here. [In France, the] simple-majority two-ballot system went hand in hand with fairly marked stability. . . . Obviously the second ballot attenuates the variations of the first. (Duverger 1964, p. 304)

In terms of relative increases in electoral volatility, however, Belgium and the Netherlands rank higher. Yet the absolute figures here seem to be of prime importance for a comparison. More revealing than the figures above were, of course, data on the volatility of voters among political or ideological blocks. Also votes cast, not just seats, need to be analyzed. This task must be left, however, to further papers that also will deal with government instability and with economic and political measures taken by governments. In any case, strong increases in electoral volatility make it more difficult, if not impossible, for governments to take measures effectively that might be needed in those very same situations.

Only for Germany and the Netherlands is there a consistent variation between higher turnout (in terms of valid votes) and greater volatility. For Britain in 1931 the number of valid votes is slightly lower than in the prior election. In France, turnout in 1932 and 1936 is only slightly higher, whereas Austria has a negative relationship and for Belgium a consistent, but almost negligible, positive relationship emerges. Overall, the evaluation does not change if turnout is standardized in terms of the electorate. Taking the possibility of the aggregate fallacy into consideration, it could at least be maintained that increased turnout in general is a weak factor when explaining the higher volatility during times of economic crisis.

Conclusion

All six European nations were gravely affected by the world economic crisis of the 1930s, but with some remarkable differences. For Germany in particular, many of the economic indicators resemble a V-pattern (or that of an inverted V-curve). Economic decline and recovery (under the Nazi reign) came about more rapidly than in the other European countries, where the relatively greater continuity in crisis indicators in general left more room for political maneuvering. Electoral volatility was also greatest in Germany, since the high figure for Britain is strongly affected by the majority system. While for all six countries increases in electoral volatility could be observed the closer an election was held near the trough of the economy, only in Germany did a majority of voters turn to the political extremes. In Britain, the Netherlands, Belgium, and France, voters were strongly committed to parties within the democratic spectrum, whereas in Austria the collapse of the polity was brought about more by specific forms of elite coalitions (and other factors) than by strong electoral pressure. Elite coalitions were, of course, important in all the six countries in forming reactions to their respective economic and political challenges. (They too will be the subject of subsequent papers.)

In describing the economic situation of the various polities and the degree of volatility, I do not necessarily wish to imply that, for example, unemployed people were either the ones voting for radical parties or primarily responsible for volatility. They may have contributed to it, but at best only aggregate data are available for such inferences. On the level of the polity, however, massive unemployment and high electoral volatility make for the cumulation of problems and thus deserve to be analyzed jointly. That widespread unemployment need not cause political turnover is demonstrated in the Netherlands where unemployment was high, but political radicalism comparatively limited.

An extension of the sample to the United States and Sweden would be of special interest, since the United States was the country most seriously afflicted by the economic crisis, even worse than Germany. But it managed to survive without the collapse of the polity. Moreover, both in the United States and in Sweden, state intervention, public work programs, and measures of employment as well as deficit spending (politics of "cheap money") played a more important role than in the six European democracies studied here. These two cases thus provide some of the necessary variation for more adequate tests of some of the theoretical notions that guide this inquiry.

Notes

1. In some countries (such as Austria) with respect to unemployment in 1926 and Germany in the years of 1923 and 1926 (Borchardt 1982, pp. 193-94), there are noteworthy forerunners of this economic crisis. Germany in general after World War I was suffering from a serious lack of investment and a shortness of capital was intensified by the collapse of the stock market.

2. In some instances, operational definitions of variables (such as unemployment) differ not only between countries, but also from period to period within country. Only after Flora's data collection will have become available and after drawing on many additional sources can more sound comparisons be made. In the present instance only some of the most severe differences in operational definitions will be noted. For further details see Mitchell (1981).

3. Mitchell (1981, p. 175) reports 4.3 percent as unemployed for 1929 (average of monthly numbers of registered unemployed). Up till 1929 he gives figures only for unemployed in trade unions. Drawing on Petzina et al. (8.5 percent—1978, p. 119) and Kocka (9.3 percent—1972, p. 343) Mitchell's figure is changed here to 9.3 percent. For subsequent years, there are some minor differences between Mitchell and Petzina et al. Kocka seems to use the same sources as Mitchell so that Mitchell's figure of 4.3 instead of 9.3 percent appears to be a printing error.

4. Petzina (1977, pp. 16-17) for 1930-32 presents considerably higher figures for unemployment in Germany, but his figures refer up till 1932 to union members only.

5. Decimal figures have always been rounded for presentation in the figures.

6. Estimation, since for 1931-33 no data are given by Mitchell.

7. For Belgium, data on GNP are available for one year only (1930) between 1928 and 1933. For comparison, industrial production went down by 34 percent between 1929 and 1933.

8. Actually these changes in the electorate had been prepared in earlier elections when conservative forces had withdrawn from the middle parties. Some of this support went to radical-regional splinter parties. This is one of the corrections Winkler (1972) raises against Lipset's thesis that the Nazis gained from the electoral losses of the middle parties. This move to the right obviously reflected a more long-term trend.

Bibliography

Aldcroft, Derek H. 1980. *The European Economy, 1914-1980.* Revised ed. London: Croom Helm.

Bombach, G., H.-J. Ramser, M. Timmermann, and W. Wittmann, eds. 1976. *Der Keynesianismus II. Die beschäftigungspolitische Diskussion vor Keynes in Deutschland.* Berlin: Springer.

Borchardt, Knut. 1983. "Zum Scheitern eines Produktiven Diskurses über das Scheitern der Weimarer Republik: Replik auf Claus-Dieter Krohns Diskussionsbemerkungen." *Geschichte und Gesellschaft* 9, pp. 124-37.

————————. 1982. *Wachstum, Krisen, Handlungsspielräume der Wirtschaftspolitik: Studien zur Wirtschaftsgeshicte des 19. und 20. Jahrhunderts.* Gottingen: Vandenhoeck and Ruprecht.

Botz, Gerhard. 1982. "Formen politischer Gewaltanwendung und Gewaltstrategien in der österreichischen Ersten Republik." In *Sozialprotest, Gewalt, Terror. Gewaltanwendung durch politische und gesellschaftliche Randgruppen im 19. und 20. Jahrhundert,* ed. Wolfgang J. Mommsen and Gerhard Hirschfeld, pp. 349-80. Stuttgart: Klett-Cotta.

Bracher, Karl Dietrich. 1957. *Die Auflösung der Weimarer Republik. Eine Studie zum Problem des Machtverfalls in der Demokratie.* 2d ed. Stuttgart: Ring-Verlag. 6th ed. Königstein: Athenäum. 1978.

Broszat, Martin et al., eds. 1983. *Deutschlands Weg in die Diktatur.* Internationale Konferenz zur nationalsozialistischen Machtübernahme im Reichstagsgebäude zu Berlin. Berlin: Siedler.

Conze, Werner and Hans Raupach, eds. 1967. *Die Staats- und Wirtschaftskrise des Deutschen Reichs 1929/33.* Stuttgart: Ernst Klett.

Davies, James C. 1962. "Toward a Theory of Revolution." *American Sociological Review,* 27 (February), pp. 5-19.

Duverger, Maurice. 1964. *Political Parties: Their Organization and Activity in the Modern State.* London: Methuen.

Flora, Peter et al. 1983/84. *State, Economy and Society in Western Europe 1815-1975. A Data Handbook.* 2 vols. Frankfurt/London/Chicago: Campus/Macmillan/St. James.

Galenson, Walter and Arnold Zellner. 1957. "International Comparison of Unemployment Rates." In *The Measurement and Behavior of Unemployment,* ed. National Bureau of Economic Research, pp. 439-581. Princeton: Princeton University Press.

Holtfrerich, Carl-Ludwig. 1984. "Zu hohe Löhne in der Weimarer Republik? Bermkungen sur Borchardt-These." *Gesichte und Gesellschaft* 10, pp. 122-41.

——————————. 1982. "Alternativen zu Brünings Wirtschaftspolitik in der Welwirtschaftskrise." *Historische Zeitschrift* 235, pp. 605-31.

Kindleberger, Charles P. 1973. *Die Weltwirtschaftskrise 1929-1939.* München: Deutscher Taschenbuch Verlag.

Kocka, Jürgen. 1972. "Amerikanische Angestellte in Wirtschaftskrise und New Deal 1930-1940." *Vierteljahreshefte für Zeitgeshichte* 20 (October), pp. 333-75.

Krohn, Claus-Dieter. 1982. "Zu Knut Borchardts Analyse der deutschen Wirtschaft in den zwanziger Jahren." *Geschichte und Gesellschaft* 8, pp. 415-26.

Kwiet, Konrad. 1970. "Zur Geschichte der Mussert-Bewegung." *Vierteljahreshefte für Zeitgeschichte* 18 (April), pp. 164-95.

Landes, David S. 1983. *Der entfesselte Prometheus. Technologischer Wandel und industrielle Entwicklung in Westeuropa von 1750 bis zur Gegenwart.* München: Deutscher Taschenbuch Verlag.

Linz, Juan J. 1978. *The Breakdown of Democratic Regimes: Crisis, Breakdown, and Reequilibration.* Baltimore: Johns Hopkins University Press.

Mackie, Thomas T. and Richard Rose. 1982. *The International Almanac of Electoral History.* 2d ed. London: Macmillan.

Mitchell, R.R. 1981. *European Historical Statistics 1750-1975.* 2d rev. ed. London: Macmillan.

Pedersen, Mogens N. 1983. "Changing Patterns of Electoral Volatility in European Party Systems, 1948-1977: Explorations in Explanation." In *Western European Party Systems: Continuity and Change,* ed. Hans Daalder and Peter Mair, pp. 31-66. London: Sage.

Petzina, Dietmar. 1977. *Die Deutsche Wirtschaft in der Zwischenkriegszeit.* Wiesbaden: Franz Steiner.

——————————————, Werner Abelshauser, and Anselm Faust. 1978. *Sozialgeschichtliches Arbeitsbuch Band III: Materialien zur Statistik des Deutschen Reiches, 1914-1945*. München: C.H. Beck.

Pollard, Sidney. 1983. *The Development of the British Economy: 1914-1980*. 3d ed. London: Edward Arnold.

Schulze, Hagen. 1982. *Weimar Deutschland 1917-1933*. Berlin: Siedler.

Svennilson, Ingvar. 1954. *Growth and Stagnation of the European Economy*. Geneva: Economic Commission for Europe.

Weir, Margaret and Theda Skocpol. 1983. "State Structures and Social Keynesianism. Responses to the Great Depression in Sweden and the United States." *International Journal of Comparative Sociology* 24, pp. 4-29.

Winkler, Heinrich August. 1972. "Extremismus der Mitte? Sozialgeschichtliche Aspekte der nationalsozialistischen Machtergreifung." *Vierteljahreshefte für Zeitgeschichte* 20, pp. 175-91.

Zimmerman, Ekkart. 1984. "Pitfalls and Promises: The Study of Crises in Liberal Democracies." *International Political Science Review* 5, p. 30.

——————————————. 1983. *Political Violence, Crises, and Revolutions: Theories and Research*. Boston/Cambridge: G.K. Hall/Schenkman.

——————————————. 1981. *Krisen, Staatsstreiche und Revolutionen: Theorien, Daten und Neuere Forschungsansätze*. Opladen: Westdeutscher Verlag.

6

The Impact of the First Oil Shock on Domestic and International Conflict

BARRY B. HUGHES

The Issues

The comparative and international literatures have attempted to document relationships between economic downturns or increased hardship and both domestic (individual, group, or governmental) and international conflict. Common sense tells us that deprivation increases tension and it is reasonable to posit that the tensions often lead to conflict with one's neighbors or to a joint effort with them against others. Surprisingly, however, the theory and evidence have been mixed.

In the comparative literature, the Davies J-curve theory (1962) provides support for such argument. Revolution is most likely, the theory posits, after periods of prolonged improvement have led to rising expectations, and these expectations are then dashed by declining circumstances. Davies has illustrated the "revolutionary gap" between expectations and reality with multiple cases (1962, 1969). At a lower level of conflict, some relationship has also been shown with economic difficulty. Haas (1968, 1974) addressed the economic downturn/domestic conflict issue and found some relationship between higher unemployment rate or lower economic growth rate and propensity for conflict. But the correlations were low. In a cross-sectional analysis of 26 countries, Parvin (1973) also found the rate of economic growth to be inversely related to political unrest (deaths from group violence). In a 108-nation study, Hibbs (1973) again

---

I thank Thomas Cusack and William Thompson for suggestions. The analysis in the domestic conflict section of this chapter was aided by the research assistance of Faith Klareich.

found a weak relationship between higher economic growth rate and lower violence levels. In a time series analysis of Britain, 1948-67, Gupta and Venieris (1981) identified a positive correlation between slower rates of economic growth or increased unemployment and social violence, especially industrial disputes. An extensive review of relevant comparative literature was completed by Zimmermann (1983).

It has also been posited that especially rapid economic growth upsets the social order and creates conflict (Olson 1963). The Feiera-bends and Nesvold (1969) documented a high association between modernization rate and instability. Such hypotheses are relevant here because the oil-exporting countries, in marked contrast to the rest of the world, experienced more rapid growth after the first oil shock than before it.

Our focus here is on the relationship between rate of growth and conflict, and it is desirable not to confuse that analysis with the relationship between level of GNP (or other economic development indicator) and conflict. It has been suggested that this latter relation-ship may be curvilinear, with violence greatest at intermediate levels of GNP per capita (Russett 1964; Hibbs 1973). Other literature has suggested either positive or negative linear relationships (see the literature review and results of Hardy 1979). There most likely exists an interaction between the effects of GNP per capita and rate of growth on conflict. Cooper (1974) concluded that short-term depri-vations become less a basis of domestic turmoil at high levels of development. Venieris and Gupta (1983) discovered that the articula-tion of frustration (with low growth) in mass violence is highest for mid-income countries.

Given a centuries-long interest in the relationship between eco-nomics and war, the international literature is not as rich as one might expect in studies linking economic downturn and conflict. Indirectly relevant, a number of studies have shown that international conflict is related to domestic conflict, perhaps implying a link to economic downturn (for example, Feierabend and Feierabend 1972). However, more often studies have found no significant domestic/international linkage (Stohl 1980). Historical literature also suggests an economic/ conflict linkage. Braudel (1973) noted that Christian-Moslem state wars in medieval Europe were most frequent in periods of depression (although intra-Christian wars increased in periods of prosperity).

Recently we have seen renewed interest in various global long economic and political cycles, including the Kondratieff cycle. Kondratieff himself felt that major wars were related to the cycle, and seemed most likely in periods of upswing. Russett (1983) has argued that Lenin's analysis of imperialism leads logically to the same concern with the period of upswing. Some empirical literature further reinforces that concern (Thompson and Zuk 1982). However, an analysis of the relationship between war and the regular, short-term business cycle for the United Kingdom, United States, France, and Germany over 1792-73 uncovered no relationship with phases (Thompson 1982).

The empirical analysis in the domestic and international conflict literature exhibits considerable methodological variation. Some analyses are case studies, many use comparative analysis or countries with widely varying economic growth, and others rely on illustrations.

Relatively seldom in modern history have we experienced periods when almost the entire world simultaneously suffered a loss of economic momentum, thus making a global longitudinal design possible. The Great Depression of the 1930s was one period. Although it occurred before social scientists routinely coded data on lower-level domestic and international conflict, and before the political independence of much of the world, there can be little doubt about the role the Great Depression played in domestic political conflict and extremism, and thereby in the events leading to World War II. Zimmermann (1984) compiled economic and political indicators for six major European countries over the depression period. Although he found that workdays lost in industrial disputes declined as unemployment rose (in contrast to the more contemporary study of Gupta and Venieris 1981), maximum volatility in electorate behavior occurred in five of the cases during the election nearest the trough of the economic crisis. However, no clear relationship with government duration was found and the overall results are not as clear-cut as one might expect.

The 1970s appear to offer another period facilitating a global longitudinal approach. The 1970s and early 1980s are a period of importance in terms of all of the above theories and empirical analyses. Some have characterized the period as being the trough of another long economic wave. Of particular interest may be the periods immediately following the two oil shocks (which occurred in 1973-74 and 1978-80), since those periods constitute major global recessions/depressions. The data now exist to allow investigation of levels of domestic and international conflict following the first shock, relative to earlier periods. Anecdotal evidence, such as the recent food store riots in Brazil or the linkage of the Falklands war to Argentine economic difficulties, also suggests the impact of the oil shock experiences (as well as the need to go beyond illustrations).

A more comprehensive empirical analysis of the oil shock impact on domestic and international conflict will serve several purposes. First, and not of least importance, the issue of the oil shock's impact is interesting in and of itself. There is every reason to believe that there will be further oil shocks over the next two decades and it will be useful to know what impact they might have. This study can also lay a foundation for further analysis as the data for the period following the second shock become available.

Second, the study will provide a further test of the propositions that economic downturns increase domestic or international conflict levels. It can do so in a manner that extends previous analyses, since many of those have been undertaken in periods during which selected countries experienced slower or faster growth. Here we deal with a period in which much of the global system underwent an economic downturn.

Third, this analysis will assist in the emerging investigation of the relationship between scarcity and conflict. Since the early 1970s there has been much neo-Malthusian argument that we are globally moving into a period of long-term (not simply cyclical) increasing scarcity of energy and food, as well as of environmental degradation. These arguments at least imply, and often explicitly conclude, that future global economic recessions/depressions are increasingly likely and may be of greater severity and length (Meadows 1972; CEQ 1981). Of course, many dispute this contention (Kahn et al. 1976; Simon 1981). For a review and analysis of the arguments, see Hughes (1984).

Should the more pessimistic positions prove correct, it will be especially useful to have begun an investigation of the global implications of scarcity-induced downturns. It has been shown that resource scarcity more generally can create pressures that lead to foreign conflict (Choucri and North 1975). Although the two oil shocks are not universally accepted as indicators of increasing global energy scarcity (many explain them as market imperfections or temporary results of energy system transformation), widespread perception of long-term energy problems makes them appropriate cases of scarcity-related economic downturns. Gurr (1983) focused on this longer-term scarcity issue in a preliminary consideration of the global impacts of the oil shocks.

The Hypotheses

Specifically, this chapter will test the following hypotheses:

1. The period following the first oil shock was one of increased domestic conflict in a wide variety of countries, relative to the period preceding the shock.

Obviously, domestic conflict could have increased for many reasons other than the oil shock and related economic hardship. Although none leap to mind that would account for worldwide increases in conflict, other than a general upward trend in domestic conflict *reporting,* the second hypothesis helps direct the investigation to the real cause of any increased conflict which might be discovered:

2. Those countries most negatively affected by the shock were those in which conflict increased the most.

Turning to the international side:

3. The period immediately following the first oil shock was one of increased international conflict, relative to the period preceding the shock.

The fourth hypothesis is formulated, like the second, to clarify the results of the general, global hypothesis:

4. International conflict increased most among those countries most negatively affected by the shock.

This chapter will undertake a lengthy justification of these hypotheses. They have support (as well as some opposition) in a considerable literature, some of which was indicated above. Obviously they constitute overgeneralizations. Various societies and polities react very differently to stress, and in some cases may even be unified by it (for instance, domestic unity resulting from perceived external threat). Among other reasons to anticipate greater conflict is that we expect economic hardship, whether or not scarcity induced, often to be correlated with greater inequalities or with a struggle over distribution (as supported by Sigelman and Simpson 1977, in a cross-sectional analysis). Domestic conflict may emerge as repression by those who have, revolt by those who have not, or simply manifestations of greater political instability such as rapid government turnover. Similarly, international conflict hardly constitutes an inevitable reaction to domestic economic distress, but seems particularly likely when the source of the distress appears clearly to have an international element, whether it be reparations paid by the Germans during the 1920s or higher oil bills paid by importing countries everywhere in the 1970s.

Of some concern is the possibility that this analysis may be a bit premature. Russett (1983) argues that conflict is likely to lag behind the economic downturn by several years. He points out that those affected by an economic downturn may initially be too involved with reaction or even survival for a turn toward domestic conflict. Similarly, Doran (1983) and others suggest that the beginning of the upswing may be a more serious threat to international peace than the downturn. Nevertheless, the period is of interest.

The Impact of the Shock

It seems appropriate to begin by verifying that the period following the first oil shock was indeed one of economic decline. Figure 6.1 shows that it was, but to a degree that varies for different country groupings. Decline stands out most clearly in the 1974-75 recession for industrial countries. In comparison with the 4.7 percent annual GDP growth rate experienced by those countries from 1963-72, the rates in 1974 and 1975 were .5 percent and − .6 percent, respectively. Figure 6.2 suggests that the decline was fairly uniform for industrial countries; the United States, Germany, and Japan all had near zero growth in 1974-75.

Nonoil LDCs also lost growth, but not nearly as much. Compared to 6 percent annual growth in the 1960s, nonoil LDC growth

Figure 6.1 Global Economic Growth Rates (Real)

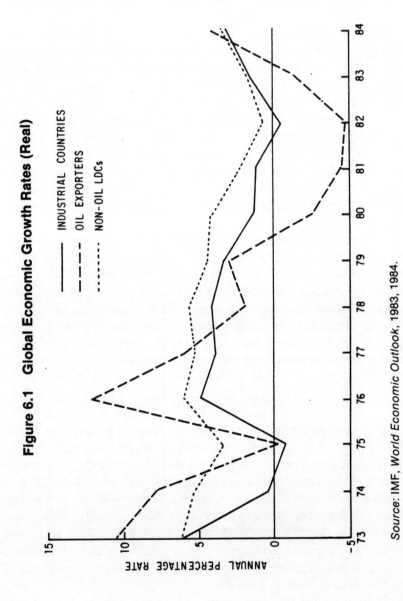

INDUSTRIAL COUNTRIES
OIL EXPORTERS
NON-OIL LDCs

ANNUAL PERCENTAGE RATE

Source: IMF, World Economic Outlook, 1983, 1984.

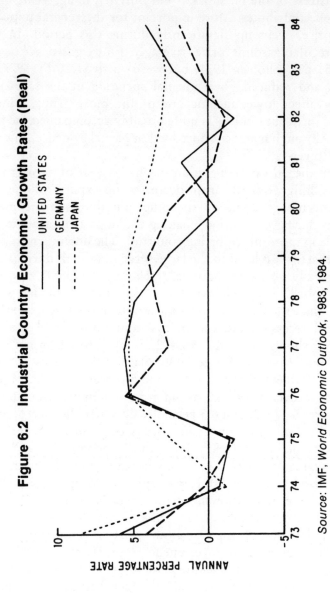

Figure 6.2   Industrial Country Economic Growth Rates (Real)

UNITED STATES
GERMANY
JAPAN

ANNUAL PERCENTAGE RATE

Source: IMF, World Economic Outlook, 1983, 1984.

was 5.4 percent in 1974 and 3.3 percent in 1975. Borrowing was a significant factor in maintaining LDC growth. However, the economic distress of the oil shock is not only felt in aggregate growth. Debt itself contributes. More important for the general population, energy prices went up significantly during this period. In nonoil LDCs, regular gasoline prices averaged (unweighted across countries) $.51 per gallon in 1971, but were up to $1.20 by 1977. Both inflation and reduced governmental spending in the face of debt generally affect lower-income groups the most. Thus, somewhat increased inequality in LDCs quite possibly accompanied the first oil shock. (Although many cite anecdotal or partial evidence, this is very difficult to verify.)

Even the oil-exporting countries had a year of zero growth in 1975, resulting primarily from decreased oil export volume. However, government domestic spending and domestic income were going up during this period, making the impact on a broad public negligible in most oil-exporting countries. The downturn is largely a statistical artifact related to the large surge in growth during 1973.

Centrally planned economies, including the USSR, also felt the first oil shock. They felt it not so much through higher prices or scarcity, since the USSR supplies most of their oil needs, but through the global recession induced in first and third world economies. Figure 6.3 shows this. The 1963-72 average growth in net material product was 7 percent for centrally planned economies as a whole. The rate fell to 6.1 percent in 1974 and 5 percent in 1975. Moreover, it did not recover in 1976-77 as did growth in industrial countries.

Figures 6.1, 6.2, and 6.3 generally do verify the macroeconomic impact of the oil shock on a wide variety of countries. Several points might be made in conclusion. First, the "economic decline" consists not in aggregate terms of actual decrease in GDP (although in industrialized countries GDP per capita did drop in 1974-75), but rather in slower than normal growth for most countries. Second, the macropicture ignores inequality effects, which most likely compounded the societal impacts. Both inflation (especially in energy prices) and cutbacks in government programs are often argued to have hit hardest the low-income groups. Third, the global recession/depression following the second oil shock has obviously been the more severe of the two. When data are available to assess conflict patterns during it, they should be analyzed carefully.

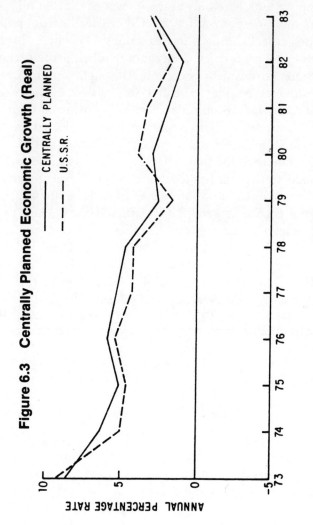

Figure 6.3 Centrally Planned Economic Growth (Real)

CENTRALLY PLANNED
U.S.S.R.

ANNUAL PERCENTAGE RATE

Sources: U.N., *Yearbook of National Account Statistics,* 1980; IMF, *World Economic Outlook,* 1983.

137

Domestic Conflict

The recently released social and political indicators of Taylor and Jodice (1983) incorporate several measures of domestic conflict that can be used here. Their time series extend only through 1977, the primary reason we look here only at the impact of the first oil shock. The indicators of domestic conflict selected are deaths from political violence, armed attacks, riots, and sanctions. The first three are measures of political protest, generally more violent protest, and the last indicator taps government coercion. Although we might expect coercion and domestic conflict to be inversely related, evidence seems to suggest a direct relationship unless lags are considered (Gurr and Duvall 1973; Hibbs 1973). These measures were selected from the larger set provided in the data base primarily because of the greater frequency of occurrence for these than for others (such as irregular executive transfers), thus facilitating some interval-level analysis.

To simplify analysis, to allow generalizations somewhat compatible with the economic groupings discussed above, and to take into account research findings that conflict relationships vary by economic development level, countries were divided into industrialized, oil exporting, net-oil exporting LDC, newly industrialized countries (NICs), and low-income LDCs (according to IMF 1983, 168-69). Within each country group and on each violence indicator, we compare violence in the 1974-77 period (postshock) with that in the comparably long 1969-72 period (preshock). Table 6.1 summarizes the results.

Industrial Countries

For industrial countries, postshock violence increases relative to preshock levels in every category except riots. Deaths from political violence increase in seven countries and decrease in five ($N = 21$); sanctions increase in thirteen and decrease in seven; riots increase in eight and decrease in seven; while armed attacks increase in nine and decrease in five. Thus it is fair to conclude that the results reflect more than change in one or two countries. In fact, in country terms, increases in conflict outnumber decreases on all four measures. It was the major decrease in U.S. riots after the Vietnam period that primarily explains the groupwide decrease in riot numbers.

Table 6.1   Measures of Domestic Conflict

	1948-52	1963-67	1969-72	1974-77	Percent Change Pre- and Post-Shock
		Deaths from Political Violence			
Industrial	179	265	806 (5)	1,020 (7)	26.5
Oil Exporting	5,692	589,274	1,000,354 (3)	713 (6)	-100.0
Net Oil Exporters	8,483	2,869	612 (4)	677 (6)	10.6
NICs	11,970	314	235	5,428	2,309.8
Low Income	32,635	48,867	459,838 (14)	63,797 (9)	-86.1
		Sanctions			
Industrial	1,316	962	900 (7)	1,490 (13)	65.5
Oil Exporting	359	838	129 (6)	79 (2)	-38.8
Net Oil Exporters	474	457	134 (3)	159 (7)	18.7
NICs	1,092	972	391 (3)	706 (6)	80.6
Low Income	530	1,789	605 (16)	484 (14)	-20.0
		Riots			
Industrial	437	637	435 (7)	396 (8)	-9.0
Oil Exporting	160	232	17 (2)	20 (3)	17.6
Net Oil Exporters	206	186	35 (4)	56 (5)	60.0

139

	1948-52	1963-67	1969-72	1974-77	Percent Change Pre- and Post- Shock
NICs	127	207	97 (3)	316 (6)	325.8
Low Income	219	676	186 (12)	138 (5)	-25.8
Armed Attacks					
Industrial	378	431	1,111 (5)	2,117 (9)	90.5
Oil Exporting	284	1,166	164 (3)	63 (4)	-61.6
Net Oil Exporters	3,421	296	83 (6)	147 (5)	77.1
NICs	790	399	237 (5)	352 (4)	48.5
Low Income	2,593	2,915	1,205 (12)	670 (11)	-44.4

Note: In parentheses are numbers of countries with a higher conflict score in the immediate pre- or post-oil shock period.
Source: Taylor and Jodice (1983).

Consistent existence of significant outliers (such as the United States on riots) was the reason for keeping the analysis simple and often nominal in measurement levels. It was tempting to throw out such "perturbing cases" or outliers. That was not done for two reasons. First, there were far too many such cases. Second, and more important, those cases must be included theoretically, because they are equally subject to the hypotheses and may be the very cases that provide strongest support or refutation of them.

A possible confounding factor would be a longer-term trend toward increasing violence, or increasingly efficient inclusion of it in the data base. No attempt has been made to detrend the data. However, two other periods are shown in Table 6.1 for comparison. (Those periods are five years in length because of aggregation by the authors of the data volume.) For industrial countries, there does appear to be a consistent pattern of increase in deaths from political violence and armed attacks, although not in riots or sanctions. This somewhat weakens the finding.

Oil Exporters

In oil-exporting countries (essentially OPEC), violence on all measures except riots decreased in the postshock period. Moreover, the postshock period proves considerably less violent than either 1948-52 or 1963-67. This not only builds some confidence in the absence of highly significant trends toward greater global violence in the data, but provides some support for the second hypothesis, that the change in violence rates would be related to the degree of negative economic impact.

However, both conclusions based on the oil exporters appear weaker when we examine the numbers of countries with greater violence in the two periods. On three of four measures, greater numbers of oil exporters experienced increased conflict levels in the postshock period than experienced decreased conflict. Only on sanctions did conflict drop in more countries than it increased. One important reason for the differences in the two measures lies in the Nigerian civil war, which inflated violence for oil exporters in the preshock period. Because sudden and major positive economic change can be as socially disruptive as decline, these results for oil exporters (in terms of country numbers) are not too disturbing. However, they do contradict the second hypothesis.

Net Oil Exporters

Net oil exporters (such as Egypt, Mexico, Peru, Syria, and Tunisia) are a difficult set of LDCs for which to form specific expectations with respect to hypotheses 1 and 2. Although the shock might benefit overall payments balances and growth rates in some cases, the secondary effects of the global recession were most often disruptive for these countries, and the microeconomic impacts of higher domestic energy prices were generally negative. In any case, violence on all four measures was up somewhat (less than for industrial countries except in the case of riots), and for three measures (not armed attacks), more countries experienced greater conflict after 1973 than experienced less conflict.

It is interesting that for these net oil exporters, conflict in both the pre- and postshock periods was sharply lower on all four measures than that in the two earlier periods. Again this supports a conclusion that the data as a whole incorporate no strong trend toward increasing conflict or reporting of it.

Newly Industrialized Countries

NICs are among those who should have been most adversely affected by the oil shock. They are all heavily dependent on trade for growth and almost all are significant oil importers. Thus it is not surprising that conflict levels increased after the shock on all four measures, and significantly. However, on only two measures did more countries experience greater violence after the shock than before, on one measure the numbers were equal, and on one measure (armed attacks) more countries experienced greater conflict before 1973 than after it. The greater conflict on all four measures after the shock proves traceable in large part to Argentina, Portugal, and South Africa, which, on different measures, suffered much greater conflict after 1973. Again the data for the NICs suggest no pattern of long-term increasing conflict; if anything, the longer-term trend appears to be toward decreasing conflict.

Low-Income Countries

The most surprising results come from low-income countries. On all four measures conflict decreased after 1973, and on all four fewer countries had increased conflict than experienced decreased conflict. These countries are almost all oil importers and, unlike the NICs, were often unable to borrow to ward off economic consequences of the shock. Aid, including the IMF's special oil window, did help somewhat, but the common (and often correct) perception is that the shock hit these countries the hardest of any group. This finding appears to contradict Cooper's (1974) conclusion that short-term deprivations result in less turmoil when they occur in more economically advanced countries.

The result appears nearly inexplicable. Perhaps there is a longer-term trend in these countries toward less violence, since the preshock period showed less conflict than in the 1960s period on three of four measures. But that conclusion, although meriting further investigation, seems unlikely. Or perhaps citizens in these countries have been so concerned with coping that violence has not been a viable option. That possibility is intriguing, but even more speculative.

Summary Results on Domestic Violence

Overall, the results summarized in Table 6.1 provide mixed support for hypothesis 1, positing increased domestic conflict after the first oil shock. Industrial countries support it consistently, net oil exporters and NICS generally do, and low-income countries consistently contradict it. Oil-exporting countries are not really appropriate test cases for hypothesis 1.

Hypothesis 2, anticipating greater conflict increases in most severely impacted countries, also receives mixed support. On the basis of the four sums of conflict for country groupings, the decreased conflict levels of oil exporters are supportive. So, too, are the relatively dramatic conflict increases within the energy-dependent NICs and the generally lower rates of conflict increases in net oil exporters than within NICs or industrial countries. However, the *numbers of countries* experiencing increases or decreases in conflict often do not. Most important, the low-income countries, generally heavily dependent on imported oil, contradict this hypothesis sharply.

As a further test of hypothesis 2, industrial countries were divided into two groups on the basis of levels of commercial energy import dependence. The median value of net imports over total consumption was used to divide them. Table 6.2 shows simple contingency tables relating above or below median import dependence to increases or decreases in conflict relative to the preshock period (numbers of countries). On each measure the relationship, summarized by Yule's Q, is in the predicted direction: greater dependence is associated with an increase in conflict.

This same intragroup approach makes no sense for the oil-

Table 6.2   Domestic Conflict and Energy Import Dependence (Country Numbers, Postshock Relative to Preshock)

	Increase	Decrease	
Deaths from Political Violence			
Above Median Imports	3	2	Q=.20
Below Median Imports	3	3	
Sanctions			
Above Median Imports	5	3	Q=.14
Below Median Imports	5	4	
Riots			
Above Median Imports	3	2	Q=.30
Below Median Imports	4	5	
Armed Attacks			
Above Median Imports	5	1	Q=.52
Below Median Imports	3	4	

Source: Taylor and Jodice (1983).

exporting and net oil exporter groups, for obvious reasons, or for the low-income LDCs, well over half of which are 90 percent or more dependent on imports for their commercial energy. In essence, these groups divide LDCs already in much the same way that Table 6.2 categorizes industrial countries. For NICs, however, a similar division into more or less adversely affected countries does have some merit. When that is done, on three of four measures dependence on imported energy correlates at low levels (Q from .33 to .50) with increased post-1973 violence; on armed attacks the sign is reversed (−.33).

Overall, hypothesis 2 receives greater support than hypothesis 1. But the support is hardly overwhelming.

International Conflict

The data used in this analysis come from the Conflict and Peace Data Bank (COPDAB) project of Azar (1980). These event data have been used in the GLOBUS project (Bremer 1983) and were aggregated in Berlin to annual summaries of conflict sent and received for 50 countries. The project provided those data series from 1948-78.

For comparability with the domestic conflict analysis, we compare the 1974-77 postshock period with the 1969-72 preshock interval. Table 6.3 also shows conflict levels in 1973 multiplied by four to make them comparable to the four-year periods on either side of 1973. In addition, 1948-51 and 1958-61 (also four-year periods) are represented so that longer-term trends become apparent. Table 6.3 uses slightly different country groupings than did Tables 6.1 and 6.2. Specifically, major powers (defined here as China, West Germany, France, Great Britain, the United States, and the USSR) are shown separately, because in preliminary data analysis they exhibited much greater average levels of conflict sent and thus tended to "swamp"

Table 6.3   International Conflict

	1948-51	1958-61	1969-72	1973-74	1974-77
			Conflict Sent		
Major Powers	39,205	50,165	30,960	34,728	18,524
Industrial (Small)	3,512	3,749	6,090	9,376	3,531
Communist (Small)	14,739	13,428	8,311	5,916	3,811
OPEC	4,309	9,139	8,928	25,556	15,264
Nonoil LDCs	11,815	14,403	32,424	22,700	14,582
Total	73,580	90,884	86,713	98,276	55,712
			Conflict Received		
OPEC	3,165	4,311	6,112	13,256	8,015
			Cooperation Sent		
Major Powers	53,678	77,715	81,574	129,928	72,883

Sources: Azar 1980 and Bremer 1983.

any variation over time in small Western industrial or communist countries.

The results in Table 6.3 are so uniform, however, that they are clearly independent of country groupings. For the four non-OPEC groupings, conflict sent in the 1969-72 period is in each case nearly double that sent in the 1974-77 period. Only for smaller industrial countries was conflict sent in 1973 significantly greater than the 1969-72 average level.

This result might be attributed to "detente." However, major power conflict levels were noticeably lower in 1969-72 than in 1958-61, and it appears from analysis of the full time series that the major impact of detente was felt immediately after 1967, when conflict sent by all major powers dropped quite sharply.

Conflict sent by OPEC did increase sharply in 1973 and re-mained high thereafter—nearly double the pre-1973 level. Moreover, conflict received by OPEC doubled in 1973 and stayed high in 1974-77, despite the drop in conflict sent by other nations.

Thus it appears that non-OPEC nation-states showed their displeasure toward OPEC during and after the oil shock; but rather than increasing their conflict levels with each other, decreased them sharply. Perhaps the domestic problems associated with the oil shock simply redirected attention normally given to foreign affairs. This is given credence also by Table 6.3. Cooperation sent by the major powers was somewhat higher in 1969-72 than in 1958-61, while conflict dropped. This is consistent with detente. However, in 1974-77, both cooperation and conflict were lower than either the 1958-61 or 1969-72 period. That suggests a withdrawal of attention to foreign affairs after the oil shock. At the level of public opinion, the tendency to decrease attention to foreign affairs in times of economic difficulty has often been noted (Hughes 1978). Here we may be seeing an extension of that to the governmental level itself.

In connection with hypotheses suggesting the economic upturn to be the most conflictual period, it should be noted that the grouping of years 1974-77 in Table 6.3 does *not* conceal any signifi-cant intraperiod variation. Examination of the annual data reveals no tendency toward increased conflict at the end of the period relative to the beginning. In 1978 major power conflict did increase somewhat, but not above preshock levels.

The aggregation of conflict here without respect to type (that is, verbal versus physical) or issue area leaves much to be desired. A more detailed analysis should be undertaken. However, the post-1973 drop in conflict is so substantial that it would be reasonable to expect decline in most categories of conflict.

We turn now to hypothesis 4, which posits that those countries most dependent on energy imports would be most likely to exhibit increased external conflict. Table 6.4 shows the 1973 dependence on energy imports as a percentage of total commercial energy consumption for all of the Western industrialized countries for which we have the COPDAB data. It also indicates the percentage change in conflict sent in 1974-77 relative to 1969-72. Pearson's r relating the two variables is − .20.

Thus the result is the reverse of the hypothesis: greater dependence in general led to reduced conflict levels. This is, however, consistent again with the conclusion drawn from Table 6.3, that the oil shock generally resulted in decreased foreign affairs activity rather than increased conflict. Moreover, it is consistent with the finding in

Table 6.4   International Conflict and Energy Import Dependence, Industrial Countries

	Dependence	*Percent Change in Conflict*
Belgium	1.025	-63.0
Canada	-.271	-3.9
Denmark	1.104	2.1
West Germany	.585	-51.7
France	.925	-14.5
Italy	.999	-67.9
Japan	1.075	-22.3
Netherlands	.291	-73.4
Norway	.541	90.7
Sweden	.899	-79.8
Switzerland	.876	-40.2
United Kingdom	.537	-31.0
United States	.178	-17.0
	Pearson's r = -.201	

Notes: Dependence is commercial energy imports minus exports over consumption. Values greater than 1 imply stock building, which was considerable in 1973. Percent change in conflict is 1974-77 relative to 1969-72.
Sources: Azar 1980; U.N., *World Energy Supplies, 1973-1978.*

Table 6.3 that only OPEC countries increased their conflict level after the shock. What we appear to be seeing is a consistent pattern of conflict directed toward and reciprocated by countries with greater oil resources (including Norway, the only country in Table 6.4 to significantly increase conflict sent), coupled with a general turning inward by most oil importers.

The same correlation for the nonoil LDCs is .06. This would actually have been negative as well except for the presence in the country group of India and Pakistan, both with relatively low import-dependence levels and dramatic (near 90 percent) decreases in conflict after their 1971 war.

Conclusions

The only expectation of this analysis truly fulfilled was that examination of postshock conflict patterns would be of interest.

Hypotheses 1 and 2 received mixed and partial support. Industrial countries fairly consistently support both propositions: that the oil shock would lead to greater domestic conflict and that the effect would be greatest in those countries most dependent on oil imports. This is perhaps stronger support for the two hypotheses than we have heretofore suggested, because Figures 6.1, 6.2, and 6.3 showed that only the industrial countries underwent clear-cut economic decline. Nevertheless, the failure of low-income countries in particular to exhibit greater postshock conflict levels raises serious doubts.

Hypotheses 3 and 4 are soundly rejected. The directions of conflict change predicted by both are simply wrong. Not only did overall global and all non-OPEC country groupings exhibit less conflict after 1973, but those countries most dependent on outside energy proved the most likely to reduce conflict levels.

Had hypotheses 1 and 2 received stronger support, it would have been possible to conclude that attention to domestic conflict was substituting for attention to international affairs. That still may be the case, and it bears further investigation. There is a large literature investigating the relationship between domestic and international conflict (Stohl 1980). Although many anecdotal references exist to an inverse relationship between domestic and international conflict—based on the proposition that international conflict is used as a diversion from domestic problems—almost all empirical work suggests a positive or null relationship between domestic and international conflict. This reinforces the possible interest of the apparently negative relationship here.

Overall, the results reported in this analysis suggest the importance of investigating the period since 1977, and especially that after the second oil shock. The economic downturn following the second shock was more universal and deeper. Moreover, the increased superpower conflict levels of the last few years (at least verbal, and implicit in U.S. defense expenditures) may have begun, at least for an important subset of countries, to support hypothesis 3. During the Great Depression many countries initially turned inward, but systemic conflict grew sharply as the economic decline persisted. It may be that the cumulative effects of the two oil shocks will be different than the results of the first alone. This issue is clearly of great importance.

Bibliography

Alker, Hayward R. and Bruce M. Russett. 1964. "The Analysis of Trends and Patterns." In *World Handbook of Political and Social Indicators*, ed. Bruce M. Russett et al. New Haven: Yale University Press.

Azar, Edward E. 1980. "The Conflict and Peace Data Bank (COPDAB) Project." *Journal of Conflict Resolution* 24 (March), pp. 43-52.

Braudel, Fernand. 1973. *The Mediterranean and the Mediterranean World in the Age of Philip II*. New York: Harper and Row.

Bremer, Stuart. 1983. *Globus Documentation*. Berlin: International Institute for Comparative Social Research, Science Center, mimeo.

Choucri, Nazli and Robert C. North. 1975. *Nations in Conflict*. San Francisco: Freeman.

Cooper, Mark N. 1974. "A Reinterpretation of the Causes of Turmoil." *Comparative Political Studies* 7 (October), pp. 267-91.

Council on Environmental Quality (CEQ). 1981. *The Global 2000 Report to the President*, 3 volumes, Gerald O. Barney, study director. Washington, D.C.: USGPO.

Davies, J. C. 1962. "Toward a Theory of Revolution." *American Sociological Review* 27 (February), pp. 5-19.

——————————. 1969. "The J-Curve of Rising and Declining Satisfactions as a Cause of Some Great Revolutions and a Contained Rebellion." In *Violence in America: Historical and Comparative Perspectives*, ed. H. S. Graham and T. R. Gurr, pp. 690-730. New York: Praeger.

Doran, Charles F. 1983. "War and Power Dynamics: Economic Underpinnings." *International Studies Quarterly* 27 (December), pp. 419-41.

Eckstein, Harry. 1980. "Theoretical Approaches to Explaining Collective Political Violence." In *Handbook of Political Conflict*, ed. Ted R. Gurr, pp. 135-66. New York: Free Press.

Feierabend, I. K. and R. L. Feierabend. 1972. "Systemic Conditions of Political Aggression: An Application of Frustration-Aggression Theory." In *Anger, Violence and Politics: Theories and Research*, ed. J. K. Feierabend, R. L. Feierabend, and T. R. Gurr. Englewood Cliffs: Prentice-Hall.

——————————— and B. A. Nesvold. 1969. "Social Change and Political Violence: Cross National Patterns." In *Violence in America: Historical and Comparative Perspectives*, ed. H. S. Graham and T. R. Gurr. New York: Praeger.

Flanigan, W. H. and E. Fogelman. 1970. "Patterns of Political Violence in Comparative Historical Perspective." *Comparative Politics* 3 (October), pp. 1-20.

Gupta, Dipak K. and Yiannis P. Venieris. 1981. "Introducing New Dimensions in Macro Models: The Sociopolitical and Institutional Environments." *Economic Development and Cultural Change* 29, pp. 31-58.

Gurr, Ted Robert. 1983. "On the Political Consequences of Scarcity and Economic Decline: Inequality, Conflict and Institutional Change." Paper presented at the 1983 International Studies Association Meeting, Mexico City.

———————————, ed. 1980. *Handbook of Political Conflict*. New York: Free Press.

——————————— and Robert Duvall. 1973. "Civil Conflict in the 1960s: A Reciprocal Theoretical System with Parameter Estimates." *Comparative Political Studies* 6 (July), pp. 135-70.

Haas, Michael. 1974. *International Conflict*. Indianapolis: Bobbs-Merrill.

———————————. 1968. "Social Change and National Aggressiveness, 1900-1960." In *Quantitative International Politics*, ed. J. David Singer, pp. 215-46. New York: Free Press.

Hardy, Melissa A. 1979. "Economic Growth, Distributional Inequality, and Political Conflict in Industrial Societies." *Journal of Political and Military Sociology* 7 (Fall), pp. 209-27.

Hibbs, Douglas A. Jr. 1973. *Mass Political Violence*. New York: Wiley-Interscience.

Hughes, Barry B. 1984. *World Futures: A Critical Analysis of Alternative Views*. Baltimore: Johns Hopkins University Press.

———————————. 1978. *The Domestic Context of American Foreign Policy*. San Francisco: Freeman.

International Monetary Fund (IMF). 1983 and 1984. *World Economic Outlook*. Washington, D.C.: International Monetary Fund.

Kahn, Herman, William Brown, and Leon Martel. 1976. *The Next 200 Years*. New York: Morrow.

Meadows, Donnella H. et al. 1972. *Limits to Growth*. New York: Universe Books.

Olson, Mancur. 1963. "Rapid Growth as a Destabilizing Force." *Journal of Economic History* 23 (December), pp. 529-52.

Parvin, Manoucher. 1973. "Economic Determinants of Political Unrest." *Journal of Conflict Resolution* 17 (June), pp. 271-96.

Russett, Bruce. 1983. "Propensity and Peace." *International Studies Quarterly* 27 (December), pp. 381-87.

———————————. 1964. "Inequality and Instability: The Relationship of Land Tenure to Politics." *World Politics* 16 (April), pp. 442-54.

Sigelman, Lee and Miles Simpson. 1977. "A Cross-National Test of the Linkage Between Economic Inequality and Political Violence." *Journal of Conflict Resolution* 21 (March), pp. 105-27.

Simon, Julian. 1981. *The Ultimate Resource*. Princeton: Princeton University Press.

Stohl, Michael. 1980. "The Nexus of Civil and International Conflict." In *Handbook of Political Conflict*, ed. Ted R. Gurr, pp. 297-330. New York: Free Press.

Taylor, Charles Lewis and David A. Jodice. 1983. *World Handbook of Political and Social Indicators*, 3d ed., 2 volumes. New Haven: Yale University Press.

Thompson, William R. 1982. "Phases of the Business Cycle and the Outbreak of War." *International Studies Quarterly* 26 (June), pp. 301-11.

———————————— and L. G. Zuk. 1982. "War, Inflation and the Kondratieff Long Wave." *Journal of Conflict Resolution* 26 (December), pp. 621-44.

Venieris, Yiannias P. and Dipak K. Gupta. 1983. "Socio-Political and Economic Dimensions of Development: A Cross-Section Model." *Economic Development and Cultural Change* 31 (July), pp. 728-50.

Zimmermann, Ekkart. 1983. *Political Violence, Crises and Revolutions: Theories and Research*. Boston: Hall.

————————————. 1984. "The World Economic Crisis of the Thirties in Six European Countries: A First Report." Paper delivered at the 25th Annual Convention of the International Studies Association, Atlanta, March 27-31.

II. Foreign Policy and Behavior

7

The Erosion of
U. S. Leadership Capabilities

MARK E. RUPERT AND DAVID P. RAPKIN

The relative decline of U.S. capabilities (or power resources) is taken as axiomatic in most recent analyses of the world political economy, international regime change, and U.S. foreign policy. Many studies converge on a form of explanation that associates preponderant U.S. capabilities at the outset of the post-World War II period with the exercise of *hegemonic leadership*[1] to create the conditions for world order. Subsequent erosion of U.S. political, military, and economic capabilities is viewed as having diminished U.S. ability and willingness to continue in the leadership role. In turn, the widely perceived disorder of the 1970s and the 1980s is linked to this retreat from leadership.[2] Some analysts apply this "rise and decline of leadership" reasoning only to the U.S. case (Krasner 1982; Keohane 1982); others compare U.S. hegemonic leadership to its nineteenth-century British antecedent (Kindleberger 1974; Gilpin 1975). The Wallersteinian version of world economic hegemony adds seventeenth-century Netherlands as a kindred case (Wallerstein 1980; Chase-Dunn 1982), while Modelski (1978, 1982) treats twentieth-century U.S. leadership as the fifth replication of a "long cycle" of world politics that includes sixteenth-century Portugal and eighteenth-century Great Britain in addition to the abovementioned cases.

Despite its theoretical centrality, capability decline is often regarded as so evident a phenomenon as to obviate the need for detailed examination beyond comparison of base and terminal year values of one or a few indicia of capabilities. There is in fact surprisingly little systematic knowledge, even of a descriptive sort, of the process of decline.[3] Important analytical and empirical questions bearing on this process are yet to be adequately addressed: At what rate has decline occurred? Has it been a steady linear process or one marked by precipitous discontinuities? Have all relevant types of capabilities declined in an approximately parallel manner and, if not, is there a particular sequence of decline? These questions must be answered before more substantive causal statements linking capabilities, leadership, and order can be meaningfully evaluated.

In this chapter we analyze a nonexhaustive compendium of capability indicators over the post-World War II period in hopes of modestly contributing to an understanding of the process of decline. Our objective here is not to account for the causes of decline, but rather to identify the rate, form, and sequence in which the process has unfolded. We abstract entirely from military and political capabilities and focus on those relating to world economic leadership. This is not to imply that economic capabilities are of superordinate importance or that the world system's economic and political-military realms can be neatly isolated and treated independently.[4] The pieces of the leadership capability puzzle will eventually have to be put together, but as a starting point we focus on measures referencing capabilities in the productive, commercial, and financial spheres of the world economy.

Two sets of indicators are examined. Share indicators are based on the premise that potential ability to lead is reflected in the hegemonic state's share of global resources and capabilities (for example, U.S. GNP/World GNP). These measures enable a rough test of Wallerstein's (1980, Ch. 1; 1982) hypothesis that hegemony unfolds in successive overlapping phases, with preponderance first gained and then lost in the same sequence: production, commerce, and finance. Interdependence indicators register the international content of the hegemonic state's aggregate economic activity (for example, U.S. trade/U.S. GNP). For reasons we will make explicit, we expect leadership activities to wane as the hegemon becomes more tightly and comprehensively integrated into the open world economy it has constructed. The two sets of indicators are juxtaposed to examine what Bergsten (1982) terms the "scissors effect." One blade of the scissors, represented by declining shares, denotes diminished ability to influence world events and outcomes; the other blade, represented by increasing interdependence, indicates greater U.S. susceptibility to events, shocks, and policies originating elsewhere in the world system. With the blades of Bergsten's scissors construed as parameters within which U.S. leadership has operated, our purpose is to determine the manner and rate at which these blades have closed. A third set of indicators—ratios of U.S. imports to exports in key industrial sectors—reflects both share and interdependence aspects of U.S. leadership capabilities.

This chapter employs the familiar and accessible "eyeball" methodology, relying upon visual examination of share and interdependence indicators arrayed against time. Though this method is prone to imprecision, in this instance the data allow relatively straightforward interpretation. We find that all the share indicators tend to decline in a more or less linear, incremental fashion, without decisive breakpoints. The interdependence indicators, however, remain at relatively low levels until approximately 1970, at which time they exhibit a clear upward change of slope. There is indeed a scissors effect, but the "share" blade closes earlier and more evenly over time, while the "interdependence" blade, dull for several decades, begins to cut sharply later in the period.

Hegemonic Leadership Capabilities: A Conceptual Discussion

The exercise of hegemonic leadership implies pursuit of extraordinary global interests and objectives that historically have been beyond the means available to all but a handful of states. Since the diffuse, expansive, and costly objectives associated with global order and stability are not found among the core objectives of "ordinary" states—even great powers—it is reasonable to infer that leadership reflects virtually unique will, purpose, and strategic design. Moreover, if it is to be successful, lesser states must afford the hegemon some measure of confidence, legitimacy, and voluntary cooperation. For these reasons, hegemonic leadership is in large part a qualitative phenomenon that does not issue simply from a preponderantly unipolar distribution of capabilities.

Though such a distribution is not a sufficient condition for leadership, it is certainly a necessary one. Hegemony depends on a base of objective capabilities that is also an historical rarity. In this sense, the theory of hegemonic leadership is a form of "power as resources" theory, "in which outcomes reflect the potential power (tangible and known capabilities) of actors" (Keohane 1980, p. 137). Given the extraordinary demands of the leadership role, however, it is difficult to specify just which capabilities are needed and in what magnitudes. One point on which there is wide agreement is that leadership requires a diversity of capabilities. Singular reliance on either military, economic, or political-diplomatic resources may suffice to achieve desired outcomes in specific issue areas or in spatiotemporally bounded situations. But hegemonic leadership, by definition, is confined within few spatial or (less than long-term) temporal bounds and encompasses a wide range of issues. The instruments of hegemony must therefore be many and varied.

Why does leadership necessitate capabilities of extraordinary scale and diversity? To what purpose are these capabilities applied? Broadly speaking, they are used to shape and influence the world political-economic environment in directions consistent with the hegemon's design for world order. More specifically, and with reference to the U.S. case, the leadership role requires extraordinary capabilities for at least the following purposes. First, the hegemon's perceived security responsibilities require the capability to control strategic space on a global scale. Second, leadership calls for initial and ongoing investments in the infrastructure of world order—that is, institutions, norms, and rules as represented by the United Nations, Bretton Woods, and GATT. Third, the hegemon may find it necessary to invest in the reconstruction of strategically critical states in order to establish a "critical mass" of allies and clients for military-security purposes and/or viable economic partners for the operation of an open, growth-oriented world economy (such as the Marshall Plan and the benevolent occupation of Japan). Fourth, incentives and "side payments" must at times be offered to induce adherence to the norms and rules of hegemonic order. The scale of the leader's domestic economy is crucial here, as access to its lucrative home market makes a particularly enticing "carrot." Moreover, "economic goods" can be traded for compliance in the military-security realm and vice versa. The qualitative characteristics associated with a "lead economy," especially technological dynamism, also comprise critical goods to be dispensed to collaborative states that aspire to competitiveness in the productive sphere. Fifth, hegemonic capabilities can also be used coercively to enforce compliance with the rules of the game. Finally, to sustain effective leadership, the hegemon at times must absorb shocks and dislocations ensuing from the operation of world markets—for example, by allocating scarce goods in times of surplus. All of these tasks, provision of which can be regarded as a public good, are expensive to perform. In Modelski's (1982, p. 104) terms, leadership "cannot be conducted on the cheap."

Another significant feature of hegemonic leadership is that it is intrinsically an unstable, transitory phenomenon. The highly skewed global distribution of capabilities that enables leadership reflects the outcome of global war in which lesser states have been emasculated while the hegemon has been correspondingly strengthened. Some degree of capability leveling is therefore inevitable as lesser states recover from war-induced weakness. Additionally, the essence of the hegemon's productive superiority is invariably diffused through the mechanisms of the open, liberal world economy created under its auspices (for example, via flows of goods, capital, and technology). It is thus an ironic feature of hegemonic systems of order that, if they function as intended, they sow the seeds of their eventual demise. Emulation and reverse engineering also contribute significantly to the narrowing of the hegemon's margin of superiority, in both the economic and military realms.

Building upon his reading of the seventeenth-century Dutch case, Wallerstein (1980, pp. 38-39) offers a conceptual framework that provides both a categorization of the capabilities constitutive of world economic hegemony and an hypothesis pertaining to the sequence in which these capabilities are gained and lost:

> Marked superiority in agro-industrial productive efficiency leads to dominance of the spheres of commercial distribution of world trade, with correlative profits accruing both from being the entrepot of much of world trade and from controlling the "invisibles"—transport, communications, and insurance. Commercial primacy leads in turn to control of the financial sectors of banking (exchange, deposit, and credit) and of investment (direct and portfolio). These superiorities are successive, but they overlap in time. Similarly, the loss of advantage seems to be in the same order (from productive to commercial to financial), and also largely successive.

Wallerstein subsequently (1982) generalizes this sequence to the nineteenth-century British and twentieth-century U.S. cases. Though there is more to Wallerstein's conceptualization of hegemony than dominant shares of productive, commercial, and financial capabilities, his formulation implies operational definition in terms of shares. Unfortunately, he offers no criteria concerning the relative amount of each type of capability necessary to attain hegemony. Were there theoretical guidance as to threshold levels, the three-phase model could be supported by demonstration that the respective thresholds were crossed in the hypothesized sequence. Lacking threshold criteria, empirical validation requires demonstration that declines (slope changes) occurred sequentially.

Another line of theoretical argument addressing the process of leadership decline directs attention to the increasing integration of the hegemon into the grid of world production and exchange. As the leader becomes more tightly enmeshed in the web of interdependence it has spun, the international content of its aggregate economic activity rises and it thereby becomes more sensitive and vulnerable to the vicissitudes of world market forces and to developments, events, and trends that are generated elsewhere in the system. As more sectors of the hegemonic society (capital, labor, regions, and communities) are impacted adversely by world market forces, they begin to pressure the hegemonic state for protection from foreign competition and from the vagaries of world markets more generally. The domestic coalition favoring leadership activities is weakened and short-term parochial interests begin to dominate the longer-term cosmopolitan interests of system maintenance and order keeping (Krasner 1982).

A more formal approach to interdependence reveals how it affects the exercise of leadership. Consider Bryant's (1980 , p. 177) hypothesis concerning the relationship between interdependence and the autonomy of a state's policy instruments:

> A structural change that increases (diminishes) the economic interdependence of a nation's economy with the rest of the world typically reduces (augments) the autonomy of its economic policy.

Bryant's analysis is framed in terms of policy multipliers that reference the effectiveness of policy instruments in influencing macroeconomic target variables. There are four sets of multipliers: home country policies/home country variables; home country policies/ foreign country variables; foreign country policies/home country variables; and foreign country policies/foreign country variables. The result of increased interdependence is to reduce the impact and heighten the uncertainty of home country policy multipliers vis-à-vis the policy multipliers of other states. For a hegemonic state, interdependence therefore translates into diminished ability to influence outcomes and other states' behavior with the policy instruments at its disposal, and heightened sensitivity and vulnerability to policies implemented by other states.

In this fashion, interdependence lessens the ability and willingness to exercise leadership. Maintenance of world order and stability becomes more problematic and uncertain as the systemic distribution of carrots and sticks shifts in a direction unfavorable to the hegemon. Though increasing interdependence does not connote erosion of a tangible capability per se, it is reasonable to posit that relative insulation from disruptive world market forces and other states' policies, as well as home country policy autonomy, constitute a form of intangible capability. It also seems reasonable to suggest that interdependence is initially more consequence than cause of capability erosion but that, once under way, it feeds back into and accelerates the erosion process.

The "scissors effect" describes the joint consequences of declining capability shares and increasing interdependence. In Bergsten's (1982, p. 13) terms:

> The United States has simultaneously become much more dependent on the world economy and much less able to dictate the course of international economic events. The global economic environment is more critical for the United States and is less susceptible to its influence.

While the scissors metaphor is a descriptive device rather than an hypothesis, comparison of the form of the share and interdependence trends provides an understanding of how the two effects have operated to progressively constrain U.S. hegemonic leadership.

Analysis of Capability Shares and Interdependence

In this section we examine a number of share and interdependence indicators that map the erosion of U.S. leadership capabilities over the postwar period. Measures of the U.S. share of selected

Figure 7.1   Ratios of U.S. to Total Core GNP (1950-67) and GDP (1960-81)

Source: Organization for Economic Cooperation and Development, *National Accounts of OECD Countries* (various issues 1970-81).

Figure 7.2   Ratio of U.S. to Total Core Gross Fixed Capital Formation (1952-80)

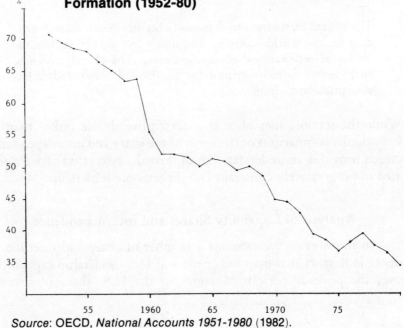

Source: OECD, *National Accounts 1951-1980* (1982).

economic capabilities, denominated in terms of either world totals or totals of the major advanced industrial states, are presented first. The order of presentation—productive, commercial, and financial—facilitates evaluation of the loss-of-capabilities side of Wallerstein's sequential hypothesis. Interdependence indicators referencing the international content of U.S. economic activity are then examined. Interspersed at several points are series based on U.S. import-export ratios in leading industrial sectors of the world economy; these measures are indicative of both share and interdependence aspects of capability decline.

A general, widely used indicator of overall productive capability is the size of the total social product (GNP or GDP). Figure 7.1 compares the aggregate output of the U.S. economy to that of the industrial "core" of the world economy, defined for present purposes as the "big seven" industrial states (United States, United Kingdom, West Germany, France, Italy, Canada, and Japan).[5] The proportion of U.S. to total core GNP (1950-67) and GDP (1960-81)[6] shows a steady decline in the weight of the U.S. economy, falling from more than 70 percent to between 40 and 45 percent—a still substantial, but no longer preponderant share. The trend is more or less linear and almost monotonic, exhibiting no decisive watersheds in the erosion of U.S. predominance of core productive capacity.

Another measure directly related to general productive capabilities, reflecting both the past experience of an economy and its adaptability to future developments, is the level of investment in new productive assets. Figure 7.2 displays the U.S. share of the gross fixed capital formation of the core as a whole from 1952 to 1980. At the outset of the period, capital formation was virtually monopolized by the United States (over 70 percent), but has subsequently fallen by about half. Given the war-decimated condition of the European and Japanese economies, the large initial U.S. share was in part artifactual and thus was bound to decline as these economies reconstructed. Nonetheless, this leveling of capital formation clearly reveals the diminished prevalence of the United States in the productive realm. Again, the decline is approximately constant in rate.

The pattern of secular decline in relative levels of U.S. output and investment is also evident in key sectors of industrial production. Space limitations and data availability preclude a more complete examination of leading sectors,[7] but the general pattern is illustrated in Figures 7.3 and 7.4 by the trends in the automobile and consumer

Figure 7.3   Ratio of U.S. to Total Core Automobile Production (1958-79), Exclusive of Japan (1946-62)

Sources: OECD, *Industrial Statistics 1900-1962* (1964); United Nations, *Growth of World Industry, 1968 Edition*, volume II (1967); United Nations, *Yearbook of Industrial Statistics, 1979 Edition*, volume II (1981).

Figure 7.4   Ratio of U.S. to Total Core Consumer Electronics Production (1958-79), Exclusive of Japan (1947-62) and Italy (1947-54).

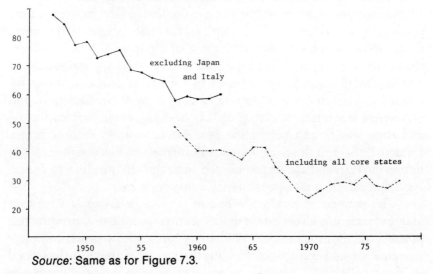

Source: Same as for Figure 7.3.

164

electronics industries. In both cases, the initial U.S. share of core production (over 80 percent) declines dramatically to around 30 percent. The apparent U.S. recovery in consumer electronics in the 1970s is somewhat misleading since Asian newly industrializing countries captured an increasing share of *world* production in this sector during that decade.

Wallerstein's distinction between productive and commercial superiority, though certainly meaningful, blurs conceptually and operationally. Productive superiority lacks significance unless it is translated into commercial dominance in world markets (and hence the imperative of an open trading system for a hegemonic state aiming to exploit its productive superiority). Nevertheless, the U.S. share of world exports, while also reflecting productive superiority, is a direct indicator of its commercial importance. Figure 7.5 exhibits U.S. shares of total world exports (1947-80) and of exports by the 14 largest developed market economies (1950-80). The former falls from 32 to less than 11 percent, with a precipitous drop in the first three years of the series (a manifestation of postwar recovery elsewhere in the world system) before stabilizing in a more gradual decline over the balance of the period. The latter measure shows a similar pattern of steady erosion. Figure 7.6 plots the U.S. share of world manufactured exports from 1958 to 1980 (pre-1958 levels can be safely presumed to have been higher than 1958's 27-28 percent). Again we find clear evidence of productive and commercial decline, with the United States losing about half a percentage point of its share per year.

The question of U.S. commercial superiority can also be addressed by looking at the ratio of imports to exports in specific categories of industrial products. Unlike the share indicators, these ratios do not directly reference the U.S. economy's relative weight in the world economy, but rather serve as rough indexes of U.S. industrial competitiveness in home and world markets. The large and affluent U.S. market has supported product and process innovations, has enabled its producers to attain economies of scale and learning, and thereby has provided a base from which goods embodying such innovations have been internationally marketed. Loss of home market space thus has direct implications for U.S. productive and commercial advantage. Lower import-export ratios denote U.S. competitive advantage, while higher ratios imply that U.S. products

Figure 7.5 **Ratios of U.S. to Total World (1947-80) and DME (1950-80) Exports**

Source: United Nations, *Statistical Yearbook* (various issues).

Figure 7.6 **Ratio of U.S. to World Exports of Manufactures (1958-80)**

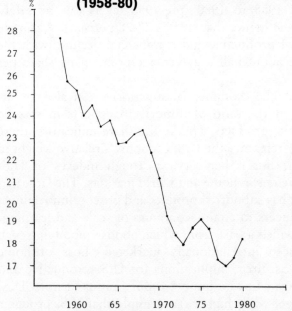

Source: U.S. Department of Commerce, *International Commerce*; *Commerce Today*; *Business America* (various issues).

166

Figure 7.7 Ratios of U.S. Imports to Exports of Capital Goods (1948-79) and High-Technology Products (1962-80)

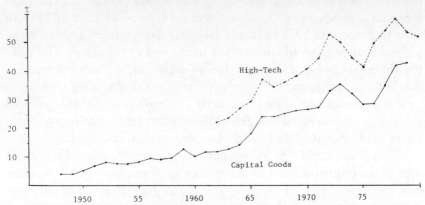

Sources: U.S. Department of Commerce, *US Exports and Imports Classified by O.B.E. End-Use Categories, 1932-1968* (1970); *Highlights of US Export-Import Trade (1970-1978)*. U.S. Cabinet Council on Commerce and Trade, *An Assessment of U.S. Competitiveness in High Technology Industries* (1983).

Figure 7.8 Ratios of U.S. Imports to Exports of Electrical Machinery and Business Machines (1948-79)

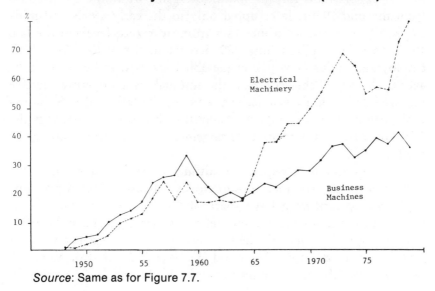

Source: Same as for Figure 7.7.

are less able to compete in domestic and foreign markets. Figure 7.7 displays import-export ratios for the crucial categories of capital goods (1948-79) and high-technology products (1962-80). The ratio for capital goods increases about tenfold from 4 percent in 1948 to over 40 percent in 1979 in steady fashion, though there appears to be a slope change from the mid-1960s to the end of the series. The ratio for the overlapping category of high-technology products traces a parallel but significantly higher path, more than doubling over a 19-year span. Since provision of these two categories of goods signifies a position at the apex of the global division of labor, we regard these series as clear evidence of productive and commercial decline.

Figures 7.8 and 7.9 tell similar, sector-specific tales. Figure 7.8 depicts the import-export ratios for electrical machinery and business machines, two types of capital goods (with the former more germane to manufacturing and the latter to service industries). The electrical machinery series begins with near-zero values in the late 1940s, increases to almost 20 percent in the early 1960s, and then climbs explosively to about 80 percent in 1979. The ratio for business machines rises sharply from negligible levels in the late 1940s to almost 35 percent in 1959, falls to around 20 percent in the early to mid-1960s, and then resumes the overall upward trend to the 35-40 percent range in the last half of the 1970s. Figure 7.9 presents the import-export ratio for automobiles. Again, we find a steep climb from the mid-1950s, interrupted only in the early 1960s and mid-1970s. Overall, the ratio increases from near-zero levels in the late 1940s to values approaching 200 percent in the 1970s. As a high employment industry with considerable backward and forward linkages to the rest of the economy, the automakers' competitive demise has provided a highly visible, symbolic manifestation of U.S. industrial decline. Further import penetration has been arrested in the 1980s only by means of quota arrangements "voluntarily" offered by the Japanese.

In addition to competitive advantages in world markets for industrial goods, commercial superiority has also enabled previous hegemons to capture a large share of "invisibles": transportation, communication, insurance, and related services (Wallerstein 1980, Ch. 2). Figure 7.10 reports the U.S. proportion of core income from invisibles over the 1950-77 period. From a 1951 high of about 36 percent, the U.S. share fell by over one-third to about 22 percent in

Figure 7.9 Ratio of U.S. Imports to Exports of Automobiles (1948-79)

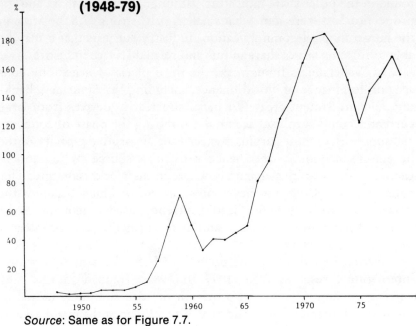

Source: Same as for Figure 7.7.

Figure 7.10 Ratio of U.S. to Total Core Income from Invisibles (1960-77) Exclusive of Japan (1950-77)

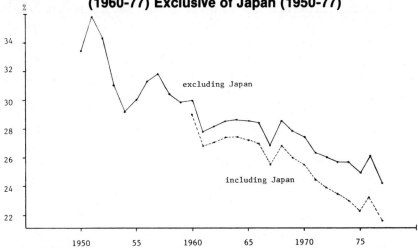

Sources: OECD, *Statistics of National Accounts 1950-1961* (1964); *National Accounts of OCED Countries 1960-1977* (1977).

169

the final year of the series. The general pattern of decline mirrors that found in the other share indicators, although the initial share and the proportion lost were somewhat smaller. (The strong U.S. position in the burgeoning telecommunications industry suggests that it may be able to regain a larger share in this and related service industries.)

In Wallerstein's framework, the third phase of hegemony consists of dominance of world finance, including the monetary, banking, and investment areas. Financial superiority derives from large current account surpluses accumulated during the phase of commercial superiority; these surpluses exceed the absorptive capacity of the hegemon's economy, and hence provide a source of investment capital for loan or investment elsewhere in the world economy. This pattern also bolsters the hegemon's currency, which becomes the world economy's "key" (or "lead") currency, used systemwide as the preferred medium of exchange and as the principal unit of international financial reserves.

Figure 7.11 displays the dwindling U.S. share of total world international reserves from 1949 to 1981. Trapped in the "key currency dilemma" between provision of adequate international liquidity and maintaining confidence in the dollar as the major reserve asset, the U.S. share fell at a steady rate from almost 60 percent in the series base year. After U.S. abandonment of the Bretton Woods fixed-rate monetary regime in the early 1970s, the decline stabilized at an asymptotic level below 10 percent. As a rough indicator of the "overhead" costs associated with world economic leadership, the linear deterioration of the U.S. reserve position reflects the changing U.S. position in the world economy. The trend in this series may overstate the decline of U.S. influence in the monetary realm since, for want of alternatives, the dollar remains the major reserve currency in the post-Bretton Woods regime of floating exchange rates. It should also be pointed out that whatever influence the United States has retained has not produced stability in the world monetary system. Since the demise of Bretton Woods—widely regarded as a landmark event in the U.S. retreat from leadership—exchange rates have been highly volatile. As Bressard (1983, p. 747), among others, contends, "Strong fluctuations in [this] key parameter—whether upward or downward—are a threat to the survival of the system."

The U.S. share of core income from foreign investment constitutes a significant exception to the overall pattern of linear decline found in previous series. Figure 7.12 reveals that though the U.S.

Figure 7.11   Ratio of U.S. to World International Financial Reserves (1949-81)

Source: Same as Figure 7.10.

Figure 7.12   Ratio of U.S. to Total Core Income from International Investment (1960-77) Exclusive of Japan (1950-77)

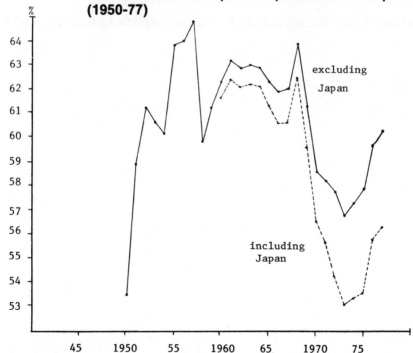

Source: International Monetary Fund, *International Financial Statistics Yearbook* (1979, 1982).

171

Figure 7.13   Ratios of U.S. Capital Outflows and Total Flows to Gross Domestic Private Investment (1960-81)

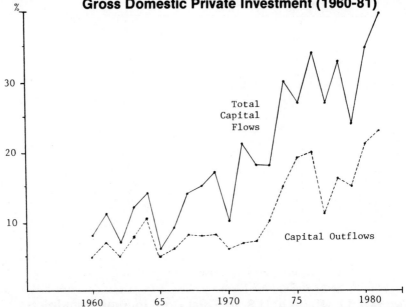

Source: U.S. Office of the President, *Economic Report of the President* (1983).

Figure 7.14   Ratios of U.S. Trade and Exports to GDP (1950-79)

Source: United Nations, *Yearbook of National Account Statistics* (various years).

share exhibits considerable year-to-year variation, no secular decline is apparent and the level of the series never falls below 50 percent. Persistent dominance of the investment realm represents the return on private capital outflows via the foreign investment activities of U.S. transnational corporations, a two-edged sword to which neomercantilists attribute the blame for the erosion of U.S. productive superiority (see especially Gilpin 1975). The pattern also provides the last phase of Wallerstein's model with some support, qualified of course by the quite different trend in the monetary area.

Turning now to the interdependence blade of Bergsten's scissors, the question is whether trends in the relative international content of U.S. economic activities are isomorphic to those we have found with respect to U.S. shares of globally or core-aggregated capabilities. We begin by examining the ratio of total capital flows (outflows and inflows, private and public) to gross private domestic investment. While we might be accused of putting "apples over oranges," the purpose of this measure is to show how much capital has flowed into and out of the U.S. economy in relation to the amount that has been invested domestically. Figure 7.13 demonstrates that outflows (the lower series) and inflows (the difference between total and outflows) each remained under 10 percent during the 1960s, but then climbed in a rapid and fluctuating manner throughout the 1970s to highs of over 23 and 16 percent, respectively, in 1981. Stated differently, bidirectional capital flows that summed to under 10 percent as a proportion of gross investment in the base year amounted to about 40 percent two decades later. The measure thus reveals that in the 1970s the productive activities of the U.S. economy not only became more integrated into the world economy, but also became more susceptible to wide fluctuations in the behavior of economic and political agents, both U.S. and foreign.

The proportion of the aggregate U.S. product consisting of exported and imported goods is a direct indicator of the degree of integration of the United States into the world economy. Figure 7.14 displays exports and total trade (exports and imports) as proportions of U.S. GDP from 1950 to 1979. Both series are virtually flat through the early 1970s, at which point they begin to ascend sharply. Trade/GNP doubles from about 8 to over 16 percent in the space of the last decade of the series. In consequence, painful dislocations and adjustments have afflicted U.S. society as more and more industries,

Figure 7.15 Ratio of U.S. Agricultural Exports to Total Farm Income (1948-81)

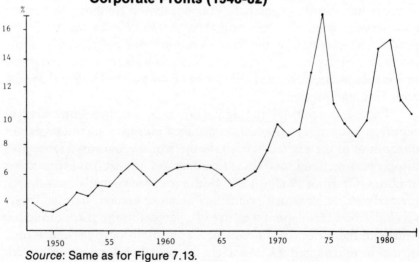

Source: Same as for Figure 7.13.

Figure 7.16 Ratio of Profits from Foreign Operations to Total Corporate Profits (1948-82)

Source: Same as for Figure 7.13.

regions, communities, and workers are subjected to foreign competition in their home market and/or are reliant on access to foreign market space for their livelihood. These developments are no doubt responsible for the proliferation of protectionist pressures to which the U.S. government has been subjected—and has increasingly succumbed to—in recent years, with the effect of undermining (at least the credibility of) the U.S. commitment to leadership of an open world economy.

As U.S. productive, and thereby also commercial, advantage in industrial goods has deteriorated, agricultural exports have assumed increasing importance in the U.S. current account picture. Figure 7.15 displays the proportion of total farm income derived from agricultural exports. From 1948 through 1972, this proportion never exceeded 15 percent and was under 11 percent as recently as 1969. From 1972 on this proportion skyrockets, passing the 27 percent mark in 1980. While superiority in agricultural production is an important U.S. strength, increasing reliance on agricultural exports in the face of ineffective global demand is also attended by costs and dislocations, as illustrated by the woes of the farm sector in recent years.

Another direct measure of the integration of the United States into the world economy is the proportion of the business sector's profits that comes from its foreign operations. Figure 7.16 reports the share of total corporate profits deriving from foreign operations from1948 to 1982. The index remains under 7 percent through 1968; climbs quickly to almost 17 percent in 1974; drops to below 10 percent in 1976-78; increases again to 15 percent in 1980; and falls to about 10 percent in 1982. Once more we find a pattern of significantly higher average levels of international content in the 1970s, accompanied by much wider year-to-year swings.

Shifting attention to the financial area, we examine the international content of U.S. banking activities. Figure 7.17 displays the proportion of total loans by U.S. banks that has gone to (public and private) foreign debtors. The series hovered in the 5 to 10 percent range from 1946 to 1973. Responding to accelerating demands for credit from oil-importing countries following the 1973 oil price shock, U.S. bank lending to foreign borrowers increased precipitously in the balance of the decade, almost tripling to over 26 percent of total lending by 1980. Recycling petrodollars has proved a risky

Figure 7.17   Ratio of U.S. International to Total U.S. Lending (1946-80)

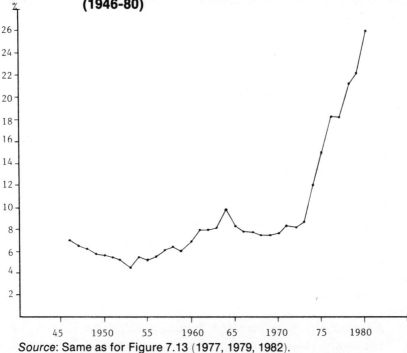

Source: Same as for Figure 7.13 (1977, 1979, 1982).

Figure 7.18   U.S. Net Balances of Merchandise Trade and Investment Income (1946-81) (Billion $ U.S.)

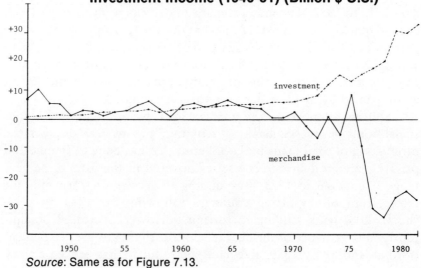

Source: Same as for Figure 7.13.

enterprise, however, as huge debt burdens among third world countries unable to service their debts imperil the solvency of major U.S. banks. With widespread fears of a collapse of the international financial system, the debate within the United States over whether the government should "bail out" threatened private financial institutions is another domestic manifestation of the increasing dependence of the United States on an unstable world economy.

Many of the changes we have discussed in the way the U.S. economy relates to the world economy are revealed by examination of the composition of the U.S. current account balance. Wallerstein's model and numerous analyses of the Pax Britannica (for example, see Gilpin 1975) suggest that aging hegemons become rentiers, increasingly reliant on returns from financial and investment activities rather than on export earnings accruing from competitive superiority in industrial production. Figure 7.18, which plots the net balances in merchandise trade and investment income,[8] supports this hypothesis for the U.S. case. Both net balances were positive and stable (under $10 billion) from 1948 through 1970. Over the next decade, the two followed sharply divergent trends: the net balance in merchandise trade plummeted to deficits of over $25 billion annually in the 1977-81 subperiod, while the net surplus on investment income rose to over $30 billion annually during the last three years of the series. These trends have continued in 1982 and 1983 as the trade deficit has deepened and investment income has increased as U.S. transnational corporations, facing high capital costs, have repatriated more of their foreign earnings.

In sum, the interdependence measures we have examined tend to follow a quite different path than the share measures. The latter, with a few exceptions, exhibit a pattern of steady decay. The interdependence measures, in contrast, are characterized by sharp discontinuities, remaining at low levels until the early 1970s, at which juncture there are sudden and significant increases in the extent to which the United States is integrated into the world economy.

Conclusion

The decline of U.S. hegemonic leadership since the halcyon days of the 1950s is usually explained as a function of the diminishing relative weight of the United States in the world economy. Our analysis suggests that the erosion of U.S. shares of leadership-enabling capabilities is a large part, but by no means all, of the story. In addition to preponderant capability shares, the United States was also extraordinary in terms of the degree of domestic insulation from the vagaries of its world economic environment. It has since become less able and willing to exercise leadership—has become more like an ordinary country—in part because it has become significantly less insulated. From our perspective, it follows that explanation of the rise and decline of hegemonic leadership as a *world systemic process* must also include this interdependence dimension.

In this context, Bergsten's concept of a scissors effect is a useful device for purposes of organization and description. One finding that emerges quite clearly from our analysis is that the two blades of the scissors have not closed in an even, symmetrical fashion over the course of the postwar period. We have also tried to provide a crude, preliminary test of Wallerstein's three-phase model of world economic hegemony (addressing only the sequence in which the three types of hegemonic capability are lost, not gained). We encountered what we think are intrinsic difficulties in operationally separating productive and commercial superiority. Our findings do provide qualified support for the hypothesized persistence of financial superiority beyond the productive and commercial phases. Again with reference to the interdependence side of the question, it is fair to say that increasing reliance on the returns from financial activities is at least as significant to an understanding of the United States as aging hegemon as is its remaining share of world financial capabilities. Longer time series and much more in the way of operational specification are needed before Wallerstein's ideas can be adequately tested.

We acknowledge that we have given but cursory attention to the various measures examined herein. Subsequent analysis will have to provide more detailed treatment of the statistical properties of each measure, its relationship to the underlying capability it represents, and the relationship of this capability to the exercise of leadership.

In closing, we take note of the "small n-size" problem endemic to the study of hegemonic leadership. This exercise, as a first cut at the question of declining hegemonic capabilities, has been framed solely in terms of the postwar Pax Americana. Within the limitations inherent to generalizing about a process that has undergone only a handful of replications, systematic comparison of the U.S. case with its antecedents is absolutely necessary. Until this is accomplished, the generalizations drawn from this case study are but descriptive contributions to the science of world systems.

Notes

1. The terms "hegemony," "leadership," and "hegemonic leadership" will be used interchangeably in the pages that follow, and should be taken to imply neither a set of purely exploitive relationships or the entirely civic-spirited provision of the public good of global order. We recognize that, to varying degrees, both elements may be present in hegemonic systems. For a useful, highly abstract treatment of leadership from a long-cycle perspective, see Modelski (1983).

2. For a fuller treatment of this line of argument, see Avery and Rapkin (1982).

3. A notable exception is Thompson's (1980) painstaking effort to operationalize the concept of seapower, which is central to long-cycle theory.

4. For a treatment of the relationship between the world system's economic and political-military subsystems, see Rapkin (1983).

5. In some of the subsequent series comparing U.S. to aggregate core capabilities, data availability precluded inclusion of all seven states over the full span of the series. Where this occurred, the omitted states were included in a separate series at the earliest possible date, and both series are reported for purposes of comparison. In general, omission affected the levels rather than the slopes of the relevant series.

6. OECD provides only GNP figures for the earlier period, and GDP for the later. The difference between GNP and GDP is equal to the net inflow of income earned on property and labor supplied by a country's citizens abroad. The higher U.S. proportion of total core GNP, as opposed to GDP, apparent for the years 1960-67 is thus due to relatively larger U.S. earnings of such income.

7. United States shares of global production of petrochemicals, energy, and agricultural products have eroded much more slowly, no doubt because of relatively abundant natural endowments.

8. We omit here, for purposes of exposition, other less significant elements of the current account; the surplus in net services, the largest of the omitted elements, increases significantly but is still small in relation to merchandise trade.

Bibliography

Avery, William and David P. Rapkin, eds. 1982. *America in a Changing World Political Economy.* New York: Longmans.

Bergsten, C. Fred. 1982. "The United States and the World Economy." *Annals of the American Academy of Political and Social Science* 460, pp. 11-20.

Bressard, Albert. 1983. "Mastering the 'Worldeconomy.'" *Foreign Affairs* 61, pp. 745-72.

Bryant, Ralph C. 1980 *Money and Monetary Policy in Interdependent Nations.* Washington: Brookings Institution.

Chase-Dunn, Christopher K. 1982. "International Economic Policy in a Declining Core State." In *America in a Changing World Political Economy,* ed. William P. Avery and David P. Rapkin, pp. 77-96. New York: Longmans.

Gilpin, Robert, 1975. *U.S. Power and the Multinational Corporation.* New York: Basic Books.

Keohane, Robert O. 1982. "Hegemonic Leadership and US Foreign Economic Policy in the 'Long Decade' of the 1950s." In *America in a Changing World Political Economy,* ed. William P. Avey and David P. Rapkin, pp. 49-76. New York: Longmans.

—————————————. 1980. "The Theory of Hegemonic Stability and Changes in International Regimes, 1967-1977." In *Change in the International System,* ed. Ole R. Hosti, Randolph M. Siverson, and Alexander L. George, pp. 131-62. Boulder, Colo.: Westview.

Kindleberger, Charles P. 1974. *The World in Depression, 1929-1939.* Berkeley: University of California Press.

Krasner, Stephen D. 1982. "American Policy and Global Economic Stability." In *America in a Changing World Political Economy,* ed. William P. Avery and David P. Rapkin, pp. 29-48. New York: Longmans.

Modelski, George. 1983. "Qualifications for World Leadership." *Voice* (Tokyo), October, pp. 210-29.

—————————————. 1982. "Long Cycles and the Strategy of U.S. International Economic Policy." In *America in a Changing World Political Economy,* ed. William P. Avery and David P. Rapkin, pp. 97-116. New York: Longmans.

—————————————. 1978. "The Long Cycle of Global Politics and the Nation-State." *Comparative Studies in Society and History* 20, pp. 214-35.

Rapkin, David P. 1983. "The Inadequacy of a Single Logic: Integrating Political and Material Approaches to the World System." In *Contending Approaches to World System Analysis,* ed. William R. Thompson, pp. 241-68. Beverly Hills: Sage.

Thompson, William R. 1980. "Seapower and Global Politics: Problems of Data Collection and Analysis." Paper read at the Annual Meetings of the International Studies Association, March 19-22, Los Angeles.

Wallerstein, Immanuel. 1982. "The Three Instances of Hegemony in the History of the Capitalist World Economy." Paper read at the Conference of Europeanists, April 29-May 1, Washington, D.C.

—————————————. 1980. *The Modern World-System II: Mercantilism and the Consolidation of the Capitalist World Economy, 1600-1750.* New York: Academic Press.

8

Recurring Influences on Economic Policy Making: Kennedy and Reagan Compared

M. MARK AMEN

In an effort to advance research on the politics of economics, this chapter outlines six factors that may provide a more comprehensive approach to the causes of and relationships between foreign and domestic economic policy.[1] The six are international market conditions, domestic market conditions, the international distribution of power, domestic politics, government decision-making, and policy beliefs. Each of these established factors has different strengths in explaining policy, but they have never been combined in interpretations that span both domestic and foreign economic policy. The balance of payments and fiscal policies of the Kennedy and Reagan administrations illustrate this framework.

Balance of Payments and Fiscal Policies of the Kennedy and Reagan Administrations

When Ronald Reagan won the presidential election of 1980, economic conditions in the United States differed considerably from

I have benefited from the comments and suggestions of several friends and colleagues, and am particularly indebted to Nancy Hewitt, John McIntyre, Lois Sayrs, and Susan Stoudinger. I also wish to thank Donald Curtis of the U.S. Treasury Department for his assistance in my research on the balance of payments files of the Treasury, and the members of the Kennedy administration who readily gave of their time in interviews over the past year. Research for this chapter was made possible in part by financial support from the University of South Florida.

conditions in 1960 when John Kennedy was elected (Table 8.1). A downward cycle in economic growth was present as both men reached the White House, but the 1960 falloff in productivity was not accompanied by inflation or budget deficits. Both of these phenomena were present in the stagflationary 1980 downturn. On the international front, both presidents were confronted with balance of payments deficits (Table 8.2), yet the characteristics and conditions under which the two deficits occurred were quite different. The 1960 deficits were due to an imbalance in the capital account, while the 1980 deficits appeared in both the capital and current accounts.

Despite the differences, both administrations were confronted with a similar problem: how to simultaneously increase domestic productivity and eliminate persistent balance of payments deficits. The two administrations' responses to this problem resulted in different mixes of fiscal and balance of payments policies.

The Kennedy administration set as its first economic priority the reduction of balance of payments deficits. Immediate steps were taken to improve the current account although the deficits were in the capital account; the two most important steps taken were the adoption of incentives for export expansion and the reduction of government spending abroad. The administration tried to expand exports by increasing Export-Import Bank credits, enlarging commercial attache activities abroad, and educating domestic producers to the potential in overseas markets. It also initiated a major drive to open up international markets by successfully lobbying Congress to pass the Trade Expansion Act of 1962. Shifts in government spending abroad were accomplished through offset agreements, expenditure switching of federal procurement from the foreign to domestic sector, and further tying of foreign aid to purchases in the United States.

Financial mechanisms were pieced together to buy time until the dollar could once again confidently provide liquidity to finance an accelerating growth in world trade (Strange 1976). These patchwork arrangements included the Gold Pool, Swap arrangements, the General Agreement to Borrow (GAB), Federal Reserve forward operations in the exchange market, and a series of liability financing methods such as Roosa Bonds, bilateral loans from European nations, and the use of standby borrowing from the International Monetary Fund (IMF).

During the early period, the administration adopted moderate

Table 8.1   Fiscal Economic Indicators[a]

	1960	1961	1962	1963	1980	1981	1982	1983
Unemployment (%)	5.4	6.5	5.4	5.5	7.0	7.5	9.5	9.5
Consumer Price Index (%)	1.5	.7	1.2	1.6	12.4	8.9	3.9	3.8
Capacity Utilization	80.2	77.4	81.6	83.5	79.6	79.4	71.1	75.3
GNP (%)[c]	2.2	2.6	5.8	4.0	-.3	2.6	-1.9	3.3[e]
Federal Receipts[b]	77.7	77.6	81.4	86.3	517.1	599.3[d]	617.8	600.6
Federal Outlay[b]	76.5	81.5	87.7	92.6	576.7	657.2	728.4	796.0
Defense Spending[b]	45.6	47.4	51.1	52.7	133.9	157.5	185.3	209.9
Surplus/Deficit[b]	1.2	-3.8	-6.3	-6.2	-59.6	-57.9	-110.6	-195.4
Prime Rate	4.82	4.5	4.5	4.5	15.27	18.87	14.86	10.79
Discount Rate	3.53	3.0	3.0	3.23	11.77	13.42	11.02	8.5

[a]Calendar year, current dollars in billions unless otherwise noted.
[b]Fiscal year.
[c]Based on 1972 dollar.
[d]Reagan modification of Carter Budget.
[e]Preliminary.
Sources: Johnson 1964; Reagan 1984.

Table 8.2 Balance of Payments Economic Indicators[a]

	1960	1961	1962	1963	1980	1981	1982	1983
Current Account Balance	2.82	3.82	3.38	4.41	.42	4.59	-11.2	-40.7[d]
Goods and Services	5.13	6.34	6.02	7.16	7.47	11.52	-3.1	-32.1[d]
Merchandise Balance	4.89	5.57	4.52	5.22	-25.54	-28.06	-36.38	-69.4
Exports	19.6	20.1	20.7	22.2	224.23	237.01	211.21	200.20[d]
Imports	-14.7	-14.5	-16.2	-17.0	-249.78	-265.08	-247.60	-260.75[d]
Investment Balance	3.37	3.75	4.29	4.59	29.57	33.48	27.30	23.58[d]
Receipts	4.61	4.99	5.61	6.15	72.44	86.24	84.14	78.03[d]
Payments	-1.23	-1.24	-1.32	-1.56	-42.87	-52.76	-56.84	-54.45[d]
Capital Account Balance	-1.8	-2.8	-2.2	-3.9	-31.1	-29.9	-30.1	-33.7[d]
U.S. Assets Abroad	-4.0	-5.5	-4.1	-7.2	-86.0	-110.6	-118.0	-49.2[d]
Government[b]	1.0	-.3	.450	-1.2	-13.2	-10.2	-10.6	-6.0[d]
Private	-5.1	-5.2	-4.6	-5.9	-72.7	-100.3	-107.3	-43.2[d]
Foreign Assets in U.S.	2.2	2.7	1.9	3.2	54.9	80.6	87.8	83.0[d]
Government[b]	1.4	.7	1.2	1.9	15.5	5.4	3.1	6.0
Private	.8	1.9	.6	1.2	39.3	75.2	84.6	76.9[d]
Official Reserves	19.3	18.7	17.2	16.8	26.76	30.07	33.96	33.75
Dollar Exchange Rate[c]	—	—	—	—	93.9	105.7	118.1	124.9

[a]Calendar year, current dollars in billions.
[b]Official Reserves and other assets.
[c]Average rate in U.S. Market, 1975 = 100.
[d]Preliminary.
Sources: Johnson 1964; Reagan 1984; U.S. Congress, 1984.

fiscal policies. The classic supply-side tools of investment tax credits and liberalized depreciation allowances were the major instruments used by the administration to bring the country out of recession. The president also supported balanced budgets, price stability, and wage-price guideposts to win the financial community's confidence. Those in charge of debt management followed the tenets of orthodox finance and, in lengthening the public debt, reduced the amount of long-term capital available for domestic investment.

In the spring of 1962, as the external deficits continued and fears were expressed that a Kennedy recession was imminent, the president became concerned about the poor results of existing policy emphasis on elimination of balance of payments deficits. At this point Kennedy endorsed tax cuts, finally submitting tax legislation to Congress in early 1963. The administration simultaneously made some minor changes in its foreign economic policy, but continued its preference for solving the balance of payments deficits without touching private capital movements. Finally, in July 1963 the Interest Equalization Tax (IET) proposal was sent to Congress. This legislation imposed a tax on U.S. private capital invested in European portfolios.

The Reagan administration, unlike its Democratic predecessor, made the domestic economy its first priority. It advocated a program to spur industrial growth by focusing exclusively on aggregate supply. The centerpiece of the administration's fiscal incentives to save and invest was the proposal for sharp reductions in taxes and government spending for discretionary and entitlement programs. In addition, the administration recommended substantial increases in defense spending and a reduction in government regulation of the economy. Congress endorsed most of the administration's proposals in the Economic Recovery Tax Act of 1981 and the Omnibus Budget Reconciliation Act of 1981, the main features of which were enactment of a 23 percent reduction in federal taxes on individual and corporate incomes, a $27.1 billion cut in nondefense spending, and an immediate $2.8 billion increase in defense spending. The combination of tax cuts and increases in defense spending conflicted, however, with the administration's commitment to balance the budget and promote a restrictive monetary policy to curb inflation.

After a strong first quarter in 1981, the economy entered a new recession, one which proved to be the most severe since the 1930s. This downturn lasted until the beginning of 1983. During the months of depressing economic statistics, only the inflation picture improved. In fiscal years 1982 and 1983, federal revenues fell while outlays increased substantially. Enlarged budget deficits, coupled with a tight monetary policy, generated high interest rates; and economic growth was crowded out by Treasury borrowing to finance the deficits. Throughout the recession, the president refused to modify either his tax or defense programs.

While signs of recovery began to appear in 1983, by the following year the outlook was uncertain. The prime rate began to climb, from 10.5 percent at the beginning of 1984 to 11.5 percent in March and 12.5 percent in May. Even the administration expressed doubts about its own fiscal 1985 budget proposals, submitted to Congress in February 1984, and called for further cuts in nondefense spending to offset its proposed 9.3 percent increase in defense outlays (*New York Times*, February 2, 1984, pp. 1, 11-13). Several sectors registered alarm that the deficits were structural and thus would not be automatically reduced if recovery continued. Budget plans proliferated as congressional leaders and administration officials vied for control over fiscal policy. The president's token "down payment" package, aimed at reducing budget deficits, was begrudgingly passed by the Senate in May, but still had to be reconciled with a House plan calling for greater cuts in defense spending and fewer cuts in discretionary and entitlement programs (*New York Times*, May 18, 1984, pp. 1, 11).

The Reagan administration's approach to the balance of payments can be characterized as a combination of benign neglect and protectionism (Cohen 1983). The president refused to modify fiscal policy in response to any of its harmful effects on the balance of payments. Instead, as higher interest rates artificially strengthened the dollar, President Reagan welcomed substantial inflows of capital that reduced not only the capital account deficit, but also the net investment position of the United States abroad. At the same time, he refused to support intervention in the foreign exchange market to correct overvaluation. A strong dollar then priced U.S. exports out of the international market, which led to severe deficits in the trade balance. The administration responded by pressuring various nations into bilateral imposition of nontariff barriers, which protected U.S. producers and exporters; but this approach did not halt expansion of the trade deficit. At the end of 1983, that deficit reached $69.4 billion and by the following April, the prognosis for the 1984 deficit was an estimated $110 billion (*New York Times*, March 30, 1984).

The Kennedy administration focused its initial attention on the balance of payments and charted a moderate course for fiscal policy. The Reagan administration manifested a clear preference for solving domestic problems and neglecting balance of payments deficits. Moreover, both administrations attempted to keep domestic and foreign economic areas separate. Yet when confronted with similar economic problems, the two administrations pursued different policies and priorities. What factors can account for the particular choices made by Kennedy and Reagan?

Constraints on Economic Policy

The first two factors bearing on economic policy identify market conditions as major determinants of policy. A market account of foreign economic policy claims that international market conditions explain government policy (Odell 1982). When the market continually moves against existing policy, the prediction is that a new policy will be adopted. The market will not be forced to conform to existing policy. International market conditions during the Kennedy period were influenced by U.S. initiatives to impose government control over international trade and finance markets after World War II. Advocates for the Bretton Woods system assumed that capital, trade, and currency exchange markets required periodic government regulation to correct imbalances. The purpose of Bretton Woods was to help the market work. More precisely, the system would help nations maintain equilibrium in their balance of payments as changes occurred in domestic growth, trade, capital flows, and exchange rates. By 1961, the role of the United States in the system was not compatible with new exchange market conditions (Wallich 1972). This incompatibility led to persistent balance of payments deficits, attributable to an excess supply of overvalued dollars, short-term capital outflows, a loss of official reserves, and government spending abroad. The market solution to these deficits was either to devalue or move to a more flexible exchange rate system, but these options conflicted with the reserve currency role in the system. Under these circumstances, advocates of a market account of economic policy would predict a change in the rules of the system.

By 1981 the transformation of the international system of trade and finance had established greater compatibility between the U.S. role in the system and market conditions. The dollar was no longer fixed, reserves were inconvertible, Special Drawing Rights (SDRs) were a major source of liquidity, and private banks had replaced the IMF as the main source for financing external deficits (Cohen 1981; Helleiner 1984). The Kennedy (1963-67) and Tokyo (1973-79) Rounds had eliminated many tariff and nontariff barriers to trade, yet the United States was again in balance of payments deficit. These deficits were due to a loss of reserves from a weak dollar, the outflow of direct investment capital, and a growing trade deficit brought on by the 1979 oil price increases and the Carter administration's refusal to impose import restrictions during its last two years in office. Under a floating exchange system, currency rates were largely determined by domestic economic policies and the financial communities' reactions to these policies. The market solution to 1980 balance of payments deficits was to adopt fiscal/monetary policies that would bring equilibrium to capital flows and provide incentives for export expansion.

Most of the evidence from the Kennedy period demonstrates that the administration did not change its balance of payments policies to fit new circumstances in the international market. Two distinct sets of data support this statement. First, the administration stopped the conversion of foreign-held dollars into gold while officially maintaining that the dollar was convertible at its existing rate of $35 to the ounce of gold. The Kennedy administration accomplished this shift from asset to liability financing of its deficits by issuing Roosa Bonds and by borrowing from nations who had international payments surpluses (Strange 1976). The Gold Pool, GAB, and Swap arrangements were additional measures the administration supported to forestall the normal course of devaluation. Second, the administration interrupted its traditional support for the free movement of trade and capital in order to force new market conditions to fit existing policy. Two examples of this were the government's foreign procurement policy and the IET proposal.

The Reagan administration's balance of payments policies were also not accommodated to changing conditions in the international market. Again, two related sets of data support this conclusion. First, the administration adopted fiscal and monetary policies primarily to influence domestic economic conditions. When its policy mix of budget deficits and tight money led to upward pressure on interest rates and a rapid appreciation of the dollar, the balance of payments moved in two directions. Higher interest rates resulted in destabilizing capital flows to the United States, which eroded the positive investment position of the United States abroad. The excessively high value of the dollar also crowded out exports and expanded the trade deficit. Yet the administration made no effort to modify its macroeconomic policies in response to the new market condition. Second, the administration responded to the growing trade deficit by moving toward bilateral reciprocal protectionism (Goldstein and Krasner 1984; Baldwin and Thompson 1984). A number of cases illustrate the administration's approach: nontariff barriers on Japanese fibre-optic equipment and automobile sales in the United States; subsidies on the sale of U.S. flour, butter, and cheese to Egypt; import tariffs on specialty steel from the European Economic Community; and the 1982 GATT initiative on Canadian foreign investment in the United States.

A second possible cause of economic policy—domestic market conditions—is premised on the assumption that developed nations such as the United States modify fiscal and monetary policy in response to changes in industrial productivity (Zysman 1983). While the promotion of industrial growth is a function of the market, since the passage of the Employment Act of 1946, U.S. policies have been expected to foster growth by promoting maximum employment, production, and purchasing power. Government policies can respond to the production-related costs of resources, capital, and labor, or they can attempt to influence the ability and willingness of consumers to purchase goods and services. In either case, the government can use fiscal spending and taxation and/or monetary policy to influence economic conditions.

A market account of domestic economic policy predicts that fiscal policies will change to eliminate either recessionary or stagflationary economic imbalances. Neoclassical and Keynesian economists disagree on how the government can accommodate recessions under conditions of either inflation or unemployment. There is even greater uncertainty about how the government ought to respond to stagflationary conditions since there is no reliable mechanism to eliminate both unemployment and inflation during a period of sluggishness (Baumol and Binder 1982). Yet the market perspective's validity is contingent upon the capacity of its advocates to demonstrate that changes in fiscal policy occur in response to these market conditions. Neither the kind nor effectiveness of government intervention is a central issue in applying this approach.

The Kennedy administration's tax policies are the most important area to evaluate in a test of the domestic market factor. Were these policies adopted to promote growth in production? The administration housed two opposing views on fiscal response to recession. The advocates of a classical response recommended the use of supply-side mechanisms to stimulate investment. They supported tax credits, liberalized depreciation allowances, and tax reform rather than tax cuts. This group also supported lengthening the public debt despite the pressure this would place on borrowing in the long-term market, and it was also preoccupied with inflation and balanced budgets. Kennedy accepted all of their recommendations until mid-1962. The Keynesian group, on the other hand, supported tax cuts and deficit spending to get the economy out of perennial sluggishness and into steady growth. They wanted to shorten the financing of the public debt and believed that unemployment rather than inflation was the immediate problem to resolve; after mid-1962 their tax cut prescriptions prevailed.

There is little doubt that the administration's fiscal policy response was at least partially based on market conditions. Yet a market account is unable to explain many aspects of the policies. Why, for instance, did the classical prescriptions of Dillon, the secretary of the Treasury, and Roosa, his undersecretary for monetary affairs, prevail until mid-1962 when the president finally decided to ask for a tax cut? Why did the president wait until early 1963 to submit the proposed tax legislation to Congress? Why were the administration's original fiscal policies based on promoting price stability when there was no inflation?

One might anticipate that a market account of the Reagan administration's fiscal policies is both necessary and sufficient since its chief spokespersons espoused a classical liberal tradition in which the market was assumed to have a high degree of self-regulation. Much of the administration's 1981 fiscal policy did appear to have as its goal the freeing of the market from government interference. Three of the administration's 1981 policies—tax cuts, reduced government spending in nondefense areas, and deregulation—were policy shifts involving less government intervention. But a market account cannot explain why these options were chosen rather than other methods to correct imbalances in inflation and unemployment. A market account also cannot clarify why the administration failed to modify its policies after the 1981 recession began. This new market condition, which lasted for almost two years, made it economically incomprehensible for the administration to continue its supply-side policy. In fact, the administration's unwillingness to modify its policies only deepened the recession as budget deficits became structural and high interest rates created disincentives for investment. Other factors must be considered to find a more satisfying account of economic policy.

While domestic market conditions had some significance in shaping economic policy, the remaining four factors seem to have far more explanatory capacity. The first of these factors is the distribution of power among political actors in the international system. Those who consider this approach focus on how the distribution of power and changes in it in the international system provide stimuli to and constraints on economic policy. If an issue-area approach to international power is adopted (Rosenau 1971; Keohane and Nye 1977; Mansbach and Vasquez 1981), the policies under consideration may be explained by reference to one of the international system's issue-areas: the balance of payments regime (Cohen 1982). The analytical difference between this and other issue-areas is based on a value typology wherein the acquisition of wealth is at the center of the balance of payments regime while different values lead to the formation of other regimes.[2] While each issue-area is the center of activity for different groupings of actors and stakes, the same resources may be used in several issue-areas. Furthermore, in each issue-area the stakes are not only concrete but also symbolic (Mansbach and Vasquez 1981).·In a given regime, actors will abide by the rules of the system to obtain the stakes unique to that regime. When upholding the rules will not allow the strongest actors to acquire the stakes, they will modify their behavior; and the regime will change when the behavior change of relevant actors becomes permanent (Keohane and Nye 1977). As regimes change, some stakes may be replaced by others, new actors and resources may enter the transformed regime, and the relative strengths of actors in the regime will undergo transformation.

Different balance of payments regimes were in operation under Kennedy and Reagan. Nation-states were the most significant actors under the fixed exchange regime in existence when Kennedy was president. The size of gold reserves, the convertibility of the dollar, control over liquidity creation, an increased share of world trade, profit from private capital flows, and balance of payments surpluses were concrete stakes for the United States. Symbolic stakes included the preservation of key currency status, the maintenance of the dollar's value at $35 to the ounce of gold, the preservation of confidence in the dollar, and the capacity to undertake liability financing of deficits without borrowing from the IMF.

Under the flexible exchange regime in operation during Reagan's presidency, the importance of nation-states has been lessened by the rise of private banking control over liquidity. Concrete stakes for the United States in this regime included the size of reserves, an increased share of world trade, profit from private capital flows, and balance of payments surpluses. Symbolic stakes included a dollar valued strongly on the basis of domestic economic growth, control over the use of private liquidity, appropriate government coordination of exchange rate policies, and maintenance of confidence in the dollar.

Much of the evidence from the Kennedy administration's fiscal and balance of payments policies can be explained as a violation of regime rules to preserve symbolic stakes in response to a loss of concrete stakes of the balance of payments regime. Several economic measures indicate the extent of this loss (International Monetary Fund 1972). The U.S. share in world trade had fallen from 18.7 percent in 1948 to 15 percent in 1961, while that of other industrialized nations in the Group of Ten had risen from 39 to 49.3 percent during the same period. Similarly, in 1948 the United States controlled 53 percent of the world's official reserves; in 1961 the amount fell to 30 percent. The Group of Ten's share in world reserves increased from 15.8 percent in 1948 to 46.2 percent in 1961. By June 1962 total foreign official and private short-term dollar holdings ($19.6 billion) exceeded the gold reserves of the United States (less than $16.9 billion). The trade/liquidity ratio was equally disconcerting. From 1948 through 1961, the three-year rates of increase in world trade surpassed comparable rates of growth in liquidity. Between 1958 and 1961, for instance, world trade increased by 10.6 percent while liquidity increased by only 5.5 percent. Trade and reserves were shifting to Europe.

Confronted with these developments, the Kennedy administration altered U.S. balance of payments policies and accommodated its fiscal policies to this change in the relative distribution of wealth in order to hold on to symbolic stakes rather than to regain concrete stakes immediately. In doing so, it behaved in violation of the regime's rules and thus set a course for the ultimate transformation of the regime: the administration insisted on maintaining dollar convertibility despite gold losses, and rejected devaluation of the dollar and any suggestion to reform the international liquidity system (Heller 1983; Samuelson 1983). At the request of Roosa, the administration shifted from asset to liability financing of its deficits. It resisted borrowing from the IMF and took the initiative to develop the Gold Pool, Swap arrangements, and the GAB. Moderate fiscal policies were added to these measures in order to retrieve confidence in an overabundant and overvalued dollar. The accommodation of fiscal to balance of payments policy also clarifies why the administration adopted government procurement and foreign aid policies that were harmful to domestic industrial growth. Two policies of the administration can be explained as attempts to actually regain a loss in concrete stakes: the emphasis on rapid export expansion and the IET proposal. The minimal efforts and results in both areas suggest, however, that the administration believed the preservation of symbolic stakes would help recoup concrete stakes. This approach nonetheless does not account for either the supply-side or tax cut policies.

In the same fashion, the Reagan administration's economic policies were violations of the balance of payments' regime rules. Trade protectionism, benign neglect of an overvalued dollar, and lack of macroeconomic policy coordination with other regime members are three of the clearest examples of behavior that deviated from the rules (Koromzay, Llewellyn, and Potter 1984). In contrast to the Kennedy policies, however, those of the Reagan administration obtained neither concrete nor symbolic stakes from the regime. The Reagan policies were undertaken to promote domestic wealth based on macroeconomic policies developed in isolation from international considerations. Interest rate policies of the administration are a critical area to assess in substantiating this interpretation. They were kept high because of tight monetary policies, instituted to curb inflation, and because of large budget deficits. Because the administration refused to address high interest rates, a sharp upswing in the trade deficit occurred. The administration chose protectionism rather than change in fiscal policy to accommodate the trade deficit.

The interest rate policy registered short-term gains in the balance of payments by shifting assets from the international to the domestic sector, resulting in the capital account moving out of deficit. The immediate beneficiaries of this were investors in the United States, private banks in the United States, and the U. S. government. The book value of direct investment in the United States, for example, rose from $68.4 billion in 1980 to $101.8 billion at the end of 1982. United States direct investments abroad during the same period rose by only $5.9 billion. Claims on foreigners by U. S. banks increased from $203.9 billion to $402.3 billion between 1980 and 1982, while bank liabilities to foreigners increased by only $33.4 billion. United States government assets abroad fell from $13 billion to $6 billion during the period (Reagan 1984). Increased direct investment in the United States was a short-term gain offset by loss of concrete stakes as the net investment position of the United States deteriorated, moving the country toward net debtor status internationally (*New York Times*, February 6, 1984, p. 34).

While an international power approach explains more about Kennedy's than Reagan's economic policies, neither administration's approach can be fully understood by the factors considered thus far. A fourth factor that has additional explanatory power is that domestic politics determines economic policy. Of all the societal forces potentially useful in explaining policy choices, interest groups are of particular concern in the field of economic policy. A weak/strong executive model (Krasner 1978) may be useful in examining the relationship between interest groups and economic policy. This model has been used to demonstrate that many interest groups, in conjunction with the legislature, have greater control over fiscal and trade policy than over international monetary policy, thereby weakening the executive in these two areas. On the other hand, strong executive control over international monetary policy would suggest that both the Kennedy administration's reluctance to address the capital account deficits and the gains in the capital account during Reagan's presidency could not be explained by interest group influence on the executive branch.

Two qualifications must be placed on this approach. With the development of modern bureaucracies in industrialized states, executive departments and agencies have increased their autonomy vis-à-vis the central executive. This change has been accompanied by greater executive autonomy from the legislature in the determination of economic policy.[3] These changes have led interest groups away from the legislature and to the executive bureaucracy. This would suggest that more interaction between executive departments/agencies and interest groups would not only occur in the areas of fiscal, trade, and international monetary policy, but that the interactions in this decentralized executive would be of an elite rather than pluralist nature. We know there are interest groups actively involved in fiscal and trade issues; I am now suggesting they may be an elite group as they move toward interactions with the executive. But are there elites from the private sector for whom the international monetary issue-area is salient, or are the consequences of such decisions so widely dispersed within society (Krasner 1978) that interests do not mobilize around the issue? This leads to a second modification, one pertinent to the strong executive aspect of the model. Commercial and investment banks as well as other foreign lenders and investors have always closely watched developments in the international monetary issue-area since the strength of the dollar and confidence in it influence this group's ability to make a profit. The domestication of international politics (Hanreider 1978) and the penetration of political and economic systems under conditions of interdependence (Rosenau 1971) not only reinforce the salience of this issue-area for banking groups, but may also open up the area to other societal groups. It may be instructive to consider the participation of commercial and investment banks in a banking complex analogous to the more familiar military-industrial complex. Other members of the banking complex could include elites in the Federal Reserve, Treasury Department, and Congress. The existence of such a complex would suggest that it, rather than a strong executive, determines international monetary policy.

The most explicit evidence from the Kennedy period that members of the executive branch participated in a banking complex is that the president, Dillon, and Roosa shared the conservative financial thinking of Wall Street investors and New York bankers. According to Dillon:

> That's why he [Kennedy] wanted me, because he said that there weren't any Democrats that the financial community both at home and abroad would trust. . . . He was rather conservative financially . . . and he wanted someone that would work to save

the dollar. The president told me when he was appointing me also that he was going to appoint very liberal people to the Council and try to build them up a bit so that he could tell his Democratic friends, "Look what I've done here. I haven't sold out to the Wall Street business people entirely." But at the same time he told me that whenever there was a real difference of opinion he would always follow the advice of the Treasury. And he always did because our positions were very similar to his own thinking. (Dillon 1983, pp. 10-12)

Paul Samuelson, Kennedy's informal economic adviser, has said of Roosa:

I felt that Roosa was going to go back to the New York financial community and he was thinking in terms of New York financial community ideology and belief. (Samuelson 1983, p. 26)

The impact of the banking community on the thinking of three officials primarily responsible for the balance of payments policies weakened the executive branch's insulation from interest group influence. Further research is necessary to determine the extent to which the sharing of common beliefs precluded the need of banking to have more formal methods of influencing the White House, Treasury, and Federal Reserve (Aronson 1977; Sampson 1982; Newton 1983). The banking complex approach can account for the administration's support for the fixed exchange rate system and the preservation of the reserve currency status of the dollar (Lanyi 1969). It also explains the administration's opposition to devaluation and reluctance to address the capital account deficits. However, a banking complex cannot explain the IET proposal. In the arena of fiscal policy, the banking complex supported balanced budgets, price stability, and supply-side mechanisms to deal with recession. The president proposed tax cuts in the spring of 1962 after the stock market decline in late May and when he feared a Kennedy recession (Samuelson 1983; Miroff 1976). In domestic policy, banking interests paralleled the perceptions of Kennedy regarding the public mood and congressional views. While the administration increased its efforts to expand exports and acquired greater authority over trade with the passage of the Trade Expansion Act, there is little evidence to suggest that during the Kennedy period trade groups shifted their lobbying efforts to the executive.

The Reagan administration's failure to respond to an overvalued dollar and high interest rates can also be seen as satisfying the interests of banking. Commercial banks were the major beneficiaries of this "do-nothing" policy in that increased demand for the dollar and the willingness of surplus nations to invest in the United States increased the capacity of banks to provide liquidity to nations in balance of payments deficit. The participation of the administration in a banking complex can be identified in activities it initiated regarding third world debts, the IMF, the GAB, and structural deficits. The temporary solutions to the debt problems of Mexico and Argentina certainly support a banking complex explanation. In August 1982 Mexico declared it was unable to make $20 billion in principal repayments due on government debt through the end of 1984. The Reagan administration arranged a $1 billion credit for the Mexican purchase of U. S. agricultural products and prepaid Mexico $1 billion for future crude oil purchases so that it could continue payment on its commercial bank debts (Lissakers 1983). During the Argentinian debt crisis of March 1984, Regan, Beryl Sprinkel, his undersecretary for monetary affairs, and other members of the administration facilitated negotiation of a $500 million loan to Argentina so that U. S. banks would not have to deduct $300 million from their earnings on these loans. The Treasury even considered ways to get around the federal laws so that the loans would not have to be classified as nonperforming (*New York Times,* March 29 and 31, 1984). Since the majority of commercial bank loans to the third world are set at a variable interest rate, the steep rise in interest rates has widened commercial bank profits from these loans.

The emerging pattern of a banking complex in the debt case is heightened by the Reagan administration's attempts to sustain private control over liquidity by expanding the secondary and supportive role of the IMF and the GAB. In November 1983 the administration successfully overcame congressional resistance to an increase in IMF quotas that required an $8.4 billion quota increase from the United States. The administration also agreed to make an additional $2.6 billion in credits available to the GAB in 1983 so that it could lend to a greater number of nations whose financial problems threatened the preservation of the existing international monetary system.

Finally, although the banking complex reacted favorably to Reagan's initial fiscal policies, its concern over the dampening effect of structural deficits on the capital market led to a stock market decline in February 1984. In light of the financial community's actions, both Paul Volcker, chairman of the Federal Reserve, and Treasury Secretary Regan encouraged the administration to take a more accommodative approach to the deficits (*New York Times,* February 8, 1984, pp. 1, 34 and May 4, 1984, pp. 34-35).

In contrast to the Kennedy period, the Reagan administration's trade policy suggests that special interests have penetrated an executive that has expanded authority over trade issues. Bilateral reciprocal protectionism has favored the interests of specific industries, such as steel and automobiles. This observation suggests that the increased authority of the executive over trade, established by the Kennedy-sponsored trade legislation of 1962, also modifies the utility of a weak executive model in the trade issue-area.

A fifth approach argues that the use of government policy-making structures and processes by members of the executive branch is a significant determinant of economic policy (Allison 1971). Policy choices can be made by using rational, bureaucratic, or organizational methods. At a minimum, the rational components of decision-making include recognition of a problem, identification and ranking of objectives, an attempt to retrieve and organize pertinent information from diverse sources, determination of possible alternative courses of action, and a cost-effective assessment of these alternatives on the basis of available information.

A bureaucratic politics model of decision-making explains policy choice by reference to the use of bargaining power among top decision-makers inside the executive branch. The choices made result from the skill with which bargainers use their positions and the resources at their disposal to get what they want. Their goals are immediately related to their own personal interests rather than to those of the organization for which they work.

Finally, an organizational approach emphasizes the extent to which policy is shaped by the machinery and procedures of the executive branch, the main determinants of policy being the interests and standard operating procedures (SOPs) of various components. Departments and agencies want to safeguard their budgetary base and promote policies that allow them to maintain the programs they have devised to fulfill their responsibilities.

The evidence refutes the proposition that the Kennedy and Reagan administrations adopted a rational approach to decision-making on either foreign or domestic economic policy. They both kept domestic and foreign economic objectives and conditions separate. Under Kennedy, the CEA was the only agency within the executive branch that took a rational approach to both balance of payments and fiscal objectives and options. Yet the CEA failed to carry the day because it lacked skill in bargaining with other members of the administration. The rest of the Kennedy executive considered a narrow range of separate options on both the domestic and international fronts and, in defending the balance of payments as a top priority, often had to manipulate information about export growth. Advocates of alternate approaches were routinely defeated.

No one in the Reagan administration behaved like the Kennedy CEA. The balance of payments policy was constructed without regard for conditions outside the United States (Cohen 1982). The administration was undaunted in the face of negative reactions to its trade and interest rates policies offered at annual summit meetings of the heads of state of industrialized nations in Versailles (1982), Williamsburg (1983), and London (1984). The lack of a rational approach to fiscal policy was acknowledged by one of the chief architects of the administration's supply-side approach to fiscal policy, David Stockman, Reagan's director of OMB. According to Stockman, "The whole thing is premised on faith . . . on a belief about how the world works" (Greider 1981, p. 29).

At the same time, the Kennedy and Reagan periods are replete with examples where bargaining skills played an important role in determining economic policy. Since President Kennedy was actively involved in economic policy-making, members of the administration used their positions and resources to win his support for their recommendations. The advocates of balance of payments priorities prevailed in getting their prescriptions adopted, in part because they had superior bargaining skills. The account of Dillon offered by Carl Kaysen, a member of the National Security Council, is particularly revealing in this regard:

> Dillon left little trace of what he did. Dillon didn't send and receive cables. He operated by phone, talked to finance ministers and heads of European central banks on the phone, had his own switchboard and his own operator. Nobody had an independent record of what he was doing. Dillon would come in and say, Mr.

President, the German finance minister says, head of the German
central bank says. . . . There was never a cable. There were no
cabled instructions and so on. . . . Dillon had it all in his vest
pocket. (Kaysen 1983, pp. 19-20)

Roosa used a similar "Kissinger" bargaining style (Tobin 1984, p. 5)
in obtaining Kennedy's support for liability financing of the deficits,
the IET, and orthodox methods of debt management. Secretary of
Defense Robert McNamara used his direct access to the president to
get Kennedy's support for a procurement program and military offset
agreements that allowed defense spending to remain at current levels
while reducing its contribution to the external deficits. Keynesians in
the council admitted they lacked skill in getting their views accepted
by the president (Gordon 1961; Pechman 1964). Ultimately, the
president endorsed the tax cuts out of fear of a Kennedy recession,
not because the council's bargaining skills improved.

A similar pattern emerges within the Reagan administration in
the establishment of fiscal policy as a priority over balance of
payments although, in contrast to Kennedy, Reagan's compliant,
cooperative, and disengaged approach to economic policy-making
eliminated his impact on outcomes (Barber 1981). In the early
months of the administration, Stockman outmaneuvered Regan as
the administration's chief economic architect (Kegley and Wittkopf
1982, p. 346). Despite Stockman's subsequent public admission of
doubt about the administration's economic program, his influence
over policy, especially the budget deficits, continued to prevail. The
Reagan council was similar to Kennedy's in that the former's members also lacked skill in effectively lobbying for their recommendations. In early 1984 Feldstein, chairman of the CEA, once again
publicly differed with Stockman's refusal to take action on the
deficits. The administration finally submitted a "down payment"
plan to Congress only after Feldstein, who later resigned, was joined
by Regan and Volcker in publicly expressing concern about the
deficits.

One of the most salient, but rare pieces of evidence that organizational factors influenced economic policy during the Kennedy
period was the administration's position on government procurement. The Defense Department pushed for a high price differential
that would allow it to procure in the domestic market and still reduce

the impact of defense spending on the external deficits. The Treasury Department also supported a high price differential to attain its responsibility for eliminating the deficits. The CEA, however, opposed this policy on grounds that it had an adverse impact on the domestic economy. Lack of consensus within the administration on this budgetary issue was resolved by letting departments adopt their own programs on procurement. In general, however, while organizational factors reinforced emerging policies, the active role of the president in economic policy-making lessened organizational constraints on economic policy.

The Reagan administration's members appear to have become captives of their departments to a greater extent than Kennedy's team (Kegley and Wittkopf 1982, p. 325). Moreover, the public display of internal, organizationally based conflict within Reagan's administration was exceptional. Sharp divisions within the administration were exemplified, for instance, in the Japanese automobile case where Reagan's secretaries of transportation and commerce pressed for trade restraints, while his economic and budget advisers opposed the voluntary quotas as a violation of deregulation (Winham and Kabashima 1982, p. 115). Much of the administration's bilateral and reciprocal approach to trade protectionism can be accounted for by an organizational approach to trade policy. A similar pattern emerges between the Treasury Department and private banking in the administration's approach to the international debt crisis.

The sixth and final explanation of policy resides in the beliefs and cognitive processes of policy-makers (Steinbruner 1974; Odell 1982). The core idea in this account of policy is that it is impossible to understand the policy recommendations of officials without reference to their beliefs. Oftentimes, when policy-makers are confronted with complex and uncertain situations, their recommendations tend to be more congruent with previously acquired beliefs than with rational, organizational, or bureaucratic factors.

Cognitive theory identifies when and how beliefs can influence policy. Individuals frequently resolve uncertain, complex situations subjectively. Either they act on strong, previously adopted beliefs or impose clear, categorical judgments rather than probabilistic ones on such situations. Policy-makers act to preserve ill-founded or contradictory beliefs already stored in their way of thinking so that consistency and stability can be upheld in their thought processes.

Sometimes decision-makers are forced to deny, isolate, or hide information and trade-offs in order to continue supporting policies that fit their beliefs rather than existing conditions. Cognitive processes involve a constrained learning approach to information wherein data are selectively gathered or interpreted to fit existing beliefs.

While several tenets of cognitive process theory are helpful in accounting for the economic policy recommendations of the Kennedy and Reagan administrations, two are particularly applicable. A cognitive account, first of all, explains policies that keep related economic conditions separate. When the relationship between domestic and foreign economic conditions is unclear, policy-makers may resolve the uncertainty by keeping the two areas apart and denying that the two are related. In isolating each area from the other, prescribers can more easily advance their own beliefs, usually favoring one area over the other. The simultaneous presence of recession and balance of payments in 1961 and stagflation and external deficits in 1981 provided ideal conditions for cognitive processes to prevail in economic policy-making. Keynesian, neoclassical, and supply-side economic theory did not provide clear prescriptions on how such simultaneous conditions could be solved under the prevailing balance of payments regimes. One possible solution in 1961 was to devalue. While this would be consistent with the domestic market need for industrial recovery and growth, devaluation would jeopardize the key currency status of the dollar. Dillon and Roosa were preoccupied with the preservation of United States control over the existing international monetary system. They therefore rejected the option of devaluation and instead advocated a series of ad hoc liability financing measures, capital controls, and a change in government procurement policy. Some of these measures, the Roosa Bonds and the IET, actually deterred capital from coming to the United States for investment purposes. Yet Dillon and Roosa isolated these effects on the domestic economy and advocated a separate set of supply-side options for recovery: the investment tax credit and the liberalization of depreciation allowances.

The Reagan administration used the separation mechanism to maintain a reverse set of priorities. When confronted with stagflation and external deficits in 1981, the administration recommended a radical fiscal program of tax and nondefense spending cuts coupled with monetary restraint. The administration's objective was to curb inflation and stimulate investment in productivity. At the same time, it took a "do-nothing" approach to the external deficits, arguing that market forces would correct the imbalance. When interest rates rose, inflation declined and massive foreign capital flowed into the United States. But the dollar became overvalued, the trade deficit widened, and the overseas investment position of the United States declined. The administration continued to hold that high interest rates had no harmful effect on the balance of payments. It made a series of bilateral protectionist moves to deal with the trade deficit, thereby isolating the trade issue from fiscal policy.

A second tenet of cognitive theory provides a plausible explanation of how policy-makers confront situations where goals cannot be simultaneously and successfully pursued. Under these circumstances, decision-makers can resolve the need to make a trade-off between goals by denying that a trade-off must or has been made. They can thus continue to hold previously acquired beliefs that are not compatible. The result is a policy that has no chance of accomplishing both goals but is purported to be able to do just that. President Kennedy claimed that trade expansion could simultaneously move the country out of recession and reduce the balance of payments deficit. Yet export increases have always been accompanied by increases in imports; the 1961 deficits were in the capital account, and the importance of the trade sector for domestic industrial growth had not been clearly established. The president nonetheless refused to acknowledge that choices had to be and indeed actually were made. In a similar vein, the Kennedy administration eventually advocated the IET but denied this was a violation of traditional U.S. support for the free movement of capital. Each of these instances can be understood by realizing that the president refused to give up two irreconcilable beliefs: that free trade and capital movements were good for the United States' pursuit of wealth and that the United States should continue its role in the Bretton Woods system.

The cognitive resolution of trade-off situations is equally applicable to the Reagan administration's supply-side fiscal policies. The administration, most insistently Stockman, held the belief that fiscal policies that were grounded in supply-side theory could simultaneously reduce inflation and unemployment, promote industrial growth, and allow the government to balance its budget. Yet the package of tax cuts and reduced government spending on discretionary and entitlement programs, coupled with monetary restraint, were proposed primarily to reduce inflation and promote deregulation. The administration refused to acknowledge either that this choice had been made or had to be made. It was thereby able to preserve consistency between two dominant beliefs generally shared within the administration: faith in the market's ability to regulate itself and the assumption that government intervention was the sole cause of economic problems.

Conclusion

The main economic policy actions taken by the Kennedy administration included a preference for solving the balance of payments problem through trade expansion, reduced government overseas spending on defense and foreign aid, liability financing of the external deficits, the IET, and moderate fiscal policies that eventually included tax cuts. The Reagan administration's economic priorities and policies included a preference for resolving domestic economic problems in isolation from international considerations, reduced government influence through cuts in taxes and nondefense spending, deregulation, support for monetary restraint, neglect of the balance of payments deficits, and adoption of bilateral trade protectionism. While both administrations adopted these distinctly different approaches to a common set of economic problems, their choices were determined by similar factors. In descending order of importance, these were unsubstantiated beliefs, bargaining skills, and instability in the economic basis of international power. While an elite banking complex emerges as potentially critical, further research is required before attributing greater significance to this factor. The rank ordering of these three factors in this manner fits the best explanation of the major fiscal and balance of payments choices made by Kennedy and Reagan. It also accounts for the way in which both administrations kept domestic and international economic policies separate.

The Kennedy and Reagan administrations kept fiscal and balance of payments policies separate, but each established different priorities because each administration housed unique sets of unfounded beliefs. President Kennedy held two irreconcilable beliefs that he refused to modify: free trade and capital movements were beneficial for the promotion of U.S. wealth, and the United States could and should continue its role as the key currency in the Bretton Woods regime to promote its international wealth and power. The dominant beliefs in the Reagan administration were that the market was automatically self-adjusting and that the government's entry into the market was the sole cause for economic problems.

Bargaining skills were a critical intervening factor in determining how both administrations upheld their beliefs in setting economic priorities and policy content. Kennedy's involvement and commitment to beliefs determined whose bargaining skills would have the greatest chance of success in lobbying for policies. The president's involvement heightened the importance of Dillon and Roosa in the Treasury Department since his first priority was to solve the external deficits. The fact that Dillon and Roosa were better bargainers than other members of the administration facilitated the accommodation of fiscal policies to international priorities. Under Reagan, the bargaining skills of his appointees were even more important since the president detached himself from decision-making. The rigidity with which the administration refused to alter its supply-side fiscal policies, despite public urging from less influential members of the administration, attested to the enduring skills of Stockman in the bargaining process. Because the president distanced himself from the process, organizational infighting abounded within the administration and, especially in trade, had a greater impact on policy than during the Kennedy period.

The economic policies of Kennedy and Reagan were established under conditions of instability in the economic basis of international power. The loss of international concrete stakes prompted Kennedy to endorse balance of payments policies to hold onto the regime's symbolic stakes, the possession of which would allow the president to maintain his belief that the United States could continue its role in the Bretton Woods system. Similarly, the Reagan administration's faith in the market led it to concentrate on regaining domestic wealth and adopting an insular approach to the balance of payments regime. While instability in the domestic economy and the balance of payments regime forced both presidents to act, the nature of instability in 1961 and 1981 could not alone explain how each administration responded. In fact, because both administrations protected previously acquired beliefs, a greater degree of international economic instability occurred during both periods: Kennedy's approach hastened the erosion of the fixed exchange rate system, and Reagan's response created disruptive capital movements and trade distortions.

These findings allow us to eliminate a number of previously potential factors as determinants of economic policy. International and domestic market conditions are not helpful in explaining the policy choices of either administration. While market conditions provided occasions that necessitated policy change, the actions taken by both administrations were not based on conditions in the market. The explanation for why this was so can be found in the processes whereby both administrations chose their respective policies. Since bureaucratic, cognitive, and organizational forces preempted a rational approach to policy-making, information about economic conditions was either eliminated or distorted in an effort to win support for recommendations. Results from the two cases suggest, furthermore, that societal forces, other than elites, have little explanatory power in the analysis of economic policy.

One final observation ought to be made regarding elite groups. Both administrations exhibited a significant amount of autonomy vis-à-vis Congress in the determination of economic policy. The shift in economic policy-making authority from the legislature to the executive, compounded by the bureaucracy's importance in policy processes, enhanced the opportunity for elite groups to have their interests satisfied through executive action. In both administrations, the banking complex appears to have consistently benefited from the fiscal and international monetary policies advocated by the executive. While additional research is needed on the existence and significance of this complex, the policies of both Kennedy and Reagan demonstrate a sufficient amount of potential in this area to warrant further analysis of relations between banking, the Treasury, and the Federal Reserve.

Notes

1. The term "factor" refers both to specific determinants at the individual, unit, and systemic levels of analysis and to less quantifiable conditions considered by various theories and approaches that analyze these levels. I have chosen to use this term since the analysis that follows includes elements from both approaches.

2. Mansbach and Vasquez (1981, pp. 36-57) have provided a thorough discussion of the development of issue typologies and the current analytical and empirical

problems related to the use of value-based typologies. My intent in using a value typology has been to draw from various theoretical developments those elements that, taken together, appear to be useful in accounting for policy change in one issue-area during two periods. In the future, a more inclusive typology can be established to treat international power. The need for a more comprehensive approach is evident even in the periods under consideration. Clearly, a defense regime issue-area based on security is required to account for the defense spending policies of the Reagan administration and how these policies were directed toward the security and/or wealth dimensions of international power.

3. More research must be undertaken to determine the extent to which executive autonomy in fiscal policy supports this statement. Congressional efforts since 1974 to gain control over the budget may be a major limit on the general trend toward executive autonomy.

Bibliography

Allison, Graham T. 1971. *Essence of Decision.* Boston: Little, Brown.

Aronson, Jonathan D. 1977. *Money and Power.* Beverly Hills: Sage.

Baldwin, Robert and T. Scott Thompson. 1984. "Responding to Trade-Distorting Policies of Other Countries." *American Economic Review* 70 (May), pp.271-76

Barber, James. D. 1981. "Reagan's Sheer Personal Likability Faces its Sternest Test." *Washington Post,* January 20, p. 8.

Baumol, William and Alan S. Blinder. 1982. *Economics.* New York: Harcourt Brace Jovanovich.

Brownstein, Ronald and Nina Easton. 1983. *Reagan's Ruling Class.* New York: Pantheon.

Calleo, David P. 1982. *The Imperious Economy.* Cambridge: Harvard University Press.

Cohen, Benjamin J. 1983. "An Explosion in the Kitchen? Economic Relations with Other Industrial States." In *Eagle Defiant,* ed. Kenneth Oye, Robert Lieber, and Donald Rothchild, pp. 105-30. Boston: Little, Brown.

——————————. 1982. "Balance-of-Payments Financing: Evolution of a Regime." *International Organization* 36 (Spring), pp. 457-78.

——————————. 1981. *Banks and the Balance of Payments.* Montclair: Allanheld, Osmun.

Cohen, Stephen and Ronald I. Meltzer. 1982. *United States International Economic Policy in Action: Diversity of Decision Making.* New York: Praeger.

Dillon, C. Douglas. 1983. Interview with the author. New York, July 18.

Goldstein, Judith and Stephen Krasner. 1984. "Unfair Trade Practices: The Case for a Differential Response." *American Economic Review* 70 (May), pp. 282-87.

Gordon, Kermit. 1961. *Papers* (Tobin to Heller and Gordon, February 7, 1961). John F. Kennedy Library, Boston.

Gowa, Joanne. 1983. *Closing the Gold Window.* Ithaca: Cornell University Press.

Greider, William. 1981. "The Education of David Stockman." *Atlantic Monthly* (December), pp. 27-54.

Hanreider, Wolfram. 1978. "Dissolving International Politics: Reflections on the Nation-State." *American Political Science Review* 72 (December), pp. 1276-87.

Helleiner, G.K. 1984. "An Agenda for a New Bretton Woods." *World Policy Journal* 1 (Winter), pp. 361-76.

Heller, Walter. 1983. Interview with the author. Washington, D.C., August 25.
—————————————————. 1966. *New Dimensions of Political Economy*. Cambridge: Harvard University Press.
International Monetary Fund. 1972-1984. *International Financial Statistics*. Washington, D.C.: International Monetary Fund.
Johnson, Lyndon B. 1964. *Economic Report of the President*. Washington, D.C.: Government Printing Office.
Katzenstein, Peter J., ed. 1978. *Between Power and Plenty*. Madison: University of Wisconsin Press.
Kaysen, Carl. 1983. Interview with the author. Cambridge, July 21.
Kegley, Charles and Eugene Wittkopf. 1982. *American Foreign Policy: Pattern and Process*. New York: St. Martin's Press.
Kennedy, John F. 1961-1963. *Public Papers of the President of the United States*. Washington, D.C.: Government Printing Office.
Keohane, Robert and Joseph Nye. 1977. *Power and Interdependence*. Boston: Little, Brown.
Koromzay, Val, John Llewellyn, and Stephen Potter. 1984. "Exchange Rates and Policy Choices: Some Lessons from Interdependence in a Multilateral Perspective." *American Economic Review* 70 (May), pp. 311-15.
Krasner, Stephen. 1978. "United States Commercial and Monetary Policy: Unravelling the Paradox of External Strength and Internal Weakness." In *Power and Plenty*, ed. Peter Katzenstein, pp. 51-88. Madison: University of Wisconsin Press.
Lanyi, Anthony. 1969. *The Case for Floating Exchange Rates Reconsidered*. Princeton: Princeton University Press.
Lissakers, Karin. 1983. "Dateline Wall Street: Faustian Finance." *Foreign Policy* 51 (Summer), pp. 160-73.
Mansbach, Richard and John Vasquez. 1981. *In Search of Theory*. New York: Columbia University Press.
Miroff, Bruce. 1976. *Pragmatic Illusions*. New York: McKay.
Newton, Maxwell. 1983. *The Fed*. New York: Times Books.
Odell, John S. 1982. *U.S. International Monetary Policy*. Princeton: Princeton University Press.
Pechman, Joseph. 1964. *Interviews with the Council of Economic Advisers* (Tobin note #5). John F. Kennedy Library, Boston.
Reagan, Ronald. 1984. *Economic Report of the President*. Washington, D.C.: Government Printing Office.
Roosa, Robert. 1983. Interview with the author. New York, July 19.
Rosenau, James. 1971. *The Scientific Study of Foreign Policy*. New York: Free Press.
Sampson, Anthony. 1982. *The Money Lenders*. New York: Viking.
Samuelson, Paul A. 1983. Interview with the author. Cambridge, July 20.
Steinbruner, John D. 1974. *The Cybernetic Theory of Decision*. Princeton: Princeton University Press.
Strange, Susan. 1976. *International Monetary Relations*. New York: Oxford University Press.
Tobin, James. 1984. Interview with the author. New Haven, March 21.
United States Congress. 1984. *Economic Indicators*. Washington, D.C.: U.S. Congress, Joint Economic Committee, May.
United States Department of the Treasury. 1961-1969. *Balance of Payments Files*. Unpublished.

Wallich, Henry C. 1972. "The Monetary Crisis of 1971—The Lessons to be Learned." Per Jacobsson Lectures. Washington, D.C.: Per Jacobsson Foundation.

Winham, Gilbert R. and Ikuo Kabashima. 1981. "The Politics of U.S.-Japanese Auto Trade." In *Coping with U.S.-Japanese Economic Conflicts*, ed. I.M. Destler and Hideo Sato, pp. 73-120. Lexington: D.C. Heath.

Zysman, John. 1983. *Governments, Markets, and Growth*. Ithaca: Cornell University Press.

9

The Political Economy of U. S. Protectionism

ROBERT THOMAS KUDRLE

No U.S. public policy has received more scrutiny from both economists and political scientists over as long a period as has the tariff. The concern continues today, with both groups presenting new theoretical and empirical findings every year. Yet the literature is remarkably disjointed. In his recent study "The Political Economy of Protectionism" (1982), written from the microeconomist's public choice perspective, Robert Baldwin cites only one work in political science. And in a discussion of U.S. foreign economic policy-making intended to cast a particularly wide theoretical net, McGowan and Walker (1981) fail even to mention the public choice approach to the interpretation of such policies.

This chapter tries to fill a void by comparing three different approaches to thinking about protection in the United States: realism, conventional political science, and public choice. I present a different trinity from the one used by Gilpin (1975) and the somewhat parallel set used by Krasner (1979); I substitute the approach most favored by economists for a Marxist or radical-left approach. The writer is both too unfamiliar with and insufficiently sympathetic toward the various schools of Marxist and related thought to do justice to their contributions. On the other hand, I am convinced that public choice cannot be ignored; it dominates the conventional approaches to interest group politics, and those who would attack pluralism should avoid dead horses and direct their fire at public choice instead.

Trade Protection in the United States

In this discussion "protection" will take a simple meaning: the official manipulation of the flow of imports, so that the volume of competing domestic production is higher than it would be otherwise. While the tariff is the most familiar instrument of protection, others have become more prominent in the United States and elsewhere as tariff rates have declined and as flexible exchange rates have made relative international prices more volatile. These other devices include import quotas, "voluntary" restrictions visited upon foreign exporters under threat of something worse, and a host of other discriminatory policies.

The Purposes of Protection

Motivations or explicit arguments for protection (and the two may be quite different in actual situations) fall into three main categories. *Distributional* motivations include the protection of the livelihoods of specific industries or a change in the factor distribution of income (say, from capital to labor). *National economic* motivations include the revenue tariff designed mainly to finance government operations, the bargaining tariff that is introduced or maintained to win concessions from others, and the optimum tariff, where the country is important enough to affect the prices at which it buys and sells. *National political* motivations include the protection of strategic industries and the use of protection to maximize gain from international trade relative to other nations.

Of all of these arguments, only the optimum tariff is generally recognized by economists as a first-best policy in the absence of strategic considerations. (For further discussion, see Lindert and Kindleberger 1982, Ch. 7.)

The Explanandum

The theoretical perspectives that follow will be evaluated by how well they illuminate the history of protection in the United States.

Until the last few years, trade protection meant almost exclusively tariff protection. Figure 9.1 shows the history of the U.S. tariff

Figure 9.1   Average Import Duties, United States, 1792-1978

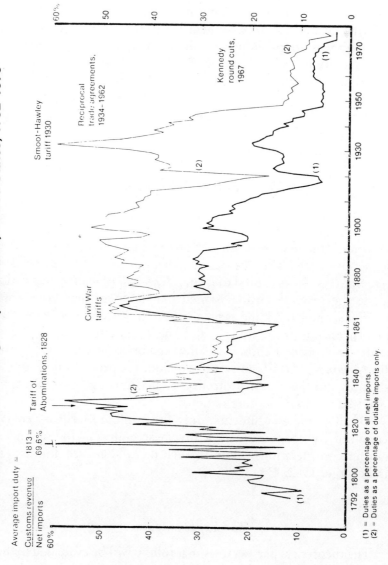

Average import duty =

$\dfrac{\text{Customs revenue}}{\text{Net imports}}$ 1813 = 69.6%

(1) = Duties as a percentage of all net imports.
(2) = Duties as a percentage of dutiable imports only.

Source: Kindleberger and Lindert 1982, p. 232.

from the founding of the republic until 1978. During the entire nineteenth century, tariffs were generally held at a moderately high level, which was viewed by many as a stimulus to industrial development and as a major source of federal revenue. Protectionist forces, mainly in the usually dominant Republican Party, maintained this "American System" at a quite stable level from the Civil War until the election of Woodrow Wilson, by which time the tariff's revenue function had ceased to be important. Wilson sponsored the Underwood Tariff that lowered the level of protection dramatically, but in 1922 tariffs were increased again under the Republicans. Herbert Hoover campaigned in 1928 on a platform of increased agricultural protection, and the special session of Congress he called in 1929 became an occasion for a drastic upward revision: the Smoot-Hawley Tariff. So many duties were set at a prohibitive level that the import of manufactures virtually ceased. In each tariff revision, the content of the "free list"—those items not subject to tariff protection—also changed.

The Smoot-Hawley Tariff triggered a fusillade of tariff increases around the world. Subsequently, the drastic reductions in world trade prompted the Roosevelt administration to begin the reciprocal trade initiatives. Eighteen treaties were negotiated between 1934 and 1945, and they were widely credited with reviving world trade (Lake 1983, p.538).

Following the war, the multilateral forum of the General Agreement on Tariffs and Trade (GATT) replaced the bilateral negotiations of the depression. After seven "rounds" under the GATT, the average U.S. tariff by 1981 had declined to 3 percent on all imports and 5 percent on dutiable imports (*Statistical Abstract of the United States 1982-83*, p. 844).

From the 1970s onwards, the principal protectionist barriers have been nontariff barriers. These include multilateral barriers against textiles, quotas against foreign steel, and voluntary restraints on Japanese automobiles. Experts in the mid-1980s disagree about whether net protectionism is rising or if the United States was holding its own as an open economy; few claim that it is liberalizing (Lipson 1982, p. 439).

The Statist Perspective

Actors and Preferences

The statist (or realist or mercantilist) perspective on international economic policy commands the sympathetic understanding of many international relations scholars because its form parallels that of national security policy. In Stephen Krasner's explanation, the statist model assumes that government leaders act with some degree of autonomy to pursue their conception of the national interest. In discussions of foreign economic policy in general and trade policy in particular, the state commands nearly exclusive attention, pursuing its objectives subject to both external and internal constraints.

The two statist models of U.S. tariff policy explored in this section attempt to interpret why the United States had high average tariffs during certain historical periods and lower ones at others. No attempt is made to explain the structure of protection during any period. In "State Power and the Structure of International Trade" (1976), Krasner suggests four unordered national objectives for U.S. foreign economic policy: aggregate national income, social stability, political power, and economic growth. In his recent model of the international economic structure from a statist perspective, David Lake suggests that nations "in descending order . . . maximize their relative gains from trade, economic security, and absolute gains from trade" (1984, p. 13). In general, realism posits a pursuit of political power for its own sake—at least in the short run—as a dominant national objective. (For further discussion, see Gilpin 1977, p. 22; Bergsten, Horst, and Moran 1978, p. 324; and Keohane 1980.)

Interest Aggregation and Policy Formulation

The statist literature frequently gives a good sense of what degree of latitude was allowed to national decision-makers *ex post*, but it usually fails to explain or predict very well why the degree of discretion varies by policy because other actors are typically only "extras" in the drama of state action. Realist writings are replete with references to "powerful private interests" (Krasner 1977, p. 170) and governments "constrained by domestic partisanship" (Lake 1983, p. 535), but interests are seldom treated in detail.[1] When Krasner comes closest to systematically discussing domestic political forces, he cites mainly the conventional political science literature (1979, pp. 85-86: 1976, p. 342). Overall, one must echo Lake's self-critical conclusion that structural arguments such as his lack "a conception of process" (1983, p. 539).

The State and the International System

Realist arguments about protection necessarily treat the state in its international context. Two major attempts have been made to develop such models; I will sketch them briefly, stressing their relevance for understanding U.S. trade policy.

Krasner (1976) relates his model to each posited state objective. He concedes that static national income will generally be maximized for states of all sizes and levels of income by the absence of protection,[2] but claims that the social instability allegedly resulting from openness will differentially affect states. Those, usually smaller, states with a larger foreign trade sector will incur more risk from openness because of the greater volatility of the international than the domestic economy. Less developed countries will suffer differentially because of relative factor immobility. He offers no evidence to demonstrate either proposition.

Political power is differentially enhanced by openness for large states, Krasner argues, because of their usually smaller economic costs of closure. This claim, based on Hirschman's research (1945), underlies the preference of large states for an open system. Large states are thus in a better position to threaten closure to others for either economic or noneconomic reasons.

While both large and small states are assumed to favor openness for growth, Krasner claims· that the relation between economic growth and openness for medium-sized states is poorly understood. He suggests that such states might grow more rapidly with a protectionist regime. Much evidence before Krasner wrote, however, and even more since suggests that openness is a correlate of high economic growth for states of widely varying size.

On the basis of these assumptions (two of which are very weak, in my view), Krasner concludes that certain configurations of states are more likely to be associated with an open world economy than are others. He suggests, for example, that a group of small developed states are likely to find openness congenial (on the proviso that some collective goods issues such as a stable monetary regime can be overcome), while a few large but unequally developed states are not likely to establish openness. Where one state dominates the others economically in terms of both size and level of development, one has the classic "hegemonic" case. Small states will follow the leader on the basis of their self-interest, and medium-sized states will be subject to the pressures of the hegemon.

The model's theoretical weaknesses are matched by problems of application. Krasner subjects it to a test of the international economy from 1820 to 1970 and finds that for 43 of the 70 years of the twentieth century, the evidence fails to meet his expectations. Particularly important for our purposes, the United States did not lead the world toward greater openness during the period 1919-33 as the model predicts for a rising hegemonic power. Just as significantly, the relative decline in power of the United States after 1960 was not accompanied by increased protectionism, but rather by vigorous attempts to lead in the direction of greater openness, at least in the early years.

In the end, Krasner abandons a strict version of his "state power" theory and concludes that systems of international economic relations are initiated and ended not immediately by changes in relative power, but rather by "external events—usually cataclysmic ones" (1976, p. 341). He cites the potato famine, World War I, and the Great Depression as relevant examples. He thus claims that inertia burdens states with outmoded policies.[3]

The Lake Model

In two complex and challenging articles, David Lake (1983, 1984) has developed a model of the international economy that claims to generate patterns of behavior solely on the basis of the preferences of the state and its situation relative to others. Lake's model, in which the United States is the actor receiving greatest attention, employs two dimensions: relative size and relative productivity. They resemble the size and development dimensions in Krasner, although Lake's focus is individual state motivation rather than the system's structural characteristics.

Lake examines relative size because he assumes that relatively smaller states are more likely to "free ride" on the efforts of others to maintain a beneficial open international economy and because they lack the capacity to provide leadership. Some ambiguity lurks in Lake's model because his focus, like Krasner's, is on the confluence of several components of openness: trade, investment, and a well-functioning monetary system. This distinction is crucial. Though concern about the provision of the collective good of what might be called "international infrastructure" lies at the root of much of the writing on hegemony, a proponent of that view such as Kindleberger (1981) otherwise assumes that states will generally adopt free trade policies as matters of their own self-interest. In Lake's model, however, the strength of this tendency depends on the relative productivity of each state and its fear of retaliation. He also assumes, with no explicit defense, that every country would like to protect some industries.

Borrowing from Gilpin (1975, 1981), Lake embraces—not without apparent misgiving—the dubious proposition that free trade is relatively more beneficial to the most technologically advanced states, at least in terms of cumulative development effects (1984, p. 11). Nations with relatively low productivity will be dissatisfied because they are not gaining relatively as much as the more productive states. They are thus assumed to close their markets, apparently both to cut down the gains for the more productive states and to spur growth (Lake 1984, p. 12). Such partial closure allows for economies of scale and greater market stability.

Lake fails to acknowledge that his assumptions about state objectives undermine much of his argument. Relative gain dominates social stability, and this dictates free trade for countries of high relative productivity. Such a state will maximize its relative economic gains from the world economy by lowering its own trade barriers, leaving others to languish in protection. Very infrequently would such unilateral action result in more gains for foreign countries than for the initiating state. This suggests that, contrary to Lake's predictions for the late nineteenth and early twentieth centuries, the United States should have examined its international initiatives to see if reciprocal lowering of barriers increased the relative advantage of the United States more than unilateral action. In fact, the United States clung to protection until 1934. Only by placing some measure of social stability at the top of Lake's objective list can more accurate predictions be generated. But this objective is given very little discussion.

Although his theoretical motivation is flawed, Lake asserts that over the entire period from 1887 to 1934, the United States was a "supporter"—that is, a country of high relative productivity that prefers openness abroad but will accept it at home *only* in return for the payoff in external openness. He argues that what changed over the period was not the category of the United States but the category of the United Kingdom. The United Kingdom remained a hegemon until about World War I, after which it entered into a period of cooperative supportership with the United States until the late 1920s; thereafter the United States was left to "support" alone—a task for which it was unprepared and unequal in resources (1983, p. 524). After World War II, of course, in common with the Krasner model, the United States is considered a hegemon.[4]

Two facts are inconvenient even if one accepts Lake's interpretation of his model's implications. First, while the United States did increasingly recognize that its openness levered the openness of others, most of its initiatives toward freer trade before World War I resulted in very little change in policy, largely because they did not enjoy sufficient support at home. Second, the two largest changes in overall tariff policy of the entire period—the dramatic Underwood reductions of Woodrow Wilson and the huge rises under Smoot-Hawley— are not at all explained by Lake's approach. He admits the latter anomaly, although only with the undocumented qualification that it may have somehow been in anticipation of the defection of the British from bilateral supportership. Lake also grants that the level of tariffs in the 1920s was higher than he would have expected on the basis of his theory.

Implications for Recurrent Behavior

If their models were persuasively constructed, both Krasner and Lake could make powerful forecasts about the future of U.S. policy as well as that of the world economy. Unfortunately, each model fails. Krasner makes questionable assumptions, and the facts fit the model very imperfectly. Far more tellingly, Krasner's conclusion that "shocks" really change the system suggests far more than he acknowledges. If shocks can jolt policy-makers into changing their positions, this and other learning may affect domestic structures and reactions to future events. If reactions can be permanently altered by experience, then similar structural characteristics in the international system may not have the same significance in different periods.

Lake's model seems to contain a fundamental contradiction. Even if that problem is ignored, however, there are anomalies in the history of U.S. protection that his approach does not explain. Significantly, neither Krasner nor Lake finds any direct evidence of relative gain as a national goal.

One must not expect any simple model to do everything. If the statist approach could persuasively explain the movement of average tariff levels over time, it would surely be counted a success. Nonetheless, one would still need other approaches to understand the structure of U.S. protection at any given time.

The Conventional Political Science Perspective

The conventional political science perspective includes two components directly relevant to U.S. protection. Lowi has developed a provocative conceptual contribution based on U.S. tariff experience designed to illuminate U.S. public policy more generally. Pastor (1980) has contributed powerfully to our understanding of the development of trade policy over time as part of a general exploration of executive-congressional relations in U.S. foreign economic policymaking. Of many other contributions in the mainstream political science tradition, Schattschneider's (1935) study of the Smoot-Hawley Tariff and Bauer, Pool, and Dexter's (1963) examination of tariff policy in the 1950s and early 1960s stand out.

Actors and Preferences

In some of the conventional political science literature dealing with foreign economic policy, the principal actors are organized interest groups, seeking, among other objectives, greater income for their members. Lowi made an important contribution by linking the way groups participate politically to characteristic issue-types. In so doing, however, he fails to solve the problem that plagues all of the pluralist political science literature: the inability to explain why some groups form and others do not, why some have greater cohesiveness and longevity, and, most important of all, why some are more effective in gaining their ends than others.

In much of informal political science writing on protection, actors other than interest groups take on importance as autonomous or semiautonomous actors. Pastor, for example, interprets the work

of Bauer, Pool, and Dexter as demonstrating congressional autonomy in the area of trade policy, and Pastor's own impressive study
argues this position. Members of Congress and their staffs exercise
latitude in the development of trade policies, and Pastor argues that
this latitude served the cause of free trade. In fact, Pastor's position
parallels that of the statist approach; he imputes to the Congress for
the past 50 years the same concern for free trade on the basis of the
national interest that statists often claim for the executive in the
pursuit of more complex goals.

Interest Aggregation and Policy Determination

Lowi (1964; see also 1967, 1972) attempts to synthesize the work
of Schattschneider with that of Bauer, Pool, and Dexter to produce a
general typology not just of trade policy, but of public policy in
general. He identifies the way in which various groups interact in the
determination of policy with the "arena of power" that the policy
involves. Both what Lowi was attempting and what he accomplished
seem open to dispute. The work has been subject to so much critical
analysis over the years (see, for example, Zimmerman 1971; Wilson
1973; Ripley and Franklin 1976) that I focus here on criticism of the
typology only as it relates to trade policy.

Lowi argues that until the reciprocal trade agreements of 1934,
the political forces surrounding tariff making in the United States
could be characterized as "distributive," by which he means that the
government grants a large number of highly disaggregated favors and
that active participants in the process—those seeking the favors—do
not compete directly with one another because they can all be
satisfied.

Lowi calls his second category "regulatory"; here both the
winners and losers are self-conscious. In Lowi's assessment this is the
stuff of most pluralist writing, and the examples he gives mainly
concern government regulation of business where policies "are usually disaggregable only down to the sectoral level and political
activity is marked by overt conflict." He claims that after 1934, tariff
policy was in this category.

The final category is called "redistributive." Here the stakes are
large in both material and symbolic terms, and "the categories of
impact are much broader, approaching social classes" (p. 691).

Lowi's approach contains flaws and lacunae that severely limit its usefulness for our purposes. Most important, the forces that allow tariff policy-making to take on different characteristics in different periods remain obscure. A clear conception of the costs and benefits of the tariff would have virtually forced Lowi to face this issue.

Analytically, all three "arenas" are largely redistributive when tariffs are the issue of attention. In fact, the tariff is perhaps the most *purely re*distributional of all of the distributional examples given. Lowi admits that "in the long run all government policies may be considered redistributive because in the long run some people pay in taxes more than they receive in services" (p. 690). But the issue is neither the long run nor tax payments. A prohibitive tariff causes an immediate transfer of income from consumers to producers, and no tax revenue is collected.

In his original work, Lowi appeared to believe that foreign policy was itself an arena. In a later article, however, he links the distributive and regulatory arenas to aspects of foreign policy, finding nonetheless, "the absence of a foreign policy variant of redistribution. . . . Devaluation might be an example of a redistributive use of resources in foreign policy" (Lowi 1967, p. 325). The real impact of devaluation, however, is identical on trade in the sense that it amounts to a uniform subsidy on exports and tax on imports. One could argue that the Burke-Hartke bill, drafted by the AFL-CIO and introduced into Congress only a few years after Lowi wrote, announced the change from Lowi's regulatory to his redistributive arena. The shift resulted from years of increased competition from foreign trade for unionized labor. Moreover, because free trade had become so much of an ideological touchstone for large sectors of society over the previous decades, the general and overtly protectionist position touched stakes much broader than merely material. Indeed, much of the rhetoric has the character of the capital versus labor argument for protection.

Lowi's arenas largely reflect the politics that result from perceptions of the impact of protection coupled with the degree of political organization of losers and gainers. This distinction goes unrecognized, and no attention is devoted to exploring these two dimensions. Lowi's confusion nonetheless suggests an important fact: the real impact of policies is frequently quite obscure to many of the affected parties.

Not only does the Lowi approach fail to clarify arena shift over time, it gives no hint about how policies might differ within the same arena. One can infer that the tariff was "distributive" in Lowi's sense over the entire period from the late nineteenth century to 1934, yet Figure 9.1 and the accompanying discussion noted considerable changes in both the average level and the structure of the tariff over this period.

Is it asking too much of the Lowi approach to assist us with an understanding of both policy outcomes and process? Some political scientists might argue affirmatively, yet McGowan and Walker (1981) not only regard such a contribution as appropriate, they imply that Lowi's work sensitizes the analyst to "short-run, incremental changes in U.S. foreign economic policy [and] the immediate surface causes of these fluctuations" (p. 378). I find little such assistance.

Pastor's Contribution

Robert Pastor's recent book on U.S. foreign economic policy (1980) presents an excellent, comprehensive account of U.S. trade policy since 1929 from an eclectic political science point of view. Pastor argues quite persuasively that the image, popular in some circles, of Congress as a barrier to a liberal international trade policy can be strongly contested.

Pastor starts with a puzzle. How can the national legislature that in 1930 passed the highest tariffs in U.S. history have supported much more liberal initiatives only two years later, and in 1934 have yielded to a sweeping initiative by the executive to liberalize international trade? Pastor readily concedes two points. First, the complexion of the legislature changed substantially in 1930 and even more so in 1932 as the traditionally low-tariff Democrats moved into solid ascendancy. Second, the 1934 Reciprocal Trade Agreements Act was only a minor part of a massive deference of the Congress to the New Deal executive. But this provides only part of the explanation. Pastor argues that the cataclysmic decline in world trade and the attendant worsening of the economic conditions of all of the major trading nations taught the entire country a permanent lesson: an open world economy is good and protectionism is bad.

While granting that the traditional protectionist forces did not dissolve overnight, Pastor nonetheless argues that the Congress over the past half-century has functioned in a fashion that is not properly characterized as more protectionist than the executive but simply as different. The difference stems from a greater sensitivity to the immediate pain of different parts of the community rather than a lower level of understanding of the beneficence of increasingly freer trade. Congressional orientation and popular misunderstanding of it have generated what Pastor calls the "cry and sigh syndrome." Congressional initiatives designed solely to get the attention of the executive or foreign governments are greeted by cries of "protection-ism." These concerns are then incorporated satisfactorily into na-tional policy, with the result of an increasingly liberal policy and the ensuing sighs of relief from free trade forces.

While Pastor's scholarship is impressive, he describes much more than he explains. In reviewing the entire period, he attributes liberal U.S. policies to a combination of four factors: First, he claims that the ideology of free trade has reigned since 1934. Second, presidential leadership replaced "Hoover's passivity." Third, Con-gress has eagerly embraced discipline in the final passage of trade bills, thus blunting a possible proliferation of protectionist initiatives or other disorder that could delay or prevent action. Fourth, mutual trust and responsiveness on trade between Congress and the execu-tive has been maintained. Pastor suggests that the second and third reasons are in fact derivative from the first, and although no explana-tion for the fourth factor is given, one might logically infer that it too derives from a common ideological commitment (Pastor 1983, pp. 37-40).

In the last analysis, then, Pastor's interpretation apparently turns on one experience: the disastrous consequences of the Smoot-Hawly Tariff, which, one infers, produced a kind of permanent ideological learning on the part of the U.S. political elite. But how plausible is this as a complete explanation? Observers could have drawn various lessons from the years 1930-33, and none of them would have provided any direct verification of the truths of David Ricardo. Free trade doctrine concerns microeconomic phenomena; the spectacular economic pathologies of the period were of an essentially macroeconomic character. Even protectionists might have later realized their folly in raising tariffs in such a precipitate and substantial fashion as to generate almost immediate and substantial retaliation.

In Pastor's view the episode not only proved the wisdom of openness, but the lesson became more powerful over time—as distance from the originating event increased—rather than less so. This could be partly attributed to the demise of traditional "American System" protectionists from the Congress, and for a couple of decades at least, to general U.S. prosperity and concern for Western solidarity. But the doctrine in Pastor's account had grown so powerful by the 1970s that even the threat to large sectors of the economy produced only tailored responses aimed at adjustment rather than general protectionism. And even those threatened sectors appear to be given protectionism more out of idealism and a sense of the national interest than political pressure. Pastor underlines his anti-pluralist message: "the best explanation of this liberal trade policy is hardly interest group theory" (1980, p. 187).

Ideological learning then bears the overwhelming burden of explanation in Pastor's account. At best, he does not explore the channels of such learning over time, and one must wonder if his dismissal of competing interests is really warranted.

International System Considerations

Most writing on foreign economic policy as interactive foreign policy stems understandably from a statist perspective. Lowi never discusses the interactive aspect of tariff making at all, and Pastor treats foreign factors only in a rather cursory fashion—mainly as the recipients of congressional "signals" to increase opportunities for U.S. exporters. He alleges, however, the acceptance of the free trade doctrine all over the world (Pastor 1983, p. 37).

Implications for Recurrent Behavior

For quite different reasons, neither Lowi nor Pastor presents a solid basis upon which to understand patterns of the past or to forecast the future. Lowi's treatment of the two major predecessor works in the tariff literature concentrates more on their ability to generate conceptual ideas than on their value to an understanding of tariffs per se. One could infer from Lowi that prior to 1934, tariff making had been a largely homogeneous pork-barrel affair; a look at the data suggests otherwise. After 1934 Lowi argues that the arena changed, but he fails to observe even whether this implied greater or lesser protection. Such failure to interpret history makes forecasting impossible.

Pastor cannot be faulted for not attempting to interpret the past or forecast the future (1980, 1983, esp. pp. 40ff.). Although he adds nothing novel to an understanding of the period prior to 1929, he does stress the strength of opposition to Smoot-Hawley as a prelude to his presentation of the history of the period beginning in 1934. In fact, his "cry and sigh" syndrome is a kind of cycle theory of politics—which must be distinguished from policy. Policies have been secularly more liberal but accompanied by the cyclical counter-point of congressional alarm and signaling. At the end of his 1983 paper, Pastor forecasts a future much like the past, but he notes the possibility that Congress might go too far and set off a series of international protectionist retaliations from which the world econ-omy might not emerge intact. If we had more than Pastor's "big bang" notion of the emergence of free trade ideology, we might be able to agree or disagree with his forecast with greater confidence.

The Public Choice Perspective

Political scientists writing about the determinants of protection in the United States have typically missed some of the richest literature on the subject: that growing out of the so-called public choice tradition, which Dennis Mueller has defined as the "applica-tion of economics to political science" (1979, p. 1). The fundamental assumption can be stated simply: if man as an egoistic maximizer serves well to explain and predict the behavior of individuals in markets, then the same approach might also serve to explain political behavior. Initial contributions to the approach include Downs (1957), Buchanan and Tullock (1962), and Olson (1965).

The Preferences of Actors

As a first approximation, microeconomics most frequently as-sumes that individuals strive to maximize their wealth in a direct and straightforward fashion. This maxim has served as the basis for a number of models of protection developed from a public choice perspective (Brock and Magee 1978). Many models, especially those associated with empirical research, however, contain a richer objective function for individuals and groups. Altruism and broader social goals such as national security or industrialization dominate these additional considerations (for a discussion, see Baldwin 1982, pp. 271-73).

Interest Aggregation and Policy Determination

The public choice approach to protection has traditionally begun with the simplest of all models: direct democracy and the assumption of a self-interested and informed electorate. In most such models, there will then be no tariffs because free trade typically maximizes national income, and income-distribution objectives are assumed to be achieved more efficiently with devices other than tariffs. Public choice then adds considerations that bring this highly unrealistic model into correspondence with observed reality.

First, there is the cost of information and political participation. Even if protection were decided upon in referenda, the impact of tariffs is not well understood (an assumption verified by Lowi); voters would rationally remain ignorant of the issues, figuring (correctly) that their own informed position would be unlikely to affect the outcome of a vote. Many would fail to register their opinion for the same reason.

Second, such issues in all countries are in fact decided by elected representatives who take stands on a wide variety of issues and are typically associated with political parties. This complication may well generate a protectionist bias when the "free rider" problem—the recognition by actors that their own behavior does not affect an outcome—is asymmetrically distributed between protectionist and antiprotectionist forces. In a complex political environment, those groups that can generate resources for their own ends can support candidates and engage in "advertising" for their position in ways that increase their potency. The ability of politicians to logroll and vote-trade introduces additional complexity (Baldwin 1982; Frey 1984).

The studies that have examined the structure of protection in the United States and other countries cover a number of periods and test various determinants. But the number of possibly relevant variables is far larger than has been yet employed. Conceptually, Baldwin (1982) has presented factors that affect either the benefits of protection for the affected parties or the costs of obtaining it. In the former category one would place such concerns as the size of the industry and the elasticities of supply and demand. If protection is expected to generate extranormal profits, then barriers into the domestic industry would take on importance. Indeed, it has been hypothesized that one of the reasons declining industries so often find protection an attractive option is that domestic entry can often be ignored.

The cost of gaining protection (or additional protection) can be expected to turn on the degree to which conditions in the industry match either the altruistic or social goals of the voters (and the degree of protection already granted to the industry), and the ability to amass the necessary lobbying funds will be driven to a large extent by the extent to which the benefiting group can overcome the free rider problem.

Most existing studies have employed only a few variables with limited data sets. Pincus (1977) found that the structure of protection in the Tariff Act of 1824 could be partly explained by higher industrial concentration. Other studies, however, have found the level of concentration to be insignificant while the number of firms, the import penetration ratio, and measures of growth perform well (slow growth or declining industries obtain more support; see research reported in Baldwin 1982 and Frey 1984).

An obvious problem with most econometric studies so far concerns functional identification. Should the fact that protectionism is higher in industries with comparatively low human capital (that is, skills and education) be attributed to altrusim or the urgency that these workers have to overcome the free rider problem and participate in the political process (Baldwin 1982)? Larger data sets and more carefully specified models are necessary to help untangle such issues.

In a pioneering study, Richard Caves (1976) tested alternative conceptualizations of the determination of Canadian tariffs. One of the variables he employed was the concentration of *buyers* on the assumption that such concentration would tend to counteract that of the protected interests. The variable performed disappointingly; but subsequently, Gerald Helleiner (1977a, 1977b) identified another pro-free-trade force: the multinational corporation. Although only very limited data were available, Helleiner adduces evidence consistent with the hypothesis that the international companies have worked most to reduce tariffs in those commodity classifications in which their "intra-industry" trade is concentrated, while not vigorously opposing increased relative protection in other labor-intensive and declining industries whose case is bolstered by organized labor.

The public choice approach can also be used to consider the development of the average level (as opposed to structure) of protection at a given time, though relatively little formal work has been done. Why did the United States have high and relatively stable tariffs until the mid-1930s and then engage in bargaining that ultimately reduced them to minor importance? The time series studies done for the United States so far do little to track such change. Unemployment in Magee (1982) and unemployment with other variables in Takacs (1981) increase the demand for protection as measured by the number of dumping cases (Magee) or petitions before the International Trade Commission (Takacs), while in the Magee model the inflation rate negatively affects the level of protection. Unfortunately, neither model employs the degree of success in achieving protection as a dependent variable, and Magee includes an unexplained shift variable in his time series.

John Stuart Mill observed that "a good cause seldom triumphs unless someone's interest is bound up with in it" (quoted in Kindleberger 1975, p. 35). Helleiner's discussion of the political economy of U.S. protection seems powerfully to complement Pastor's account by emphasizing the importance of specific interests working in favor of free trade. Over the postwar period, the share of foreign trade accounted for by corporations rose from an unknown but minor fraction to as much as 50 percent by the early 1980s. While Helleiner presents no political model of any kind, his plausible hypothesis is worth careful attention. Moreover, the increasing role of foreign trade to national income in the United States vastly increased the sectors of U.S. business with a profound interest in continuing international openness just as many other firms were hit more heavily with foreign competition. The ratio of exports to GNP moved from 4 percent in 1960 to 8.2 percent in 1980, with nearly all of the growth after 1970. Over the same period, imports grew from 3 percent to 9.6 percent (Lipson 1982, p. 423). Because Pastor eschews particularistic interests as an explanation, he largely ignores these forces. And without such an understanding one cannot really gauge the permanence of openness or track the shift of leadership toward freer trade from the Democratic to the traditionally "big business" Republican Party as the period wore on.

All accounts of the departure in U.S. protection policy in 1934 assign great importance to the willingness of Congress to yield flexible initiative to the executive—something quite unprecedented in U.S. history (Pastor 1980). The public choice approach provides a persuasive (if not necessarily unique) explanation for the change of national strategy. In his *Rise and Decline of Nations* (1982), Mancur Olson develops the idea of "distributive coalitions" that take account of the national economic interest only when the coalitions are of such substantial size that the general interest cannot be ignored. Olson has suggested in a private communication that this is the essence of the tariff arena issue: individual members of Congress may be under constant pressure from parochial interests, the service of which would directly reduce national income or generate retaliation. Those most concerned with national outcomes, however, the executive and party leaders, will take the broader view (Olson 1982). When this characterization is married to the events of the 1931-34 period, the outcome makes sense. The ideological "lesson" could be seized by those with the most encompassing view to pressure for a change in executive-congressional relations on trade.

Furthermore, as Finger (1979) has argued, from an explicitly public choice point of view, once the tariff issue was securely placed in a framework of reciprocity, an entirely different political calculus could be employed by the executive and Congress than when tariffs were treated piecemeal. Now the *net* benefits from reciprocal concessions could be calculated, and exporting interests and multinational corporations were immediately provided with the ammunition needed to promote their positions most effectively.

Few would quarrel with Pastor's contention that a general sympathy for freer trade has prevailed in elite circles in the United States since the 1930s. Yet the precise motivation, intensity, and sophistication with which these biases are held by various agents in the government is poorly understood. What follows seems to me a plausible account employing a public choice perspective; a definitive treatment remains to be developed.

Public choice theory has not dealt very satisfactorily with the problem of ideological learning. This failing, however, seems no more serious than in other traditions attempting to explain the same phenomenon, and some progress has been made. Stigler and Becker (1977) attempt to reduce ideological change to alterations in economic magnitudes and direct reactions to them, but, as Douglass North (1981) has pointed out, their argument omits two crucial considerations. Most individuals develop much of what they believe, even about the economic world, without benefit of direct logic or experience. Moreover, ethical and moral concerns, which Becker and Stigler ignore, loom large in an individual's ideological makeup.

North proposes an approach to ideology and ideological learning that is firmly grounded in the economic approach to politics. He stresses three critical features of ideology. First, it provides a "world view" that simplifies and economizes decision-making. Second, important elements of ideology necessarily inhere in notions of fairness that (one infers) cannot be reduced to the individual's direct self-interest. Third, ideologies have strong inertial properties; individuals alter their ideological outlook only when experiences accumulate.

All three tenets help interpret the present case. "The American System" of tariff protection was accepted by a broad spectrum of politicians during most of the nineteenth century and as late as the election of 1932. The Democrats favored generally lower tariffs, but at no time did the party completely embrace the free trade ideology of the mid-Victorian British Liberal Party. In the main, the United States prospered under the prevailing system, and those who advocated a really dramatic change in the prevailing system could be branded as radicals. (For a discussion of "ideological consonance" that bears a strong resemblance to North's approach, see Kudrle and Bobrow 1982.)

Second, most of the cross-section studies of the structure of protection find evidence of the power of "fairness" thinking. North here bolsters the arguments advanced by Baldwin. Finally, one can interpret the cataclysm following Smoot-Hawley as a triggering episode rather than a completely self-contained lesson. Forces favoring freer trade, mainly in the suddenly ascendant Democratic Party, could powerfully bolster their arguments by the international disaster. The presumption of elites and mass alike about the benefits of openness changed rapidly, thus giving comfort both to professional economists and those interests benefiting from freer trade.

In the postwar years, protectionism commanded too little allegiance in either party for "fairness" to dictate anything other than ridicule at the hands of economic textbook writers (see, for example, the first edition of Samuelson [1948]). Most first-year economics students now learn the benefits of free trade as a virtually unqualified truth, and one assumes an increasing proportion of congressional staffs had been exposed to such a course as the postwar period wore on. Persons thus prepared could interpret the stream of studies from the Congressional Budget Office, the Congressional Research Service, and various executive agencies demonstrating the cost to the nation of protectionist devices.

Perhaps the simplest account of the postwar period combining the elements just recounted would stress for earlier years a general commitment to freer trade based mainly on the ideological lesson of the 1930s, bolstered by a concern about Western solidarity and the alleged contribution of trade to peace. Most of U.S. industry and organized labor did not feel threatened because this was a time of severe dollar shortage and a general excess demand for U.S. goods. As time wore on and more U.S. industries and an increasing share of unionized labor became threatened by import penetration, the increasing interest of MNCs in freer trade and the interdependent stakes of myriads of other interests generated a powerful counterforce to growing protectionist sentiment.

Some might question whether the public choice perspective makes an essential addition to the general argument advanced by Pastor. I argue that it does. Pastor's emphasis on the role of common ideology in the development of mutually acceptable congressional-executive positions commands assent. But for the forecast of both protectionist pressure and congressional response to the problems of specific industries, an interest calculation is essential. Baldwin (1976) found congressional voting on the Trade Bill of 1973 to be heavily influenced by the situation in a representative's own constituency, despite the fact that particular problems are now frequently dealt with through congressional activity such that the bills themselves pass with overwhelming margins.

Public choice theory has also been used with considerable effect to study the apparent determinants of discretionary protection within governments, in the United States (Finger, Hall, and Nelson 1982) and in Europe (Messerlin 1981). In these rather complex studies, one frequent feature of public choice models is quite apparent: although the dependent variables are political, the analysis necessary to produce the model as a whole frequently involves quite sophisticated economics.

Public Choice and the International System

Public choice has provided some clear perspectives on the international economic system. The approach contributes to an understanding of the structure of tariff cuts made under the various negotiating rounds of the GATT and hence to the structure of U.S. protection. Finger (1979) has explained progress in liberalization to date and the difficulties of continued advance. He stresses the internalization-coverage trade-off. Internalization emphasizes the extent to which GATT bargaining has involved the United States in reciprocal actions with major trading partners, most of whom are within the GATT, hence avoiding the free rider problem of giving benefits to countries that do not "earn" them with concessions of their own. As the barriers have been reduced on such items, coverage becomes a more difficult problem because a larger fraction of protected world trade involves the developing countries for whom reciprocity is largely rejected on both ideological and practical grounds.

Public choice also casts light on the issue of whether declining U.S. hegemony dictates increasing protection. Oligopoly theory, based on the concept of mutual dependence recognized, suggests doubt that the decline of the United States from its position of hegemony would have a profound effect on the prospects for international trade cooperation. A rather small number of major actors whose interest would be served by an active attempt to preserve and perhaps even extend a liberal regime would continue to dominate the system (McKeown 1983). Each would be important enough to affect the actions of others, and this reality can be expected to galvanize resistance to protectionist interests. Recent analyses of protectionist pressure in the United States and other countries assign it to the difficulties of specific sectors rather than declining U.S. hegemony (Strange 1979; Cowhey and Long 1983).

Recurrent Behavior and Public Choice

The configuration of forces now favoring free trade seems to overdetermine the U.S. political system, and it is difficult to foresee a set of developments that would move the country sharply in a protectionist direction. Although U.S. foreign direct investment does not now grow at rates vastly in excess of the U.S. economy, U.S. business continues to become more multinational in both trade and investment. Reciprocity, construed in the liberal multilateral sense, will continue to remain overwhelmingly important. Protectionist rhetoric per se in the United States seems virtually dead outside of the AFL-CIO. Short-run protectionism as a lever for greater openness on the part of trading partners appears to be all the major politicians can muster.

In short, a public choice perspective stresses the extent to which ideological learning and powerful economic interests have conjoined to produce a U.S. position that is wedded to a very high degree of openness. Short of some totally unforeseen catastrophe, the present mix of ideology and interest seems no more likely to allow widespread protection than a return of legislation designed to protect small shopkeepers from the competition of chain drug stores and supermarkets. As Evan Luard (1984) has recently pointed out, openness produces pain, but protectionism remains intellectually unrespectable.

An Overall Assessment

The earlier discussion criticized realist models quite severely on grounds of assumptions, internal logic, and evidence. Societies may undergo episodes of ideological learning that alter international strategies and deprive intertemporal models of consistency. Moreover, statism's quest for a national interest divorced from particularistic interests may be inappropriate. Public choice theory illustrates structural circumstances in which the national interest may come into close correspondence with the outcome of domestic politics, and the shift in approach to tariff making in 1934 and later represents one such example. Finally, statism cannot claim exclusive concern for international structure. The oligopolistic elements in international economic relations form an important part of the public choice approach.

The statist perspective contains valuable insights. Executive leadership based on notions of the national interest has played a role in the development of U.S. trade policy. Attempts by each U.S.

president since Roosevelt to lead the nation toward a more open system undoubtedly had some effect. One may question, however, whether that leadership reflected a conception of the national interest that was quite distinct from the dominant views of Congress or the most powerful interests in society. Statism helps one understand leadership but not followership.

Lowi's typology of U.S. public policy using the tariff as the prime example illuminates little that is important for the understanding of the content of U.S. protection policy. Instead, Lowi indirectly suggests important puzzles that he leaves to other approaches to solve. The most one can gain from Lowi is that there was a period of U.S. history in which—within limits—tariff favors were distributed almost as if no one were paying. Why such a situation existed and why it changed remains unexplained. Lowi's work inspires inquiry about why issues are seen as they are by both citizens and elites. The public choice approach, stressing individual interest and perception, provides an underpinning for Lowi's "arenas" and also illuminates arena shifts.

Pastor's sweeping account of the history of U.S. protection policy in the context of executive-congressional relations casts valuable light on a broad range of relevant issues. His central failing is to denigrate the direct and indirect role of material interest in the formation of U.S. trade policy. Pastor treats ideology and interest as if they were competing explanations, while the public choice interpretation favored here regards their complementarity over the past 50 years as a satisfactory explanation for observed policy. The challenge remains, however, to trace more carefully the means whereby interest and ideology have reinforced each other in the service of openness.

The author favors the public choice approach. The reader, however, may have concluded that the term has been given an excessively loose and encompassing meaning. This is a danger. While I believe that only some form of "bottom-up" approach can really illuminate trade policy or forecast its course, public choice has clear limitations as developed so far. It can explain the structure of tariffs better than other approaches, *faute de mieux*, but much statistical work has been poorly specified and only moderately successful in accounting for observed variation.

The interpretation of ideological and institutional change presents the most ambitious face of public choice—and perhaps its most suspect. In largely qualitative interpretations of historical change, public choice must borrow heavily from existing literature. Its methodology, however, also dictates a focus on individual actors at every level of decision-making. In principle, public choice could contribute to a quantitative understanding of the development of protection over time, but this goal remains almost entirely unachieved.

The growth of vested interests in openness along with an ideological understanding of its general value make a distinction between the two as determinants of policy very difficult. But both determinants appear robust, and the most probable departures from openness are of only two kinds. First, "breathing space" protection, introduced for adjustment or renewal in specific industries such as steel and textiles, may prove quite difficult to remove. Second, some retrogression could develop as the result of unsuccessful strategic attempts to wrest openness from others. Overall, however, economic interdependence cannot be reversed. United States policy, which in the past fostered the restructuring of the world economy, now must necessarily reflect it.

Notes

1. Lake's discussion of U.S. tariff policy before World War I, for example, never discusses regional economic interests and their relations to the major political parties complicated by the bitterness of the Civil War.

2. Krasner expresses concern that complete openness in the form of an outflow of technology and capital may undermine the domestic economy of advanced states, but the point is not pursued.

3. One apparent implication is that Britain would have benefited from closure as early as the turn of the century.

4. Lake never makes the case that the relative productivity of the United States played an important role in either its behavior or that of the United Kingdom's. The role of relative size in the model is also somewhat suspect. The United States saw its total share of world trade rise steadily from 9 percent in 1870 to 14 percent in 1929, and although it fell again to 11 percent in 1938, it was only 18.4 percent at the height of its hegemony in 1950, falling subsequently to 13.4 percent by 1977. This was, however, the period of maximum advantage in relative productivity.

Bibliography

Baldwin, R. E. 1982. "The Political Economy of Protectionism." In *Import Competition and Response,* ed. J. N. Bhagwati, pp. 263-92. Chicago: University of Chicago Press.

——————————————————. 1976. "The Political Economy of U. S. Trade Policy." *Bulletin.* New York University Center for the Study of Financial Institutions.

Bauer, R., I. de Sola Pool, and L. A. Dexter. 1963. *American Business and Public Policy.* New York: Atherton.

Bergsten, C. F., T. Horst, and T. H. Moran. 1978. *American Multinationals and American Interests.* Washington D.C.: Brookings Institution.

Brock, W. A. and S. Magee. 1978. "The Economics of Special Interest Politics: The Case of the Tariff." *American Economic Review* 68, pp. 246-50.

Buchanan, J. M. and G. Tullock. 1962. *The Calculus of Consent.* Ann Arbor: University of Michigan Press.

Caves, R. E. 1976. "Economic Models of Political Choice: Canada's Tariff Structure." *Canadian Journal of Economics* 9, pp. 278-300.

Cowhey, P. F. and E. Long. 1983. "Testing Theories of Regime Change: Hegemonic Decline or Surplus Capacity?" *International Organization* 37, pp. 157-88.

Downs, A. 1957. *An Economic Theory of Democracy.* New York: Harper and Row.

Finger, J. M. 1979. "Trade Liberalization: A Public Choice Perspective." In *Challenges to a Liberal International Economic Order,* ed. R.C. Amacher, G. Haberler, and T.D. Willett. Washington D.C.: American Enterprise Institute for Public Policy Research.

——————————————————, H. K. Hall, and D. R. Nelson. 1982. "The Political Economy of Administered Protection." *American Economic Review* 72, pp. 452-65.

Frey, Bruno S. 1984. "The Public Choice View of International Political Economy." *International Organization* 38, pp. 199-223.

Gilpin, R. 1981. *War and Change in World Politics.* Cambridge: Cambridge University Press.

——————————————————. 1977. "Economic Interdependence and National Security in Historical Perspective." *Economic Issues and National Security,* ed. Klaus Knorr and F. A. Trager, pp. 19-67. Lawrence: Regents Press of Kansas.

——————————————————. 1975. *U.S. Power and the Multinational Corporation.* New York: Basic Books.

Helleiner, G. K. 1977a. "The Political Economy of Canada's Tariff Structure: An Alternative Model." *Canadian Journal of Economics* 4, pp. 318-26.

——————————————————. 1977b. "Transnational Enterprises and the New Political Economy of U.S. Trade Policy." *Oxford Economic Papers* 29, pp. 102-16.

Hirschman, A. O. 1945. *National Power and the Structure of Foreign Trade.* Los Angeles: University of California Press.

Keohane, Robert O. 1980. "The Theory of Hegemonic Stability and Changes in International Economic Regimes, 1976-1977." In *Change in the International System,* ed. Ole Holsti, Randolph Siverson, and Alexander George, pp. 131-62. Boulder, Colo.: Westview.

Kindleberger, C. P. 1981. "Dominance and Leadership in the International Economy: Exploitation, Public Goods, and Free Rides." *International Studies Quarterly* 25, pp. 242-54.

——————————————————. 1975. "The Rise of Free Trade in Western Europe, 1820-1875." *Journal of Economic History* 35, pp. 20-55.

Krasner, S. D. 1979. *Defending the National Interest: Raw Materials Investments and U.S. Foreign Policy.* Princeton: Princeton University Press.

——————————————————. 1977. "Domestic Constraints on International Economic Leverage." In *Economic Issues and National Security,* ed. Knorr Klaus and Frank Trager, pp. 160-81. Lawrence, Kansas: Allen Press.

——————————. 1976. "State Power and the Structure of International Trade." *World Politics* 28, pp. 317-47.

Kudrle, R. T. and D. B. Bobrow. 1982. "U.S. Policy Toward Foreign Direct Investment." *World Politics* 34, pp. 454-83.

Lake, D. A. 1984. "Beneath the Commerce of Nations: A Theory of International Economic Structures." *International Studies Quarterly* 28, forthcoming.

——————————. 1983. "International Economic Structures and American Foreign Economic Policy, 1887-1934." *World Politics* 35, pp. 517-43.

Lawson, Fred H. 1983. "Hegemony and the Structure of International Trade Reassessed: A View from Arabia." *International Organization* 37, pp. 317-37.

Lindert, P. H. and C. P. Kindleberger. 1982. *International Economics.* Homewood, Ill.: Irwin.

Lipson, Charles. 1982. "The Transformation of Trade: The Sources and Effects of Regime Change." *International Organization* 36, pp. 417-55.

Lowi, Theodore. 1972. "Four Systems of Policy, Politics and Choice." *Public Administration Review* 32, pp. 289-310.

——————————. 1967. "Making Democracy Safe for the World: National Politics and Foreign Policy." In *Domestic Sources of Foreign Policy,* ed. James N. Rosenau, pp. 295-331. New York: Free Press.

——————————. 1964. "American Business, Public Policy, Case-Studies, and Political Theory." *World Politics* 16, pp. 677-715.

Luard, Evan. 1984. *Economic Relationships Among States.* London: Macmillan.

Magee, S. P. 1982. "Protectionism in the United States." Dept. of Finance, University of Texas at Austin.

McGowan, P. and S. Walker. 1981. "Radical and Conventional Models of U.S. Foreign Economic Policy Making." *World Politics* 33, pp. 347-82.

McKeown, Timothy. 1983. "Hegemonic Stability Theory and 19th-Century Tariff Levels in Europe." *International Organization* 37, pp. 73-91.

Messerlin, Patrick A. 1981. "The Political Economy of Protectionism: The Bureaucratic Case." *Weltwirtschaftliches Archiv* 117, pp. 469-96.

Mueller, Dennis C. 1979. *Public Choice.* Cambridge: Cambridge University Press.

North, Douglass C. 1981. *Structure and Change in Economic History.* New York: Norton.

Olson, Mancur. 1982. *The Rise and Decline of Nations: Economic Growth, Stagflation, and Social Rigidities.* New Haven: Yale University Press.

——————————. 1965. *The Logic of Collective Action.* Cambridge: Harvard University Press.

Pastor, Robert. 1983. "The Cry and Sigh Syndrome: Congress and U.S. Trade Policy." In *Making Economic Policy in Congress,* ed. Allen Schick. Washington: American Enterprise Institute for Public Policy Research.

——————————. 1980. *Congress and the Politics of U.S. Foreign Economic Policy, 1929-1976.* Berkeley: University of California Press.

Pincus, J. J. 1977. *Pressure Groups and Politics in Antebellum Tariffs.* New York: Columbia University Press.

Ripley, Randall B. and Grace A. Franklin. 1976. *Congress, the Bureaucracy and Public Policy.* Homewood, Ill.: Dorsey Press.

Samuelson, P. A. 1948. *Economics: An Introductory Analysis.* New York: McGraw-Hill.

Schattschneider, E. E. 1935. *Politics, Pressures and the Tariff: A Study of Free Enterprise in Pressure Politics, as Shown in the 1929-30 Revision of the Tariff.* New York: Prentice-Hall.

Statistical Abstract of the United States. 1982-83. Washington D.C.: U.S. Government Printing Office.

Stigler, G. J. and G. S. Becker. 1977. "De Gustibus Non Est Disputandum." *American Economic Review* 67, pp. 76-90.

Strange, Susan. 1979. "The Management of Surplus Capacity: Or How Does Theory Stand Up to Protectionism 1970s Style?" *International Organization* 33, pp. 303-34.

Takacs, Wendy E. 1981. "Pressures for Protectionism: An Empirical Analysis." *Economic Inquiry* 19, pp. 687-93.

Wilson, James. 1973. "Organizations and Public Policy." In his *Political Organizations*, pp. 327-46. New York: Basic Books.

Zimmerman, William. 1971. "Issue Area and Foreign-Policy Process: A Research Note in Search of a General Theory." *American Political Science Review* 67, pp. 1204-12.

10

International Economic Long Cycles and American Foreign Policy Moods

ROBERT E. ELDER, JR. AND JACK E. HOLMES

Recent years have seen a great deal of research done on topics relating to international economic long cycles as initially developed by Soviet economist N.D. Kondratieff. The authors of this chapter at the same time have done extensive research on American moods as part of a cycle crucial to U.S. foreign policy. It was felt that a relationship could be found between these two long-cycle theories, Kondratieff's long waves and U.S. foreign policy moods. The 1983 ISA presidential address by Bruce Russett helped us solidify plans in this regard.

U.S. Foreign Policy Moods

Frank Klingberg (1983, 1979, 1952), Jack Holmes (1985, 1976), and more recently, Jack Holmes and Robert Elder (1983; Elder and Holmes 1982), have authored a series of books, articles, and papers

The authors are most appreciative for the help of their research assistants at Hope College. Paul Bolt, Sally Budd, and Dirk Weeldreyer made special contributions. Sally diligently worked through numerous versions of the tables. Dirk and Paul were extremely helpful as we prepared the chapter for publication. Lon McCollum, Patricia Cecil, and Brian Crisp made helpful editorial suggestions. Sandy Tasma was our most patient typist. Editor William Thompson and ISA panel commentator Harold Guetzkow made several useful suggestions. While we are most grateful for this assistance, all matters of fact, interpretation, and error herein remain the responsibility of the authors.

directed at explaining and documenting a historical pattern of behavioral changes in the making of U.S. foreign policy. Klingberg's writing in 1952 suggested that since 1776 the United States has moved between periods of intense involvement in foreign policy and periods where involvement was considerably less. Klingberg divided U.S. foreign policy history into four "extrovert" and four "introvert" phases:

Introvert	Extrovert
1776-1798	1798-1824
1824-1844	1844-1871
1871-1891	1891-1919
1919-1940	1940-

Klingberg identified these periods on the basis of statistics he compiled in regard to percentages of state of the union messages and inaugural addresses devoted to foreign policy, increases or decreases in naval expenditures, armed expeditions, and diplomatic pressures. Such activities increase during extrovert periods and decrease during introvert periods. Extrovert periods span an average of 27 years, and introvert periods last an average of 21 years.

Jack Holmes (1985, 1976) visualized Klingberg periods as a fluctuating curve driven by popular opinion and called it a mood curve. Our democratic institutions are affected by popular moods and respond with either increased or decreased interest in the area of foreign policy. Holmes's mood curve indicating introversion and extroversion in foreign policy against a backdrop of increasing foreign policy interests appears in Figure 10.1.

Elder and Holmes (1982) divided each extrovert and introvert period into three stages in order to better understand the dynamics of this cyclical pattern that has been repeated four times in U.S. history. Introvert stages last an average of seven years, while extrovert stages are approximately nine years in duration.[1]

Holmes (1976) attributed shifts between introversion and extroversion to mood changes in a basically Lockean liberal society. But what were the forces behind this tendency to first live in relative peace with our neighbors and then to fight wars and annex territory? One plausible hypothesis is found in psychological research in motivation as developed by David McClelland and David Winter. Mc-

Figure 10.1 The Mood/Interest Conflict

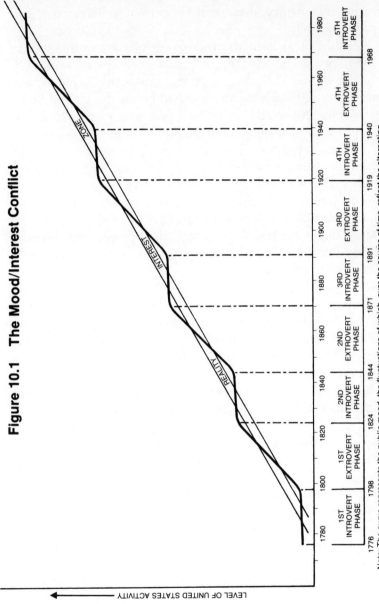

Note: The curve represents the public mood, the fluctuations of which, over the course of time, reflect the alternating attempts of U.S. liberalism to change international politics. The shaded area (reality/interest zone) represents the interim periods during which liberal mood and politicomilitary interests are in harmony. The curve extended above or below the reality/interest zone reflects periods of excessive extroversion or introversion, respectively, demonstrating that a new introvert or extrovert phase begins at a time when overall mood leans strongly in the opposite direction.

Source: Holmes (1985), Chapter 3.

241

Clelland (1961) successfully isolated three basic motives within human beings: a desire to have power over others, a desire to achieve concrete results in solving specific problems, and the need to be loved and cared for. He named these motives power, achievement, and affiliation, respectively.

McClelland (1975) used the techniques of content analysis to identify high power, affiliation, or achievement periods in U.S. literature. He argued that the wider the gap between power and affiliation, the more likelihood there would be for the United States to engage in wars. Although McClelland posited a 15-year lead time between appearance of the motive in the literature and the occurrence of war, Elder and Holmes see the relationship as more immediate. When examining foreign wars of the United States, high power/low affiliation literature was found in the last mid-decade year prior to the war's start in five out of six instances coded by McClelland. Our research has shown that high power years have a tendency to relate to periods when the mood is changing, while low power years seem to occur during the second (middle) stage of introvert and extrovert phases (Elder and Holmes 1982).

David Winter and Abigail Stewart (1977) applied content analysis techniques to the inaugural addresses of all twentieth-century presidents. Using the president's leadership in foreign policy as a gauge for motivation in the making of foreign policy, Elder (1981) and Elder and Holmes (1982) modified Winter's method and content analyzed nineteenth-century presidential inaugurals from Polk through McKinley for purposes of making comparisons with the last three Klingberg-Holmes cycles. Table 10.1 demonstrates the tendencies toward high power, low affiliation inaugural addresses in extrovert periods and particularly during Holmes-Elder first and third extrovert stages. Higher affiliation scores tend to occur during all second stages and in first-stage introvert periods. The gap between power and affiliation is shown by the power divergence score, obtained by subtracting the affiliation score from the power socre.

The discovery that the motivation scores of presidential inaugurals and popular literature matched shifts in foreign policy with a fair degree of regularity across 150 years was interesting, but left us no closer to what brought about these motivational changes. Were we examining underlying motivations or were presidents simply responding to politics in their inaugurals? Our 1983 paper incorporated

James David Barber's (1977) work on presidential personality and posterity rankings of presidents into our analysis. We concluded by suggesting that foreign policy behaviors might be influenced by changing motivational patterns and were also part of larger domestic policy cycles (Holmes and Elder 1983).

Kondratieff International Economic Cycles

While we were working on the several cyclical relationships noted above, most literature relating to 50-year cycles seemed to concentrate on the Kondratieff economic cycles. We clearly needed to see whether we could relate our research to some of this literature. This is our initial effort at identifying relationships between international economic conditions and U.S. foreign policy moods.

The initial methodological challenge we faced when comparing various authors on Kondratieff cycles with Klingberg and Holmes material on introvert/extrovert phases was to make a clear distinction between U.S. and international considerations and data. Kondratieff's cycles and most material written about them are based on international data. Since one of the countries looked at by Kondratieff and those who write about him is the United States, American data contribute to the international data. The material by Klingberg and Holmes is primarily American and is based on the study of U.S. moods regarding international involvement. For our initial comparison of Kondratieff material to Klingberg-Holmes material, we believed it best to concentrate on the relationships between international forces represented by the Kondratieff international cycles and U.S. forces represented by the Klingberg-Holmes material on foreign policy moods.

Our comparison of Kondratieff international economic cycles and Klingberg-Holmes U.S. mood cycles is designed to explore the degree to which there is some relationship. If a close relationship is indicated, then it is appropriate to suggest additional research. In particular, a comparison of U.S. foreign policy moods to U.S. price cycles might be productive. However, the authors believe the initial comparison should proceed from the base strength of each theory.

Kondratieff, who wrote during the early part of the twentieth century, fell out of favor with his Soviet colleagues because he saw the dynamics of capitalism as cyclical rather than dialectical. He

Table 10.1 Presidential Inaugural Scores (elected presidents with one or more years in office)

Mood/ Interest Cycle	President and whether Second Stage Only[a] (SSO)	Years in Office (dates inclusive)	Achievement Score	Power Score	Affiliation Score	Power Divergence	Average Power Divergence Score for Cycle Presidents	Average Power Divergence Score for Cycle Second-Stage-Only Presidents	Average Power Divergence Score for Cycle Non-second-Stage-Only Presidents
2nd Extrovert 1844-70	Polk	1845-48	28.4	55.3	16.3	39.0			
	Taylor	1849-50[b]	36.4	45.5	18.2	27.3	23.94	8.15	34.47
	Pierce (SSO)	1853-56	32.9	44.3	22.8	21.5			
	Buchanan (SSO)	1857-60	47.4	23.7	28.9	-5.2			
	Lincoln	1861-65[b]	22.3	57.4	20.3	37.1			
3rd Introvert 1871-90	Grant	1869-76	28.5	43.0	28.5	14.5			
	Hayes (SSO)	1877-80	30.5	27.8	41.7	-13.9	-0.15	-13.9	4.43
	Cleveland	1885-88	27.8	33.4	38.8	-5.4			
	B. Harrison	1889-92	29.2	37.5	33.3	4.2			
	Cleveland	1893-96	26.8	62.5	10.7	51.8			
3rd Extrovert 1891-1918	McKinley	1897-1901[b]	53.2	18.2	28.6	-10.4	31.48		
	T. Roosevelt (SSO)	1901-08	37.5	50	12.5	37.5		37.5	29.98
	Taft	1909-12	25.1	54.9	20.1	34.8			
	Wilson	1913-20	31.3	56.2	12.5	43.7			
4th Introvert 1919-39	Harding	1921-23[b]	25.8	41.9	32.2	9.7			
	Coolidge	1923-28	26.9	50	23.1	26.9	22.35	11.1	26.1
	Hoover (SSO)	1929-32	44.4	33.3	22.2	11.1			
	F. Roosevelt[c]	1933-45[b]	41.7	50	8.3	41.7			

	President	Years							
4th Extrovert	F. Roosevelt[c]	1933–45[b]	41.7	50	8.3	41.7			27.5
	Truman	1945–52	27.0	48.6	24.3	24.3	21.3	-3.5	27.5
	Eisenhower (SSO)	1953–60	25.0	35.7	39.2	-3.5			
1940–67	Kennedy	1961–63[b]	33.4	40.7	25.9	14.8			
	L. Johnson	1963–68	45.8	41.7	12.5	29.2			
	Nixon	1969–74[b]	45.0	27.5	27.5	0			
5th Introvert	Carter (SSO)	1977–80	36.4	30.3	33.3	-3	2.73	-3	5.6
1968–	Reagan	1981–	45.8	32.7	21.5	11.2			
	Average of all Presidents						17.56	6.36	21.91
	Average of Extrovert Presidents						25.57	12.58	30.3
	Average of Introvert Presidents						8.82	-1.93	12.85

Notes: Achievement, power, and affiliation scores, the three components of the total motive score, may not add up to 100 because of rounding.

[a] A second-stage-only president is one who is classified exclusively in a second stage. Therefore, Coolidge and Truman, even though they are classified as second-stage presidents, are not counted as second-stage-only presidents because they are also classified in other stages. Stage classifications are based on the following criteria: presidents who spent two full terms or more in office must spend more than three years in the phase to be put in that phase. Presidents spending more than one full term, but less than two full terms, must spend more than two years in a phase to be so classified. Presidents with one term or less are placed according to where they spent most of their time in office; in the instance of ties, presidents are included in the phase during which they were elected. Years are worked so as to not overlap in the case of elected succession. In cases where a president dies in office or resigns, the transition year is allowed to overlap. Because the fifth introvert phase is still in progress, we are relying on the average 21-year pattern of introvert phases and are using seven years for these stages. President Garfield, who served less than seven months, is not included in our analysis.

[b] These presidents died or resigned while in office, and their successors took over in midyear.

[c] F. Roosevelt is included in both the fourth introvert cycle and the fourth extrovert cycle according to the rules of classification. Therefore, his score is used once when finding the average of all presidents and once in each average when finding the average of introvert and extrovert presidents.

Sources: Winter and Stewart (1976, p. 53). Scores for Polk-McKinley, Carter, and Reagan were derived by our own coders who followed Winter's manual (1973, pp. 247–66).

argued that over a 150-year period three cycles of price rises and falls could be traced, each lasting between 40 and 60 years (Kondratieff 1935). Kondratieff's long-wave dates are as follows:

First Long Wave: The rise lasted from the end of the 1780s or beginning of the 1790s to 1810-17. The decline lasted from 1810-17 until 1844-51.
Second Long Wave: The rise lasted from 1844-51 until 1870-75. The decline lasted from 1870-75 until 1890-96.
Third Long Wave: The rise lasted from 1890-96 until 1914-20. The decline probably begins in the years 1914-20.

Although the literature on economic long cycles is extensive, we have selected the dates offered by five long-cycle researchers as a basis for a comparison with the Klingberg-Holmes foreign policy and motivational long cycles. Table 10.2 gives the trough and peak dates of these five long-cycle researchers.

As Table 10.2 demonstrates, economic long cyclists have some difficulty agreeing on the dates for turning points of their price cycles. However, in most cases they follow the general pattern of long waves set by Kondratieff. Jacob Van Duijn's figures were chosen as the basis of comparison for most of the remainder of our analysis for several reasons.[2] His dates are generally close to those of Kondratieff. Also, Van Duijn's analysis covers the entire period of our comparison. Finally, Van Duijn (1981, p. 268) breaks his cycles into four stages, which provide a good basis for comparison with the Klingberg-Holmes mood cycle and Holmes-Elder stages of that cycle.

Table 10.3 charts Van Duijn's phases of economic long cycles and provides major macroeconomic characteristics for each phase. Although the first three characteristics in Table 10.3 are Van Duijn's, the last four (employment, productivity, propensity to innovate, and prices) have been added to his original chart in order to create a more complete economic picture.

Van Duijn's stage dates are similar to the Holmes-Elder mood-stage dates and provided an opportunity for comparison. On this basis we hypothesized that we would find a fit between domestic periods of recovery and Holmes-Elder third-stage introvert periods. Periods of prosperity would be linked to Holmes-Elder first- and second-stage extrovert periods. Third-stage extrovert periods would

Table 10.2 Economic Long-Cycle Theorists: Peak and Trough Years in Price Cycles Compared to Klingberg-Holmes Transition Years in Foreign Policy Cycles

	Trough	Peak	Trough	Peak	Trough	Peak	Trough	Peak
Rostow	1790	1815	1848	1873	1896	1920	1933	1951[a]
Mandel	—	—	1848	1873	1893	1913	1940	1970
Kondratieff (average of two ends)	1789	1813	1847	1872	1893	1917	—	—
Van Duijn	1782	1825	1845	1873	1892	1929	1948	1973
Modelski[b]	1792	1815	1848	1873	1913	1946	1973	—
Klingberg-Holmes	1798	1824	1844	1871	1891	1919	1940	1968

[a]Most sources consulted by the authors do not agree with this early peak. See Forrester (1981) for a development of the dominant viewpoint.

[b]Modelski classifies the entire 1913-46 phase as one of war. Most sources do not view this as correct, and indeed Klingberg (1952) and Holmes (1985) place a United States introvert phase between the two world wars.

Sources: Elder and Holmes (1982, p. 3); Rostow (1978, pp. 20-37); Kondratieff (1935, p. 111); Van Duijn (1981, p. 268); Mandel (1981, pp. 332-38); and Modelski (1981, p. 73).

Table 10.3   Fiscal Economic Indicators[a]

	Depression	Recovery	Prosperity	Recession
Gross National Product	Little or no growth	Increasing growth rates	Strong growth	Decreasing growth rates
Investment Demand	Excess capacity rationalization	Increase in replacement investment	Strong expansion of capital stock	Scale-increasing investment
Consumer Demand	Growth at expense of savings	Purchase power seeks new outlets	Expansion of demand in all sectors	Continued growth in new sectors
Employment High/Low	Down	Up	Up	Down
Prices High/ Low	Low	Up	Up	Leveling
Innovations High/Low	Up	Up	Slowing but continue and change in nature	Low
Productivity High/Low	Low	Up	Up, but slowing in upward ascent	Decreasing

Source: Van Duijn (1981, p. 268). The last four characteristics were added by the authors in order to form a more complete macroeconomic picture.

have the greatest predisposition toward recessions and depressions would fall predominantly within Holmes-Elder first- and second-stage introvert periods.

Table 10.4 compares Van Duijn phases of Kondratieff cycles with Holmes-Elder cycle stages in Klingberg-Holmes extrovert and introvert periods from 1798-1974.

Out of 19 possible phase-stage relations, agreement was found 13 times. The other six cases all occurred after 1913 and appear one phase late. If the Van Duijn phases after 1920 are moved up one position, agreement is found in all 19 cases. One possible explanation for this occurrence is that the prosperity/war phase of 1913-20 (World War I) interrupted the normal sequence of economic phases. Another possibility is that the expanding role of the U.S. government in this century makes economic patterns less distinct over time.

Although small discrepancies do exist between the Klingberg-Holmes cycles and economic long cycles, the relationship between the two is very suggestive. For example, positive international economic signals precede U.S. movements into extroversion in all four instances for which comparative data are available (1792-1802, 1836-45, 1883-92, and 1937-48).

Small and Singer War Data

If the Klingberg-Holmes U.S. mood cycle is related to Kondratieff's international economic cycle, how do the two compare to patterns of international violence? To test this we looked at Small and Singer's (1982) data for interstate wars under way and begun and total battle deaths, and compared these indicators to Klingberg-Holmes mood cycles and the direction of Kondratieff's long waves. Our results appear in Table 10.5.

This table shows that data for wars have some relationship to mood cycles and international economic flow, with the most graphic demonstration found in battle deaths, an indicator of the severity of conflict. However, these results did not prove conclusively a connection between international violence and specific economic trends.

Van Duijn's divisions of economic long waves were used in Table 10.6 in an attempt to find more definite results. We took the three major indicators of interstate war from Small and Singer from the previous table and applied these to both international and American wars. First we looked at the instances of conflict by each specific Van Duijn phase and then in terms of action by each of the four major economic phase types.

When war data were examined in this manner, a clearer picture emerged, especially for nation months begun per year and battle deaths, also counted in the years war began by Small and Singer. These indicators showed a tendency for nations to get involved in wars in recovery and prosperity phases; these wars may drag on, as evidenced by the differences between figures for war begun and war

Table 10.4 Holmes-Elder Stages Matched with Van Duijn Long-Cycle Stages

Holmes-Elder Extrovert and Introvert Stages	Van Duijn Dates		
1st Extrovert Phase 1798-1823			
1st Stage 1798-06	1792-1806	Prosperity	Fit
2nd Stage 1807-14	1802-15	Prosperity/War	Fit
3rd Stage 1815-23	1815-25	Recession	Fit
2nd Introvert Phase 1824-43			
1st Stage 1824-30	1825-36	Depression	Fit
2nd Stage 1831-36			
3rd Stage 1837-43	1836-45	Recovery	Fit
2nd Extrovert Phase 1844-70			
1st Stage 1844-52	1845-57	Prosperity	Fit
2nd Stage 1853-61	1857-66	Prosperity	Fit
3rd Stage 1862-70	1866-73	Recession	Fit
3rd Introvert Phase 1871-90			
1st Stage 1871-77	1873-83	Depression	Fit
2nd Stage 1878-83			
3rd Stage 1884-90	1883-92	Recovery	Fit
3rd Extrovert Phase 1891-1918			
1st Stage 1891-99	1892-1903	Prosperity	Fit
2nd Stage 1900-08	1903-13	Prosperity	Fit
3rd Stage 1909-18	1913-20	Prosperity/War	No Fit
4th Introvert Phase 1919-39			
1st Stage 1919-25	1920-29	Recession	No Fit
2nd Stage 1926-32			
3rd Stage 1933-39	1929-37	Depression	No Fit
4th Extrovert Phase 1940-67			
1st Stage 1940-48	1937-48	Recovery	No Fit
2nd Stage 1949-57	1948-57	Prosperity	Fit
3rd Stage 1958-67	1957-66	Prosperity	No Fit
5th Cycle 1968			
1st Stage 1968-74	1966-73	Recession	No Fit
			13/19 (68.4%)

Sources: Van Duijn (1981, p. 268) and Elder and Holmes (1982, p. 10).

under way. This suggests that during times of economic upswings wars are begun much more frequently than during downswings. Thus, the availability of money during upswings may promote expansion of the military establishment of nations, leading to an increased tendency toward war. During harsher economic times, money is not as easily channeled to defense spending. The fact that recovery periods evidence nearly as much war as times of prosperity (war that is usually more severe as evidenced by the amount of battle deaths) is due greatly to events in the twentieth century. One possible explanation of this is that the widespread knowledge of Keynesian economics has enabled governments to spend money to advance politicomilitary aims as soon as economic signals begin to brighten, using the argument that such deficit expenditure "primes the pump."

It is important to note that American wars are more closely related to Van Duijn phases than are the wars of the entire international system. Indeed, specific patterns are discernible. First, an American war has occurred before every economic downturn. The Civil War, not listed in Table 10.6, fits this pattern. One conflict, the Vietnam War, started before the downturn and continued through a large part of it. Second, there has been an American war after every recovery. World War II is the one exception, a war during recovery that the United States was, for the most part, forced to enter. Thompson and Zuk (1982) also note that recovery precedes wars, while downturns follow. Certainly these conclusions apply to the results found in U.S. data. The fact that we found battle deaths to be an important indicator shows that their emphasis on major wars rather than all wars is well placed.[3]

When major American wars are related to moods, several interesting relationships are suggested (Holmes 1985). Major wars that occur in the first third of extrovert phases (Mexican-American War, Spanish-American War, and World War II) tend to be won decisively. Major wars at the end of extrovert phases (Civil War, World War I, and the Vietnam War) tend to end in bitterness and alienation, while major wars in the middle of extrovert phases (War of 1812 and the Korean War) tend to end in stalemate. The precise interaction between U.S. public mood and international economics cannot be delineated on the basis of the data in this chapter, but it appears that the patterns operate in a mutually supporting manner.

Obviously there are important patterns in the relationship be-

Table 10.5   Klingberg-Holmes Mood Curves Compared to Small and Singer Interstate War Data and Kondratieff Waves

Klingberg-Holmes Cycles	Nation Months of International War per Year of Phase[a]		Total Battle Deaths per Year of Phase (thousands)	Kondratieff Waves
	Under Way	Begun		
1st Extrovert 1798-1823	No data	No data	No data	Up
2d Introvert 1824-1843	.576	.506	11.1	Down
2d Extrovert 1844-1870	.710	.719	40.08	Up
3d Introvert 1871-1890	.672	.541	18.28	Down
3d Extrovert 1891-1918	.780	.800	322.71	Up
4th Introvert 1919-1939	.379	.708[b]	171.1[c]	Down
4th Extrovert 1940-1967	1.017	.871[b]	586.50[c]	Up
5th Introvert 1968-	Not complete	Not complete	Not complete	Down

[a]Normalized by system size by Small and Singer. Their methodology was to determine total nation months of war under way or begun for each year and divide this number by the number of nations in the international system during that year. This procedure yielded the "nation months of war" figure "normalized by system size."

[b]Nation months of war begun for World War II were distributed between the 4th introvert and 4th extrovert phases according to the years in which each individual country entered the conflict. Thus, for example, all nation months for the United Kingdom and Germany were counted in 1939 while all nation months for the United States were attributed after 1939. This was done because nations did not enter the conflict at the same time, and since WW II had the highest incidence of nation months of any entry in Small and Singer's data, it was hoped this procedure would yield a more accurate picture of the violence involved.

[c]Battle deaths for World War II were averaged by year from 1939 to 1945 in order to provide a more accurate representation of battle deaths in the 4th extrovert phase. This was necessary because Small and Singer place total battle deaths for each war in the year in which the war began. In this case all

252

tween international economic cycles and war, both international and American, that require further investigation. However, the regularity of American patterns as compared to other nations suggests that internal dynamics such as U.S. mood are quite important.

Motivation

In line with our earlier suggestion that mood change was a function of the intensity of power, achievement, or affiliative motivation, we also tested for statistical relationships between U.S. motivations and international economic indicators.

In earlier papers, a close relationship had been found to exist between David McClelland's high-power–low-affiliation years and Klingberg-Holmes's extrovert phases. Similarly, McClelland's low-power years seemed to tie in with introvert phases (Elder and Holmes 1982). Since Van Duijn's prosperity phases normally appear during extrovert phases, it was natural to suppose that we might find a relationship between Van Duijn's prosperity phases and McClelland's high-power years, while low-power years would correspond to periods of economic downturn.

There was also evidence in McClelland (1961) indicating that those people who are labeled high achievers do not tend to be risk takers, while those persons with high-power tendencies, although more daring, are less oriented to problem-solving in systematic ways. We hypothesized that achievers, being less oriented to taking gambles, would not attempt high levels of innovation during prosperity since there was no need to take a chance. On this basis it would be proper to suppose high levels of both achievement motivation and innovation might occur together during economic downturns because depression and recovery necessitate new and more efficient methods of operation. Conversely, during high-prosperity periods when systematic economic problem-solving and innovation are less necessary, heightened power scores by presidents and values relating

---

the World War II battle deaths were attributed to 1939 (the last year in the 4th introvert phase), a year that definitely did not have the greatest amount of actions in the war.

Sources: Small and Singer (1982, pp. 118-22, 151-54); Table 10.2, Table 10.4.

to power in literature would be more readily tolerated by the U.S. population.

In order to test this hypothesis, we looked at McClelland's literary high- and low-power years and also examined presidential inaugurals under the system developed by Winter as they appear in Table 10.1. By doing this, we hoped to get a representation of the predominant motive of the U.S. public as expressed by the president in his inaugural address and best-selling literature. Winter's presidential motives and McClelland's high-low years are compared to Van Duijn's phases and innovative behaviors in Table 10.7.

McClelland's decades of high- or low-power divergence agree with Van Duijn's phases of economic growth in 10 of 15 instances where comparative data are available (66.7 percent). Power divergence scores derived from Winter's scoring of presidential inaugurals agree on 9 of 14 instances (64.3 percent). Periods of recession and recovery are characterized by lower power divergence scores in both U.S. literature and presidential inaugural addresses. Seeming to challenge our own hypothesis was the strong relationship in some cases between economic depressions and power predispositions in both best-selling literature and presidential inaugurals. It is possible that depressions, as major crises, call for strong actions and daring, and so high-power leaders are therefore chosen. Also, please note that high-power scores in such presidents are often matched by equally high scores in achievement. Franklin Roosevelt (power 50, achievement 41.7) is one case in point. The possible relationship between power-achievement balance, Van Duijn's periods, and tendency to innovate is suggested more clearly in the columns in Table 10.7 where separate power and achievement averages of Winter's inaugural addresses and predispositions to innovate are averaged by Van Duijn's periods of prosperity and depression. Although data are available only for two cycles of prosperity and depression, note that there is a rough parity between achievement and power in periods of economic downturn, which becomes an imbalance favoring power during periods of prosperity. Similarly, Van Duijn's innovations for these same periods follow the expected pattern rising during periods when the balance between achievement and power is close and falling relative to each cycle as power begins to predominate. Thus, although illustrative data are sparse, they do correspond to rather than contradict our hypothesis.

The relationship we expected to find between increases in presidential power-divergence scores and low levels of innovation is also present. The higher the power divergence evidenced in presidential inaugurals, the lower the innovative tendency. However, when we compared combined achievement plus affiliation scores with innovative behaviors, a clear pattern emerged only after we looked at the total average scores for all four of Van Duijn's phases. Our results appear in Table 10.8.

Table 10.8 shows the power-divergence scores to be highest during prosperity phases and lowest in depression phases. Conversely, the lowest combined achievement and affiliation scores occur in periods of prosperity, and the highest in depressions. Van Duijn's findings relating innovations to economic phases are essentially borne out. When we checked the relationship our hypothesis predicted between innovations and combined achievement and affiliation scores, we found that with the exception of recessions, the higher the combined affiliation and achievement scores, the greater the propensity to innovate. Recessions simply do not reward innovations.

Summary and Conclusions

What can we learn from the set of relationships discussed and outlined above? The fact that we found U.S. wars, as opposed to international wars, having a stronger relationship to both the Klingberg-Holmes U.S. mood phases and the Van Duijn divisions of the Kondratieff waves argues for the importance of U.S. trends, as does Holmes (1985). It is our impression that the close agreement between Klingberg-Holmes and economic cycles stems from the existence of a relationship between money made available for defense expenditure, predisposition toward an expansionist foreign policy, and war, and a relationship between introversion, postwar economic deterioration, declines of government revenue, and less foreign involvement. It should be remembered that Klingberg (1952) originally utilized naval expenditure data as well as information about armed expeditions to construct his introvert and extrovert phases. Figure 10.2 demonstrates the close relationship between money spent on arms and economic upturns or downturns by adapting the naval expenditure chart utilized by Klingberg and overlapping it with troughs and peaks in U.S. price cycles. Note that price rises appear to

Table 10.6 Van Duijn Phases Matched with Small and Singer Interstate War Data

Van Duijn Phases[d]		International War			American War			Major American Wars
		Nation Months Under Way	Nation Months Begun	Battle Deaths (thousands)	Nation Months Under Way	Nation Months Begun	Battle Deaths (thousands)	
1782-1814[b]	Prosperity/War	No Data	No Data	No Data	No Data	No Data	No Data	(1812-14 War of 1812)
1815-24	Recession	.394	.656	3.67	0	0	0	
1825-35	Depression	.655	.481	16	0	0	0	
1836-44	Recovery	.4	.536	5.11	0	0	0	
1845-56	Prosperity	.567	.511	30.76	.047	.047	.92	(1845-48 Mexican-American)
1857-65	Prosperity	.618	1.108	43.28	0	0	0	
1866-72	Recession	1.046	.586	46.23	0	0	0	
1873-82	Depression	.963	1.023	35.05	0	0	0	
1883-91	Recovery	.331	.067	1.68	0	0	0	
1892-1902	Prosperity	.441	.442	11.23	.013	.013	.46	(1898-Spanish American, 1900 Boxer Rebellion)
1903-12	Prosperity	.239	.268	24.6	0	0	0	
1913-19	Prosperity/War	2.259	2.511	1261.04	.061	.064	18	(1917-18 World War I)
1920-28	Recession	.357	.173	3.67	0	0	0	
1929-36	Depression	.241	.244	26.65	0	0	0	

1937-47	Recovery	1.707	1.645	1490.19	.073	.073	37.12	(1941–45 World War II)
1948-56	Prosperity	.978	.962	219.15	.054	.055	6	(1950–53 Korean War)
1957-65	Prosperity	.157	.659	135.98	.01	.09	6.22	(1965–73 Vietnam War)
1966-73	Recession	.644	.135	8.03	.08	0	0	

	Averages by Van Duijn Phase Type[c]			
	Prosperity	Recession	Depression	Recovery
International				
Nation Months Under Way	.681	.583	.647	.874
Nation Months Begun	.833	.383	.603	.811
Battle Deaths (thousands)	196.29	13.75	25.51	567.35
American				
Nation Months Under Way	.026	.019	0	.028
Nation Months Begun	.036	0	0	.028
Battle Deaths (thousands)	3.76	0	0	14.08

Note: All figures are averaged per year in stage. Nation months of war per year are normalized by system size. Small and Singer's methodology is found in note a, Table 10.5. American nation month data were normalized for system size by the authors in the same manner. Battle deaths are in the year the conflict was initiated.

[a]For statistical counting reasons, transition years have been included in the new phase.
[b]Small and Singer data begin with 1816; thus Van Duijn phase for the period 1815-25 is short one year in the calculations.
[c]Average is total battle deaths or normalized nation months per phase type divided by total years.
Sources: Small and Singer (1982, pp. 82–95, 118–22, 151–54) and Table 10.4.

Table 10.7 Van Duijn Phases Compared to McClelland Years, Inaugural Scores, and Innovative Behaviors

Van Duijn Economic Phases	Presidential Power and Achievement Scores Averaged by Van Duijn Periods of Prosperity and Depression			McClelland High/ Low Power Years[a]	Presidential Power Divergence Scores[b]	Presidential Achievement Scores (Achievement plus Affiliation in parentheses)[b]	Innovative Behaviors per Year in Van Duijn Phase[c]	Innovations per Year Averaged for Van Duijn Phases by Prosperity and Depression
	Ach.	Gap	Power					
1792–1801 Prosperity	—	—	—	1795 High (Fit)	—	—	—	—
1802–14 Prosperity/War	—	—	—	1805 High (Fit)	—	—	—	—
1815–24 Recession	—	—	—	1815 Low (Fit)	—	—	—	—
1825–35 Depression	—	—	—	1825 High (No Fit)	—	—	—	—
1836–44 Recovery	—	—	—		—	—	.111	—
1845–56 Prosperity	33.48	11.76	45.24	1845 High (Fit)	29.27 (Fit)	32.5 (51.67)	.167	.250
1857–65 Prosperity				1865 Low (No Fit)	15.95 (No Fit)	34.85 (59.45)	.333	
1866–72 Recession	—	—			14.5 (Fit)	28.5 (57)	.143	—

258

Period	Van Duijn phase				Year	McClelland						
1873-82	Depression	29.0	6.42	35.42	1875	Low (Fit)	.3	(Fit)	29.5	(64.6)	.4	.4
1883-91	Recovery	—	—		1885	Low (Fit)	-.6	(Fit)	28.5	(64.55)	.778	—
1892-1902	Prosperity	34.78	13.58		1895	High (Fit)	20.7	(Fit)	40.	(59.65)	.545	.4225
1903-12	Prosperity			48.36	1905	Low (No Fit)	36.5	(Fit)	31.3	(47.6)	.3	
1913-19	Prosperity/War				1915	No Data	43.7	(Fit)	31.3	(43.8)	.714	
1920-28	Recession				1925	Low (Fit)	18.3	(Fit)	26.35	(54)	.889	
1929-36	Depression	43.05	1.39	41.66	1935	High (No Fit)	26.4	(No Fit)	43.05	(58.3)	1.111	1.111
1937-47	Recovery				1945	Low (Fit)	33	(No Fit)	34.35	(50.65)	1	
1948-56	Prosperity				1955	Low (No Fit)	10.4	(No Fit)	26	(57.75)	1.667	
1957-65	Prosperity				1965	High (Fit)	13.5	(No Fit)	34.73	(60.60)	.333	
1966-73	Recession						14.6	(Fit)	45.4	(65.4)	.286	
						10/17 (66.7%)		9/14 (64.3%)				

[a]If a Van Duijn phase contained two McClelland high/low power years, only the first year was considered.

[b]Presidential power divergence, achievement, and affiliation scores are classified into Van Duijn phases according to the same rules as their classification into Holmes-Elder stages. See Table 10.1, note a, for rules of classification. A power divergence score of 18.73, the average of all presidents (Polk–Nixon), or higher is considered high, while 18.72 and below is considered low.

[c]Van Duijn lists major innovations in 13 industrial sections since 1840. The authors calculated innovative behaviors per year for each Van Duijn phase.

Sources: McClelland (1975, p. 46); Van Duijn (1981, pp. 271-73); Table 10.1 and Table 10.4

259

Table 10.8   Average of Power Divergence, Innovative Behaviors, and Combined Achievement and Affiliation by Van Duijn Phase

Van Duijn Phase	Power Divergence Score	Achievement and Affiliation	Innovation
Recovery	16.2	57.6	.655
Prosperity	24.42	54.66	.552
Recession	16.06	59.16	.458
Depression	13.35	61.45	.778

Note: Averages are derived as sums divided by total number of years in each type of Van Duijn phase.
Sources: Table 10.1, Table 10.4, and Table 10.7.

precede naval expenditures during the first two cycles. In the third cycle, both prices and expenditures peak in the same year, although prices rise later than naval expenditures. In the fourth cycle, prices again rise before naval expenditures.

Other persons have pointed to the strong importance of domestic policy in examining international trends. For example, work by Namenwirth (1973) and Weber (1983) analyzes U.S. and British economic and issue cycles respectively in the context of Kondratieff. Weber (1983, p. 46) notes that, taken together, these studies of British and U.S. trends "provide powerful empirical evidence for Wallerstein's (1974) observation that although states in the world-system are linked via the world-economy, their internal political dynamics are much more independent." Interestingly, the Namenwirth study identifies four U.S. parochial value phases that, on the average, start within two years of the Holmes-Elder third-stage introvert phases and three cosmopolitan value phases that start within two years of the Holmes-Elder third-stage extrovert phases. This relationship points out the fact that more work needs to be done on interactions between national and international cycles. A useful starting point would be to compare U.S. price data and data on innovations to U.S. moods and motives.

The important consideration for practitioners of foreign policy formulation is to keep public attention on such long-range tendencies. Our basic power interests do not change with shifts in moods, motives, or economic prosperity. They have been relatively consistent across time (Holmes 1985, Ch. 3).

Currently, President Reagan, a conservative Republican, has been playing a role that Franklin Roosevelt, a liberal Democrat, played in the 1930s by attempting to rearm the United States during its worst economic downturn since the Great Depression. The hostility of nuclear freeze advocates and many Democrats to Reagan's positions on El Salvador, Nicaragua, Lebanon, the MX and

Figure 10.2 Klingberg's Naval Expenditure Chart and American Price-Cycle Turning Points

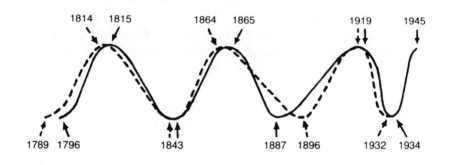

―――――――――― = Klingberg
- - - - - - - - - - -= Hartman and Wheeler

	Trough	Peak	Trough	Peak	Trough	Peak	Trough	Peak
Klingberg U.S. Naval Expenditure Analysis	1796	1815	1843	1865	1887	1919	1934	1945
Hartman and Wheeler U.S. Price Cycle Analysis	1789	1814	1843	1864	1896	1919	1932	—

Sources: Klingberg (1952, p. 259) and Hartman and Wheeler (1979, p. 47).

Pershing missile options, and his increases in defense expenditures are as strong as the tirades that isolationists of both parties leveled at Roosevelt in the 1930s. On this occasion, however, the menace to U.S. security, if not greater, is certainly closer to home.

The current increase in U.S. defense spending and economic upturn could represent a new Kondratieff upswing. We cannot, of course, predict the future, but if past patterns continue, a new U.S. extrovert phase will begin during the coming decade. Readers can, no doubt, imagine potential problems in the nuclear age. Possibly the best way to avoid such problems is to anticipate them by an informed understanding of long-term trends.

We can wish neither war nor human nature away. We need to pay consistent attention to our strategic interests, neither over- nor undercommitting defense expenditures along the way. This takes politically wise statesmen with a sense of history who are willing to work for bipartisanship in foreign policy over time. In a democracy this takes considerable courage. Are we asking for more than is realistically possible? A useful beginning would be for specialists in foreign affairs to take off short-term ideological blinders in the interest of understanding long-term economic relationships and motive shifts as they impact on U.S. foreign policy.

Notes

1. Each introvert-extrovert cycle spans approximately 50 years. Introvert periods, which average 21 years, are divided into three seven-year stages with short or extra years put in the second stage. Extrovert periods, which average 27 years, are divided into nine-year segments with short or extra years put in the third stage.

2. Van Duijn bases his phases on Schumpeterian concepts (1939). The concepts are originally Schumpeter's and are expanded on by Van Duijn. Van Duijn places two wars under prosperity, but does not include the wars in prosperity dates. In our calculations, based on the idea that wars extend prosperity, we included the wars within prosperity dates.

3. We did not test Thompson and Zuk's (1982) conclusions about wars as a cause of the magnitude of the Kondratieff waves.

Bibliography

Barber, James D. 1977. *The Presidential Character.* Englewood Cliffs, N.J.: Prentice-Hall.

Donley, Richard E. and David Winter. 1970. "Measuring the Motives of Public Officials at a Distance: An Exploratory Study of American Presidents." *Behavioral Science* 15, pp. 227-36.

Elder, Robert E. 1981. "A Comparison of Winter's Motives and Barber's Character: Toward a Unified Theory of Presidential Personality." Presented at the Political Science Section, Michigan Academy, University of Michigan, March, Ann Arbor, Michigan.

———————————— and Jack E. Holmes. 1982. "Presidential and Societal Motives Related to U.S. Foreign Policy Moods: Toward a Combined Theory." Presented at the Annual Meeting of the International Studies Association, March, Cincinnati, Ohio.

Forrester, Jay W. 1981. "Innovation and Economic Change." *Futures* (August), pp. 323-31.

Hartman, Raymond S. and David R. Wheeler. 1979. "Schumpeterian Waves of Innovation and Infrastructure Development in Great Britain and the United States: The Kondratieff Cycle Revisited." *Research in Economic History* 4, pp. 37-85.

Holmes, Jack E. 1985. *The Mood/Interest Theory of American Foreign Policy.* Lexington: University Press of Kentucky.

———————————. 1976. "The Mood/Interest Theory of American Foreign Policy." Presented at the Annual Meeting of the International Studies Association, March, Toronto, Canada.

———————————— and Robert E. Elder. 1983. "Classifying Presidents and U.S. Foreign Policy Moods." Presented at the Annual Meeting of the International Studies Association, April, Mexico City, Mexico.

Klingberg, Frank L. 1983. *Cyclical Trends in American Foreign Policy Moods.* Lanham, Md.: University Press of America.

———————————. 1979. "Cyclical Trends in American Foreign Policy Moods: Policy Trends and Their Policy Implications." In *Challenges to America: United States Foreign Policy in the 1980's*, ed. Charles W. Kegley, Jr. and Patrick J. McGowan, pp. 37-55. Beverly Hills: Sage.

———————————. 1952. "The Historical Alternation of Moods in American Foreign Policy." *World Politics* 4 (January), pp. 239-73.

Kondratieff, N. D. 1935. "The Long Waves in Economic Life." *Review of Economic Statistics* 17 (November), pp. 105-15 (trans. W. F. Stolper).

Mandel, Ernest. 1981. "Explaining Long Waves of Capitalist Development." *Futures* (August), pp. 332-38.

McClelland, David C. 1975. "Love and Power: The Psychological Signals of War." *Psychology Today* 8 (January), pp. 44-48.

———————————. 1961. *The Achieving Society.* Princeton, N.J.: Van Nostrand.

————————————, ed. 1955. *Studies in Motivation.* New York: Appleton-Century-Crofts.

Modelski, George. 1981. "Long Cycles, Kondratieffs, and Alternating Innovations: Implications for U.S. Foreign Policy." In *The Political Economy of Foreign Policy Behavior,* ed. by Charles W. Kegley, Jr. and Patrick McGowan, pp. 63-83. Beverly Hills: Sage.

Namenwirth, J. Zvi. 1973. "The Wheels of Time and the Interdependence of Value Change." *Journal of Interdisciplinary History* 3 (Spring), pp. 649-83.

Rostow, W. W. 1978. *Getting From Here to There.* New York: McGraw-Hill.

Russett, Bruce. 1983. "Prosperity and Peace." *International Studies Quarterly* 27 (December), pp. 381-84.

Schumpeter, Joseph. 1939. *Business Cycles I.* Philadelphia: Porcupine Press.

Small, Melvin and J. David Singer. 1982. *Resort to Arms: International and Civil Wars, 1816-1980.* Beverly Hills: Sage.

Thompson, William R. and L. Gary Zuk. 1982. "War, Inflation, and the Kondratieff Long Wave." *Journal of Conflict Resolution* 26 (December), pp. 621-44.

Van Duijn, Jacob J. 1981. "Fluctuations in Innovations Over Time." *Futures* (August), pp. 264-75.

Wallerstein, I. 1974. *The Modern World System.* New York: Academic.

Weber, Robert P. 1983. "Cyclical Theories of Crisis in the World System." In *Crises in the World System,* ed. A. Bergesen, pp. 37-55. Beverly Hills: Sage.

Winter, David G. 1973. *The Power Motive.* New York: Free Press.

——————————————— and Abigail J. Stewart. 1977. "Content Analysis as a Technique for Assessing Political Leaders." In *A Psychological Examination of Political Leaders,* ed. Margaret G. Herman, pp. 27-61. New York: Free Press.

11

Short-Term Cycles and Long-Run Consequences: A Reformulation of the Theory of Capitalist Imperialism

PAT McGOWAN

This chapter establishes the groundwork for and then specifies a political-economic model of British imperialism in the period 1870-1914. The theoretical model is in the form of eight equations that are open to evaluation by standard econometric time-series techniques. The model assumes: the existence of a short-term, eight-to-nine-year business cycle in Great Britain; that during this historical period Britain was a laissez-faire political economy in which the government did not consciously engage in countercyclical macroeconomic policies; and that there existed in Britain a social class of investors—individuals and institutions—possessed with discretionary income seeking the best possible returns for their investments. From these historically plausible assumptions flow long-run generalizations about British economic growth (capitalist accumulation), the growth of the British Empire after 1870, British arms spending, and British conflict with other capitalist powers (imperialism).

The model seeks to capture in a "testable" form the theories of Lenin (1917/71) and Bukharin (1917/1973) associated with the Marxist critique of monopoly capitalist imperialism. By combining basically Marxist theoretical arguments with a systematically empirical model specification, the chapter brings together two intellectual traditions that have seldom been joined, perhaps to the detriment of our understanding of world politics and the world economy (for bibliographies of the imperialism literature, see Owen and Sutcliffe 1972 and Brewer 1980).

Theoretical Orientation

As the chapters in this book illustrate, social scientists and specialists in international studies have rediscovered the possibly cyclical nature of social, economic, political, and international life. While historians such as Ibn Khaldun, Oswald Spengler, and Arnold Toynbee have long speculated on patterns in the rise and fall of civilizations, the modern, empirically grounded study of cycles derives from the work in the 1920s of the Soviet economist N. D. Kondratieff (1926, 1935; Maddison 1982, pp. 66-73). Focusing on price and production series since the mid-eighteenth century, Kondratieff claimed to have identified and explained "long-waves" of from 40 to 60 years in length, characterized by half-length phases of "rise" and "decline" in prices and economic output.

The clearly cyclical nature of economic life in the capitalist West inspired other research based upon Kondratieff by economists who uncovered a 22-year-long "secondary secular movement" (Kuznets 1930) and cycles of 50-year "Kondratieffs," eight-to-nine-year "Juglars," and 40-month-long "Kitchin" cycles (Schumpeter 1939). After a long period of neglect by professional economists, the post-1973 downturn in the world economy has sparked renewed interest in economic cycles by both conventional (Rostow 1978; Lewis 1978; Maddison 1982) and Marxist economists (Mandel 1975).

Coincident with this renewed interest, historically oriented sociologists and political scientists have returned to the study of long waves and cycles. Sociologists interested in the origins and development of both the capitalist world economy and its political expression, the interstate system, have posited A and B phases of economic growth and then economic stagnation or slower growth in the world economy of some 100 to 150 years in length, and approximately equally long cycles of political-economic "hegemony" by one core capitalist state followed by a period of competition among roughly equal core powers (Hopkins and Wallerstein 1979; Bousquet 1980; Chase-Dunn and Rubinson 1977). Two other sociologists even claim to have identified empirically "long waves" of colonial expansion and contraction since the 1400s (Bergesen and Schoenberg 1980).

Not to be outdone, political scientists at about the same time began to write about "the long cycle of global politics" in which five 100-year-long cycles of rising and falling world political leadership by a succession of dominant global powers are said to exist (Modelski

1978, 1981). The timing of these cycles approximates shifting "moods" in public support for active and passive U.S. foreign policies (Klingberg, 1952, 1979) and Kondratieff's long waves (Modelski 1980, 1981). The richness of recent theorizing by all these "cyclicalists" has inspired a series of empirical studies (Elder and Holmes 1984; Goldstein 1984; Rasler and Thompson 1983; Singer and Cusack 1981; Thompson 1982; and Thompson and Zuk 1982a), as well as debates between those who see these cycles as the expression of a single political-economic logic (Wallerstein 1979, Chs. 1 and 8; Chase-Dunn 1981) and those who see political and economic cycles as related but analytically distinct phenomena (McGowan and Kegley 1983, various chapters; Thompson 1983a, various chapters, 1983b, 1983c).

While much of this debate represents misguided "economism" (Ashley 1983), it has had the great benefit of bringing history back into the study of international relations. Gone forever, it is hoped, are the days in which a model could be advanced that was intentionally *ahistoric* in that it was meant to apply to any social formation throughout recorded history experiencing "lateral pressure," whether that formation was precapitalist, capitalist, or socialist (Choucri and North 1975, pp. 19-20).[1] *Such a position denies the existence of history*—that is to say, social change in fundamental social structures and processes that, however long such changes may take, makes the imperialism of Rome in the time of Christ a different phenomenon from British imperialism in the era of Salisbury.

If our discipline is, indeed, becoming more historical, then the question arises of how to treat time in our research. The great French historian Fernand Braudel has elaborated the notion of "social time," which is a function of the rate of change observable in the phenomenon we study. If our subject matter is the development of capitalism or cycles of world political leadership, then we are working with the *long-duree* in which time is "slow-moving, sometimes practically static" (Braudel 1972, p. 20). A decade or even a generation does not normally evidence much observable change in phenomena of the *long duree*; therefore, knowing that the European "new imperialism" of the 1880s and 1890s that partitioned Africa and Southeast Asia happened toward the end of the fourth cycle of world power leadership (Modelski 1978) does not take us very far in explaining why then and not before or after.

At the other extreme of social time from the *long duree* is episodic or short-term time (Braudel's *evenementielle*), which is "the tempo of individuals, of our illusions and rapid judgment— . . . the chronicler's and journalist's time" (Braudel 1972, p. 14). This is the time of most conventional political science with its preoccupation with periodic elections, or coups d'etat, or international conflict episodes and crises. A model of international crises (Hermann 1972) based upon episodic data can, perhaps, account well for such short-term crises, but it obviously cannot be applied to other "crises" such as that of capitalism in the twentieth century.

Braudel also has a medium-term conception of time, the *conjunctural*, which involves either turning points in cyclical movements such as the onset of a Kondratieff decline between 1870 and 1875 and the onset of a rise between 1890 and 1896 (Maddison 1982, p. 72), or specific historical periods, such as that from 1870 to 1914—the stage of monopoly capitalist imperialism, according to Lenin (1917/1971) and other Marxists. Because social science "models are of varying duration: they have the same time-value as the reality they record" (Braudel 1972, p. 32), model building in the political and social sciences must expressly take time into account by stating the time scope to which the theoretical model is meant to apply.

Thus, in what follows I shall present a model of capitalist imperialism that covers the medium term between 1870 and 1914, which has as its driving mechanism short-term shifts in the eight-to-nine-year business cycle, which seeks to account for long-run consequences such as capital accumulation in the core of the world system and the world-system-transforming event of World War I, and which is further concretized to apply only to one core power, albeit the most important, Great Britain. In so doing I hope to illustrate convincingly the advantages of historical model building and to show that a logically consistent and plausible theory of capitalist expansion and conflict with other expanding capitalist powers, consistent with the well-known theories of Lenin, Bukharin, and Luxemburg, can be created. The roots of this model are found in Marx, however, not in Lenin and other early twentieth-century Marxists. This essential background must, therefore, be presented first.

Marx's Analysis of Capitalism as a World System

To theorize about capitalist imperialism is to address one of the central global issues of our time—international inequality (Tucker

1977)—because only the Marxist tradition argues that such inequality is the theoretically necessary consequence of international economic exchanges (Brewer 1980).[2] Yet, as recently as 1800, after some 300 years of the organization and development of the modern capitalist world system, international inequalities were not yet very large. According to the recent estimates of Bairoch (1979, pp. 164-66), the wealth ratio of poor to rich preindustrial societies was only about 1 to 1.5 or 1.6. Economic inequalities between larger regions such as Europe, India, and China were even less, in the range of 1 to 1.2 or at most 1 to 1.3.

It is not at all unreasonable to argue that the present state of affairs (where the ratio of wealth is 1 to 30 or worse) is to a great degree due to the geographically localized industrialization of one part of the world *in combination with* the full integration of the entire world into one world economy after 1870 because of imperialism and colonialism by the European capitalist powers and the associated revolution in transportation, represented by the iron steamship and the spread of railroads beyond Western Europe and the United States.

While the concern of Marxists since Lenin's time with the related issues of imperialism and international inequality are well known if often ignored by the social science mainstream, it is much less well recognized that the origins of international inequality and a proto-theory of imperialist expansion can be found in the writings of Marx himself (Brewer 1980, pp. 27-60; Hodgart 1977). As early as 1848 Marx said that

> If the free-traders cannot understand how one nation can grow rich at the expense of another, we need not wonder, since these same gentlemen also refuse to understand how within one country one class can enrich itself at the expense of another. (McClelland 1977, p. 269)

Harvey (1977) has shown in brilliant detail that the writings of Marx contain a theory of capitalist imperialism emphasizing the processes of accumulation, crises of accumulation, and the geographical spread of capitalist relations of production.[3] The advantage in starting with Marx when one wishes to construct a theoretical model of imperialism is that he alone has so far developed a general theory of the dynamics of the capitalist mode of production as a totality.

This model of the *long duree* can serve as the groundwork for more historically specific model building, as is done in this chapter. At the heart of Marx's theory is the process of capital accumulation which, because of crises of accumulation, is inherently cyclical in character.

For Marx, capital is not a physical entity, nor is it a set of institutions. Rather, it is a *circulation* process involving the *production* of agricultural and industrial commodities via capitalist relations of production and the *realization* of the value embodied in these commodities by selling them in national and foreign markets. Value is embodied in commodities because the labor power of workers who produce the commodities is not fully compensated. But such value is potential and can be "realized" by the capitalist who "owns" the product only if he can circulate it to markets and then sell it. If, for some reason, the product cannot be sold, then its value is negated and capital as a process of production, circulation, realization, and subsequent expanded production comes to a halt. Such an outcome is contrary to the interests of any given capitalist and of the capitalist class as a whole. Therefore, capitalists are driven to seek means to accumulate capital in whatever fashion is made possible by the forces and relations of production currently in place (Harvey 1977, p. 291).[4]

That capitalists are driven to accumulate capital is well recognized as the central theoretical assertion of Marx's theory of capitalism as a whole. As is also well known, Marx did not believe that the process of accumulation was smooth and automatic. Rather, it was his view that there were contradictions within the dialectical whole of the capitalist system that produced periodic interruptions in the circuit of capital, leading to crises of accumulation. An instance is a realization crisis wherein the capitalists' desires to accumulate have resulted in overproduction and goods remain unsold, thereby negating their value. Such crises are a necessary feature of the capitalist system because they are a consequence of the capitalists' contradictory drives, such as to maximize production and to minimize their wage bill, thereby dampening effective demand.

Realization crises resulting from overaccumulation manifest themselves in unemployment and underemployment, falling rates of profit, accumulating inventories, cutbacks in production, capital surpluses, and lack of investment opportunities. Marx's realization crisis represents the downturn and trough in the conventional economist's business cycle; each has the same appearance and are what we today call recessions. Marx believed that the trend in capitalist economies was upward, but not smoothly so. Periodic realization crises—such as the eight-to-nine-year business cycle of pre-World-War I Great Britain and the more profound stagnations such as the so-called Great Depression of 1873-94—are necessary features of the system not only because they are produced by the contradictory drives of capital, but also because such crises represent the only source of order and rationality in the process of capitalist economic development.

If capitalism as a system is to survive, profits must be enhanced, business cycle troughs must become crests, and recessions must become booms. In short, new conditions for expanded capital accumulation must be created. Historically, the capitalist class has achieved this objective by a combination of the intensification of capitalist relations of production and their spatial expansion. Intensification has proceeded by three means: enhanced labor productivity via the application of labor-saving, high-technology machinery and equipment; creating new social wants and needs through advertising and coordination with other sectors of capital and the state; and promoting population growth at a rate consistent with long-run accumulation. Expansion as a fourth means of overcoming crises in accumulation has involved the creation of what Marx called the "world market" by means of foreign investments, foreign trade promotion, and the incorporation of new regions into the capitalist commodity market (Harvey 1977, pp. 267-68).

These means are not mutually exclusive and are often seen in common, even though there exist trade-offs among them—expansion is not necessary if population growth and the easy creation of new needs and wants within a country work adequately to meet the capitalists' need for a "sound business climate." For the purpose of this chapter I shall focus on the process of spatial expansion beyond national boundaries, which we have seen is driven by the business cycle and other crises of accumulation.

The capitalists' drives to find new opportunities for accumulation by means of expansion lead to constant inventions and innovations in the technology of transportation and communication (McGowan 1984b). Circulation of commodities from the point of production to the market in which they will be sold to realize value is part of the total production process. Circulation obviously has costs, which can be reduced by speedier and safer means of transportation and communication. Marx called the period between production and final sale the "turnover time of capital." He noted that capitalists are driven to reduce turnover time as much as possible by more efficient transportation, and in particular by means of sophisticated credit mechanisms that often result in payment to the producer before the delivery of the product to its final destination.

In their efforts to reduce circulation costs and turnover time, capitalists are driven to "annihilate this space with time" (Marx, *Grundrisse*, p. 539; in Harvey 1977, p. 270). This is done in two ways: the penetration of distant markets via speedier transportation and communication, and the geographical concentration of production in great urban centers and industrial regions to annihilate space with time through economies of scale. Thus, expanded accumulation necessarily leads to the geographical expansion of markets and the geographical concentration of production, or in Marx's words, "flows in space [rapidly increase, while] the market expands spatially, and the periphery in relation to the center . . . is circumscribed by a constantly expanding radius" (Marx, *Theories of Surplus Value, 3,* p. 288; in Harvey 1977, p. 272).

Thus, we see that a center-periphery structure emerges as a necessary consequence of the process of capital accumulation. This has been argued recently by writers such as Baran (1957), Amin (1974), Frank (1978 1979), and Wallerstein (1979, Ch. 1). The process that creates and reproduces imperialistic core-periphery relations is

> a new and international division of labor, a division suited to the requirements of the chief centers of modern industry . . . which . . . converts one part of the globe into a chiefly agricultural field of production, for supplying the other part which remains a chiefly industrial field. (Marx, *Capital, 1,* p. 451; in Harvey 1977, p. 276)

But if this division of labor leads to economic growth for core capitalist states and underdevelopment for the peripheral but increasingly capitalist states and regions, does it not follow that at some point in time this system of exchange will break down as the result of growing impoverishment in the periphery? The answer must be yes if only commodity trade is considered, but it is decidedly no if capital flows are added to the picture.

As Marx noted, "the English are forced to lend to foreign nations in order to have them as customers" *(Grundrisse,* p. 415; in Harvey 1977, p. 276). Lenin, too, recognized the key role of capital exports as opposed to commodity trade. Indeed, he thought it was so central that he made it one of his five defining features of capitalist imperialism: "(3) the export of capital as distinguished from the export of commodities acquires exceptional importance" (Lenin 1917/1971, p. 233). The export of capital transfers effective demand from the core to the periphery of the capitalist world system in exchange for claims on property and incomes in the periphery. This borrowing by peripheral governments and firms pays for a significant part of core exports, thereby reproducing the hierarchical division of labor so central to Marx and Lenin.

Besides directly fostering accumulation via spatial expansion, the mobility of capital has a significant and indirect impact on the overall process of capitalist accumulation in the core. The ultimate threat to capital comes from class struggle and revolutionary action by the proletariat. In times of class struggle in a core country, capital can try to escape the consequences of such class conflict by being mobile and moving to safer havens elsewhere in the core. Or capital can simply threaten to do so, thereby weakening any anticapitalist thrusts by social democratic and nationalist governments in both the core and the periphery. Finally, as emphasized by Lenin, repatriated profits from earlier foreign investments and trade can be used to "buy off" militant workers' movements and political parties by means of genuine material advances, without in any way lessening the consumption of the capitalist class or the long-term profitability of their system. All of these mechanisms have been used in the past, leading to the inference that when imperialism permits increased capital exports and foreign trade, it reduces class conflict at home and thereby facilitates the accumulation process in core countries such as Great Britain.

The theoretical contribution of Bukharin and Lenin was to take Marx's general theory of the necessity of capital to accumulate, and if necessary to do so on an intensifying and expanding spatial scale, and then to apply it creatively to a specific historical period or conjuncture: the late nineteenth-century stage of capitalist development they both called imperialism.

Arguably more original than Lenin (Brewer 1980, pp. 101-17),

Bukharin (1917/1973, p. 110) defined imperialism as both the international policy of finance capital and the ideology that justified expansion by the "civilized powers." The cartelization and monopolization of national industry beginning in the Great Depression between 1873 and 1894 and the scramble for colonies in the 1880s and 1890s created "a few consolidated, organised economic bodies ["the great civilized powers"] on the one hand, and a periphery of underdeveloped countries with a semi-agrarian or agrarian system on the other" (1917/1973, p. 74). However, at the same time that these imperial blocs were being consolidated, production and transportation advances created a global system of production and exchange, Bukharin's "world economy." The resulting contradiction between the nationalization and the internationalization of the capitalist world system at this time was but a new form of the ultimate Marxian contradiction of capitalism: private appropriation based upon social production. In true Marxian fashion, Bukharin argued that the contradiction between these two opposed tendencies was driving the system toward interstate war and ultimate breakdown (Brewer 1980, p. 103).

Lenin's much better known pamphlet may not have the theoretical coherence of Bukharin's analysis,[5] but it is deservedly famous because of its "popular" synthesis of the ideas of Marx, Hobson, Hilferding, and Bukharin, its succinct definition of imperialism as the highest and most recent stage of capitalism (1917/1971, p. 233), and its abundant and forceful descriptions of the operation of the imperialist system over the previous 20 years. For beter or worse, Lenin's identification of Western political and economic expansion after 1880 with the concept of capitalist imperialism has stuck, in spite of all the ink spilled over the years, from Schumpeter to the present, intended to refute both the logic and the details of his analysis.

Taken together, the books by Bukharin and Lenin present a coherent theory-sketch of the forces behind the late-nineteenth-century economic expansion of key capitalist powers such as Great Britain and the political and military consequences of that expansion. Yet, as stated, their theoretical arguments cannot be evaluated other than by historical case studies, of which there have been hundreds. One more such study will not add much to our knowledge base. This suggests that empirical evaluations of their arguments could benefit by the application of different research techniques, such as econometric model specification and estimation. My test case will be the British one, for, as the first industrial nation and the leading capitalist and imperial power from the 1770s to 1914, Great Britain is the closest instance history provides to a "crucial experiment."[6]

A Model of British Imperialism, 1870-1914

The Marxist theoretical orientation I have presented views capitalism as an inherently dynamic system in which accumulation goes forward by expansion beyond national boundaries in an effort to organize a world market. These tendencies are both theoretically inevitable according to Marxists and empirically demonstrable (Kuznets 1973). Once capitalism has reached the stage of imperialism, spatial expansion leads to conflict and violence among the expanding powers. Thus, a hierarchical set of relationships among the key concepts of accumulation, expansion, and conflict is suggested by this theory-sketch. Technically, this notion of causal hierarchy can be modeled in the form of a block-recursive system of equations (Hibbs 1974).

The theoretical viewpoint a block-recursive model is intended to capture is that the process of capitalist accumulation is the taproot of imperialism, that it leads to economic and political-military outreach and expansion, and that both accumulation and expansion result in the long run in conflict and violence among the states that organize and represent accumulation and outreach.

Because I am trying to be as faithful as possible to the classical Marxist tradition, I must posit accumulation as the driving force in my model. However, such a theoretical stance is not incompatible with a recognition that feedbacks within the model may well exist and that interstate conflict in "global wars" (Modelski 1978; Gilpin 1981) has a profound effect upon the opportunities for accumulation and expansion. In my view, however, the way to capture the impact of such possibly system-transforming events is to recognize that they represent conjunctural turning points and to treat them as break points that may require entirely different model specifications, rather than to specify them as "feedback loops" in what would then be a fully recursive model.

Figure 11.1 represents my view of the process of accumulation under conditions of laissez-faire capitalism. This specification draws

Figure 11.1 The Process of Capitalist Accumulation

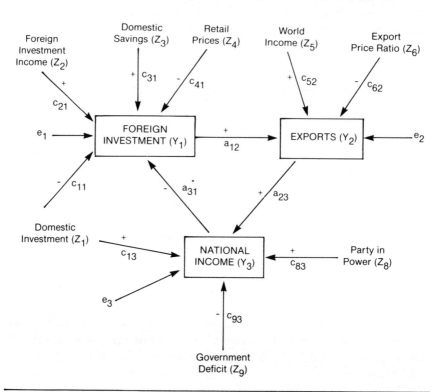

upon the little-known article of Zimmerman and Grumbach (1953) and requires three rather reasonable assumptions. First, it is assumed that the political economy is one of the "night watchman state" of laissez-faire in which governmental decision-makers may well come from the capitalist and aristocratic classes, but they do not consciously engage in macroeconomic management. This assumption leads to a second: that the British national economy will manifest a trade or business cycle of roughly nine years in length in which periods of economic prosperity and domestic investment opportunities alternate with periods of recession and "surplus" capital.[7] Third, I assume that there existed in Britain a property-owning class of individuals, households, and institutions that received incomes beyond its consumption needs and which, therefore, had discretionary income available to it that it sought to invest profitably.

All three of these theoretical assumptions are historically accurate for Great Britain between 1870 and 1914. The beginnings of the welfare state in the United Kingdom date only from David Lloyd George's "peoples" budget of 1909. The entire time period was characterized by a nine-year business cycle that resulted in periodic unemployment rates in the range of 5.7 to 10.7 percent (Sayers 1967, p. 32; Maddison 1982, pp. 74-75, 88-89). Regarding the distribution of income, Hobsbawm's data (1968, Appendix Nos. 43–44) indicate that between 1885 and 1899 only 3 percent of the British public were "rich and very rich," whereas 10 percent were "comfortable middle class," and fully 87 percent were "struggling and poor."

The following theoretical argument can be derived from these assumptions: because of the business cycle, domestic investment was not always attractive to the British middle class and rich. Yet, if their incomes were to grow without periodic interruptions, outlets for profitable investment in times of domestic decline must exist. Foreign investment provided such an outlet. Intentionally or not, foreign investments created foreign demand for British exports, which when paid for increased British national income (however maldistributed) and ended the cyclical decline. That another downturn always occurred was a result of the contradictions of capitalism, particularly those that produce realization crises. Nevertheless, without the equilibrating relationships among domestic and foreign investment, exports, and national income depicted in Figure 11.1, the situation might well have been worse and business-cycle downturns might well have caused system-threatening upturns in class struggle and conflict. In short, British ability to invest abroad smoothed out the business cycle and made British economic growth both more rapid and more steady than it would have been otherwise. Not yet having Keynes, the British consciously (Marxist) or unconsciously (mainstream) invented him in their formal and informal Empire (for these distinctions see Gallagher and Robinson 1953).

Equation I.1 of Table 11.1 and Figure 11.1 is designed to explain the *annual supply* of new British Foreign Investment (Y_1) overseas. Depending upon the state of the domestic business cycle in any year, the capitalist class will invest at home (when the cycle is favorable) or abroad (when it is unfavorable). This leads to the prediction that the coefficient linking domestic and foreign investment ($-c_{11}$) should be significantly negative through time. So should the relationship be-

Table 11.1   An Econometric Model of Capitalist Imperialism

Block I: Capitalist Accumulation

(I.1)   FOREIGN INVESTMENT (Y_1) = constant - a^*_{31} national income (Y^*_3) - c_{11} domestic investment (Z_1) + c_{21} investment income (Z_2) + c_{31} domestic savings (Z_3) - c_{31} retail prices (Z_4) + e_1

(I.2)   EXPORTS (Y_2) = constant + a_{12} foreign investment (Y_1) + c_{52} world income (Z_5) - c_{62} export price ratio (Z_6) + e_2

(I.3)   NATIONAL INCOME (Y_3) = constant + a_{23} exports (Y_2) + c_{13} domestic investment (Z_1) + c_{83} party in power (Z_8) - c_{93} government budget (Z_9) + e_3

Block II: Imperial Expansion

(II.4)   TOTAL FOREIGN INVESTMENT (Y_4) = constant + b_{14} foreign investment (X_1) - b_{24} exports (X_2) + b_{34} national income (X_3) + c_{74} unemployment (Z_7) + c_{104} world imports (Z_{10}) + e_4

(II.5)   SIZE OF EMPIRE (Y_5) = constant + a_{45} total foreign investment (Y_4) + a^*_{55} size of empire (Y^*_5) + b_{15} foreign investment (X_1) - b_{25} exports (X_2) + c_{85} party in power (Z_8) + e_5

(II.6)   ARMAMENTS (Y_6) = constant + a_{56} size of empire (Y_5) + a^*_{66} armaments (Y^*_6) + b_{36} national income (X_3) - c_{96} government budget (Z_9) - c_{116} alliances (Z_{11}) + e_6

Block III: Interstate Conflict

(III.7)   BRITISH COLONIAL CONFLICT (Y_7) = constant + a_{87} violence behavior (Y_8) - b_{27} exports (X_2) + b_{57} size of empire (X_5) + c_{77} unemployment (Z_7) + c_{127} other's colonial conflict with U.K. (Z_{12}) + e_7

(III.8)   BRITISH VIOLENCE BEHAVIOR (Y_8) = constant + a_{78} British Colonial Conflict (Y_7) + b_{58} size of empire (X_5) + b_{68} armaments (X_6) - c_{118} alliances (Z_{11}) + c_{138} other's violence toward U.K. (Z_{13}) + e_8

Key to terms: a_m coefficients go with Y_m endogenous variables; a^*_m with Y^*_m lagged endogenous variables; b_k with X_k predetermined variables; and c_i with Z_i fully exogenous variables.

tween earlier changes in National Income and Foreign Investment $(-a^*_{31})$ for the same reason. Income from previous foreign investments (z_2) was, according to Lenin (1917/1971, pp. 241-48), in part used to corrupt the upper strata of the British working class. There nevertheless remained what we can think of as an "imperial slush fund" that could be recycled each year into new Foreign Investments, hence the positive coefficient c_{21}. These are my three central theoretical expectations about the determinants of annual British Foreign Investment.

One should not, however, ignore conventional theories of foreign investment in that they represent counterhypotheses to the ones just presented. Therefore, the rate of Domestic Savings should positively affect all investments, including new Foreign Investments (c_{31}), and strong domestic Prices should make domestic investment attractive and thereby reduce Foreign Investment $(-c_{41})$. Finally, and for all my equations, some part of annual British Foreign Investment is caused by other variables not included in the model (e_1).

Equation I.2 indicates that the *annual demand* for British Exports (Y_2) is determined primarily by the annual supply of British Foreign Investment, which transferred effective demand abroad (as Marx said, "the British are forced to lend to foreign nations in order to have them as customers." *Grundrisse*, p. 416).[8] Besides new Foreign Investment, conventional economic theory suggests that the foreign demand for British products should be augmented by rising World Income (c_{52}) and depressed when British Export Prices are less competitive $(-c_{62})$. Thus, I have theoretically specified that the annual amount of British Exports will be driven by the endogenous variable of Foreign Investment (a_{12}) and two exogenous variables suggested by conventional economic theory.

The last equation (I.3) in Table 11.1 for National Income attempts to capture the essence as opposed to the appearance of capitalist accumulation in Great Britain.[9] In accordance with conventional economic theory, the variables that drive National Income are Domestic Investment (c_{13}) and expanded Exports (a_{23}). Yet, in the context of the entire model so far developed, such relationships operate only because of the export of capital by the British capitalist class. While I do not expect either the political party in power (z_8) or its fiscal policies (z_9) to have any impact on National Income because this was an era of laissez-faire in which neither Liberals nor Tories practiced welfare capitalism, two counterhypotheses can be posited: the Conservatives were more interested in capital accumulation than the Liberals (c_{83}) because they comprised the majority of the "rich and very rich," and Government Deficits may enhance accumulation via unconscious Keynesianism ($-c_{93}$).

In terms of its economic consequences, Figure 11.1 and equations I.1 to I.3 of Table 11.1 represent a microtheory of *economic imperialism* in which financial imperialism (the export of capital) equilibrated the otherwise dangerous business cycle of laissez-faire British capitalism and produced a steady accumulation of capital in Britain. As such, however, the theory so far developed does not involve territorial expansion and interstate conflict. It is therefore an incomplete Marxist model, a problem I shall now address.

Figure 11.2, showing the equations of Block II in my model (which are also given in Table 11.1), is based upon the Marxist hypothesis that the process of capitalist accumulation creates interests overseas of a financial, political-territorial, and military character, whether or not this is the conscious intention of the capitalist class and its government leaders. Trapped in a system they can barely comprehend, some capitalists such as Cecil Rhodes or Joseph Chamberlain may knowingly seek Empire, but others, perhaps the majority, only seek reasonable returns on their investments without any conscious intent to dominate "lesser breeds." Indeed, they may willingly contribute to their "betterment" via support of missionary societies and other philanthropic ventures.[10] Yet, the logic of the system they are embedded in and that they do, almost to a man, ideologically defend (Bukharin 1917/1973, p. 110) leads to domination, inequality, and violence. At least that is the Marxist positon.

Equation II.4 explains the growing British financial stake (Y_4) in the world economy between 1870 and 1914, in which year British investors owned 50 percent of all foreign investments worldwide ($20 billion at 1913 exchange rates). All three endogenous variables representing capitalist accumulation from the first block (now treated as predetermined) should affect this vital British interest, but in different ways. Annual Foreign Investment (b_{14}) should add each year to the stake abroad unless annual repatriations were greater than new investments, which they were not. Kuznets' finding (1973) that "modern economic growth" (X_3) has invariably been associated with economic outreach should also positively affect Total British Foreign

Figure 11.2 The Process of Imperial Expansion

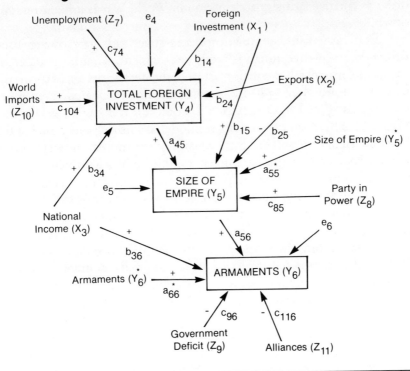

Investment (b_{34}). In contrast to these augmenting forces, years in which the British economy was competitive internationally should be years in which Exports did not have to be financed by foreign lending and, therefore, the over-time relationship between the two variables should be negative ($-b_{24}$).

Conversely, years in which British products were not competitive were years of business stagnation. The entirely exogenous business cycle should therefore be in a downturn, with its best indicator, Unemployment, increasing. This would predict the direct relationship between Unemployment and Total Foreign Investment (c_{74}) stated in equation II.4 because, as I have argued, the way out of periodic economic declines was to invest overseas. Finally, world demand for British investment, as represented by the proxy variable of World Imports, should increase the British foreign economic stake (c_{104}). The sum total of these forces should be to create a steady increase in Total British Foreign Investment up to 1914 when, in order to finance British participation in World War I, it had to be run down.

That capitalist accumulation necessarily leads to growing Total British Foreign Investment is really self-evident. That both accumulation and financial expansion caused the territorial growth of the British Empire after 1870 is, in contrast, hotly debated. Nevertheless, this is what I have specified in equation II.5 of Table 11.1 and Figure 11.2 because I am trying to model as faithfully as possible the Marxist theory of imperialism. It should be noted, however, that while I specify that the parameter linking Total Investment and the Size of Empire (a_{45}) will be positive and significant, this does not mean that British investments were going exclusively or even primarily to the new possessions acquired after 1870. What (a_{45}) implies is that as growing British foreign investments internationalized capitalism by elaborating the world economy, the British state also engaged in preemptive imperialism to create a nationally controlled bloc in competition with other expansive national capitals (Bukharin 1917/ 1973). Particularly important in this "defensive" territorial imperialism was British concern for the security of India and the routes to India through Suez and around South Africa (Robinson and Gallagher 1965).

Other factors consistent with the theoretical orientation of Marxists also should have affected the growth of the formal British Empire. Why acquire new populations and territories, which entails expenditures and governance duties, if one can trade with them without such involvements? This traditional Liberal Party position suggests that the Empire grew more rapidly when they were out of power (c_{85}) and that annual Exports should negatively relate to the Size of Empire ($-b_{25}$). Finally, as Hobson and subsequent Marxists argued, to the extent that investment did go to the new territories, this prompted their annexation by the capital-exporting power (b_{15}).

Modern colonial empires are bureaucratic "going concerns" (Mackinder 1962), perhaps created by precapitalist aristocratic military elites in search of glory and careers (Schumpeter 1919/1955) who continually push back the "turbulent frontier" in search of secure imperial borders (Galbraith 1960). This conventional wisdom suggests the competing hypothesis that British empire-building was primarily autoregressive (a^*_{55}).

Empires in a world of competitive capitalist nation-states engaged in empire-building must be protected, hence the specified positive impact of growth in the British Empire on British Armaments in the period after 1870 (a_{56}). Equation II.6 of Table 11.1 also sees military expansion as a direct consequence of capitalist economic growth (b_{36} linking National Income to Armaments) because modern states are violence-controlling *enterprises* (Lane 1979) that will spend part of their growing national wealth on weapons in order to ensure continued economic expansion.

As is well recognized in the conventional literature, military establishments are bureaucracies that thrive on incrementalism, hence the autoregressive parameter a^*_{66}. Futhermore, international crises and wars can lead to step-level increases in arms spending, often by Bank of England-financed Budget Deficits ($-c_{96}$) (Rasler and Thompson 1983). Finally, while the processes of capitalist accumulation and imperial expansion ultimately produce interstate conflict and violence, annual Alliances may foster a sense of security and thereby dampen the need to arm ($-c_{116}$).

Figure 11.2, then, sees the process of imperial expansion as an interrelated whole in which growing financial interests result in additional territorial interests, which are both protected by expanded military force. In explicit contrast to theories such as that of Choucri and North (1975), I specify that British overseas expansion after 1870 is the long-run consequence of a particular historical political economy—advanced British laissez-faire capitalism—and not a generic feature of all societies experiencing growth in population and technology.

Figure 11.3 presents the final block in my model. Following Lenin and Bukharin, I see British interstate conflict and violence behavior as being the long-run result of British capitalist accumulation and imperial expansion. I have chosen to distinguish between specifically Colonial Conflicts with other expanding capitalist and semicapitalist great powers (Y_7) on the one hand and British Violence Behavior toward all states after 1870 (Y_8) on the other hand. General British Violence Behavior ultimately resulted in World War I, whereas the British never fought a war with another great power over colonial issues in the period under examination (unlike the seventeenth- and eighteenth-century British colonial wars).[11]

Three aspects of capitalist imperialism are represented in equa-

Figure 11.3 The Process of Interstate Conflict

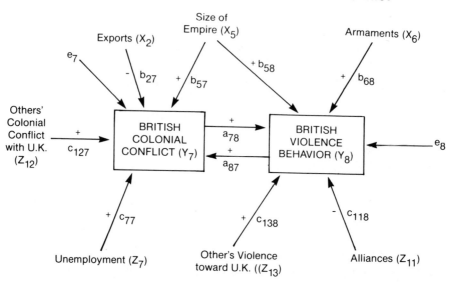

tion III.7 for British Colonial Conflict. First, factors involved in the process of capital accumulation should have predisposed the British for or against the use of force in colonial disputes. Second, when British Exports lagged ($-b_{27}$) and when Unemployment was high (c_{77}), British leaders, as members of the capitalist class, should have been more willing to take an aggressive stance in pursuit of their colonial interests than when the world economy was more favorable to the British economy. Third, the very expansion of the British Empire (Y_6) should have provoked tensions and conflict with other empire-building capitalist powers (b_{57}) as the British slid into the "territorial trap" of excessive defensive commitments to imperial real estate (Thompson and Zuk 1982b).

Since the logic of the interstate political system cannot be reduced entirely to the logic of the world economy, factors associated with international political behavior also ought to affect British Colonial Conflict. These factors are represented in equation III.7 and in Figure 11.3 by Others' Colonial Conflict with Britain (c_{127}) and general British Violence Behavior itself (a_{87}). The hypothesis represented by these two specifications derives ultimately from Richardson (1960), who pioneered the study of international conflict as an action and reaction process.

The final equation in my model, III.8, draws upon ideas already articulated. Overall British Violence Behavior is driven in part by past imperial expansion in the areas of Armaments (b_{68}) and Territory (b_{58}) and by the Richardson action (a_{78}) and reaction (c_{138}) processes associated, respectively, with simultaneous British Colonial Conflict (Y_7) and all Other States' Violence toward Britain (Z_{13}). Finally, as in the case of Armaments, I expect that as the British increased the number of their allies, this enhanced British security perceptions in the short term and lessened the annual British need to engage in Violent Behavior toward Other States ($-c_{118}$).[12]

Table 11.1 summarizes my model in the form of a block-recursive system of eight linear additive equations in three recursively organized blocks. Given the complexity of my theoretical orientation—based as it is upon Marx, Bukharin, Lenin, and contemporary "Marxists" such as Amin, Frank, and Wallerstein, and the possible alternative specifications of each equation presented in this section—Table 11.1 reveals that the model is about as simple as possible. That is to say, I have not specified any variable transformations nor have I incorporated interaction terms or nonlinear relationships in the variables (such as X_k^2) or in the parameters (as in X_k^b).

The reason for the technical simplicity of my model is the absence of "strong theory" in this area of research. To my knowledge, no one has ever tried to combine the theoretical Marxist tradition of capitalist imperialism with the systematically empirical techniques of contemporary social science model building.[13] The models that do exist in this area are mainstream ones that implicitly (Richardson 1960) or explicitly (Choucri and North 1975) deny the driving role of capitalism, its contradictions, and class conflict in the explanation of macrosocial processes such as economic growth, empire-building, and war. In such circumstances, small and simple models, while perhaps not beautiful, are prudent.

Conclusions

The model developed and presented in this chapter was constructed in order that it might be evaluated against appropriate time-series data on annual British economic, political, and military behavior over the period 1870 to 1914. These data exist in a publicly available form[14] and preliminary empirical results have been reported elsewhere (McGowan 1984a).

This chapter therefore accomplishes two rather important tasks. First, it elaborates the setting, the theoretical orientation, and the actual model specification in far greater detail than would be possible in an article or chapter that also reported empirical results. This was necessary because the two traditions of Marxist and mainstream social science I have worked with are so unrelated, both in the literature and among actual researchers, that it was essential for me to develop my arguments at some length.

Perhaps, therefore, the Marxists and neo-Marxists who may read this chapter will accept my argument that methods other than theoretically informed, historical case studies can be applied usefully to the study of capitalist imperialism. Perhaps the mainstreamers who read this chapter will have had their appreciation of the theoretical richness of the Marxist tradition enhanced, as well as their understanding of how one can relate Marxist theories to systematically empirical methods.

If this is the case, then my second objective will have been accomplished as well. Mainstreamers will have by now noted that I have not set out to "falsify" Marxist theory by somehow trying (as if it were possible) to model econometrically the contradictions of laissez-faire capitalism that I would then propose to "test" with a statistical package and a convenient data set. This cannot be done because the international political economy is a historically fashioned articulation of a politically organized states system and an economically organized division of labor and mode of production (Wallerstein 1974, 1980). While both the states system and the world economy have their own rules of operation, neither can be completely explained by the other nor by its own rules alone. This is so because the two expressions of capitalism as a global, historical system comprise a totality in which each has its own internal contradictions (opposing tendencies) and in which their articulation is itself profoundly contradictory (Ashley 1983).

Because of this, it is often the case that actions and policies that "make sense" in terms of the logic of the states system, such as securing strategic points of influence within the world system (Egypt, South Africa, Singapore for the British), may also lead to territorial involvements and military expenditures that seriously disrupt the circuit of capital (such as the Boer War; Thompson and Zuk 1982b). Similarly, the dictates of capital, such as "trading with the enemy," may contradict the imperatives of state security.

Since this is almost always the case, mainstream methods can only explore the expected consequences of contradictions, such as how the nine-year-long business cycle is assumed to generate an inverse relationship between Foreign and Domestic British Investment. In modeling and evaluating the expected consequences of unmeasurable contradictions, a sensible approach is to attempt to incorporate the best available ideas, whatever the source—as I have done with the counterhypotheses that feature in many of my equations—as long as one is also sensitive to certain basic incompatibilities among theoretical traditions that differ as much as do Marxism and its mainstream critics (McGowan and Walker 1981).

Notes

1. Unfortunately, the current fashion for expected utility behavior analysis from microeconomics, in which it is assumed that individuals, groups, classes, states (in short, all political actors) "evaluate the costs and benefits associated with choices to obtain the largest net gain (expected utility) at an acceptable level of risk" (Bueno de Mesquita 1984, p. 228, and 1981) suggests otherwise.

2. It is, of course, the position of neoconservative (Tucker 1977) and neorealist (Waltz 1979) students of international studies that international political *and* economic inequality is the sole result of international power differentials.

3. Marx did not use the concept of imperialism in the sense that it has acquired since Hobson and Lenin wrote their famous books. For him it was the rather traditional empire-building of the most advanced states and the pretensions to grandeur of Louis Napoleon.

4. When capitalism is viewed in this light, the debate between "productionist" (Brenner 1977) and "circulationists" (Wallerstein 1974, 1979, Ch. 1, 1980) is nonsensical.

5. Internal evidence, such as the dating of Lenin's "Introduction" to Bukharin's book as "December, 1915," makes almost certain that Lenin had read Bukharin before writing his own pamphlet on imperialism in 1916.

6. It is, of course, true that both the United States and Germany surpassed the British national economy in gross national product before 1900. But even by 1914 they were not Britain's equal in naval power, international finance, or scope of empire (Hobsbawn 1968; McGowan 1981).

7. I would stress that this model is not one that accepts the underconsumptionist thesis of Hobson (1902/1965). I merely posit temporary periods of ineffective domestic demand caused by being in the trough of the business cycle and not any such long-term tendency.

8. This specification says something about current debates over the role of capitalism in "developing" the periphery (Frank 1969; Cardoso 1973; Warren 1973).

The transfer of effective demand to the periphery via British portfolio investment before 1914 probably did stimulate capitalist development there, at least if a_{12} is positive and if some of the exports were capital goods, as we know they were. The direct private investment of global corporations today (Gilpin 1975) may be an altogether different matter.

9. British National Income must be regarded as a proxy for capital accumulation, but it is not a bad one because the period 1870-1914 saw very little redistribution of income in Britain; therefore growth in net national product meant expanded production and at least constant returns to scale for the capitalist class in the United Kingdom.

10. Such humanitarian efforts are, of course, perhaps the "highest" form of cultural imperialism.

11. It should be noted that my intended operationalizations of Colonial Conflict and General Violence Behavior are based upon scaled event data from Choucri and North (1975) in which only the highest scale values involve the actual use of military force. Most scale values are closer to diplomatic disputes.

12. One must distinguish between the number of allies the United Kingdom had and the rigidity of the opposing alliance systems prior to the outbreak of World War I.

13. Not everyone agrees that joining these two traditions is a good thing (Cardoso 1977), but it can be done if concepts such as capitalist accumulation and dependency are seen as orienting terms that suggest a frame of reference and not measurable variables (Duvall 1978).

14. ICPSR 7738 "British Economic Imperialism, 1869-1914." Ann Arbor, MI: Inter-University Consortium for Political and Social Research, 1979.

Bibliography

Amin, Samir. 1974. *Accumulation on a World Scale: A Critique of the Theory of Underdevelopment.* New York: Monthly Review Press.

Ashley, Richard K. 1983. "Three Modes of Economism." *International Studies Quarterly* 27, pp. 463-96.

Bairoch, Paul. 1979. "Ecarts internationaux des niveaux de vie avant la revolution industrielle." *Annales: economies, societies, civilisations* 34, pp. 145-71.

Baran, Paul. 1957. *The Political Economy of Growth.* New York: Monthly Review Press.

Bergesen, Albert and Ronald Schoenberg. 1980. "Long Waves of Colonial Expansion and Contraction, 1415-1969." In *Studies of the Modern World-System,* ed. Albert Bergesen, pp. 231-77. New York: Academic Press.

Bousquet, Nicole. 1980. "From Hegemony to Competition: Cycles of the Core?" In *Processes of the World-System,* ed. Terrence K. Hopkins and Immanuel Wallerstein, pp. 46-83. Beverly Hills: Sage.

Braudel, Fernand. 1972. "History and the Social Science." In *Economy and Society in Early Modern Europe,* ed. Peter Burke, pp. 11-42. New York: Harper and Row Torchbooks.

Brenner, Robert. 1977. "The Origins of Capitalist Development: A Critique of Neo-Smithian Marxism." *New Left Review* 104, pp. 25-92.

Brewer, Anthony. 1980. *Marxist Theories of Imperialism: A Critical Survey.* London: Routledge and Kegan Paul.

Bueno de Mesquita, Bruce. 1984. "Forecasting Policy Decisions: An Expected Utility Approach to Post-Khomeini Iran." *PS* 17, pp. 226-36.

———. 1981. *The War Trap*. New Haven: Yale University Press.

Bukharin, Nikolai. 1917/1973. *Imperialism and World Economy*. New York: Monthly Review Press.

Cardoso, Fernando Henrique. 1977. "The Consumption of Dependency Theory in the U.S." *Latin American Research Review* 12, pp. 7-24.

———. 1973. "Associated-Dependent Development: Theoretical and Practical Implications." In *Authoritarian Brazil*, ed. Alfred Stepan, pp. 142-76. New Haven: Yale University Press.

Chase-Dunn, Christopher. 1981. "Interstate System and Capitalist World Economy: One Logic or Two?" *International Studies Quarterly* 25, pp. 19-42.

——— and Richard Rubinson. 1977. "Toward a Structural Perspective on the World-System." *Politics and Society* 7, pp. 453-76.

Choucri, Nazli and Robert C. North. 1975. *Nations in Conflict: National Growth and International Violence*. San Francisco: Freeman.

Duvall, Raymond D. 1978. "Dependence and Dependencia Theory: Notes Toward Precision of Concept and Argument." *International Organization* 32, pp. 51-78.

Elder, Robert E. and John E. Holmes. 1984. "Economic Long Cycles and American Foreign Policy." Paper presented to the Annual Meeting of the International Studies Association, Atlanta.

Frank, Andre Gunder. 1979. *Dependent Accumulation and Underdevelopment*. New York: Monthly Review Press.

———. 1978. *World Accumulation 1492-1789*. New York: Monthly Review Press.

———. 1969. *Capitalism and Underdevelopment in Latin America*. New York: Monthly Review Press.

Galbraith, John S. 1960. "The 'Turbulent Frontier' as a Factor in British Expansion." *Comparative Studies in Society and History* 2, pp. 150-68.

Gallagher, John and Ronald E. Robinson. 1953. "The Imperialism of Free Trade." *Economic History Review* 6, pp. 1-15.

Gilpin, Robert. 1981. *War and Change in World Politics*. Cambridge: Cambridge University Press.

———. 1975. *U.S. Power and the Multinational Corporation*. New York: Basic Books.

Goldstein, Joshua S. 1984. "Long Waves and War Cycles." Master of Science thesis, Massachusetts Institute of Technology.

Harvey, David. 1977. "The Geography of Capitalist Accumulation: A Reconstruction of the Marxian Theory." In *Radical Geography: Alternative Viewpoints on Contemporary Social Issues*, ed. Richard Peet, pp. 263-92. Chicago: Maaroufa Press.

Hermann, Charles F., ed. 1972. *International Crises: Insights from Behavioral Research*. New York: Free Press.

Hibbs, Douglas A., Jr. 1974. *Mass Political Violence: A Crossnational Causal Analysis*. New York: Wiley.

Hobsbawm, Eric J. 1968. *Industry and Empire: The Making of Modern English Society, Vol. II: 1750 to the Present Day*. New York: Random House.

Hobson, John A. 1902/1965. *Imperialism—A Study*. Ann Arbor: University of Michigan Press.

Hodgart, Alan. 1977. *The Economics of European Imperialism.* New York: Norton.
Hopkins, Terrence K. and Immanuel Wallerstein. 1979. "Cyclical Rhythms and Secular Trends of the Capitalist World-Economy: Some Premises, Hypotheses, and Questions." *Review* 2, pp. 483-500.
Klingberg, Frank L. 1979. "Cyclical Trends in American Foreign Policy Moods and Their Policy Implications." In *Challenges to America: United States Foreign Policy in the 1980s,* ed. Charles W. Kegley, Jr. and Pat McGowan, pp. 37-55. Beverly Hills: Sage.
——————. 1952. "The Historical Alternation of Moods in American Foreign Policy." *World Politics* 4, pp. 239-73.
Kondratieff, N. D. 1935. "The Long Waves in Economic Life." *Review of Economics and Statistics* 17, pp. 105-15.
——————. 1926. "Die Langen Wellen der Konjunktur." *Archiv fur Sozialwissenschaft und Sozialpolitik* 55 (December), pp. 573-609.
Kuznets, Simon. 1973. "Modern Economic Growth: Findings and Reflections." *American Economic Review* 63, pp. 247-58.
——————. 1930. *Secular Movements in Production and Prices.* Boston: Houghton Mifflin.
Lane, Frederic C. 1979. *Profits from Power: Readings in Protection Rent and Violence-Controlling Enterprises.* Albany: State University of New York Press.
Lenin, V. I. 1917/1971. *Imperialism: The Highest Stage of Capitalism. (A Popular Outline.)* New York: International Publishers, one-volume edition of Lenin's *Selected Works.*
Lewis, W. Arthur. 1978. *Growth and Fluctuations 1870-1913.* London: Allen and Unwin.
Mackinder, Halford J. 1962. *Democratic Ideals and Reality.* New York: Norton.
Maddison, Angus. 1982. *Phases of Capitalist Development.* Oxford: Oxford University Press.
Mandel, Ernst. 1975. *Late Capitalism.* London: New Left Books.
McClelland, David, ed. 1977. *Karl Marx: Selected Writings.* Oxford: Oxford University Press.
McGowan, Pat. 1984a. "The Political Economy of Appropriate Technology." In *Appropriate Technology: Choice and Development,* ed. Mathew Betz, Pat McGowan, and Rolf Wigand, pp. 31-47. Durham: Duke University Press.
——————. 1984b. "Marx and Lenin Meet the Computer: An Econometric Study of British Imperialism, 1870-1914." Paper presented to the Annual Meeting of the International Studies Association, Atlanta.
——————. 1981. "Imperialism in World-System Perspective: Britain 1870-1914." *International Studies Quarterly* 25, pp. 43-68.
—————— and Charles W. Kegley, Jr., eds. 1983. *Foreign Policy and the Modern World-System.* Beverly Hills: Sage.
—————— and Stephen G. Walker. 1981. "Radical and Conventional Models of U.S. Foreign Economic Policy Making." *World Politics* 33, pp. 347-82.
Modelski, George. 1981. "Long Cycles, Kondratieffs, and Alternating Innovations: Implications for U.S. Foreign Policy." In *The Political Economy of Foreign Policy Behavior,* ed. Pat McGowan and Charles W. Kegley, Jr., pp. 63-84. Beverley Hills: Sage.
——————. 1980. "On the Interdependence of Political and Economic Fluctuations." *Economie Appliquee* 35, pp. 47-70.

—————————. 1978. "The Long Cycle of Global Politics and the Nation-State." *Comparative Studies in Society and History* 20, pp. 214-35.

Owen, Roger and Bob Sutcliffe, eds. 1972. *Studies in the Theory of Imperialism*. London: Longman.

Rasler, Karen A. and William R. Thompson. 1983. "Global Wars, Public Debts, and the Long Cycle." *World Politics* 35, pp. 489-516.

Richardson, Louis Fry. 1960. *Arms and Insecurity*. Pittsburgh: Boxwood Press.

Robinson, Roland E. and John Gallagher. 1965. *Africa and the Victorians: The Official Mind of Imperialism*. London: Macmillan.

Rostow, Walt W. 1978. *The World Economy: History and Prospect*. Austin: University of Texas Press.

Sayers, R. 1967. *A History of Economic Change in England, 1880-1939*. London: Oxford University Press.

Schumpeter, Joseph. 1939. *Business Cycles*. New York: McGraw-Hill.

—————————. 1919/1955. *Imperialism and Social Classes*. New York: Meridian.

Singer, J. David and Thomas Cusack. 1981. "Periodicity, Inexorability, and Steermanship in International War." In *From National Development to Global Community*, ed. Richard L. Merritt and Bruce M. Russett, pp. 404-22. London: Allen and Unwin.

Thompson, Willian R., ed. 1983a. *World System Analysis: Competing Perspectives*. Beverly Hills: Sage.

—————————. 1983b. "Uneven Economic Growth, Systemic Challenges and Global Wars." *International Studies Quarterly* 27, pp. 341-56.

—————————. 1983c. "World War, Global Wars, and the Cool Hand Luke Syndrome." *International Studies Quarterly* 27, pp. 369-78.

—————————. 1982. "Succession Crises in the Global Political System: A Test of the Transition Model." In *Crises in the World-System*, ed. Albert Bergesen, pp. 93-116. Beverly Hills: Sage.

————————— and Gary Zuk. 1982a. "World Power and the Territorial Trap Hypothesis." Paper presented to the Annual Meeting of the International Studies Association-West, San Diego.

—————————. 1982b. "War, Inflation, and the Kondratieff Long Wave." *Journal of Conflict Resolution* 26, pp. 621-44.

Toynbee, Arnold J. 1954. *A Study of History, Volume 9*. London: Oxford University Press.

Tucker, Robert W. 1977. *The Inequality of Nations*. New York: Basic Books.

Wallerstein, Immanuel. 1980. *The Modern World-System II: Mercantilism and the Consolidation of the European World-Economy, 1600-1750*. New York: Academic Press.

—————————. 1979. *The Capitalist World-Economy*. Cambridge: Cambridge University Press.

—————————. 1974. *The Modern World-System: Capitalist Agriculture and the Origins of the European World-Economy in the Sixteenth Century*. New York: Academic Press.

Waltz, Kenneth N. 1979. *Theory of International Politics*. Boston: Addison-Wesley.

Warren, Bill. 1973. "Imperialism and Capitalist Industrialisation." *New Left Review* 81, pp. 3-44.

Zimmerman, Louis J. and F. Grumbach. 1953. "Saving, Investment and Imperialism." *Weltwirschaftliches Archiv* 71, pp. 1-19.

Power Cycle Theory
And Systems Stability

CHARLES F. DORAN

Introduction

This chapter will attempt to show that the structure of the international system changes drastically when a number of the leading actors pass through critical points on their respective power curves at approximately the same time; further, that governments have a difficult time coping with the decision consequences of great upward and downward mobility within the system (the vertical decision plane); and finally, that in such historical intervals, the probability of anarchy and systemwide tumult of a violent sort correspondingly increases. World Wars I and II can therefore be seen as the aftermath of the decline of the nineteenth-century balance of power system on the one hand, and as the prelude to the establishment of the twentieth-century bipolar system on the other.

In policy terms, the principal conclusion to be drawn from this study is: both the bipolar and the multipolar systems, for reasons intrinsic to each system, may be quite stable. This conclusion challenges much of the traditional literature that argued in favor of the exclusive stability of either one or the other type of system (Waltz 1964; Deutsch and Singer 1964; Rosccrance 1966). But this study also suggests that the occurrence of major war is perhaps most likely during periods of massive systems transformation. Moreover, regarding the future, the probability of major war may increase somewhat during the period of transition away from bipolarity toward some new international system, until that new system develops its own accompanying source of equilibrium. Equilibrium is not complete in a mature international system until that equilibrium is satisfactorily established, legitimized, and accepted by the salient members of the newly emergent system.

Elaborated in terms of the behavior of the single actor, power cycle theory prepares the theoretical and empirical foundation for the analysis at the systems level presented here. This chapter generalizes from the individual actor to the systems level the findings on the relationship between state power and involvement in major war.

Power Cycle Theory

What are the essentials of power cycle theory? Power cycle theory (Doran 1971; Doran and Parsons 1980; Doran 1983a, 1983b) accounts for some of the dynamics of international statecraft and the importance of these dynamics for why major war occurs. According to power cycle theory, the components of national capability such as gross national product, population size, and military expenditures for the leading states have increased by some nonlinear power function over time. But national capability of one state relative to the aggregate capability of the other leading actors over long time periods follows a cyclical pattern of rise, maturation, and decline. Governments such as the Netherlands and Sweden traversed this path in the seventeenth century, while France reached the peak of its relative power in the mid-eighteenth century and Britain reached the apex of its power at the very beginning of the nineteenth century. Upward and downward mobility of states along their power cycles has become a structural characteristic of the international system.

Power cycle theory also holds that critical points occur on each state's cycle where abrupt shocks occur in the society's whole perspective toward foreign policy. At the upper and lower turning points and at the two inflection points on the curve, the conventional linear extrapolation of the state's future position and prospects within the international system proves starkly incorrect. At these points the government and society are forced to make adjustments to their expectations and assumptions about international politics. These adjustments are painful, causing anxiety, frustration, and even visions of foreign policy grandeur (lower turning point). None of these responses is conducive to foreign prudence. The consequence is that the state is susceptible to incautious statement and action. Because the foreign policy stakes for the state at these points are viewed as extremely high—involving core values about power, status, and security—the state is subject to a higher than average probability of entanglement in major war. Power cycle theory therefore provides insight into when and how a government is likely to get enmeshed in the most serious types of conflict within international politics. No determinism exists here. The probability of major war involvement for the state is simply greater than at other times in its history. Power cycle theory thus relates changes in the power position and foreign policy outlook of the state to the likelihood that the state will become entangled in an extensive war.

Causation

According to Marc Bloch (1941/1953), the brilliant economic historian who died in the French Resistance, the concept of causation can be divided into a "particular cause" and into the "conditions" that surround that cause. "There is," he notes, however, "something extremely arbitrary in the idea of a cause par excellence, as opposed to mere 'conditions'." It is for this reason that we explore in this chapter the set of conditions and not the "particular cause" underlying major war. These conditions are not totally deterministic of the war outcome, but neither are they purely arbitrary or subject to unfettered choice. If on a mountain road a misstep that leads to calamity—to use a Bloch example—is likened to the particular cause of war, then the reality that the path had to be constructed in this way, at this place, necessitating great caution on the part of the traveler, is the kind of causation we have in mind here. Constructed differently, constructed elsewhere, or traversed by a more experienced traveler, the road might have led to different results. Hence the engineering and planning that underlie the construction of the road represented constrained choice, just as much as did the attitude toward safety assumed by the traveler, or the decision that led to the original misstep. An understanding of the conditions surrounding the incidence of major war (Stoll 1980; Vasquez 1984) is as important to interpretation and prediction as an isolation of one or two permanent causes indexed by the variance explained in a dependent variable.

Two Planes of Foreign Policy Decision-Making
And Interaction Relevant to the Preservation of Order

The Horizontal Plane

Conditions relevant to the avoidance of major war are commonly associated with a view of international politics that can best be described as horizontal. Horizontal thinking perceives the central system as a club of members whose relationships, however competitive, are nonetheless orderly and well-defined. In the early and mid-nineteenth century these actors included Britain, France, Prussia, Russia, and Austria-Hungary. In the post-1945 period only the United States and the Soviet Union constitute the central system. Regardless of the identity of the system or that of its principal actors, the predominant concern involved with horizontal thought about international politics is the maintenance of balance. In the nineteenth century this preoccupation is with the maintenance of a balance of power among the actors. Britain is described as a "holder" of the balance since it had interests and capability that set it apart from the Continental powers and ensured its desire for peace and equilibrium in Europe. It had no territorial ambitions on the Continent unlike most of the other governments. Alternatively, the British role was described as one among five, each of which reacted against an actor that tried to challenge the stability of the system or to expand beyond the boundaries of its territory. Overseas competition was continuous and, as in much of the eighteenth century, violent. However, the primary focus was European. No matter how much European politics spilled over into the colonies or vice-versa, the stability of the international system was determined largely by events within Europe and not elsewhere. The comparatively small number of actors, their relative equality of national capability, the lack of deep ideological division among the societies, and the close geographical proximity of the countries all contributed to the ease of balance and coalition formation. Alternatively, governments would attempt to preserve the balance in the short term by mobilizing military resources internally and then demobilizing them when the threat of misadventure had passed. But regardless of how the process of balance took place, thinking remained horizontal—the system was viewed as though all of the primary actors could be identified and were located on a plane of interaction where the principal calculation was that of short-term balance.

This perspective on international politics as though it were a horizontal plane is common in the contemporary system as well. It is the perspective which holds that politics between the Soviet Union and the United States are primary. In arms control talks, for example, the concern is with "mutual, *balanced* force reduction." Little anxiety exists in Washington or Moscow about challenges from other states to the dominance of these two actors. Moreover, despite tensions and cold war rhetoric, the stability that has prevailed since 1945 is perhaps the result of the capacity of these two governments to manage their rivalry in a fashion that does not get out of hand. Implicit rules of statecraft have emerged, for instance, regarding the acknowledgment of spheres of primary and comparatively exclusive influence and regarding the decision—tested in the October 1973 war—never to field troops together, face to face, in the same region. While the contemporary system is in no sense a "balance of power system," concern about the maintenance of equilibrium between the superpowers dominates informed thought about contemporary statecraft. The horizontal mode of thought—treating the two superpowers as though they were on a horizontal plane of relative equality—comes easily because of the comparative simplicity of decision-making involved and because of the comparative security that emerges out of the rigid and durable coalitions surrounding each of the poles. As long as each of the superpowers feels comfortable with its position vis-à-vis the other, disputes elsewhere in the system appear susceptible to management and the fundamental stability of the system is not endangered. Although other types of systems in other periods have not been examined here, it might not be too much of a speculative leap to theorize that these also are susceptible to the horizontal interpretation when structural stability in the central system enables governments to concentrate on the rough mechanics of balance.

The propensity to analyze international politics in terms of interdependence fits nicely into the horizontal perspective as well, both in terms of the use of interdependence as an analytic device and as a goal of foreign policy. States are once again, especially because of the diversity of issue-areas involved where asymmetries of influence are allegedly offset, conceived as lying upon a plane horizontal to the viewer and bound there by mutual and involuntary forces such as trade and exchange. Implicit within the concept of interdependence is relative equality: an equality of power, an equality of opportunity to obtain benefits, and an equality of responsibility. For an effort to bring together interdependence and dependence ideas, see Modelski (1983).

The Vertical Plane

The other way of viewing international relations is along a vertical perspective. This perspective emphasizes the upward and downward mobility of states within the international system. It also stresses long-term rather than comparatively short-term and idiosyncratic developments, since upward and downward movement on the power cycle is very incremental. Hundreds of years are encompassed in the full manifestation of a single cycle, such as in the instance of France. But if change along the vertical plane is slow, it is also profound in that it shapes the entire structure of the international system.

Vertical movement by states along their power cycles determines membership in the central system. Indeed, the striking change between the international system of the mid-eighteenth century and the mid-nineteenth century was that the upward and downward mobility of states had completely transformed the character of the central system and the identity of the leading members. The United States was not even a member of the central system in 1850, whereas by 1950 four of the prior five members had dropped out, leaving only Russia/Soviet Union as the other remaining member of the twentieth-century central system. Moreover, the members of the earlier central system that dropped out did so at different times and rates. The first to leave the central system was Austria-Hungary, formally at the Treaty of Versailles but in actuality decades earlier in spite of the reluctance of the nineteenth-century central system to admit this reality.

The remarkable aspect of the vertical perspective on international relations is the profound impact that upward and downward mobility of states has had on the structure of the international system, combined with the gradualism of the change spread over very long time intervals. It is the interplay between profound effect and gradualism of perception that especially marks the vertical perspective. Both a sense of inertia and a sense of determinism characterize the slow movement of states upward or downward on their respective power cycles. In essence, however, both the apparent inertia and determinism are more a product of the collective political and economic choices of the governments and societies, some of which choices have unanticipated consequences, than of ineluctable social forces operating within the international system. But the capacity of governments to effect the shape of the long-term power curve is far less than their capacity to effect power balancing on the horizontal plane. The vertical perspective contains an aura of inevitability not conveyed by observations about change on the horizontal plane of state behavior. Variation occurs in terms of the amplitude and the periodicity of the power curves so as to accentuate differences across states, even though the generalized pattern of rise, maturation, and decline remains the same.

Vertical thinking about international relations is inhibited not only by the slow pace of change on the power cycle but also by the difficulty associated with making forward projections of position and assessing the implications for role. There is a tendency to assume that what happened in the past will continue. The adage that the best predictor of next year's budget is this year's budget prevails. Governments tend to think in terms of linear extrapolations of the past into the future. But if these tendencies persist among government policymakers and analysts who are alerted to the vertical manner of thought about international relations, how much more common is this tendency for those accustomed to thinking of international relations as though it were carried out on a horizontal plane? How much more common are these shortcomings of perception for those who are locked into the calculations of balance and coalition formation facilitated by the horizontal conception of international relations?

In practice, both the vertical (Midlarsky 1984) and horizontal conceptions of international relations ought to shape foreign policy thought. Neither view of international relations is wrong. Each is a partial view. Each is essential to a fuller and more comprehensive understanding of the dynamics of international relations. On the other hand, taken by itself, each is a useful simplification of international political reality, but only a simplification. In practice, since the horizontal perspective is frequently more useful for policy prescription, it is probably the conception of international relations most often employed by the decision-maker. It lends itself to judgments that can readily be followed up by foreign policy action. Its simplicity and apparent precision in the context of known actors in the central system and familiar interactions is also clearly an asset to policy choice. How far this conception of international relations alone can take the policy-maker, and what kind of distortions the partial view of the system can inculcate, is a matter to which we turn in a subsequent section.

World War and its Causes: Two Contemporary Views

According to Nazli Choucri and Robert North (1975), the concept of *lateral pressure*, namely the expansion of foreign activity, accounts for international conflict and violence. This activity may involve the deployment of troops into foreign territory, investment by subsidiaries, or even the dispatch of missionaries. Conflict thus results when two or more nations extend their activities outward and these collide. Employing simultaneous equations, Choucri and North undertake a simulation of the nineteenth- and twentieth-century international systems. They find that violent international behavior is best accounted for by five variables additively related: intensity of intersections; military expenditures; military expenditures of nonallies; alliances; and violence of others. Depending upon period, country involved, and the independent variables selected, the study accounts for between 31 and 91 percent of the variance explainable in the dependent variable. A number of interesting anomalies are also reported. For example, no rising level of violence between Britain and Germany precedes the outbreak of World War I. Violent behavior seemed to emerge largely from a response to the actions of other countries (see Holsti, North, and Brody 1968), particularly to military expenditures of nonallies and to violence of others and not to the hypothesized effect of "lateral pressure." In these conclusions, the two scholars were appropriately cautious. Hence their observations about what they were not able to achieve analytically in terms of the simulation are as interesting as their findings.

In the context of analysis previously elaborated, the Choucri and North conceptual framework strongly expresses the horizontal pattern of thought. Lateral pressure almost perfectly describes behavior on the horizontal plane. Lateral pressure undoubtedly explains a great deal of comparatively low-level conflict quite effectively. It may account for the frequency of conflict between governments with some reliability. But what lateral pressure was not very helpful in describing was the sudden buildup of war on a monumental scale (Levy 1983). Extensive war is not the kind of systemic disruption that lends itself to analysis primarily through preoccupation with the horizontal perspective. Hence the carefully stated conclusions of the Choucri-North study emphasizing the difficulty in accounting for the onset of World War I serve to illustrate and reinforce the need for other variables or another perspective that highlights the conditions leading to this particular form of massive confrontation and violence.

Singer and Small (1968), in a well-known article on the relationship between alliance aggregation and the onset of major war, concluded that alliances and war were strongly correlated in the twentieth century but *inversely* correlated in the nineteenth century. While this study was criticized by younger scholars who preferred to work with multivariate statistical designs where many independent variables impinged simultaneously on a dependent variable, the essential elegance of this pioneering study was not challenged by this criticism. At the level of analysis explored in this initial study, the bivariate approach was valid; if "spuriousness" was present it was up to subsequent researchers to demonstrate this, or alternatively to demonstrate the validity of the century dichotomization. The dichotomization was again reinforced in a study employing a more complex model (Singer, Bremer, and Stuckey 1972), which concluded that there was something fundamentally different about the relationship of the structure of the international system to war in the nineteenth and the twentieth centuries. According to these findings, greater "parity and fluidity" in the nineteenth century seemed to be a useful antidote to war, whereas in the twentieth century greater "preponderance and stability" seemed to reinforce peace. These latter findings, based again on a large component of alliance intermediation combined with an index of relative capability and systemic concentration, tended to reinforce the earlier work in terms of the need to treat the centuries differently. But the latter findings seemed to contradict the earlier ones in terms of direction and interpretive substance. If alliances are to be equated with the preponderance and stability (bipolar) view regarding the maintenace of political order, then one would have expected the preponderance and stability model to have held in the nineteenth century where the earlier work showed that greater alliance aggregation led to less war. Similarly, one might have expected the opposite of the actual 1972 study results for the twentieth century. If alliances lead to war in the twentieth century, then perhaps the parity and fluidity approach would make more sense in policy terms because this approach would appear to have made war less likely.

What Singer and his associates have done is to bring together the horizontal and vertical perspectives on international relations. In so doing, they have underlined the significant structural differences in the two centuries, but they have also illustrated the difficulties of integrating these two complex international political perspectives within a single model so as to obtain consistent interpretations over time (Siverson and Sullivan 1982). The work highlights the theoretical question: Why is the relationship between structure and conflict different in the two centuries and what are the factors that best explain the occurrence of major war at the beginning of the twentieth century? Put somewhat differently: Why did major war erupt at the beginning of the twentieth century rather than in the nineteenth century after 1815 or in the twentieth century after 1945? And what is it about the different structures before and after the world war period that accounts for the comparative peace in each of these other intervals? Does a more intense focus on the vertical plane of international political change hold any clues to the questions so effectively raised by Singer and his colleagues?

An Alternate View

We hypothesize that major war in the first half of the twentieth century resulted from the failure of the central system to cope with the rise and decline of states. We further hypothesize that this change in systemic structure was most severe prior to World Wars I and II and was not equalled in its magnitude and scope at any other time in recent historical experience. Hence if the international system highlights verticality, the reasons for the outbreak of total war during the early twentieth century are observed in the changing structure of the international system. This changing structure is in essence the movement of the leading states upward or downward on their power cycles, a movement that the central system of actors finds difficult to adapt to in the context of the balancing process that is so familiar from the horizontal international relations perspective. In sum, at those times when the cumulative effect of vertical upward and downward mobility of states is greatest and least anticipated, international political order is likely to be most threatened by massive confrontation and world war.

Nineteenth-Century Structural Change and Twentieth-Century War: Some Evidence

A Note on Data Handling and Operationalization

This chapter is an outgrowth of a project that began more than a decade ago (Doran 1971). Data employed in the construction of the indices on national capability were drawn from more than 40 sources. Based on prior empirical research relating perceptions of national power to aggregate indicators of capability, two dimensions—size and development—were shown to underlie this capability. The variables iron and steel production, population, and size of armed forces were used to index size; energy use and urbanization indexed development. In order to avoid problems of inflation and exchange rate conversion encountered in attempting to work across long time periods, actual units of output were substituted for monetary units whenever possible.

In the original empirical study (Doran and Parsons 1980), war data were obtained from the excellent Correlates of War data bank. Major war was coded in terms of intensity, duration, and magnitude (rank of actors times the number involved in the war). A significant positive relationship was found for the initiator of a conflict as it passed through a critical point and major war as defined in any of the three ways. Handling of the data in the present chapter differs in that no attempt at direct association is made between initiator and conflict. Rather, we attempt to show that aggregate structural change within the central system preceded the largest of the major conflicts as indexed by roughly coterminous passage through critical points on the respective power cycles of many of the actors.

Data Analysis and Results

All of the following results facilitate examining the hypothesis that rapid and unanticipated structural change near the top of the international system tends to precede and to establish preconditions for major war experienced during the first half of the twentieth century. The reasons these data are so helpful in this empirical task is that they represent the focus of change in the power position and role of the major actors. The data index the critical points where a linear extrapolation of past experience proves radically and incontestably wrong. At these points a government is obliged to reassess its evolutionary position within the international system, its base of national capability, its goals of foreign policy, and its capacity to reach those goals (Taylor 1979). This is not a simple or casual undertaking. It cuts to the core of what is essential and important in foreign policy conduct. It involves security questions at the highest levels. It also involves the necessity to readjust and to reformulate strategies about the future place and position of the government within the international system. It requires a capacity for flexibility and control that a number of governments perhaps struggle to muster. On the one hand, this awareness of changed circumstance at the lower turning point, for example, may create the setting for aggravated nationalism, xenophobia, and visions of grandeur that stimulate expansionist thought. On the other hand, at other critical points this new awareness of changed power circumstance may generate excessive pessimism and anxiety over the future course of foreign affairs conduct and the eventual place of the actor within the international system. This latter kind of experience is the type of response that leads to misperception, exaggerated foreign policy conduct, paranoia, and a higher probability of conflict involvement as well.

The reason that conflicts once triggered at these points tend to become major conflicts is that the issues at stake are felt by the affected governments to go to the heart of their security situation and role in the system. This kind of perception about the seriousness of the stakes means that the governments are willing to devote massive military effort to the objective of winning the conflict. Moreover, since the big powers are involved, and a large number of actors become entangled, the wars also become far more extensive than is true on the historical average. In short, to borrow a phrase, these are felt by the participants to be the kind of wars "to end all war."

The four points where these climactic involvements in violent conflict are most probable are the two inflection points and the upper and lower turning points on the curve (see Table 12.1). Recorded by five-year intervals, there are some 23 critical points in all for nine advanced industrial nations between 1815 and 1975. In the absence of any other organizing principle, one might expect the points to be randomly distributed across the entire interval. A glance at Figure 12.1 tells us that this assumption is incorrect. Lumpiness of distribution occurs especially in the period 1875 to 1915, with nine critical points falling in those years.[1] Indeed, within five years of the outbreak of World War I, four of the critical points occurred, and within ten years an additional point occurred. What does this distribution of critical points mean for conflict theory?

According to these results, an astonishing amount of abrupt and unanticipated change occurred within the structure of the interna-

Table 12.1 Type and National Identity of Critical Points, 1875-1914

Austria-Hungary	Inflection Point (2) Low
France	Inflection Point (2)
Germany	High
Great Britain	Inflection Point (2)
Italy	Inflection Point (2) Low
Russia/Soviet Union	Low
United States	Inflection Point (1)

Note: The ideal and actual placement of these critical points are identified in Figure 12.1.

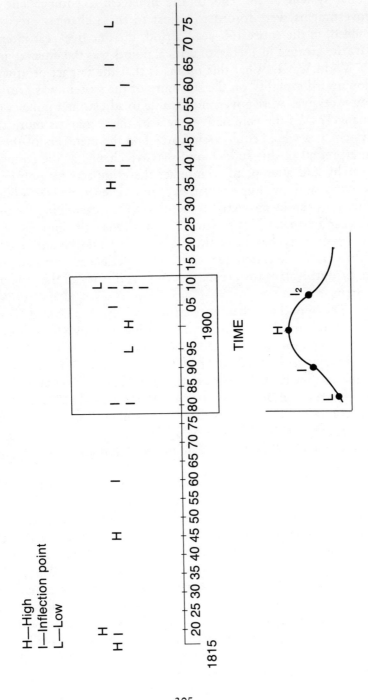

Figure 12.1 Distribution of Critical Points by Type and Temporal Occurrence

H—High
I—Inflection point
L—Low

TIME

305

tional system at the end of the nineteenth century. The leading governments were forced to adjust to these changes precipitously. Indeed, in the entire 160-year period, the one five-year interval that saw the greatest incidence of critical points was the interval just prior to World War I. What this means is that the impact of upward and downward mobility on the structure of the system was great, possibly excessive. Were governments able to adjust their policies to these changes? Was the cumulative effect of these changes more than the system as a whole could assimilate? Did the members of the system interpret all of this sudden and massive change as the equivalent to anarchy and attempt to counteract these impacts by political over-reaction and by hypersensitivity and defensiveness? While these questions can be answered in depth only by examining communications and dispatches of the time (Zinnes 1968), the impression left by this analysis is that all of these questions could be answered in the affirmative. The system seems to have experienced overload just prior to the outbreak of the greatest war in the history of the modern state system.

The hypothesis that more structural change preceded World War I than occurred at other times during the two centuries under examination can be subjected to a bit more rigor. The little statistical test known as the Student t is perfect for a small sample comparison of means (Snedecor 1956; Kalton 1966). We postulate the existence of two interval samples, one prior to World War II (1875-1910) μ_a and one composed of the years that fall outside this interval and the war period (1815-1870; 1950-1975) μ_b. We draw upon the critical point data in Table 12.1 and formulate our null hypothesis as follows:

$$H_o : \mu_a = \mu_b \qquad \mu_a - \mu_b = 0$$

The null hypothesis is that there is no difference between the two population means. We shall try to reject this hypothesis that there is no more structural change prior to World War I than at other times. The alternative hypothesis to be accepted if the null hypothesis is rejected is that there is greater structural change during the 1875-1910 interval than at other times. We selected that .01 confidence level for the test indicating that if the null hypothesis is rejected, there is only a 1 in 100 chance that we will have done so in error. (Actually, the one-tailed test we employ allows an even more conservative estimate since we are able to identify direction.)

$$\bar{x}_a - \bar{x}_b = .62 > .50$$

The sample difference falls within the 1 percent critical region and the null hypothesis is rejected. We accept the argument that structural change prior to World War I was unusually severe.

What evidence is there that structural change within the international system was similarly marked prior to World War II? Clearly, on average, there was more upward and downward mobility through critical points in the World War II period than at other times for the whole 1815-1975 interval. Indeed, there were nearly twice the number of critical points in the World War II interval. Using the same two control periods (1815-70 and 1950-75), the Student t test was performed for the 1930-45 interval. The Student t test upholds the observation of above-average structural change prior to and during the World War II period as well as the .025 confidence level.

Turning to Figure 12.1, we observe a number of additional facts regarding structural change prior to World War I. First, contrary to much commonplace historical interpretation, Germany was not the only government experiencing the wrenching strains of mobility and role adjustment. Seven of the nine countries included in this sample passed through at least one critical point during this prewar interval. Structural change was very broadly distributed both inside and outside the old balance of power central system. Germany may have set the wheels of war rolling with its aggressive policies, but this evidence suggests that the other leading actors were probably in no mood to respond with coolness and firm restraint. Structural change of an aggravated sort was just too widespread and disruptive.

Second, two of the weakest and thus presumably most compliant members of the central system, Austria-Hungary and Italy, passed through not one but two critical points in this comparatively short interval. These two governments passed through a second inflection point and a lower turning point in that order. The psychology associated with such passage perhaps gave to these governments on the eve of the war a kind of confidence that things could not get worse and they could play power politics with the larger states without having to fear immediate defeat. Such passage perhaps reduced the caution these two governments normally would have had regarding active participation in belligerency.

Third, at least six of the nine critical points in this period of 40 years were inflection points (points occurring on the side of the power curves). Four of these occurred within a decade of the outbreak of the war. A total of four of the inflection points were second points, meaning that they signified a change in the rate of decline rather than in the rate of ascendancy. The significant observation here is that *rate of change* in relative national capability was extremely important immediately prior to World War I. A lessened rate of decline for some of the actors, especially in the face of ascendancy on the part of others, probably stiffened the backs of the governments that were facing a continuing falloff in their relative capability.

The overall impression left by the findings in Figure 12.1, however, is that structural change was very widespread as well as interwoven, and that it probably affected the foreign policies of the declining powers as much as those of the ascendant actors. However, this analysis should not obscure the very important observation that German power apparently peaked in this interval. The Germans were aware that Britain outranked them at sea and that the Russians had the potential for a larger army on land. But Germany was not prepared to heed these realities in the face of the prospect of real future declines relative to rivals in terms of national capability. The shock of the German discovery of imminent relative decline must be factored into any larger statement of the causes of World War I.

In Figure 12.2, critical points are distributed according to national identity and percentage share of the total national capability accounted for by country and temporal occurrence. Several additional observations about pre-World War I structural change are possible in terms of these data. Clearly the system faced a squeeze between the declining powers Britain, France, Austria-Hungary, and Italy on the one hand, and the recently ascendant powers Germany, the United States, Russia/Soviet Union, and Japan on the other. Moreover, the rivalry between Germany and Britain is apparent in that they shared relatively equal amounts of national capability in the 1900-05 interval. In the longer term, relatively speaking, both were declining powers, although the British decline had begun long ago from a higher apogee and would proceed more rapidly as the twentieth century wore on. Germany's greatest potential rival, the United States, had not even been a member of the central system in 1890 and was isolationist until its late entry into World War I, with strains of this isolationism still affecting Wilson's diplomatic efforts at Versailles.

Figure 12.2 Percentage Share of National Capability Accounted For by Countries Passing Through Critical Points

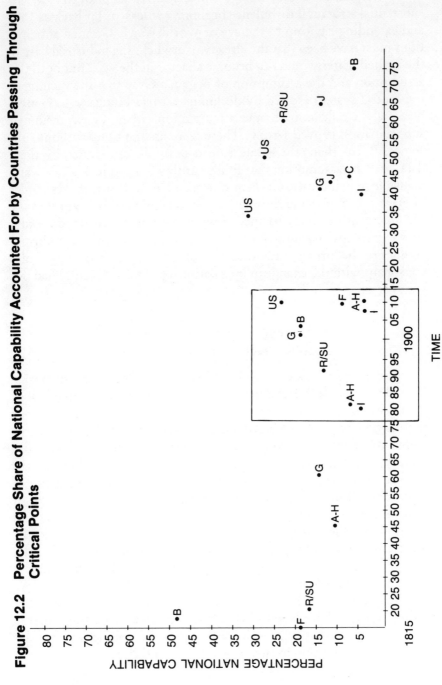

The upshot of these findings is that the decades prior to 1914 saw substantial structural turbulence beginning at least as far back as 1880 and extending right up to the eve of World War I. German anticipations must have been that the already overwhelming industrial base of the United States would not become a factor in the war. But both this assumption and the assumption of Britain's Grey that the vacuum in the central system created by declining Austria-Hungary and enfeebled Italy would not become a temptation either for expansion or subordination proved wrong. These were assumptions without substance. But perhaps the greatest mistake of all, as revealed by these data, was the assumption that France at this stage in its history was a plausible match for the German war machine. In short, the dynamics of great power rise and decline were so pronounced by 1914 that the old nineteenth-century balance of power system existed in idea only. It was perhaps the ultimate failure of the system that equilibrium could not be preserved under the old rules and that new rules consonant with the change in international political structure had not yet evolved.

Systems Transformation as a Possible Precondition of Major War

Returning to the discussion of historical causation at the beginning of this chapter, an important cause of total war in the first half of the twentieth century, insofar as we attempt to fathom the origins of the conflict in terms of *preconditions*, was the inability of governments to adapt to rapidly changing systems structure. Put more sharply, the nineteenth century experienced the flourishing of the balance of power; the twentieth century witnessed the emergence of bipolarity. World Wars I and II resulted from the inability of governments to adapt to rapid and unexpected changes in role and position on their respective power cycles. In a word, both the nineteenth- and twentieth-century systems at maturity were stable. The problem was getting from one system to the other; the problem was systems transformation.

Returning to the Choucri and North study, the reason the authors observed no "snow-balling" of conflict to tip off the analyst or policy-maker that truly major war was in the making was that the trigger or precondition for major war was found elsewhere: not in the dynamics of conflict relationships per se, but in the governmental response to the changing structure of the international system. The reason Singer and associates have repeatedly discovered differing international political and conflict models to be applicable in the nineteenth and early twentieth centuries is that different structural circumstances did prevail in each century and ultimately would provide different international political solutions to the problem of world order. What neither statesmen nor analysts have been able to generate, however, is a model or formula to ease the transformation of international systems.

While the architects of different systems may arrive at different but equally plausible solutions to world order (see Thompson 1983a), the transition from one type of mature system to another appears to be difficult and tumultuous. Largely a function of shifts of state power and position in relative terms on their respective capability cycles, systems transformation is tempestuous and uncertain. Governments have yet to learn how to integrate horizontal thought about balance with vertical analysis regarding state entry in and out of the central system. History provides warnings regarding these matters but fewer policy guidelines.

Note

1. The "lumpiness" in the data distribution of critical points across time was noted in Thompson (1983b, p. 158). The implications regarding structural change at the systemic level and the incidence of World Wars I and II were drawn by the author thereafter.

Bibliography

Bloch, Marc. 1941/1953. *The Historian's Craft*. New York: Vintage.
Choucri, Nazli and Robert C. North. 1975. *Nations in Conflict: Natural Growth and International Violence*. San Francisco: Freeman.
Deutsch, Karl and J. David Singer. 1964. "Multi-polar Power Systems and International Stability." *World Politics* 16, pp. 390-406.
Doran, C. F. 1983a. "Power Cycle Theory and the Contemporary State System." In *Contending Approaches to World System Analysis*, ed. William R. Thompson, pp. 165-82. Beverly Hills: Sage.
——————. 1983b. "War and Power Dynamics: Economic Underpinnings." *International Studies Quarterly* 27, pp. 419-41.
——————. 1971. *The Politics of Assimilation: Hegemony and Its Aftermath*. Baltimore: Johns Hopkins Press.

——————————————— and Wes Parsons. 1980. "War and the Cycle of Relative Power." *American Political Science Review* 74, pp. 947-65.

Holsti, Ole R., Robert C. North, and Richard A. Brody. 1968. "Perception and Action in the 1914 Crisis." In *Quantitative International Politics*, ed. J. David Singer, pp. 123-58. New York: Free Press.

Kalton, G. 1966. *Introduction to Statistical Ideas*. London: Chapman and Hall.

Levy, Jack S. 1983. "World Systems Analysis: A Great Power Framework." In *Contending Approaches to World System Analysis*, ed. William R. Thompson, pp. 183-201. Beverly Hills: Sage.

Midlarsky, Manus I. 1984. "A Hierarchical Equilibrium Theory of Systemic War." Paper delivered to the Annual Meeting of the International Studies Association Atlanta, Georgia, March 27-31, 1984.

Modelski, George. 1983. "Dependency Reversal in the Modern State System: A Long Cycle Perspective." In *North/South Relations: Studies of Dependency Reversal*, ed. Charles Doran, George Modelski, and Cal Clark, pp. 49-72. New York: Praeger.

Organski, A. F. K. and Jacek Kugler. 1980. *The War Ledger*. Chicago: University of Chicago Press.

Rosecrance, Richard. 1966. "Bi-polarity, Multi-polarity, and the Future." *Journal of Conflict Resolution* 10, pp. 314-27.

Singer, J. David and Melvin Small. 1968. "Alliance Aggregation and the Onset of War, 1815-1945." In *Quantitative International Politics: Insights and Evidence*, ed. J. David Singer, pp. 247-86. New York: Free Press.

——————————————, Stuart Bremer, and John Stuckey. 1972. "Capability Distribution, Uncertainty and Major Power War, 1820-1965." In *Peace, War, and Numbers*, ed. Bruce Russett, pp. 19-48. Beverly Hills: Sage.

Siverson, Randolph and Michael P. Sullivan. 1982. "War, Power and the International Elephant." Paper delivered to the Annual Meeting of the International Studies Association, Cincinnati, Ohio.

Snedecor, G. W. 1956. *Statistical Methods*. Iowa: Iowa State College Press.

Stoll, Richard J. 1980. "Two Models of Escalation of Serious Disputes to War, 1816-1976." Paper delivered to the Annual Meeting of the International Studies Association, Los Angeles, California.

Taylor, A. J. P. 1979. *How Wars Begin*. New York: Atheneum.

Thompson, William R., ed. 1983a. *Contending Approaches to World System Analysis*. Beverly Hills: Sage.

——————————————. 1983b. "Cycles, Capabilities, and War: An Ecumenical View." In *Contending Approaches to World System Analysis*, ed. William R. Thompson, pp. 141-63. Beverly Hills: Sage.

——————————————— and Gary Zuk. 1982. "War, Inflation and the Kondratieff Long Wave." *Journal of Conflict Resolution* 26, pp. 621-44.

Vasquez, John A. 1984. "The Role of Capability in the Preservation of Peace and the Onset of War." Paper delivered to the Second International Congress of Arts and Sciences (Peace Science Series), Rotterdam, Netherlands.

Waltz, Kenneth. 1964. "The Stability of a Bipolar World." *Daedalus* 83, pp. 881-909.

Zinnes, Dina A. 1968. "The Expression and Perception of Hostility in Prewar Crisis: 1914." In *Quantitative International Politics*, ed. J. David Singer, pp. 85-122. New York: Free Press.

13

Cycles of War in the Reproduction of the World Economy

ALBERT BERGESEN

> What I cannot forgive . . . is . . . their treating an essentially pathological international system as if it were normal and inevitable. The essence of Marx's critique of classical economics was that it treated a system with deep pathologies as if it were normal and healthy. . . . Compared with any economic system, however, the international system is sick unto death, whereas the worst economic system is only sick unto misery. The present international system is an indeterminate sentence of death, not only on the human race but on the last billion years of evolution. (Boulding 1983, p. 84)

Boulding has struck a nerve, although one not as yet fully comprehended by international relations theorists seeking to understand the origin of great power wars in the modern state system. The world of states is also a world of war, such that war almost appears as a natural outgrowth of the very existence of states themselves. This idea, classically articulated by Hobbes in 1651, has constituted the basic set of assumptions upon which today's explanations of war have arisen. This Hobbesian Consensus sees global politics as a utilitarian world composed of a plurality of competitive states each seeking to maximize its own interest, making the world system prone to struggle and war. This chapter begins to sketch an alternative theory of

I would like to thank Doug McAdam, Walter L. Goldfrank, Mike Hout, Ned Muller, Chris Chase-Dunn, William R. Thompson, Paul Johnson, and Terry Boswell for helpful comments on an earlier draft.

313

war, which is rooted in the reproductive dynamics of the world political economy. Before turning to a preliminary exposition of these ideas, the Hobbesian Consensus on the nature of international order and its decomposition into war will be briefly examined.

States and power—the two terms are almost synonymous. From the point of view of many international relations theorists they are, for the struggle for power has been understood as the animating principle and principal interest of all states. It is an idea that goes back at least as far as Thucydides, and can be traced through Machiavelli to Clausewitz, Morgenthau and his neorealist successors. The interest in power is assumed to be a pre-international given, much like the early utilitarians imputed innate and universal interest in gain and profit to economic actors in capitalist society. Gilpin articulates this theoretical logic when he asserts, "actors enter social relations and create social structures in order to advance particular sets of political, economic, or other types of interests" (Gilpin 1981, p. 9). What is important to note here is that the interests of states are given and precede the state's participation in the international system. But it is not the national interest that determines the structure of the state system, but the structure of the state system (and world economy) that determines the national interest. The logic of Gilpin and other neorealists is the perspective of the early utilitarians who posited individuals in a precontractual state of nature endowed with primordial wants, needs, and desires, who then, in the process of their satisfaction, went on to contractually form the division of labor, civil society, and a host of other social institutions. Utilitarian theoretical logic moves from individual actors to collectivities, from nature-given wants and desires to contractual social order—society. In realist and neorealist international relations theory we encounter the same logic. Instead of the rational utilitarian individual, we now have the utilitarian state and rational choice statesman; instead of attributing universal motives for economic gain and profit to individuals, we now have the attribution of universal motives for power to states, or uneven economic growth propelling states toward collisions with each other in contests for power (Choucri and North 1975; Ashley 1980; Organski and Kugler 1980; Gilpin 1981); and instead of having institutions like the division of labor and civil society arising from the pursuit of individual interests, we now have international institutions—like the balance of power and international regimes—arising as states pursue their national interest. From this point of view, war becomes the collision of national interests that seems to inevitably occur given the assumption of a universal state interest in power and an international environment of anarchy.

But the economic and political dynamics generating war are not universal and constant throughout historical time, for different political units *are* the historical epochs in which they appear. Greek city-states and modern nation-states are political forms reflecting different historical political economies, and as we wouldn't say capitalism and slavery operate according to the same social principles, we shouldn't claim that twentieth-century nation-states and fifth-century B.C. city-states follow the same logic. This comparison is only plausible when a transhistorical force is inserted as a common cause of state behavior, like, for example, ideas that "the drives . . . to dominate are common to all men," or "the struggle for power is universal in time and space," or that "it cannot be denied that throughout historic time, regardless of social, economic, and political conditions, states have met each other in contests for power" (Morgenthau 1978, pp. 36, 37). Obviously, political entities have engaged in war before the modern state system. But these wars have to be understood in terms of the dynamics of the historical periods in which they arose. To reduce all political conflict to a common set of motives negates the organizational dynamics of the historical epoch under consideration, and masks the workings of the historical system in question.

War is no more a product of universal desires for power than, say, exploitation and oppression are a product of a universal desire to truck and barter. Both modern war and economic exploitation are generated in historically bounded social systems, whether feudalism, slavery, or capitalism for economic exploitation, or the modern international state system for war. There is a remark, attributed to Marx I think, to the effect that a man seeking profit and gain does not make capitalism, but capitalism makes a man seek profit and gain. The same general reasoning holds for states seeking power and engaging in conflict. Centuries of international struggle and conflict do not make the state system, but the state system makes for centuries of struggle and war. States are not national Robinson Crusoes, plopped down on some global island where, pursuing their national interest, they create international order and collide in war. That was a utilitarian myth then and its reincarnation in IR theory today is a continuation of that fiction. This myth simply masks the historical dynamics of the world political economy and international state system. The exploitation of man by man is neither natural nor an inevitable consequence of universal motives for economic gain and profit. Human relations are shaped by the socioeconomic system in which they appear. These systems are not eternal, but historical arrangements that can, and must, be changed. This is also true for war and the world system. International conflict and violence is not something that will always be with us, because war is not the product of a universal drive for power and as such is not an inherent aspect of human relations. Contrary to Hobbes and his descendants, modern war does not originate because of the anarchistic state of nature (which itself is a utilitarian fiction), but in the social relations among states that manifest themselves as the world economy and international state system. Both of these are historical systems, which arose during the fifteenth and sixteenth centuries, and will someday be transformed into some other global historical system with a very different logic (that may or may not generate war). War is not caused by the world system; it is part and parcel of the very operation of the world system. Its existence is dependent upon cycles of conflict and war. The modern world economy and international state system produce death and destruction as they are crises-prone economic and political arrangements. To understand the origins of war, therefore, requires a dissection of the inner logic of this historical world system that has been in operation since the end of the fifteenth century.

War and the World Political Economy

Political scientists studying international relations tend to emphasize the autonomy of the state system from the dynamics of the capitalist world economy, while the sociologists of the Wallersteinian world system perspective tend to argue that the logic of the world economy directly affects the logic of world politics (for arguments on both sides, see the papers in Thompson 1983). Here the state system and world economy will be considered not only interdependent, but more fundamentally different dimensions of a singular social formation on a global scale, the international political economy. To understand the place of war in the reproduction of this world political economy, we begin with the fact that the world economy does not exist in a state of equilibrium. Its past history shows periods of sustained growth and expansion followed by stagnation and contraction. Further, these movements are roughly synchronized with other long-wave phenomena. While different global cycles with various periodicities have been the object of much recent scholarship (Modelski 1978; Thompson 1982; Thompson and Zuk 1982; Rasler and Thompson 1983; Doran 1983; Goldstein 1984), I wish to discuss the interrelationship of six particular cyclical movements. One of these is a cycle of major power wars, and it is the synchronization of this cycle with other more economic cycles that is the key to the claim that war is produced by the world economy.

Long Waves of Colonization/Decolonization

Long waves of colonization are mentioned first because their periodicity has been established with quantitative data (Bergesen and Schoenberg 1980). Colonialism is an important indicator of the collective dynamics of the world system because it is a linkage between the system's core and periphery, making it a distinctly structural property of the world system as a whole. These waves have also covered most of the world system's history, providing a constant indicator of long-term change. Figure 13.1 presents these long waves of formal colonial rule. In theory there are any number of ways to measure colonialism: square miles of territory, number of people under colonial control, or number of colonies in any particular year. Because of the practical difficulty of estimating colonial territory (particularly for the early centuries) and the skimpiness of historical demography for colonial areas, I will use information on years in office of colonial governors as an indicator of the formal existence of a colony. The data come from an exhaustive study (Heinge 1970) of all colonial governors since the first Portuguese colony established in Ceuta in 1415 through 1969 when the study ended. Heinge listed the years during which governors held office. The first and last year in which a colonial governor held office was taken as an indicator of the duration of colonial rule. The total number of colonial governors per year from all core countries is presented in Figure 13.1. (For the rest of this chapter, references to the first and second cycles will refer to the periodicity of these colonial waves.) These data reveal that colonialism came in two general waves, and although the particular

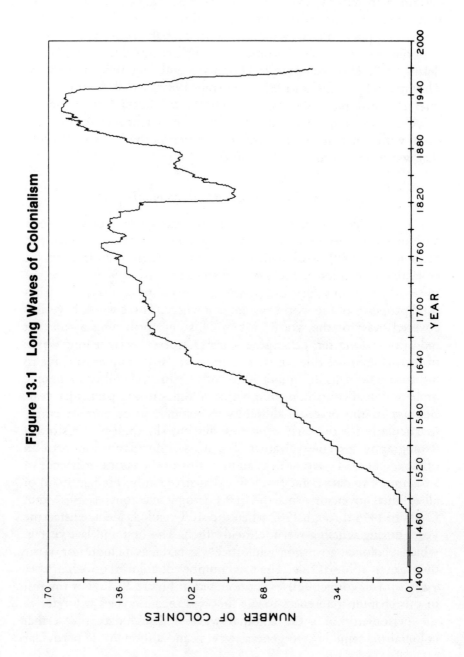

Figure 13.1 Long Waves of Colonialism

data set ends in 1969, by then most of the second wave of European colonialism had ended.

The important point here is the assumption that these long waves tell us something about the rhythmic inner logic of the world system as a whole. As Schumpeter (1937, p. v) observed about business cycles, "cycles are not, like tonsils, separable things that might be treated by themselves, but are, like the beat of the heart, of the essence of the organism that displays them." This is true of colonial cycles and the larger world system. Since formal colonial rule has virtually disappeared, if these are of the essence of the world system, where is today's colonialism? The answer lies in the fact that, at a deeper level, colonialism represents the domination of core states over peripheral areas. In the growing Soviet-U.S. competition for influence around the world, it can be argued that we are, in fact, entering yet another wave or cycle of struggles by the major powers for more explicit political control of the weaker states of the third world. It is, of course, impossible to gain the same kind of quantitative data on this more informal colonialism.

Long Waves of War and Peace

Like colonialism, warfare between the great powers has not been randomly distributed across the history of the world system (for a recent review of cycles of war, see Goldstein 1983). Using Quincy Wright's (1942) definition of major wars as lasting at least two years with at least one major power on each side, and having a minimum of 50,000 troops, we can see that major wars appeared intermittently during the first wave of colonialism, by and large ceased during the 100 years peace of 1815-1914, and then recurred during the second wave of colonialism (see Figure 13.2). Levy's (1983, p. 75) dates for what he calls "general wars" also fit this general pattern. The association between war and colonies is not perfect. War is an almost constant feature of the first cycle, whereas it only appears twice at the peak of the second. In general, though, when colonialism increases, the chances of war seem to increase; when colonialism declines, war declines. In and of itself this is not all that significant, but when we find other wavelike movements with similar periodicities, the discovery of each additional wave adds support to the idea that the world

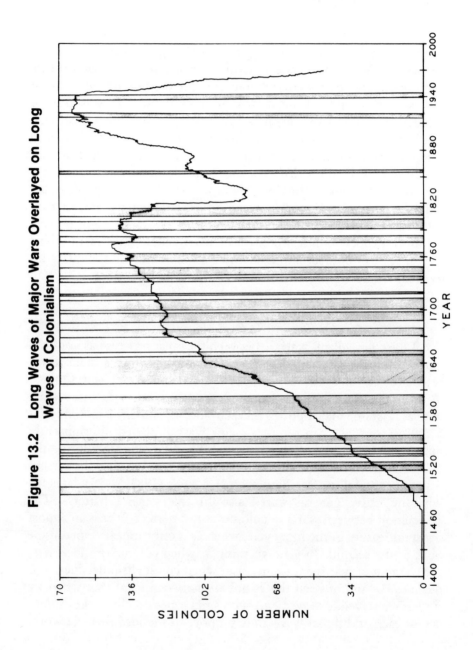

Figure 13.2 Long Waves of Major Wars Overlayed on Long Waves of Colonialism

system has a general cyclical nature and that war is somehow a fundamental part of these rhythms.

Long Waves of Mercantilism and Free Trade

Over the history of the world economy, trade relations between core and periphery (and among core states) have swung back and forth between periods of relatively free trade and more closed, politically regulated exchanges under mercantilism and protectionism. During the first cycle, trade between core and periphery was politically regulated under mercantile trade policies. But as that wave declined in the early nineteenth century, there appeared a period of relatively free trade, the so-called Era of Free Trade (1820s-1870s), which toward end of the century gradually gave way to another long wave of rising tariffs, protectionism, and trade wars (1870s-1947), which corresponded to the second wave of colonialism. Then, with the decline of colonialism, protectionism also declined and there was another era of free trade negotiated under GATT, that seems, in the 1980s, to be giving way, once again, to yet a third cycle of protectionism and neomercantile state policies, correlating with growing U.S.-Soviet competition for control over sections of the third world. Mercantilism and protectionism (Krasner's 1976 more closed world economy) can be seen as similar to both colonialism and overt war. If we see colonialism as a formal regulation and control by the core of peripheral areas, then mercantilism and protectionism represent a similar formal regulation, but of trade and exchange rather than overseas territories. But mercantilism and protectionism are also known as "trade war" and these policies reflect—like the scramble for colonies—struggle and competition among core states. From this point of view, mercantile economic relations reflect more than just a formalization or political regulation of trade; they also represent struggle among core states.

Long Waves of Hegemony

Hegemony is the dominance of a single state in world production and political/military strength. From Wallerstein (1980) to Modelski (1978), it has been suggested that the world has passed through at least four hegemonies: the Spanish of the sixteenth century (for

Modelski the Portuguese), the Dutch of the seventeenth, the British of the mid-nineteenth, and the United States of the mid-twentieth century. From the point of view of my cyclical rhythms, though, there have only been two such combined political and economic hegemonies: the British of the mid-nineteenth and the American of the mid-twentieth century. During the first wave, the almost constant presence of war (see Figure 13.2) suggests the absence of any clear military hegemony that could pacify core rivalries for any length of time. When British dominance began to wane during the last quarter of the nineteenth century, the distribution of power in the core became more multicentric and unstable, eventually decomposing into the second Thirty Years War of 1914-45. The result of this wave of struggle was the emergence of American, as opposed to German, hegemonic succession to Britain. By the mid-1970s, though, it was increasingly clear that U.S. economic dominance was being challenged by the Japanese and military hegemony by the Soviet Union.

Emphasizing only the hegemonies of Britain and the United States is not to deny the leading position of the seventeenth-century Dutch in world production. But could they be considered to have exercised both commercial and military dominance at the same time? It may very well be that in the early centuries of the world system the cycles of productive and military dominance were not as well synchronized, but as the world system became more tightly integrated over the centuries, the two cycles came to be lodged in a single country, first Britain and then the United States. There is a certain appeal to this sort of reasoning, although it is clear that at present the economic and military challenges to the United States come from different states, Japan and the Soviet Union. If we are in fact repeating the cycle of the last century, then it appears that the United States is playing the role of Britain, the hegemonic state in decline, the Soviet Union is repeating Germany's position as the principal military challenger, and Japan is repeating the past American position as the principal economic challenger. All of this is conjecture, of course. What is clear, though, is that the United States by any measure (percent of world trade, world production, number of top corporations, and so forth) is in objective economic decline, and that this same decline in world production occurred about a hundred years ago with Britain.

Long Waves of Economic Expansion and Contraction

Many have linked economic cycles with war (Thompson 1982; Goldstein 1984; Thompson and Zuk 1982; Rasler and Thompson 1983). In terms of the cycles I am dealing with, the British and U.S. hegemonies were also periods of generalized economic expansion, while their decline was associated with economic stagnation and contraction. This is not to say there were not upswings and down-swings during the first general cycle of Figure 13.1. Many have speculated that the sixteenth century was one of generalized expansion in world trade and production, while the seventeenth century was a period of stagnation and depression (Frank 1978; Wallerstein 1974, 1980; among the many). It has also been suggested that Kondratieff cycles can be traced prior to the 1790s, the date Kondratieff thought the cyclical ups and downs of capitalism began. But if these sorts of business cycles are generated by capitalism, then what of the earlier centuries where the distinctly capitalist mode of production was not as yet fully established? How can you have capitalist business cycles racing through a precapitalist economic system?

The height of British hegemony corresponded to the boom years of 1849-72, while the beginning of British decline corresponded to the Great Depression of 1873-93. While there was a short upturn from 1894-1914, the remaining years of the second wave were of stagnation and outright depression. Similarly, U.S. hegemony corresponds with the postwar boom of 1945-73, and the decline of that hegemony is correlated with the world economy slump of the late 1970s and early 1980s. The British mid-nineteenth-century hegemony also corresponds to the drop in colonization as does the U.S. hegemony of the mid-twentieth century. These two hegemonies, then, are correlated with the troughs of the waves of Figure 13.1.

Long Waves of Mergers Among Business Firms

The business enterprise grows in different ways depending on whether the larger world economy is expanding or contracting (Bergesen 1982). When the world economy is expanding, the firm's growth takes place internally, as the firm expands its size and scale of operation within an already existing organizational framework. Many new firms also enter the market. When the world economy is stagnating, the firm continues to expand, but now principally through mergers with other firms. This process appears cyclical, as the expansion of the firm plants the seeds for a later saturation of given markets leading to recession and downturn, which in turn lead to waves of mergers as smaller firms combine and larger ones swallow the weakened.

From the point of view of the waves of Figure 13.1, the mid-nineteenth-century trough was a period of overall economic expansion and a proliferation of family or joint partner firms pioneered in Britain—England as the workshop of the world. The overexpansion of the previous mid-century boom resulted in overproduction and downturn at the end of the century, setting off a wave of mergers that created the modern multiunit corporation, this time pioneered in the United States. Then, during the upturn of 1945-73, this corporation itself underwent dramatic internal expansion, becoming more multinational or transnational. This mid-twentieth-century expansion, like the one a hundred years ago, planted the seeds for overproduction, and by the mid-1970s the world economy was again stagnating and experiencing another significant wave of mergers—like Conoco Oil and Dupont or Marathon Oil and U.S. Steel. (The conglomerate merger wave of the 1960s was more a financial rearrangement.) The size of the firm has grown with each cyclical downturn I have identified. I do not think the present merger of firm with firm, though, is the final form of industrial reorganization of the elongated period of stagnation the world economy entered in the mid-1970s. During the remainder of this growing third wave, I think we will see the consolidation of a relationship between the state and firm, as exemplified by the role of MITI in Japan and the whole idea of "Japan, Inc." where the state orchestrates growth and guides production decisions. This state-managed production will become, I think, the new pillar of the world economy, much like the giant corporation was at the turn of the last century. Today's hegemonic state, the United States, will fall behind and fail to adopt to this new industrial format, much like the British earlier failed to adapt the multiunit corporation that was pioneered in the United States. In effect, with transformations in the organization of production there is also a shift of hegemonies, as we have gone from Britain to the United States and now possibly on to Japan.

The Interrelationship of These Cycles

The world system, then, goes through cycles that could be said to have the following A and B phases:

A-Phase	*B-Phase*
Peace ---------------------------->	War
Economic Expansion ------------->	Economic Contraction
Free Trade------------------------>	Trade Wars
Decolonization-------------------->	Colonization
Hegemony ------------------------>	Multicentric Core
Growth of the Firm -------------->	Mergers of the Firm

While there is an obvious sequence to these phases, the overall process is cyclical, such that an earlier B-phase makes the present A-phase possible, and in that sense you cannot really say, except in the short run, that A precedes B. How, then, do these different cycles fit together, and what is the role played by war? This is an obviously complex issue and one for which it must be said there is no conclusive answer. Much remains to be learned and the exact interconnection of these cycles is yet to be precisely determined. Nevertheless, it is possible to sketch out some preliminary ideas as to how these wavelike movements might fit together in the global process of producing and reproducing the world economy and international state system.

As stated earlier, the capitalist world economy does not exist in a stationary state. The wavelike movement of the world economy appears to be cyclical—that is, the activity of one phase plants the seeds for the later phase, making the two interdependent (like the world economy and international state system). In general, the A-phase economic upturn results in overproduction leading to the B-phase downturn, the violence of which removes blocks to further capital accumulation, allowing the system to proceed to yet another expansionary A-phase. The downturn creates severe strains on the institutional structure of the world economy and forces its reorganization. The world system either reorganizes or permanently breaks down. So far, it has managed to reconstitute itself and continue. The convulsions of the downturn, what Schumpeter referred to as "creative destruction," involve the appearance of intense political struggle at all levels of the system, from the shop floor to the international state system. In effect, the organizational outcome of yesterday's reorganization is today's roadblock. While the restructuring process will facilitate yet another period of relative peace, the new period of expansion will eventually run past its old limits, creating yet another period of stagnation and global crisis.

In terms of war, the central point is that the Schumpeterian convulsions and reorganizations of the downturn are not solely limited to economic institutions. Recessions/depressions do bring about intensified struggle between capital and labor over wages, benefits, and working hours, and between factions of capital as firms engage in price wars, takeovers, and mergers. But they also bring about struggle and conflict between states too, because the international state system is the backbone of the world economy. That is, while the state is somewhat *external* to a national economy, the state system is *internal* to the world economy, constituting its very skeletal structure of force and power, which upholds and enforces its economic logic. Relations between states in the core, and between core and periphery as a whole, constitute the principal political relations of the world system, and the crises, competition, and struggle of the downturn restructure these relations. The competition between core states over spheres of influence and outright control of peripheral states (colonialism) reorganizes and expands the outer boundary of the world economy by incorporating new areas. War among core states also ends the plural distribution of power, creating a new hegemonic state, which in turn provides the political power to allow the growth and expansion of the reorganized business enterprise that grows under its protection (the family firm in Britain, the corporation in the United States, and maybe the state/firm in Japan). Hegemony also opens up the markets of other core and peripheral countries to the newly reorganized firm that was created during the previous convulsive downturn. Mid-nineteenth-century British power backed the expansion of English enterprises into Latin America, which had been formally incorporated into the world economy by the previous wave of Spanish and Portuguese colonialism (the first cycle of Figure 13.1). In the mid-twentieth century, with the collapse of European colonial holdings after 1945, American hegemony allowed the rapid penetration of these new markets by American multinationals the same way Britain did for its firms a century earlier.

The key theoretical point is this: the movement from economic downturn to upturn involves the use of coercion, force, and struggle, which are the by-products of struggles not only between capital and labor, but between states too. At the national level, more purely Schumpeterian economic convulsions take place within more narrowly defined economic sectors; but on a world scale, the presence of Schumpeterian reorganization requires the forceful reorganization of the system's skeletal structure—the international state system—and this struggle takes the form of major wars. The political power of an extant hegemony is itself rooted in a period of previous economic expansion and growth, such that in this cyclical fashion the exercise of political power in the world economy sets in motion processes that both undermine the economic base of the existing hegemonic state and provide conditions allowing a new hegemony to emerge.

Nineteenth-century British power politically constructed and enforced the mid-century free trade expansion, which saturated given world markets creating the following downturn, which started mergers, which in turn created a new enlarged firm in another country that went on to become the next hegemonic state. Britain was not the locus for the new form of industrial organization. What merging Britain did was more a federation of firms that kept local family control intact rather than collapsing smaller family firms into the multiunit corporation as was occurring in the United States with the formation of Standard Oil and US Steel, and to a lesser extent in Germany with industrial cartels. In this way the free trade a world hegemony guarantees undermines that hegemony's very position, by creating an expansionary world economy that will eventually crash and set up a new form of industrial organization in a new country. The United States underwrote the 1945-73 boom, which paved the way for the downturn starting in the mid-1970s. As Britain did earlier, the United States tends to reaffirm older industrial formats, principally the private multinational (like bailing out Chrysler), rather than moving to the new form of industrial organization, as seen in the industrial policy of Japan.

The reason upturn leads to downturn is that aggregate world demand is politically set during the convulsive reorganization of the previous B-phase downturn, and, given the overall anarchy of world production decisions, world supply eventually outruns this structural limitation. The present runs into the past and the world economy's booming expansion races past the level of demand set during the previous downturn, such that there are now too many producers for the aggregate level of world demand. The result is overproduction, stagnation, and heightened struggle for survival. If this were all that was involved, the world economy could move from contraction to expansion and only experience the friction and conflict of forceful reorganization within the market economy narrowly defined; the creative destruction of the downturn would be limited to the economy and thus avoid world wars. But the movement from downturn to upturn involves competition and struggle between states. There cannot be recovery and sustained expansion without reunifying the world market and that takes force, which means hegemony, which is established through war.

Global war creates a new hegemonic state that then reunites the world market and reconstructs what appears to be a naturally arising free trade division of labor. But the seemingly self-regulating international division of labor masking as free trade is a myth. The division of labor is not self-generating nor self-regulating, but politically constructed and forcefully guaranteed. Buying and selling are the consequences of an already constructed social system; they are not the acts that construct the system. The seemingly self-regulating world of a free trade division of labor is not a natural outcome of voluntary agreements among equals, but the product of struggle and force, where the victor opens up world markets with newly acquired force. The proof of this is clear when the hegemonic advantage declines, for then the whole regime of free trade grinds to a halt as each state pushes its own national interest in the form of trade wars and competition over control of the periphery (colonial rivalries). The uncontested penetration of the markets of other core states by the hegemonic state during the upturn does not go unchallenged when that hegemonic power begins to decline. Other states now actively pursue their own claims for influence and market shares, as the colonial rivalries of the B-phase begin, whether the European "rush for Africa" of the late nineteenth century or the Soviet-U.S. competition of the late twentieth century.

The self-regulation of the free trade world division of labor, then, is a fiction covering the exercise of power that can be seen when that power declines, as the seemingly peaceful economic competition of the upturn becomes the political competition of the downturn, and the struggle for market shares turns to a struggle for political shares, and market war turn to political war. The irony here is that the closer one approximates the condition of a true equality among states, the further one gets from a self-regulating division of labor and free trade. Equality brings bickering, trade wars, colonial and neocolonial rivalries, and eventually open conflict. Equality does not generate peace and free trade but conflict and protectionism. When there was some peace, the relative peace of the upturn, it was only because one state dominated the others. War ends that equality, creates a victor, establishes a new hegemony and a new inequality, which ironically is the very political substructure for renewed "peaceful" economic expansion.

From this point of view, the expansion and prosperity of a free trade upturn does not naturally arise, but is underwritten by the power of a hegemonic state. Not, I might add, as some suggest to provide "world order" or global "public goods," but to further the economic interests of that hegemonic state. When Canning said, "Spanish America is free and if we do not mismanage our affairs sadly she is English" (quoted in Gallagher and Robinson 1953), he was not speaking of providing public goods for the rest of the developed world, but of underwriting access to Latin American markets for British capital. The British, and the Americans in the next century, encouraged, often with gunboat diplomacy, stable governments that were favorable to British capital and provided good investment risks.

What is important to remember is that hegemony does not just arise because of the independent and autonomous economic development of various states that rise and challenge the previously most developed state. The world system is not the Hobbesian jungle depicted in conventional international relations theory. Periods of growth and free trade do not last, and this is not just a matter of a winding down of energy (Modelski 1978) or added overhead costs of hegemonic imperium (Gilpin 1981), but rather a direct consequence of the earlier cycle of expansion. The six cycles that have been identified in this chapter are all casually interconnected and reflect the overall movement and laws of motion of the global system as a whole. To repeat, if you cannot have a new period of economic expansion without a reunification of the world market and a pacification of core rivalries, and if that politically comes about through the dominance of a single state, then war becomes the means through which the bickering and protectionism of the downturn is turned into the seeming peace and free trade regime of the succeeding upturn.

From this point of view war, and the relative peace of the

upturn, are but different forms of competition and struggle within the world economy, with each making the other possible. The expansion of the upturn is based on the reorganizations of the previous downturn, when the world economy restructured itself. War is part of the downturn and establishes the new hegemony, which in turn reunites the world market, pacifies core rivalries, provides a common currency for world exchanges, and eliminates the colonial structure that was part of the downturn expansion of the system's boundaries. War, then, is not an accident, nor a rational calculation of gain. It is one phase in the cyclical reproductive policies of the world economy. It makes for peace, but the ensuing peace makes for further war, and the cycle continues. The peace here is not a real peace, not an absolute peace, but the relative peace that appears when a single state exercises hegemony and enforces "peace" and order in international relations. Contrary to conventional international relations theory, war is not a rupture of the system, not a colliding of self-seeking national interests, but a moment when the global economy reorganizes itself. War is part of the continuity of the global system, not a breakdown.

We have, since the end of the fifteenth century, entered into a period of historical organization that we refer to as the world of modern states and the modern world economy. This division of our species into 160 or so political units, and the grouping of them into classes of states—a core and a periphery—is not natural nor inevitable. Most of all, the manner in which this particular world economy reproduces itself and resolves its inherent crises through war makes it a pathological form of human organization. The problem of war and peace is not one of accidents, demonic leaders, nor the war-trap myth of rational-choice statesmen freely deciding whether it is in their interest to go to war. Instead, the problem lies in the very organization of this historical system: in its political-economic structure that manifests itself in recurring cycles of war and peace.

Bibliography

Ashley, R.K. 1980. *The Political Economy of War and Peace: The Sino-Soviet-American Triangle and the Modern Security Problematic*. London: Frances Pinter.

Bergesen, A. 1982. "Economic Crisis and Merger Movements: 1880s Britain and 1980s United States." In *Ascent and Decline in the World-System*, ed. E. Friedman. Beverly Hills: Sage.

————————————and R. Schoenberg. 1980. "Long Waves of Colonial Expansion and Contraction, 1415-1969." In *Studies of the Modern World-System*, ed. A. Bergesen. New York: Academic.

Boulding, K. 1983. "Review of R. Gilpin, *War and Change in World Politics.*" *Society* (March-April), p. 84.

Bueno de Mesquita, B. 1981. *The War Trap*. New Haven: Yale University Press.

Choucri, N. and R. North 1975. *Nations in Conflict: National Growth and International Violence*. San Francisco: Freeman.

Doran, C.F. 1983. "War and Power Dynamics: Economic Underpinnings." *International Studies Quarterly* 27, pp. 419-41.

Frank, A.G. 1978. *World Accumulation, 1492-1789*. New York: Monthly Review.

Gallagher, J. and R. Robinson, 1953. "The Imperialism of Free Trade." *Economic History Review*, Second Series, 5, pp. 1-15.

Gilpin, R. 1981. *War and Change in World Politics*. Princeton: Princeton University Press.

Goldstein, J. 1983. "Long Waves and War Cycles." Unpublished manuscript. Cambridge, Mass.: Department of Political Science, M.I.T.

————————————. 1984. "War and the Kondratieff Upswing." Paper presented at the Annual Meeting of the International Studies Association, Atlanta, March 27-31.

Heinge, D. 1970. *Colonial Governors*. Madison: University of Wisconsin Press.

Krasner, S. 1976. "State Power and the Structure of International Trade." *World Politics* 28, pp. 317-47.

Levy, J. 1983. *War in the Modern Great Power System*. Lexington: University of Kentucky Press.

Modelski, G. 1978. "The Long Cycle of Global Politics and the Nation-State." *Comparative Studies in Society and History* 20, pp. 214-35.

Morgenthau, H. 1978. *Politics Among Nations: The Struggle for Power and Peace*. New York: Knopf.

Organski, A.F.K. and J. Kugler 1980. *The War Ledger*. Chicago: University of Chicago Press.

Rasler, K.A. and W. R. Thompson. 1983. "Global Wars, Public Debts, and the Long Cycle." *World Politics* 35, pp. 489-516.

Schumpeter, J. 1937. *Business Cycles*. New York: McGraw-Hill.

Thompson, W.R. 1983. *Contending Approaches to World System Analysis*. Beverly Hills: Sage.

————————————. 1982. "Phases of the Business Cycle and the Outbreak of War." *International Studies Quarterly* 26, pp. 301-11.

————————————and L. G. Zuk. 1982. "War, Inflation, and the Kondratieff Long Wave." *Journal of Conflict Resolution* 26, pp. 621-44.

Wallerstein, I. 1980. *The Modern World-System*, Vol. 2. New York: Academic.

————————————. 1974. *The Modern World-System*, Vol. 1. New York: Academic.

Wright, Q. 1942. *A Study of War*. Chicago: University of Chicago Press.

Index

achievement motive, 242, 253-55
affiliation motive, 242, 254-55
AFL-CIO, 221
Aldcroft, Derek H., 114
Allison, Graham T., 198
Amin, Samir, 272, 285
Archibold, G., 75
Aronson, Jonathan D., 196
Ashley, Richard K., 267, 314
Azar, Edward E., 145

Bairoch, Paul, 269
balance of power system, 296
Baldwin, Robert, 189, 210, 226-27, 230
Baran, Paul, 272
Barber, James D., 200, 242-43
Bauer, R., 220
Baumol, William, 189
Becker, G. S., 230
Beksiak, Janusz, 24
Bergesen, Albert, 266, 317, 323
Bergsten, C. Fred, 156-57, 161, 178, 214
Bingham, Richard D., 10
Blinder, Alan S., 189
Bloch, Marc, 294
Block, Fred, 5
Bobrow, Davis, 230
Bombach, G., 97
Borchardt, Knut, 89, 92-94
Botz, Gerherd, 86
Boulding, Kenneth, 313
Bousquet, Nicole, 266
Bracher, Karl D., 115
Bradbury, Katherine L., 16
Braudel, Fernand, 129, 267-68

Bremer, Stuart, 145, 300
Bressard, Albert, 170
Bretton Woods, 158, 170, 187
Brewer, Anthony, 265, 269, 273
Broadbent, Andrew, 11
Broaden, Noel, 14
Brock, W. A., 225
Brody, Richard A., 299
Broszat, Martin, 115
Brown, Alan A., 62
Brown, M., 81
Brüning, Heinrich, 94, 96-97, 115
Bryant, Ralph C., 160
Buchanan, James M., 225
Bukharin, Nicolai, 24, 265, 268, 274, 280, 282, 283, 285
bureaucratic politics model, 198
business cycle, 25, 26, 130, 270-71
business firm mergers long wave, 323-24

Canning, George, 329
capital accumulation process, 3-4, 269-70, 280
capital mobility, 273
Carter, Jimmy, 188
Castells, Manuel, 3, 6
Caves, Richard, 227
Cawson, Alan, 7
Chamberlain, Joseph, 280
Chase-Dunn, Christopher K., 155, 266, 267
Chelinski, R., 24, 65
Choucri, Nazli, 131, 267, 283, 285, 299-300, 310-11, 314
Clark, Gordon, 6

333

About the Editors and Contributors

M. MARK AMEN is Assistant Professor of International Studies at the University of South Florida (Tampa). He has published a monograph on United States foreign policy in Greece after World War II and is currently writing a book on U.S. economic policies during the 1960s.

ALBERT BERGESEN is Associate Professor of Sociology at the University of Arizona (Tucson). Recent publications include *Studies of the Modern World-System* (1980), *Cultural Analysis: The Work of Peter Berger, Mary Douglas, Michel Foucault and Jurgen Habermas* (1984), and *The Sacred and the Subversive: Political Witch-Hunts as National Rituals* (1984). He is currently writing a book on long waves of war since the sixteenth century.

CHARLES F. DORAN is Professor of International Relations at the School of Advanced International Studies, Johns Hopkins University. He recently co-edited *North/South Relations: Studies of Dependency Reversal* (1983).

ROBERT E. ELDER, JR. is Professor of Political Science at Hope College (Holland, Michigan). He has published *Development Administration in a North Indian State: The Family Planning Program in Uttar Pradesh* and has a research interest in political theory.

ZBIGNIEW FALLENBUCHL is a Professor of Economics at the University of Windsor (Windsor, Ontario, Canada). He has published extensively in the field of Soviet and East European economics and East-West economic relations.

TED ROBERT GURR is Professor of Political Science and Director of the Center for Comparative Politics at the University of Colorado

(Boulder). The author or editor of a dozen books and monographs on political conflict, governmental authority and performance, and criminal justice, he is now working on a series of theoretical and empirical essays for a book on the *The State and the City.*

JACK E. HOLMES is Associate Professor of Political Science at Hope College (Holland, Michigan). He is the author of *The Mood/Interest Theory of American Foreign Policy* (1985).

BARRY B. HUGHES is a Professor at the Graduate School of International Studies, University of Denver. In addition to numerous articles, his recent publications include *World Modeling* (1980) and *World Futures: A Critical Analysis of Alternatives* (1984).

ODED IZRAELI is Associate Professor of Business and Economics at Oakland University (Rochester, Michigan). He specializes in urban and macropolitical economics.

PAUL M. JOHNSON is Assistant Professor of Political Science at Florida State University (Tallahassee). He specializes in Soviet/East European politics, and his previous publications deal mainly with the foreign and domestic determinants of economic policy-making in this region.

TIMOTHY KEARNEY is a Research Assistant in the Country Risk Assessment Section of Mellon Bank (Pittsburgh). He received his M.A. in Economics from the University of Pittsburgh in 1983.

MITCHELL KELLMAN is Associate Professor of Economics at City College of New York and at the Graduate Center of the City University of New York. He specializes in international economics and economic development.

DESMOND S. KING is completing a Ph.D. dissertation at Northwestern University on "State Autonomy in Advanced Capitalism: National Penetration of the Local State in a Period of Fiscal Stress."

ROBERT THOMAS KUDRLE is Professor of Public Affairs in the Hubert H. Humphrey Institute at the University of Minnesota (Minneapolis). He specializes in international economics and recently completed a term as a co-editor of *International Studies Quarterly.*

PAT MCGOWAN is Professor of Political Science at Arizona State University (Tempe). He has published recently in *American Political Science Review, Review,* and *Journal of Modern African Studies* on a variety of topics in comparative and international political economy.

ANTONI MOSKWA is Professor of Economics at Allegheny College (Meadville, Pennsylvania) and the author of *The Direction of Economic and Political Changes in Poland.*

DAVID P. RAPKIN is Associate Professor of Political Science at the University of Nebraska (Lincoln). He has co-edited *America in a Changing World Political Economy* (1982) and is currently studying the politial economy of the factory automation industry.

MARK E. RUPERT is working toward a Ph.D. in International Relations at Claremont Graduate School (Claremont, California). His primary research interests concern questions pertaining to world political economy processes.

BRUCE RUSSETT is Professor of Political Science at Yale University. The author of numerous publications on international politics, he is a past president of the Peace Science Society (International) and the 1983-84 President of the International Studies Association.

WILLIAM R. THOMPSON is Professor of International Relations at Claremont Graduate School (Claremont, California). He has edited *Contending Approaches to World System Analysis* (1983) and is currently writing monographs on the role of seapower in global politics and the impacts of global war on major power state-building processes.

EKKART ZIMMERMANN is Professor of Sociology in the Hochschule der Bundeswehr Munchen (University of the Federal Armed Forces, Munich). In addition to works in German, he is the author of *Political Violence, Crises, and Revolutions: Theories and Research* (1983). Currently, his research focuses on European political responses to the economic shocks of the 1930s depression.

Other titles in this series:
Donald Sylvan and Steve Chan, eds.,
FOREIGN POLICY DECISION MAKING
(New York: Praeger, 1983)